THE PASSPORT REPORT

OVER 100 WAYS AND MANY GOOD REASONS TO OBTAIN A SECOND FOREIGN PASSPORT

EIGHTH EDITION
Revised for 1993

Dr. W.G. Hill

SCOPE
INTERNATIONAL
LIMITED

Scope International Ltd.,
62 Murray Road,
Horndean,
Waterlooville PO8 9JL, UK

8th Edition 1993
By Dr. W.G. Hill J.D.
Investigator and Consultant

For questions and further information contact the author by mail in care of the publisher

British Library Cataloguing in Publication Data

Hill, William G.
    The passport report : over 100 ways to
    obtain a second foreign passport.___8th ed.
    1. Passports
    I. Title
    342'.82   JX4251

ISBN 0 906619 19 X

Phototypeset by Barbara James Typesetting, Rowlands Castle, Hampshire
Printed by Hartnolls, Bodmin, Cornwall

TABLE OF CONTENTS

Part XIII: CASE HISTORIES

PART XIV: PARTING WORDS

SUMMARIES OF OTHER REPORTS

PT 1: How to Avoid Bureaucrats & Taxes
PT 2: Freedom and Privacy Tactics
Campione: Switzerland's Secret Semi-Tropical Tax Haven
Monaco: The Glitzy Tax Haven
Lloyd's of London: How to Earn £50,000 p.a. With No Investment
Channel Islands: Residence/Domicile for £50 per Month
Think Like a Tycoon: How to Make a Million
Andorra/Gibraltar: The Cheapest European Tax Havens
Free Cars: How to Own A New Luxury Car Every Year of Your Life, For Free
Swiss Report
Tax Exile Report
Tax Haven Report
Order Form

A MESSAGE TO PASSPORT OFFICERS
AND FOREIGN MINISTERS

If you represent a young or small country, you already know that many of your most productive and wealthy citizens have been lured away, moving their capital or talent to major industrial countries. The flight of some of your best people may be inevitable for reasons explained in *The Passport Report*. Paradoxically, your country can turn the tables and generate significant funds by offering citizenship to the same sort of productive people you would most like to keep.

Both your government and private citizens who assist in the project will benefit significantly.

WE STRONGLY URGE THAT YOU MAKE ARRANGEMENTS FOR A "CITIZENSHIP BY REGISTRATION" PROGRAM. At our suggestion, one small country did this and raised US $25,000,000 in three years from about 1,000 well screened reputable new citizens who gladly contributed to the National Treasury. The majority of these new citizens may never live in your country, but the relationships will surely stimulate commerce, investment and tourism. The bureaucratic tendency to make a simple program complex and unworkable should be resisted. We can show you how to set up the project without any cost or new staff and make it a major source of revenue within three months.

At the present time most small countries realize only negative benefits because their passports are marketed and distributed illegally by individuals who violate the public trust for strictly personal profit. When national laws make it impossible to acquire citizenship and passports legally, only then do scoundrels and criminals get involved. A legitimate program would generate desirable applicants and raise large sums to finance national projects.

The author will assist your country in setting up such a program at a nominal charge. Because of the wide circulation of *The Passport Report,* we have a pool of interested future citizens, well qualified financially, of good moral character, with desirable technical skills and access to millions of dollars in capital. These individuals will get second passports somewhere. Why not from your country?

Comments, questions, additions and constructive criticism should be sent to: W.G. Hill, c/o Scope International, 62 Murray Road, Waterlooville, Hampshire, PO8 9JL, Great Britain.

FOR YOUR COUNTRY:
ELEMENTS OF A SUCCESSFUL PASSPORT PROGRAM

Most government officials and bureaucrats are not used to the concept of creating a product or service that will appeal to a "user". The obvious reason is that they see themselves as *dispensers of privileges* that people are willing to pay any price for. This was the mistake made by Jamaica. With some fanfare a few years ago, Jamaica launched its passport program. The deal called for an investment of US $100,000 in a program (similar to Dominica's proposed program I read about in the newspapers). This was generally perceived as a deal where the "investment" was sure to be a dead loss for the investors. Further, there were many unnecessary requirements like "5 years prior residence in a commonwealth country". The Jamaica program, as we understand it, was a complete flop. It has been in effect for several years without one single applicant having been approved.

In contrast, Singapore (an attractive destination) attracted thousands of Hong Kong Chinese and others with a program that allowed immediate immigration and citizenship with an investment of US $500,000 or "free" with a transfer of technical skills. The most important feature of the Singapore program was that it allowed complete freedom to the applicants. They were not obliged to actually move to or live in Singapore.

Likewise, Canada with a much cheaper required investment has had enormous success with a similar program. It allows investor-immigrants to live and invest where they please instead of imposing restrictions on travel and freedom. Citizenship and a passport are granted after three years. The long wait is the most undesirable feature of this program, although Canada waives the three year residence period in some cases. An important aspect of Canada and Singapore is that they both have political stability, excellent locations relative to major markets, a first class infrastructure and non-corrupt, non-socialist, low tax governments favoring entrepreneurial activity. Finally, their passports offer the facility of visa-free travel to Europe, Japan, the US or most other places a businessman might wish to visit. No country in Central or South America can come close to offering similar enticements. Accordingly, there should be no illusions that the funds and quality of people attracted by a less developed country would be as good as Canada unless other factors were involved. One of these factors is of course, the PRICE.

Your writer personally came up with the idea for the Belize Program which was a financial success attracting, in about two years, direct contributions (not investments) of approximately US $40,000 each from approximately 1,000 successful candidates for citizenship. The amount of money contributed was in excess of $24 million US dollars. This in spite of a program that was inefficiently administered, badly priced and beset with bureaucratic meddling and inefficiency. The cost to the country was the cost of printing around 1,200 little booklets or around US $12,000 for the passports themselves. This program was, however, ruined by the intervention of politicians. It must be remembered that Belize had (and still has) little to offer the international businessman as a place either to settle, vacation or invest. The Belize passport offered only visa-free travel to most Commonwealth countries. This is important to English speaking clients. The Belize program was a minor success, while it lasted. Why? Because the original price (of US $12,500 to Belize, with a similar sum paid to the marketing agents) was not unreasonable. However, at a lower price, the amount of revenues raised would have been multiplied by many times as you will see from the Panama example which follows. Note: While the official Belize "price" was originally US $12,500 + US $12,500 for administration, additional family members and upgrades within the program ultimately cost the candidates, on average, US $40,000 each. The Belize program was abruptly shut down with a lot of hard-feelings and litigation for quite irrational political reasons. It is important that other countries anxious to raise money from new citizens learn from and do not repeat the errors of Belize, Jamaica and the others.

A large number of countries have come up with passport and investor programs that were total flops. I was involved in some, but am pleased to note that the disasters were caused not because of our basic plan or concept but only by failure of the locally responsible politicians and public officials to use any common sense! The main reason for failures observed by this writer is that *local politicians and bureaucrats often sell citizenship and passports on a "private* basis.'' Thus, powerful and well connected private individuals will work to sabotage any legally authorized programs that interfere with their private source of revenue. The most outstanding example of this is in Panama where just *one consular official of the Noriega régime personally sold 60,000 legally issued and renewable passports at approximately US $8,000 each.* These documents were recognized and approved by the past as well as the current Panama administration (which derives substantial financial benefits from the passport holders). None of the approximately ONE BILLION DOLLARS raised during the past five years (and still being raised) from the sale of Panamanian citizenships benefited the *public* treasury however. The Panama passport is still being effectively marketed, and many people associated with the government are profiting. The program is essentially one where officials (who have discretion to grant citizenship) are being privately compensated for doing so. In the case of Panama, passports thus issued are fully recognized by the government and internationally as well.

In contrast, to the quasi-legal Panama Program, a consular official of Ireland recently issued several hundred Irish passports to young and attractive oriental ladies who wished to lived in the European Community. This went on from about 1984 to 1987. In exchange for a combination of money (approximately US $1,000 per passport) and sex, Irish passports were issued. The Consul was fired when his game was discovered by the Irish Foreign Ministry. They are now seeking to recall these passports – or not renew them when they expire ten years after issuance.

The writer has many stories to tell on the above subject, but *our main interest is in helping governments set up a legally authorized programs which will benefit the participating countries.* Such programs will also be a force for justice and right thinking in the world. By facilitating travel and investment for legitimate business people whose rights are being restricted by political situations they have had no role in creating, these countries will be facilitating a world of free trade and unrestricted travel. There are many individuals who are not able to live, invest, or travel freely due to an accident of birth or parentage. They hold the ''wrong'' passport or perhaps no passport at all. While many of these individuals are penniless refugees in United Nations camps, others are highly skilled people with assets and substantial resources. Some have wealthy friends and family abroad.

A successful passport program, in our opinion, should offer good travel documents in exchange for economic or other equally valuable contributions. Political and marketing considerations should also allow private individuals associated with the program to openly and legally earn substantial commissions for their marketing and administration efforts.

In the real world, unless ''go getter'' people can be motivated by the prospect of earning something, the program is doomed to be less than a success. Good hearted leftist people may be fine at slogans and speeches, but only a businessman can put together and administer a program that will earn a poor country some serious money. The writer is available to help write appropriate legislation. We have an honest sales and administration team that will raise very substantial sums for a visible and beneficial specific project like a hospital or university that would be supported by all political factions. Without unanimous support and public popularity, a passport program is bound to be attacked by opposition politicians on the outside and revoked by a later administration. The choice of a suitable national project or ''object'' where the money raised could be spent is for the country to decide. This writer would suggest a new free hospital for delivering babies or a clinic where the people can all come for free dental care or anything that is VISIBLE, free to all the people and NON-CONTROVERSIAL. The project must not offend any existing interests. For instance, a medical facility should be staffed by local doctors if available. The local professionals should be well paid for delivering their services. If foreign medical personnel are perceived as stealing business from local professionals, there will be trouble. **The idea is to gain the total support of all political factions and backing of everyone** associated with or affected by the project.

The "product" itself, your passport, must be good for visa free travel to Europe and as many countries as possible. Normally this is accomplished by diplomatic accords removing all your own visa requirements appertaining to the citizens of those countries. Free and unrestricted travel rights have always brought benefits to the countries liberal in granting such rights. For instance, the tourism industry in Spain or Great Britain is many times bigger than in equally attractive countries like the US where they shortsightedly require visas of most foreigners for entry.

Passports, which must be conceived of as "A Product You are Selling", must be made attractive. These are some additional elements of any successful program:

1.   The entire program must be kept Simple. In one country a program was ruined when each official of the ministry began inserting his pet restrictions. A health minister insisted upon an AIDS test for new citizen-prospects. The Minister of Justice insisted upon unreasonable background checks. Bureaucratic delays added months of waiting time. It must be remembered that individuals who acquire second passports, in most cases *will never wish to visit the country of their new citizenship*. If a country is worried about these people bringing in disease, it could require medical testing before *all* non-resident passport holders return home. There are many simple ways to screen out criminals, but to make the initial acquisition of a travel document too difficult, too costly or too long a process simply turns away potential customers who must be courted, not discouraged.

2.   The price to the consumer must be competitive and set to maximize revenues. It is better to sell 10,000 units of a product at $10,000 than 50 units at $25,000. There are many products on offer! Passports are available from African countries for as little as US $500 each. While a European Community passport may be worth US $50,000 or more and a US passport worth around US $25,000 in a free market, it should be remembered that almost any civilized country with a useable passport could sell a few documents at a high-end price. But a more reasonable price will maximize national revenues. Remember, few if any of the "new citizens" will ever even visit, much less live in the country of their second citizenship.

3.   The cost to the user should not be in the form of any "investment" where the return is not definite. It is simpler and more attractive for all to *sell* a "medical clinic construction bond", for instance, which bears **no interest** and will **never be redeemed**. If this **contribution** can be made "tax deductible" in the applicant's home country the price charged can be higher, as the writer will explain in a presentation to any Foreign Ministry officials if requested to do so.

4.   There must be no **residence requirement, no requirement to visit** the country and **no restrictions** upon the absolute freedom of your citizen abroad to engage in any legal activity.

5. The passport must be **renewable for life** and **irrevocable**. This must be guaranteed by a constitutional provision that can't be changed by a succeeding administration. The program itself can be terminated, but citizenships granted under it should not be revocable except in the event of a conviction for a felony crime committed within the country of issuance.

6. Citizenship must pass to later-born children and new spouses the same as for native-born citizens.

7. Family and children should be included in the program although there can be an extra charge for extra family-member passports (perhaps at 50 per cent of cost of head-of-family). A spouse or children should be included on the passport of the main individual if this is requested by the client.

8. The **life of the passport should be at least ten years** before renewal is required.

9. There is nothing wrong with "a charge in lieu of income tax" for non-residents, of say US $500 per year, payable on renewal of passports. The amount must be definite and set in advance. This concept will keep public support for the project alive for many years and provide a stream of income to support the hospital, clinic, housing program or other project chosen as the object of funds raised by this program. The fact that there is a good cash flow coming in without any cost to the country will make it harder for later politicians to attack or terminate the program.

10. **Confidentiality of names of new citizens is essential**. Their "old" country must **not be notified**.

11. **There must be no required oath of allegiance nor military service**. Taxes if any must be reasonable, definite and in the range of #9 above. Naturally, the writer has a great many ideas and very good reasons for all these points which will be explained and presented in detail if your government desires to institute a successful program using our services.

12. The program must grant exactly the same rights and protections for "new citizens" as exist for natural born citizens. For instance, if a native cannot be extradited, the new citizen must have the same protections against extradition, deportation or rendition.

13. There can be no "exit visa" requirement nor restrictions on travel.

14. ANY INVESTMENT PROGRAM SHOULD BE SEPARATE FROM, AND NOT CONFUSED WITH THE PASSPORTS!
    There are many good reasons for this as the writer and his clients have learned from the Canadian experience. These can be explained, upon request.
    If investment in the local economy is desired, it must be made attractive by such things as, for instance, a 25 year tax holiday, freedom from exchange controls, ability to hire and fire without interference, freedom from import or export duties (as for instance in a free port), etc. This is a complex subject, and the author has considerable expertise that would require several volumes to set out. But the point is, **investment will not flow to places where corruption, high taxes** or bureaucratic restrictions make investment less desirable than the places where such investments already are in place.

15. Your country should be liberal in appointing honorary consuls and in issuing diplomatic and service passports. A program that I have in mind and have masterminded for several countries could bring great benefits to the country with no costs or negative aspects. It could be related to your passport program.

HOW TO MAKE IT HAPPEN

In the event that your country is interested in my proposals, I suggest that I visit your decision makers to lend my services and expertise in setting up and marketing your program. This could be in return for an annual cash retainer of US $500,000 per year plus expenses. *Alternatively, I would work for free!* But I would then ask for your government to show good faith with a non-cash commitment to me. I am open to all suggestions, but one possibility would be in the form of an appointment as "official advisor to the government" with diplomatic status – revokable only for misconduct. It would be understood that this document would be used only by the author for personal travel or in connection with any passport program ultimately adopted. I feel that some serious offer to me (of a role in the marketing of this program) on the part of responsible officials would be desirable in the event I was to devote a lot of time and money to promoting this project, without the usual cash retainer.

Finally, my feeling is that if any passport program I drew up and implemented was actually adopted, a small neutral nation with good international recognition could raise approximately ONE BILLION US DOLLARS, net of all expenses. There would be no negative aspects. It is my belief that if handled correctly, in a businesslike manner, the program would bring in far more money than one billion dollars. Why? Because some of your new citizens, attracted by the enlightened policies of your government would take advantage of free port and other investment facilities. The above figure would then just be a small proportion of the total economic benefits to be received. Because of my unfortunate experience with many governments, I know how difficult it is to get local politicians to agree on anything that makes sense. But a simple passport program is easy to start and could be done on a small-scale experimental basis for a year or two.

With your assistance I would like to try to make it happen. The potential benefits to your country and to all persons associated with a passport sales program would be very great.

If you will forward a copy of my proposals to the proper people, I will be at their service.

Sincerely yours,

Dr. W.G. HILL

A MESSAGE FOR LAWYERS AND THOSE ABLE TO OBTAIN PASSPORTS OR RESIDENCE PERMITS

We receive several inquiries a week from readers who request referrals and assistance in passport and immigration matters. If you can be of service and work on a "contingent fee" arrangement (with no money taken out of escrow unless you can accomplish the objective), we will keep information about your services on file and send referrals of readers who are interested in what you offer. Your sheet should contain as much of the following information as possible:

1.   Name of country(s)
2.   Full price of passport(s)
     Including extras for spouses and dependants
     Volume discounts for groups
3.   Escrow or payment arrangements
4.   Which of the documents listed below are needed from client?
5.   Which of these documents are **issued** as part of your package? Indicate by (✓) after the above. Use a photocopy of this page for your reply.

	NEEDED	ISSUED
Cedula or ID card	☐	☐
Copy of old passport	☐	☐
Birth Certificate	☐	☐
Naturalization Certificate	☐	☐
Tax Clearance	☐	☐
Exit Visa	☐	☐
Health Certificate	☐	☐
Police Good Conduct Certificate	☐	☐
Driving License	☐	☐
International Driving License	☐	☐
Visa for the US, Europe, or other	☐	☐
Proof of Residence (state time required, if any)	☐	☐

6.   Basis upon which the passport you offer is legally issued:
          Investment (give details)
          Meritorious Service (give details)
          Military Service
          Ancestry
          Religion
          "Special Arrangements"
          Birthplace
          Parent's Nationality
          Other
7.   Validity period of passport, how renewed, cost of renewals.
8.   List of countries holder can visit without a visa.
9.   Restrictions on issuance: for example, racial or religious barriers, if any.
10. Languages spoken and races living in country.
11. Your name, address, phone, fax or other means of contact.
12. Your references.
13. Would you like your firm's name published in future *Passport Reports?*

Part I

WHY YOU NEED A SECOND PASSPORT

HOW IT ALL STARTED

The first refugee travel document was the "Nansen Passport" issued in 1917 to white Russian refugees in Europe. It was named after Fritzjof Nansen, the Norwegian explorer and delegate to the League of Nations. This passport successfully served hundreds of thousands of refugees as a document of identity for travel until the outbreak of World War II.

While the International Refugee Organization (IRO) replaced the defunct Nansen Passport Office from 1930 to 1945, it had no authority to issue identity or travel documents to refugees.

The 1951 treaty, Convention of the Status of Refugees, defined the rights of refugees. It only became operative in 1960 after the required 35 countries had ratified it. According to this convention, only those ratifying countries are authorized to issue travel documents to refugees. These countries are further authorized to determine which individuals are "eligible" to be recognized as refugees.

The result has created a large refugee population and economic pressures for some of the ratifyers. In turn, some have refused to accept the legal responsibilities implied under terms of the Convention when declaring these refugees "eligible". In some cases, the United Nations High Commissioner for Refugees Office (established in 1945 to replace the IRO), has given, without authority, the title "refugees-in-orbit" to those who are not recognized as "eligible."

International law's UN Universal Declaration of Human Rights Article 13 states: "Everyone has the right to freedom of movement and residence within the borders of each state. Everyone has the right to leave any country, including his own, and to return to his country."

Article 15 says: "Everyone has the right to a nationality. No one shall be arbitrarily deprived of his nationality nor denied the right to change his nationality."

However, countries the world over have spent most of their time restricting movement, and making freedom of travel as difficult as possible. Hence this report.

WHO NEEDS A SECOND PASSPORT?

You, if your present passport or travel document
1. Makes you a target of terrorists
2. Could be revoked, confiscated or suspended
3. Restricts your basic human right to travel in any way
4. Subjects you to tax on your worldwide income, to currency controls or other confiscations
5. Allows your government to control, restrict or monitor your travels
6. Causes you delays, harassment or denies entry at any border
7. Prevents you from working or settling anywhere you prefer
8. Requires visas to visit places where you want to go
9. Forces you into unwanted military obligations
10. Identifies you as a citizen of an unpopular, immoral, aggressive or despotic nation
11. Needs to be renewed or validated more than once each decade
12. Limits your freedom to invest your money or borrow when and where you please

13. Interferes with your freedom to pursue any investment opportunities or other activity that brings you happiness without harm to others

14. Last but not least, if your present citizenship requires too much bookkeeping and paperwork, making life a hassle . . .

Then you may want to opt for more freedom. A second passport can be your passport to freedom.

DO AMERICANS NEED A SECOND PASSPORT?

Perhaps people in countries facing civil war or political uncertainty, such as Hong Kong, may need a place to go. But what about Americans? Don't Americans believe that everyone in the rest of the world wants an American passport?

The truth is, some huddled masses and the wretched refuse of some third world shores may want to become Americans. But according to knowledgeable international lawyers and passport consultants, wealthy people (even those who might want to live part-time in the US for tax reasons) know better than to seek American passports. In fact, wealthy Americans create the greatest demand for second passports. Does this mean that American citizens are giving up their birthright in order to become citizens of banana republics and tin-horn dictatorships? Far from it!

During five years of in-depth research and interviews the author has uncovered a fascinating story – the story of a trend by freedom-seeking individuals to imitate the multi-national corporations. A surprisingly large number of these individuals are Americans. But they come from all over the world . . .

WHY BRITS DO IT

Over 600,000 United Kingdom citizens have been driven into exile because of high taxes. Once domiciled abroad, in Italy, Portugal, Singapore, Bermuda (and hundreds of other locations favoured by the English), many Brits at first came home like migratory birds to spend six months each year (tax-free) "vacationing" in England. The tax collector (Her Majesty's Inland Revenue) then passed rules making long stays by former Brits more difficult. Today if a Brit maintains a home or apartment within the UK, even a single day's visit results in full income tax on worldwide income. Without a home the allowable vacation visit has been reduced to 90 days per year (after a three year continuous absence). Many Brits found that if they entered and left the UK on a non-British passport, the record of their entry and departure was never linked up with their income tax files. They could come and go in greater freedom, without counting the days.

Brits are individualists and freedom lovers. They don't like to be told they can't visit their old haunts or grandchildren unless they surrender up to 40 per cent of their income for the privilege. Thus (ironically), Brits who love their Kingdom the most, those who like to spend time in the Motherland, are today most likely to have become citizens of another country. UK law allows unrestricted dual citizenship.

WHEN DO SWISS NEED A SECOND PASSPORT?

Swiss men who want to avoid lifetime military summer camps may wish to change citizenship. There are other reasons as well. Swiss citizens have found numerous instances where they are discriminated against. Switzerland does not permit foreigners to own land or hold a job in Switzerland (with a few exceptions). Thus, other countries, playing tit-for-tat, have reciprocity laws. The Swiss are thus prevented from owning land or seeking employment in a long list of countries. This sort of restrictive legislation is of course stupid and self-defeating, but it goes on all the time.

BEATING THE COMPUTERS

Many countries have lately tried to trap more people in their tax nets. To do this they have shortened the periods that tourists or visitors can stay from the previously almost universal six months to much shorter periods. In the US after 1987, a foreigner who stays for over 122 days per year may be held liable for heavy US income taxes on his worldwide income. He will have to go through an unpleasant grilling to get a tax clearance before being permitted to leave. In that tropical paradise Thailand, a similar rule requires tax clearance and a $50 fee payable by those who spend over 90 days per year in the country. For Perpetually Tax-free Tourists who wish to avoid such paperwork and expense, **all such problems and confrontations are avoided by having a second passport**. One departs before the maximum allotted time on passport number one and re-enters later on passport number two, thereby keeping the annual visits, as recorded in passport entry-exit stamps, to the short periods allowed – at least insofar as the computers which record such matters are concerned. Some individuals prefer name variations on their different passports to assure even greater privacy and freedom of movement.

AVOIDING DISCRIMINATION

During the Falklands defense, British passport holders were discriminated against and detained in jails all over South America. Similar indignities are **always** suffered by South Africans – this **regardless of the fact that their personal convictions may oppose those South African government policies** that have caused undeserved discrimination against individual travelers. There is scarcely a country in the world whose citizens are not regularly victims of international tensions. During the 1986-89 period any prospective visitor to France had to stand in long lines to get a French visitor's visa – unless he held an EC passport. Previously (before an outbreak of bombing and terrorism) France had allowed visa-free entry from a long list of countries.

An individual who has a drawer full of passports can choose the most suitable for the time and circumstances. Why shouldn't you always travel with minimum inconvenience?

CUTTING THROUGH THE RED TAPE

Pakistan denied entry to hundreds of British tourists stranded at the Karachi airport after Britain attempted to halt illegal Pakistani immigration by imposing visa requirements on Pakistanis. Brazil requires American tourists to get a personal letter of recommendation from the US Ambassador in Brasilia after the US imposed a similar requirement upon Brazilian tourists in the US. The diplomats and politicians play games while travelers must incur extra costs and spend hours in airport transit lounges and embassy queues trying to cope.

Government officials are constantly throwing up more barriers to property ownership and freedom of movement. Insulation from bureaucratic harassment is sought by individuals. Those who have the intelligence and money to procure alternate travel documents will do so. Second passports can circumvent many miles of red tape.

THE MULTI-NATIONALS

A multi-national corporation has several citizenships. By incorporating in more than one political jurisdiction, a company becomes a legal entity able to do business in each country of incorporation. The company may be "owned" by a parent in a foreign country, but local governments generally treat it as one of their own domestic corporations, i.e. a "local" citizen.

To induce a foreign company to set up shop, many governments offer special concessions. These may include up to twenty-five year tax holidays, discounts on energy and raw materials, free land, subsidized local labor, cash grants, and other attractions. Why? Principally because ruling powers tend to stay in office when the populace is employed and prosperous. High rates of unemployment bring unrest and riot, whereas full employment is a mass anaesthetic. The cost of giving a twenty five year tax holiday to a company that creates jobs and would otherwise not come, is zero.

The impetus to form multi-nationals, however, did not arise because of courtships and extravagant inducements. The movement didn't even grow primarily to exploit localized opportunities for profit. Instead, explosive growth of the multi-national movement came about to evade restrictions and high taxes. These were initially justified and imposed upon corporations, largely to pay for World War Two.

CURRENCY CONTROL

In order to retain assets within their borders, all countries have at one time or another restricted capital outflows. One reason for moving money from one country to another is fear of loss due to political changes or relative inflation rates. For instance, all currencies tied to the US dollar were in a serious decline during 1984-1987. Sensible French or Italian corporate treasurers and individuals looked to the currencies of low inflation countries such as Japan, West Germany and Switzerland for a hedge.

Foreigners and foreign subsidiary corporations can manage currency hedging easily without running foul of laws that often provide criminal as well as civil penalties for doing no more than prudently protecting one's capital. Very few countries in the world permit their citizens to have foreign bank accounts, foreign currencies or foreign investments of any kind – without strict controls, costly permits and special taxes. Dual citizens, like multi-national corporations, can usually circumvent all currency controls.

HIGH TAX RATES

Governments imposed tax rates after World War II that generally soared to over 50 per cent. These rates would have been considered confiscatory prior to the war when international rates topped out at 10 per cent or so. No company can maintain a competitive edge and a healthy growth rate when over half of its profits are used to pay taxes.

The multi-national corporate structure allows a company to make component parts and sell profitable services in a low tax jurisdiction, thereby minimizing taxation. For example, suppose a plastic part costs 2 cents to manufacture. It sells for $1.00. If that part is wholly manufactured in the US, UK, Germany, Sweden, or any other high tax jurisdiction, the 98 cents profit is eroded by a tax of 40 per cent or more.

If however, the component part costing 2 cents is made in a no-tax zone such as Panama, and the home company is billed for $1.00, a 98 cent tax-free "transfer payment" profit is accumulated and retained "offshore". Loan transactions, insurance, shipping and other services are typically rendered by offshore corporations or individuals. Profits from these offshore activities thus build up capital abroad.

THE WHOLE WORLD IS A TAX HAVEN

A high income individual American could change nationality, move part or full-time to a tax haven and continue to render services to his old company. He could be paid tax-free offshore.

A TAX HAVEN CAN BE ALMOST ANY COUNTRY OTHER THAN ONE'S NATIVE LAND

An individual can and should be a multi-national if his tax payments are of greater value than the benefits received from his home country.

The Rolling Stones moved to France in order to escape high British income taxes. Yet many wealthy Frenchmen are in the UK in order to avoid high French taxes. This anomaly is caused by the fact that most high tax countries exempt foreigners who reside there less than six months a year.

Thus, a "foreigner" who winters in California for four months, travels or lives outside the US for three months and then spends the remaining five months in his own country will typically pay no taxes anywhere! More important, this individual will not be subject to currency controls, investment restrictions and burdensome paperwork brought about by bureaucratic tax and accounting requirements.

The multi-national (two passport) individual has the same advantages as a multi-national corporation.

In order to enter and live in a foreign country for six months as a tourist, one generally needs a passport. Several countries also require visas from tourists. And in order to remain longer, to work or purchase a home a Residence Permit is often needed.

"Non-work residence permits" are typically granted to entrepreneurs and others who do not compete on the local job market. *A citizen of any country (with the exception of the US and the Philippines) need never acquire a second passport for tax reasons. He simply* **moves** *and can then live anywhere outside of his homeland to escape taxes.*

Further details of the advantages of changing domicile are in *The Tax Exile Report,* published by Scope International.

WHAT'S THE MOST EXPENSIVE PASSPORT IN THE WORLD?

The US, however, is the only major country in the world that imposes the same tax rates upon US citizens who live abroad as it does upon US residents.

The resulting equation becomes a simple one for non-resident wealthy Americans. By giving up US citizenship, their net income is, at minimum, doubled. Even with Reagan era tax reductions in the US, the 28 per cent federal rate is but a component of the total bite. State and local taxes typically run around 20 per cent. Then there is a 5 per cent federal surcharge for large incomes. Thus, for unsheltered taxable income in the US, the effective rate will still be well over 50 per cent. Why pay it when one can just be a "tourist" visiting the US on a non-US passport?

If past history is a guide, the "low" 50 per cent effective tax is only temporary. US tax regulations will continue to change constantly and will continue to be complex and confusing. Retainers for tax lawyers and accountants will still be expensive – and *necessary* – in order to protect American taxpayers from making small mistakes that quickly mushroom into huge fines and severe criminal penalties.

US tax collectors, known as the Internal Revenue Service (IRS), are notorious worldwide as a law unto themselves, behaving as extremely difficult and disagreeable tyrants. They have the power to make administrative seizures and confiscations that require the defendant taxpayer to go to court or to prove his innocence. IRS power is totally contrary to the US theory of "presumption of innocence until proven guilty by due process of law". Constitutional protections (privacy, no self incrimination, freedom of speech) have no application to tax matters in the US.

A second passport and less than six months (now reduced to 122 days) annual stay in the US avoids these confrontations and eliminates the myriad of full disclosure and detailed financial filing requirements. One may own real property in the US, hold securities and open US bank accounts without being a citizen of the US. It is best to accomplish this through nominees such as foreign banks or trustees, for complete privacy.

Foreigners who become US citizens must give up their freedom, privacy and at least half their taxable income for the rest of their lives – even if that income was generated by assets accumulated prior to becoming a US citizen. It is easy to see why the US passport is often called "the most expensive passport in the world"!

Naturally, US tax rates fluctuate and so-called tax shelters are available to US citizens and resident aliens. Yet it is far easier to avoid all US taxes and the tyranny of the IRS if one is not a US citizen and has no taxable assets there. Knowing all of this, would you still want to become or remain a US citizen? The clear answer for anyone of substantial means is "no".

In 1990, the US Justice Department ruled that FBI agents may enter foreign countries and arrest Americans or foreign nationals wanted for federal offences. This "snatch authority" will require presidential sanction in each case. Tax-dodgers have less security too, now the IRS has right of access to passport renewals information made abroad. Within a few years, as current passports expire, all non-filing US-non-residents can be traced.

FOREIGNERS ARE ALWAYS TREATED BETTER THAN CITIZENS

Generally, anyone with papers identifying him as a "foreigner" can avoid most unpleasant police and bureaucratic contacts. My driving licence was once taken by a pickpocket in an English-speaking country. The policeman taking the theft report insisted upon arranging for me to obtain a replacement licence issued by the local authorities so that I could continue my Australian tour with a rented car. The test was difficult, and I flunked it. Locals would have to wait six months before applying again. I was given a short oral course by the friendly director of the department and an oral re-examination. The result was an immediate licence. "We try to help our overseas visitors," I was told.

Foreigners are more likely to obtain friendly, if not red carpet treatment since most governments encourage tourism. Nasty, local bureaucrats or customs officers may do their worst to their own countrymen, but few will harass foreigners. One exception may be the world infamous US immigration officers, they are **mean** as junk yard dogs **to everyone**. But guardians of the United Kingdom's borders and the Spanish Civil Guard, for instance, are always kind and helpful to tourists of obvious substance, although not always so nice to natives. Backpackers do not always get the same welcome! In any event, local citizens, backpackers or otherwise are far more likely to be strip-searched or abused than "foreigners".

Americans coming home from Panama or the Cayman Islands can expect the proverbial third degree, complete with body search. Any affluent American, unless he is otherwise protected, is suspected of being in the money laundering business. He will be grilled. Any other nationality can import and export as much currency as they please with no reaction from US officials. Incidentally, cash bundles do show up on those airport X-ray machines. Customs officials of the country you are leaving will often seize large amounts of cash (over $30,000) if you can't prove it was legally obtained, i.e. tax paid money. The "crime" of money laundering is always the flavor of the year.

HOW A DUAL NATIONAL MADE US $175,000 ON A US $600 INVESTMENT IN 3 WEEKS

While a second passport is not being touted as the way to make a great fortune, reports from many of our clients indicate that a second nationality can lead to unexpected cash-making opportunities.

One unusual situation occurred in 1985 when United Airlines announced a promotional contest. Anyone who could touch down in all fifty states of the US within fifty days, using United Airlines, would win unlimited first class air travel for one year.

An individual we'll call "Joe" had just acquired his second nationality. He was already aware of a "See the USA" airpass promotion that provided 30 days of US air travel for US $600. This promotion was limited to non-US citizens or non-residents – a qualification that Joe could now meet.

He entered United's contest using his non-citizen's "See the USA" airpass and became one of seventy-three individuals to win. During the awards ceremony, Joe learned that he was the only one to make it on a $600 airpass. Other entrants had spent over $6,000 on air tickets.

Joe then rang up over US $175,000 in first class airline trips in 1986 and 1987, all of which were paid for by United Airlines.

United's contest ended long ago. However, at this writing, the "See the USA" airpass program is still operating for non-US citizens. Other countries have similar deals for "foreigners". In Italy for instance, tourists obtain free road insurance and 15 per cent discount coupons for gasoline. Non-EC citizens may purchase autos in Denmark at a substantial discount and obtain free two year international tax-free tourist plates that give *de facto* immunity on parking and traffic tickets. (See our *Free Car* Report).

Another example of the money-making potential of dual nationals involves an American-Paraguayan. He bought a fully loaded top-of-the-line Mercedes Benz in Stuttgart for US $30,000, drove it all over Europe and the US, and sold it in the US after one year for a neat US $20,000 profit – after paying for shipping, EPA conversions and customs. He then bought a "tax-free" Cadillac convertible in the US which he sold in Switzerland for a similar profit. Although he could probably have accomplished this without a Paraguayan passport, he knows through experience that US customs authorities aren't so easy going with a US passport holder. Instead, they tend to impound an imported auto in order to find fault with its smog conversions.

In addition to ever-present situations to turn opportunities into cash, respectable "foreign visitors" who maintain their good humour and politeness will normally obtain exceptional courtesies from immigration, police and customs officials.

BANKING PASSPORTS

In the course of writing the *Passport Report,* we often heard lawyers use the term "BANKING PASSPORT". Until then, we had never heard of it. But after our initial rejection of the concept as something possibly illegal and certainly unpatriotic, we have had a change of thinking.

Especially for people who live in unfree countries, the concept of a *Banking Passport* now seems quite reasonable.

Let's say that Mr Smith is a citizen of the UNITED STATES OF ALBANIA. As you know, ALBANIA, hereafter called USA has all sorts of currency laws and restrictions. USA makes the unreported transfer of cash abroad a major felony-crime of "money-laundering" punishable by 25 years in the pokey. It makes having a secret account abroad to preserve assets against government confiscation (by inflation or otherwise) a crime. Incredibly, failure to file detailed reports of all activities four times a year and pay one-third of your income to "the State" is also a crime. One can file all these reports and pay, but such disclosure defeats the whole purpose of most Albanians – to have a nest-egg that is judgment proof and above all, government proof.

There are persistent rumors that the USA will follow the example of its mentor the former USSR and simply declare all bank-notes over $20 to be null and void because cash is something only used by criminals and drug dealers. Confiscation of private property is the logical solution of bureau-rats to all conceivable civic problems.

In our example, Mr Smith is an Albanian who has wangled the right to travel abroad freely. He also makes an occasional deal where the profits could be paid into a foreign account. He would probably be glad to pay a reasonable tax on such profits. But if he did pay a tax and reveal the nature of his foreign business (or publicly report where he keeps his assets), he would never have anything squirreled away for emergencies or retirement. So he stashes his cash and unwillingly accepts the risks of being a "criminal" by depositing some of his wealth outside of USA. The father of President John F. Kennedy once remarked that there were so many laws, it was impossible for any businessman not to be a criminal. That was sixty years ago! Now, laws on the books have multiplied 10,000 times.

As a result the US (as in United States of America) has a prison population ten times as big as the average country in Europe and is in fact the number one jailer on a per-capita basis, in the world, surpassing by far South Africa and the Soviet Union who were the old champs at keeping their citizens in the pokey. The United States of Albania is only slightly better. Thus, Smith wants to be low profile.

"Offshore Financial Advisers" tell Mr Smith that he can control yet conceal, secret assets by means of trusts, holding companies, foundations and other expensive legal entities requiring annual costs of at least £2,000 or more to set up and around £1,000 or more per annum for care and feeding. The disadvantage of such arrangements (necessary for active businesses, but not needed for mere asset management) is that not reporting such activities is illegal anyway. To make things worse, with offshore trusts or other vehicles:

a) *Someone else knows your business.* Those persons are not necessarily:
   1) Discreet
   2) Honest
   3) Cheap to feed

b) Your advisers (or new partners in crime) will say they "need" to be able to sign checks (to insulate you, they say) and control your funds. But all too often the adviser:
   1) Makes bad business decisions
   2) Makes mistakes

3) Is not available when you need him

4) Steals, or at best

5) Gets into some difficulties unrelated to you and to save his hide gives you up. You can't sue anyone for telling your secrets without stirring up an even bigger can of worms.

As Ferdinand and Imelda Marcos learned when their personal financial records were splattered all over the newspapers, they could be charged with many crimes even though advisers assured everything was "legal". [Moral of story: There is little or nothing one can do in business, politics or tax-avoidance that can't be turned into a criminal prosecution. Once you are in court, you will be financially ruined before you are finished – win or lose.] *The best protection may be to do whatever you are doing without witnesses or paperwork. Avoid giving information to friends and confidants. They could turn into enemies!*

THE 'BANKING PASSPORT' IS AN OPTION FOR ACHIEVING PRIVACY AND CONTROL.

The old alternative was setting up a corporation, foundation or trust. You create a separate "legal entity". Perhaps it was "offshore" which just means, not in your native country. The corporate treasurer (not you) signs checks. You are supposed to control things behind the scenes. It works, sometimes. **But what if you create another *person* with another nationality and a full set of identification? Will this serve the same purpose more cheaply and effectively? Can this be done legally? For the person with "passive" investments, the answer is, yes! So let us now return to Mr Smith.**

Assume that the Grand Duchy of Freedomia will accept any (rich) person as a citizen and issue them a passport. Assume further that Freedomia (like most English speaking countries) permits its citizens to use any name they like on their passports. **Presto! Shazam! You have created something like a corporation or holding company or foundation, but you have *complete control*. The new person you have created is the only completely reliable and trustworthy person in the whole world. Why? Because it is YOU, yourself!**

Thus Mr "P.T." Smith, instead of telling his lawyer, "Set me up with an offshore holding company", says, "Set me up with a new passport from a truly free country, or if none is available, then at least a country that does not care about its offshore citizens. That way, I won't have to serve in any army to kill people, spend half my time filling out silly forms, pay any more income tax or inheritance tax, VAT etc. or allow myself to be treated like some sort of "resource", exploited to pay for things I don't even believe in. Give me a new name and a new passport." For a **one-time** fee in the $20,000 range, that is exactly what many lawyers can do. If Mr Smith read *Passport Report* he might do it himself, for free! Either way, Mr Smith, now stops at his safe-deposit box just across the border whenever he leaves Albania. He deposits his passport. Then, like Superman, he switches passports, thus changing identity to (for instance) "Sherlock Holmes Acourt, Earl of Freedomia". The *noble title* is of course an optional extra, and for low profile purposes is definitely *not recommended!* But we like a little humor in our otherwise dull presentations. So as a sideline we help deposed ex-monarchs peddle noble titles. Titles can impress young girls, sometimes. But we digress, back to that new PT with the new ID, Mr Smith.

If Sherlock Holmes Acourt, also known as Smith of Albania is a PT, he probably never visits either Albania or Freedomia with his new Freedomia Passport. He keeps the two identities completely separate. When back in Albania for rare visits, Sherlock Holmes Acourt doesn't exist, at least not on any Albanian computer. If any Albanian spy should ever learn that someone named Sherlock has an account at the *Terribly Secret Bank & Trust Company of Liechtenstein, Ltd.,* the Albanian investigator will ignore it. What does he care if some citizen of Freedomia has a secret account. Everyone knows that the Freedomia government is a bunch of anarchists who don't tie up their citizens with the heavy Albanian ball and chain of taxes on worldwide income, currency restrictions and long jail sentences for almost everything. For those readers who haven't figured it out, Freedomia is every country in the world except the ''Socialist Republics'' and the Union of Socialist Albania (USA).

Getting back to Smith and his new passport. What has he accomplished? Smith has a new identity. With it he can judgment-proof his assets and do things that have no connection with Mr Smith of Albania. He can even do things that are legal everywhere else, but might be slightly illegal in the eyes of the despots of Albania. Even if those dastardly secret snooper agents of Albania (planted in Swiss banks etc.) should intercept a communication or letter regarding 'Sherlock Holmes Acourt' there would be no connection between Sherlock and Smith – unless Smith sent out communications direct from Albania in his alias or blabbed about his new arrangements.

If some day the vicious Albanian dictator, Cardinal Flimsy Wolsey decided to torture all citizens by making them come home to Albania and listen to incessant rock music, Smith would have the option of staying abroad as Sherlock. If the Albanian government decided it would not renew the passports of citizens abroad unless they paid some exorbitant sum (like 50 per cent of their income) just for the privilege of having an Albanian passport, Smith could simply become Sherlock for good, stay away from his native country and put his expensive Albanian passport to its highest and best use – perhaps as toilet paper.

As a dual Albanian-Freedomian, it is possible that many countries would accept Smith as a tourist (without requiring a visa) or resident just because he was a citizen (and/or noble) of Freedomia. In any event, with two passports to choose from, he can travel or immigrate more easily in an emergency than most people.

If you read *PT 1* you know why having a second passport is such a good idea. The concept of a **banking passport** is simply that for a **one-time expense and/or effort, one can become a ''new person''**. This separates one from activities or assets best kept confidential.

In the perfect world of our imagination, private property would of course be a ''sacred protected right''. There would be no laws against an individual using (or hiding) his legally acquired assets any way he wants to, but unfortunately, the rulers of Albania think (and have passed laws to support their views) that all property is theirs to re-distribute. Your ass and your assets are equally the ''property'' of the State.

Politicians can always figure out new ways to squander your money. National budgets expand to absorb available resources. A favorite boondoggle is to hire more bureaucrats who don't work or produce anything but are very good at tying us up in red tape.

If we are to exercise our natural right to own property and the DUTY to provide first for our family and our own comfortable retirement, we must figure out some way to place our nest egg somewhere beyond the grasp of those socialist minded officials who now have power over our A+A (Ass and Assets or, if you prefer, Property and Posterior).

The "banking passport" is just one of many tools available in the pursuit of freedom. It is nothing magical, and it is nothing new. International types have been using "passports of convenience" ever since passports were invented by Napoleon to prevent Frenchmen from leaving their country to avoid excessive taxation and military service. Passports have always been nothing more than a way to restrict freedom and to control people. In order to overcome unnatural barriers to the basic human rights of free travel and freedom to move assets, we can consider obtaining second or third sets of travel documents. Circumventing restrictions with appropriate paperwork is the traditional job of lawyers. It has always been the way to regain freedom or keep assets that governments would steal.

Only wicked governments restrict travel. Only criminal governments who fear having their citizens living freely abroad force their citizens to return in person to renew passports. Only greedy and unreasonable governments make passport renewals dependant upon the payment of large sums of money (like an income tax on worldwide income – without any benefits). Only the most evil, despotic governments forbid or make dual-citizenship difficult for their citizens to obtain.

If your government does any of these things, it may be time to vote with your feet and move your Ass and Assets elsewhere. Or at least position yourself to be *able to move* when the time is ripe. Who, these days, can seriously argue that their government will "provide for and protect them"?

Only people who do not love freedom submit to the dictates of despots. The PT will make governments exercise some restraint upon their greed and arrogance. If more people had the paperwork in hand to put A+A out of the jurisdiction, governments would no longer be the number one cause of misery and premature death in the world. Just as citizens of the ancient Mayan civilization disappeared into the jungle when the government began claiming all the best young virgin girls for human sacrifice (as a form of tax payment), such wasteful misuse of our A+A must be stopped today, in the same manner. We hope this has given you some food for thought!

The author welcomes all input, suggestions, improvements. As Ben Franklin said, "If we don't all hang together, we will hang separately!"

EXTRADITION: NO MATTER WHAT YOU DO, IT NEEDN'T AFFECT YOU

Someone who considers leaving friends and family, home and hearth in order to escape from persecution or jail also fears being dragged back home to face the music. The truth is that with over two hundred different countries in the world, no one need ever know where to begin looking. Even if they did know where you went, legal extradition is not available for most of the situations that people run away from.

There is no extradition for:
1.   Private debts or civil matters.
2.   Quasi-criminal matters such as failure to pay alimony, child support or taxes.
3.   Political matters such as treason or fiscal offences such as currency control violations.

4. Victimless or moral crimes such as prohibited sexual relations, slandering the state or refusing to abide by restrictions imposed upon racial or religious minorities.
5. Offenses which aren't serious (felonies) in the sanctuary jurisdiction. "Sanctuary" is the place where you go **after** committing an offense elsewhere.

Some nations prohibit or criminalize conduct that others consider to be normal or even beneficial. In Quebec, Canada, a seller of English language books was convicted of having a sign in his window in English. All signs in Quebec have to be in French. No nation would extradite this "criminal".

In the US, individuals receive stiff sentences for selling vitamin pills if they claim that health benefits accrue to users – even if the claims are true. In some countries, private commercial transactions or ownership of a foreign bank account is a capital crime, as is defection. Most countries do not extradite for these offences.

Extradition might be possible in the following cases:
1. If an extradition treaty exists.
2. If the treaty specifically includes the alleged or convicted crime.
3. If friendly relations exist between the two countries.
4. If the "criminal" can't escape the host country or "go underground" upon learning that the local police may be looking for him.

Any extradition treaty which might affect you is available for reading in any public law library. In practice, extradition is granted only in connection with criminals considered to be dangerous to the sanctuary country.

These would include:
1. Contract murderers.
2. Major narcotics dealers.
3. Individuals the sanctuary wants to be rid of. Child pornographers and child molesters, for instance, tend to be very unpopular.

Whenever a sanctuary wants to be rid of an individual, deportation or rendition is the normal method of exporting criminals. The undesirable is simply placed on an outbound boat or plane. While destination may be negotiable, relations with the "wanting" country can come into play. **Unlike extradition and deportation, "rendition" is an administrative, police affair without the formality of judicial review or appeals**.

If relations are friendly such as between the USA, Canada and England, law enforcement officers will ensure that the first stop on the outbound mode is in the country where the deportee is sought. Notification is provided so that law enforcement agents can arrange for a proper welcome on arrival. **Although extradition gets a lot of publicity, it is a relatively rare event**.

FUGITIVES: HOW THEY AVOID CAPTURE INDEFINITELY

We will not dwell upon justifying someone becoming a fugitive. Suffice to note that for all of the situations where someone is properly accused and deserves to be brought to justice, there are also some situations which are clearly a miscarriage of justice and common sense, if not also a mistake of law. The point is that some people who have been falsely accused or have made a mistake or have paid their debt to society probably deserve a chance to start anew. If they arrive in a new country and live a clean trouble-free life for many years, generally past problems will fade away. A fugitive is generally "home free" if he can keep a low profile and separate himself from his past.

YOUR INDIVIDUAL GOALS

95 per cent of the solution to any problem lies in clearly writing it down and then listing your options.

W.G. Hill

Would you drive a car without a spare tire? Probably not! The cost of emergency protection is low when you consider the inconvenience it may save you. Being stranded just once makes anyone a believer in spare tires. Unfortunately, you usually won't get a second chance to consider the merits of a second passport. Too often people put off taking the necessary steps to protect themselves against crisis situations.

Adversity occurs with unfortunate and increasing regularity – terrorist incidents, kidnappings, hijackings, revolutions, wars and social changes are the most obvious. But what about divorce? Child custody disputes? Unjust accusations of crime? Crippling litigation? Confiscatory tax claims? For any business person who achieves an above average level of wealth, these problems are becoming almost inevitable.

A proliferation of laws and regulations seems to almost make even breathing a criminal offence. *You don't have to be a "bad person" to face jail or the loss of all your property any more.* Growing the wrong crops on your farm, selling goods at the "wrong" prices, inadvertently causing a negative environmental impact, overhearing a conversation and not reporting it to the authorities, causing a traffic accident while under the influence of a prescribed medicine – all of these newly-defined crimes and many inadvertent acts or omissions could mean financial disaster or even a jail term. This is true in all first world countries.

It may seem unlikely now, but like cancer, **getting caught in the grindwheels of a bureaucracy is an unpredictable thing. Until it happens, you don't believe it could happen to you**. Our usual belief is that problems will happen to the next guy – or the folks in the next country. This means that the majority of people are not prepared. They do not have an escape route. They do not have options.

Of course it is foolish to run away from every problem at the first sign of trouble. It is equally foolish to place yourself in a vulnerable position. Why take a beating that could have been avoided? Having a second passport, like having spare cash for emergencies, is just a type of self-preservation.

Do you need diversification? Clearly you do. Consider this . . . simply being a banker, a respectable enough profession in most places, was declared a crime *punishable by death* in Iran, a result of the Ayatolla's strict enforcement of the Islamic ban on moneylending. Bankers who couldn't get a visa or second passport to leave the country were shot or tortured to death. **Obtaining the right to travel – to be able to leave a country – is extremely important!**

Communist countries prohibit most travel. In the "ex" communist countries of Eastern Europe, there is theoretical freedom to travel, but the paperwork and costs do not allow the "average Ivan" much latitude. Even respectable and civilized countries like Italy, France and the UK have in recent years effectively restricted travel by limiting amounts of cash that can be taken out, deposited or spent abroad by their citizens. These regulations wax and wane. Accordingly, it goes without saying that in addition to a second passport, a good PT (see back pages of this book for a summary of the PT theory developed by Dr Hill) must keep enough assets abroad to support himself for a year or more.

During the past fifty years, ownership of a second or spare passport would literally have saved the lives of millions of people. Today you can benefit from business and tax saving opportunities with a second passport. You can in any emergency embark on a new life, leaving behind personal or national problems.

A passport is only a "piece of paper". It is easy to obtain at nominal cost – if you are not in a hurry or in an emergency situation. But when crisis hits and you need it most, a second passport can be nearly impossible to get in time for effective use.

Ideas and alternatives outlined here will ensure that you and your family will not only ride out most storms, but will actually profit and enjoy life more.

Once our simple ideas are implemented, newly opened business and tax pathways will lead to higher material standards and possibilities. There will be association with like-minded, intelligent, internationally-oriented people. Most importantly you will experience a personal sense of security and well-being. You will know that you have prepared yourself and your loved ones with tools, options and resources to deal with those inevitable crises and tragedies of life. You will gain a freedom of action and an expanded world view.

DO YOU WANT TO CONTROL YOUR OWN DESTINY – OR BE FLOTSAM AND JETSAM, TOSSED AROUND BY FORCES YOU NEITHER UNDERSTAND NOR CONTROL?

If you seek freedom from governmental whims and restraints, obtaining your second passport is a most important step. There are other intelligent moves to make. You must:
1. Protect and diversify your assets internationally.
2. Arrange for a source of livelihood, credit and a business at a second location.
3. Acquire a comfortable and suitable foreign residence, ready and waiting when you need it.
4. Develop an alternative lifestyle and a new identity.

You can be totally prepared – financially, mentally and physically – with your fallback social and economic contacts in place. This is PT – the "Perfect Thing". But first you must have the papers (i.e. passport) and know-how to be able to go somewhere else.

You must have somewhere to go and something pleasant waiting for you at your destination point. But for now, let's concentrate on the paperwork – namely how to go about obtaining your second passport.

Comments, questions, additions and constructive criticism should be sent to:
Scope International, 62 Murray Road, Waterlooville, Hampshire PO8 9JL, Great Britain

Part II

HOW TO GET YOUR SECOND PASSPORT

PATRIOTISM OR A PIECE OF PAPER?

For some individuals, the decision to seek a second passport can be an emotional one. Changing former allegiances can be as gut-wrenching as changing religions or getting out of one marriage into another. But emotional difficulties are not necessary, since it is "all in the way you look at it".

For our purposes a passport should be regarded as nothing more than a piece of paper. An important paper certainly – but one without mystical qualities. There is no need to get blubbery or flagwavingly patriotic over it. **Your basic loyalties and priorities need not be affected in any way by these little cardboard booklets**. The decision to get a new passport (or more likely, a second passport in addition to your present passport) should be viewed as a purely economic or survival decision. It is a private matter.

A LITTLE KNOWLEDGE IS A DANGEROUS THING

This book contains many helpful hints, anecdotes that may apply to you and several serious warnings intended to keep you out of trouble. Reading time is several hours. I urge you to read this report from cover to cover in one sitting. Skimming may cause you to miss a most important item that applies to you. Mark passages of interest and those sections advising action appropriate to your individual situation. Then think about the situation and what you have read. Mull over the possibilities for one day.

During the following day, set your own plan in motion by writing letters, making telephone calls and visiting Consulates and libraries. All too often we procrastinate and lose opportunities which exist for only a short time. Other distractions pop up and we become diverted. If you have a large supply of money and a limited amount of time, you may wish simply to "buy" an instant passport as explained in this report. Several reliable sources for legally issued instant passports are available from Scope International. Such arrangements cost from $6,000 to $500,000 these days. BUT THIS BOOK WILL ALSO SHOW YOU HOW TO OBTAIN A SECOND PASSPORT LEGALLY, FOR THE PRICE OF A GOOD LUNCH.

IF YOU DON'T ACT UPON THIS INFORMATION WITHIN 48 HOURS . . . YOU PROBABLY NEVER WILL!

For maximum effectiveness, your intentions or actual possession of a second passport should not be discussed with anyone – particularly your spouse, especially if there is the slightest chance of a future divorce or financial dispute between you. Having a second passport can provide a smooth and easy escape route, lower taxes, freedom to travel to places where your government might not allow you to go and freedom from military service – a veritable bouquet of unexpected advantages.

MOST BENEFITS WOULD BE LOST IF THE FACT OF YOUR SECOND PASSPORT WAS COMMON KNOWLEDGE. ACCORDINGLY, KEEP IT TO YOURSELF!

Your purpose is to insure your survival and prosperity. In the face of a hostile plaintiff, tax collector or divorcing spouse. If it were known that you had a second passport, you would be ordered to surrender it or go to jail. Obviously the fact that you have a second passport is for you alone to know.

It would be a shame if, after considerable work and expense, you were unable to use your passport because it was confiscated, destroyed or stolen from you by a wrongly trusted business partner or spouse.

Your passport should be kept at an accessible location, preferably *outside* your country of residence. A telephone call or code message to its custodian should cause it to be delivered to you on short notice. It should be kept in a sealed envelope and upon your instructions, it should be delivered where you direct.

Most bankers or a mail collection and forwarding service can act as custodian. Your Channel Island landlord (see *The Channel Island Report* published by Scope International) would be an ideal custodian.

THE FIRST STEP – YOUR PSYCHOLOGICAL PREPARATION FOR THIS PROJECT

Let's suppose there was a general hostility in your community to people like you. What do I mean? Suppose you are a wealthy person – a property owner or employer. It is possible that you could be labelled an "exploiter". It has happened before, in many times and places with many variations.

Perhaps people of your particular politics, ancestry, religion or skin colour became unpopular. Let's assume that the situation got so bad that you were facing immediate physical injury or jail unless you, for instance, signed a deed, a confession or a declaration against your will.

Obviously, in this world, there are and always have been people who would rather die than give up their property, become an informant or take a distasteful oath. Many were burned at the stake for refusing to do what the Inquisition required of them. Joan of Arc was such an idealist. Galileo, on the other hand, decided to live a while longer. He signed a statement recanting his belief that the Earth revolved around the Sun.

Our proposition is that it is better to sign any document to escape and go on living (or staying in one piece) than to be an idealist. "I regret I have only one life to give for my country" is a fine line for a movie actor, but nothing is more important than self-preservation – Nothing! This book is not aimed at super-patriots or idealists who would rather take gas than take necessary protective actions to survive. The "Glorious Dead" and the "Financially Ruined" gave up their chance to fight on for truth and justice.

The world belongs only to the living. You are reading this because you already think like a survivor. **If you want to be a dead hero, stop here.** This is information for pragmatists. We don't encourage or believe in doing anything unpatriotic, illegal or immoral, unless it is the price of survival. When your survival is in doubt (financial or physical) you must be ready to emigrate, pay a bribe, take an oath you don't really believe or do whatever it takes to keep yourself together. **We feel that governments who oppress citizens to the point of desperation are criminal and immoral. There is nothing immoral about escaping from a place where life, liberty, property rights and the pursuit of happiness are restricted.**

For the average Johnny Lunchbucket or Tillie the Toiler, the whole idea of a second passport and survival is irrelevant. His horizon does not extend beyond the next beer and ball game. He goes to his routine job or takes the dole. His taxes are deducted at the source and he has no idea that they could or should be less. If there's a war, regardless of what it's about, he will without serious objection fight and bleed for his country, right or wrong. Johnny and Tillie are what the government calls the proverbial good, responsible citizens.

Because you are reading this report, **you always question authority. Blind obedience is not one of your virtues**. Politicians tend to regard us, their subjects, as an expendable natural resource. You presumably value yourself and will resist any attempt to liquidate or expend you. You are a sovereign individual who can and will control your own destiny with as much freedom as possible in an unfree world.

You don't want to be sent into combat (or have your child disfigured or killed) over a dispute that ten years later will be perceived as insignificant, petty and unnecessary. You probably feel that most wars, laws and regulations for the ''national benefit'' cause more problems than they solve. Military conscription, matrimonial, moral and sexual conduct laws (what you can read, see, drink and smoke), currency controls and travel and investment restrictions are all examples of these. You correctly sense that all these unwarranted intrusions on your liberty, as well as confiscatory taxes, can be legally avoided with a second passport.

WHY COUNTRIES ''SELL'' PASSPORTS

Virtually every country in the world wants to attract preferred residents, including investors and those with critical skills who will bring with them a capability to increase employment, enhance tourism or stimulate local exports.

Some politicians have realized that their countries lack the charm and attractiveness of a Monte Carlo. They do not have a superb climate, cultural attractions, political stability or a cosmopolitan community of ultra-wealthy tax exiles.

Countries such as Belize, Bolivia, Haiti, Tonga and most African nations are **very unattractive to multi-national companies and wealthy individuals seeking a second home. Such countries are discovering that they can raise money abroad by selling passports.** These documents cost little to produce, but have high value to foreigners.

For countries seeking an extra few million dollars above their usual tax collections, the sale of documents and such is a natural response to a growing demand for:
1. Passports.
2. Diplomatic appointments (honorary and otherwise).
3. Precious metal coins for collections.

4. Postage stamps.
5. Tax haven registrations (banks, shipping, corporations).

Smaller and poorer countries sell passports and diplomatic appointments which are linked with national bonds or contributions to the government. An entire national debt can be eliminated in any one year by such a move. Important national projects can be financed. Individual lawyers and other agents (citizens of the country involved, naturally) also profit personally by administering the programs. Private fees are paid by foreign clients in addition to government charges.

Governments are increasingly attuned to the fact that wealthy foreigners may never want to settle or invest in their countries, no matter what inducements they may offer. Residence and investment requirements are beginning to disappear, having fallen victim to competition. Some countries have amended their policies to suit the marketplace.

Because foreigners are willing to pay US $10,000 or even US $50,000 and up for a quick passport or diplomatic appointment, demand is today creating an abundant supply.

Where there is a need, someone will fill it. **The demand for second passports is being satisfied by formal programs in some countries and by informal ''special arrangements'' in many others.** It is expected that more countries will join this bandwagon in the near future.

This book is updated once or twice a year to dispense new information. Scope International is available to consult with representatives of national governments on how to implement their programs. We also refer individuals desiring personal assistance in obtaining legal second passports to specialist consultants.

THOSE WHO ADVERTISE AND CLAIM TO PROVIDE SECOND PASSPORTS

Advertisements appear regularly in international publications offering passports or travel documents. The most notable and regular source for such notices appears to be the classified section of the *International Herald Tribune,* published in English. It is printed in Hong Kong, Singapore and Paris and is available at most international news-stands. Whether the advertisers are reliable is not known but we would be glad to hear of your experience with these or any similar agencies.

To obtain the information given below we responded to an advertisement. Without advancing any money or information about ourselves, we received the prices and terms by mail. These firms are neither recommended nor criticized. For all we know they could be excellent, they could be sting operations set up by Interpol to catch fugitives, or they could be swindlers. Please let us know of any experiences you have with them.

SPECIAL NOTE:
Kenneth K. Kirk & Company: A ''Passport Good For Travel To Many Countries'', was advertised as recently as January 1991 in the *International Herald Tribune* for the ''incredibly cheap price of $1,600''. Despite the fact that this gentleman has a similar Bermuda mail-drop to our own, we stress that there is no connection whatsoever between us. Further he is not related in

any way to our research assistant, Ronald Kirk. We invite our readers to read our section on WORLD SERVICE AUTHORITY passports (in this report under ODDBALL AND TAX HAVEN PASSPORTS) and then to judge for themselves if this Mr. Kirk is offering a righteous deal on a WSA travel document.

SUMMARY OF FIRMS ADVERTISING SECOND PASSPORTS.AND OTHER RELATED SERVICES

A-Z AND COMPANY
Austria: US $250,000, requires six to nine months, visit and Oath of Allegiance (citizenship granted by Act of Parliament). Previous government is notified.
Costa Rica: US $65,000, requires three months and visit.
Dominican Republic: US $87,000, requires three months, but no visit.
Honduras: US $38,000, requires three months, but no visit.
Paraguay: US $26,000, requires two months, but no visit. Honorary Consul General and Diplomat passports also arranged.

BENJAMIN PIKE AND COMPANY
Dominican Republic: US $28,000, requires 90 days and visit, includes national identification, driver's license and baptismal certificate.
Honduras, Nicaragua: US $20,000, requires two weeks, but no visit. No longer believed to be trading.

BUREAU OF PRIVATE INVESTIGATION (BPI)
Central and South American Countries (unspecified): US $18,500 to US $50,000, requires 6 to 8 weeks. US $72,000 for Diplomatic Passports. US $95,000 to US $150,000 for Honorary Consul.

BUSINESS BUREAU INTERNATIONAL (BBI)
Argentina, Bolivia, Brazil, Costa Rica, Dominican Republic, Ecuador, Honduras, Panama, Paraguay and Venezuela: US $25,000, passport issued with identity card, naturalisation certificate and international driving license. US $60,000 for documents with Diplomatic Credentials.
Anguilla, Bahamas, Cayman Islands, Jamaica, Turks and Caicos Islands: Assistance with residency applications.

CONSOLIDATED FINANCIAL SERVICES
Iceland: US $100,000.
NOTE: There is reportedly no legal Icelandish program in force.

FIDELITY MANAGEMENT
Dominican Republic: US $57,000 total. Condo US $40,000. Bonds US $10,000. Fees US $7,500.

Panama: Negotiable, but over US $50,000. Two months residence required. Passports issued to entire family group six months later.

Costa Rica: US $50,000 to be invested in Costa Rica mutual fund.

NOTE: In 1988, some four million US dollars was reportedly lost by investors who never got their passports when the manager of this company absconded to Spain.

FINANCIAL ENGINEERING CONSULTANTS INC.

Bolivia: US $25,000, includes passport, police identity card and naturalization certificate

Taiwan: US $23.00, non-resident passport, only for those of Chinese origin.

NOTE: Although imitation is the sincerest form of flattery, we note that this firm seems to be in the habit of rehashing what our readers discovered in past editions of this report, often now out of date! Definitely not recommended.

HANIMAN-CENTRO

Dominican Republic: US $50,000 home or condo to be selected and purchased by applicant. US $10,000 purchase of Dominican Bonds at 5 percent maturing in ten years. Fees of US $8,000 to US $14,000. Two visits required, one for application, the other for "Award of Citizenship". Requires 6 months. Passports provided for entire family, including all dependents under 18. Must prove net worth of at least US $100,000.

NOTE: Our personal investigation reveals that the purchase of a property is **not** necessary. This is just a way for real estate developers and brokers to make more money from you.

Brazil: US $40,000. No visit required.

INDEPENDENT MANAGEMENT CONSULTANTS LIMITED

Belgium: Involves property purchase and three years residence.

Bolivia: US $12,000, includes identity card, certificate of health and certificate of good conduct. US $50,000 for Honorary Consulate.

Brazil: US $25,000, available in any name with any date of birth. US $150,000 for Honorary Consulate.

Burkina Faso: US $60,000 for Honorary Consulate.

Columbia: US $24,000, knowledge of Spanish is necessary, 12 months required for naturalization.

Ecuador: US $25,000, requires knowledge of Spanish and residency of one year.

Guatemala: US $28,000, not necessary to visit country, but will take six months.

Honduras: US $32,000, must travel at least once to Honduras and have knowledge of Spanish.

Nicaragua: US $30,000, must travel at least once to Nicaragua and have knowledge of Spanish.

Paraguay: US $12,000, must travel to Paraguay, knowledge of Spanish is necessary, passport valid for two years.

Panama: US $40,000, must travel to Panama.

Switzerland: Various programs to obtain residence.

INTERNATIONAL STATE PARLIAMENT

Latin America, Africa, few European and North American Countries: US $12,000 to US $35,000 plus US $5,000 for travel and other expenses, also offers Honorary Diplomat and Member of Parliament titles for US $500 to US $2,500.

KAROPART
Paraguay, Ecuador: US $30,000, two month visit and police certificate of good conduct required.

McCULLOCK AND COMPANY
Legal Consultants and Private Attorneys: Requires a £2,500 professional fee up-front before doing anything!.

MIDI INTERNATIONAL
Bolivia: US $25,000 non-refundable contribution for National Agricultural Development. Requires 2 months for full processing.
Costa Rica: US $74,000 to purchase a condo. A provisional passport will be issued after approximately two months.
Dominican Republic: US $57,000 total. Condo US $40,000. Bonds US $10,000. Fees US $7,500.
NOTE: This company, based in The Isle of Man is no longer trading.

NATURALIZATION INTERNATIONAL
Bolivia: US $28,000, no visit required.
Costa Rica: US $50,000 time deposit in a Costa Rican bank, US $4,000 fee and two month visit required for a provisional passport. A regular passport may be issued after five years of physical residence of at least four months per year.

NEW CONCEPTS
Dominican Republic: US $12,900.
Venezuela: US $13,900.
Panama: US $14,900.

ROCHESTER GROUP
Choice of "Respected" Countries: US $26,500, 60 day service for global visa free travel, includes ID card and driver's license.

SAGE AND COMPANY
Argentina, Bolivian, Brazil, Dominican Republic, Ecuador, Honduras and Swaziland: US $25,000, no visit required.

SDG AND COMPANY
Honorary Consulships, Royal Titles, Noble Titles and Knighthoods.

STRAIGHT TOGETHER COMPANY
Bolivia: US $25,000. Information lifted "straight" out of *The Passport Report*. Caveat emptor.

SWISS INTERNATIONAL INVESTMENTS INC.
Dominican Republic: US $17,900, discount for three or more individual orders, four to six week delivery. US $25,000 for Diplomatic Passport. US $45,000 for Honorary Consulate.
Panama: US $19,900, discount for five or more individual orders, eight to twelve week delivery.
Paraguay: US $8,000, discount for six or more individual orders, four to six week delivery. US $25,000 for Diplomatic Passport. US $45,000 for Honorary Consulate. US $1,650 for Driver's License.
Venezuela: US $18,900, discount for four or more individual orders, six to eight week delivery.

❋❋❋❋❋

OUR ADVICE ON WHO TO DEAL WITH AND WHO TO AVOID

To obtain current information and our "off-the-record" comments on the deals offered, please write to Scope International. We do not "sell" passports or act for you but offer this service free to registered report buyers only. Please supply registration number on this book's first page to receive this service and/or details of from whom you purchased *The Passport Report*. Also, state in writing that you are not a journalist or an agent for any undisclosed principal and that the information being sought is for your personal use and will not be disclosed to any third person.

OTHER PASSPORTS FOR SALE? MAYBE!

Every month or so, we get a fax or call about some special citizenship "deals" or one-time passport programs. These are usually open for a limited time only, sometimes just twenty-four hours! Often, appointee-bureaucrats of a politician who has been defeated will "sell" passports (and anything else) while they are lame ducks awaiting replacement. In almost all cases, a very tiny number of people will get in under the wire. Usually there are only a few people "in the know" who learn of these special offers. We seem to be on the list of people to whom these deals are offered.

One such deal came up in the fall of 1990. East Germany was about to unite with West Germany. This meant that all East Germans, on October 3rd, automatically would become EC citizens. A back door to the EC? Obviously!

With the help of a very understanding communist mayor anxious to secure his financial independence, several thousand people including a few of our personal consulting clients were alerted to this opportunity. For $50,000 cash they became East Germans "overnight". A special provision in DDR law stated that those who did any *meritorious service* for the Communist Regime could be rewarded with East German citizenship at the discretion of the local mayor. It was all "legal". With their full set of Deutsche Demokratische Republik identity papers, these new East German citizens then got full West German (EC) citizenship and new passports. The deal was done in an escrow, and the ''ex''-communist officials who set up the deal absconded with five hundred million dollars (we hear). Not a bad retirement package for half a dozen rotten communist bureaucrats!

Special cases like this come and go.

A recently independent Pacific Island will sell you an instant passport without any need to go there. This scheme may be all over by the time you read this. But there will always be a veritable boutique of other offers for our consulting clients. Why is this possible? The Pacific Island republic mentioned here is a politically stable small democracy. It says it desperately needs venture capital to establish a world class resort/casino. Local politicians have promised their constituents jobs in the casino. They are convinced that selling passports abroad is the way to raise the money needed. They are prepared to cooperate fully with anyone who will peddle their passports on a commission basis. Both the present government and the opposition party are involved in the scheme. Every politician in this little nation will doubtless have their hands in the cookie jar. The passports of this country are recognized all over the world. But the country does not want it to become widely known that they are ''selling'' full citizenship and genuine passports at $35,000 a pop. Thus, this deal is a one-time opportunity for a limited number of people to apply for a limited period of time. We have seen a dozen of these programs come . . . and go!

Prices to the client are usually about $20,000 a piece or $40,000 per family. No doubt a lot of the money raised will stick to the fingers of hungry bureau-rats and politicians. But this author, for one, isn't going to try and eliminate all the crooks in governments. It's impossible! We go with the flow. ''If you can't lick 'em, join 'em''.

Our consulting clients will get updates on what's new and what may be coming up on request. We try to keep abreast of all new passport deals. We can also refer clients (no criminal record, please) who wish to become diplomats. If you would like to become an Honorary Consul in your home town, or a small nation's Ambassadorial rank representative to the United Nations in Europe or New York, contact Scope International and we will put you in touch with a consultant who can assist you in this.

HOW TO DETERMINE WHICH PASSPORT SUITS YOU BEST

1. Read what the various countries have to offer. Then determine your top three passport choices. Let's call them your ''targets''. Your determination of target passports will probably be based upon your national origin, race, religion or language skills. Obviously, you will feel more comfortable and be questioned less at borders if you look, sound and act like the particular nationality matching your passport. English or Spanish speakers have many desirable choices available to them.

The reason for choosing three targets instead of one is that your first choice may not work out. Your passport application may be rejected or the rules of the game may change against you while your application is in progress. You will end up with at least one new passport in addition to the one of your present country if you try for three. If you should get all three, so much the better. You might have problems with renewal or replacement. If you get into any legal or financial difficulties your second passport might be revoked, confiscated or lost. Having two "spares" is a good idea.

2. Obtaining the passport of your home country plus a duplicate passport of your home country is desirable before you start the process of going after your second foreign passport. Some countries require the surrender of a prior passport before your new one can be issued. This makes an expendable duplicate essential.

3. By letter, contact the nearest Consulate of the "target". Your letter should say something like this:

> "Dear Sirs, I understand that your country welcomes investors as residents and citizens. I would like to find out the current status of all your immigration and passport programs. Please send me the necessary forms to make an application. I am willing and able to visit . . . (the capital of the target) if necessary and would appreciate receiving the name, address and telephone number of the appropriate officials or government authorized agents who deal with matters of immigration and naturalization. If you know of a private attorney who speaks English (if not an English speaking country) and can be recommended, please let me know."

> (SIGN) YOUR PEN NAME AND BOX NUMBER.

4. If the target has a local branch office of their bank, airline, government tourist office or trade/commercial office, you can visit them personally. Call and make an appointment to see the manager. Ask them to identify individuals who can be of assistance to you. Pump for all the information you can get. Take written notes. It is easy to forget details and confuse countries if you don't organize and file your information.

5. Know your target and its history. Read about it, its main cities and historical figures. Start with the encyclopaedias. Check out books from your library. See if National Geographic Magazine has ever done an in-depth picture story on your target country. Read all periodicals/newspapers at the library.

6. Buy a set of language course cassette tapes from Audio Forum or (cheaper) the US State Department Foreign Service Institute Language Study Division, Washington DC 20520, USA. Start learning the language if your native tongue is not spoken at the target. Order a copy of the US State Department's exhaustive "Area Handbook" on your target country from the US Government Printing Office Bookstore, telephone (202) 275-2091 in the US, or the equivalent in your home country.

7. Get together the necessary application forms, papers, personal documents, transcripts and certificates. Do it yourself. It will save you considerable legal fees.

8.   If you want your hand held and have enough money to pay other people to do all the work, contact an immigration lawyer at one of the big, reputable firms in the target country. This will be provided if you write for a list of recommended lawyers from your own consulate or embassy in the target capital. For example, if I were an English speaking person and was considering Australia, Belize, Denmark or Ecuador, I might write and ask my own British Consulate in the target country for a list of reputable local lawyers.

Many British and American law firms have offices and partners in almost every major city where a business proposal is needed. One international law firm with offices in major cities is Hightower, Baker and McKenzie. Another firm is Clifford Chance (London-NYC-Tokyo-Hong Kong-Paris-Singapore).

Lawyers representing multi-national companies are usually well informed about immigration, expatriation and passports.

Also helpful would be representatives of major public accounting firms or international banks in the target country. You can make an appointment to talk to a partner or manager who can often direct you to proper contacts.

The big accounting firms usually know what is going on. These include Klynveld Peat Marwick (now known as KPMG), Price Waterhouse, Arthur Anderson, Ernst & Young, Coopers & Lybrand, Deloitte or Touche Ross. These familiar names will be listed as ''certified public accountants'' or ''chartered accountants'' in the *Yellow Pages* (commercial phone directory). If you are already a customer of any international bank, a bank manager of their branch in the target country will surely know the ins and outs of local immigration and perhaps be able to help you with information booklets, short-cuts or special arrangements.

9.   As a last resort you can send Scope International your questions, with £200 consulting fee. For best results clearly define what you see as your major problems and goals as well as your time frame and budget for the project. You may (and should) use a pen-name in such correspondence. If we know your educational background, marital status, ethnic ancestry, race, language skills, assets and liabilities and criminal record (if any), it will help us give the best advice.

We will refer you to the best talent (or at least try to), giving several options where possible. Please allow up to six weeks for a response. We strongly urge that you also read *PT*. It was written after *The Passport Report* and answers many questions asked by readers. See back of this report for further details.

10.   Generally, it is a good idea to visit the target for a month if possible. Sniff around at business opportunities, real estate prices, banking and financial practices, etc. Visit bankers, accountants and lawyers. Your visit will be more productive if, before you go, you have read the local daily papers (particularly the ads) and have made appointments to meet at least a dozen people by mail before you arrive. Colleagues in your own line of work that you seek out could open many doors.

Another possibility for meeting helpful people is through religious groups, affinity groups or professional associations such as Toastmasters, Rotary, Lions, the British-American Club and Knights of Columbus. LOCAL SPONSORSHIP AND GOOD CONTACTS CAN MAKE THE DIFFERENCE BETWEEN SUCCESS AND FAILURE. Normally you don't need to pay anyone a large fee for obtaining a second passport for you if you simply put in some time and effort to do it yourself.

To help future readers, please let us know of your successes and failures. You can write us your story using a "pen name" or alias. Share information with us for the benefit of people like you! We will reciprocate with a swell gift for you!

HOW TO AVOID THE WRONG PASSPORT

For someone who has not researched the subject, the obvious choice of a passport would often be the wrong choice. For the individual who has made enough money to avoid working for a living, there are quite a few places blessed with superb climate, political stability, safety from terrorist bombs, high sanitation standards, sporting activities, sophistication and culture. As a result, the wealthiest people in the world have flocked to certain popular cosmopolitan resort colonies.

Take two popular choices . . . California, USA and the Riviera in Southern France. A harassed South African businessman might say, "An American or French passport is the one for me". If the purpose was to live in any of the two regions mentioned above, seeking either the US or French passport would be a big mistake! Let me show you why.

A wealthy South African will have a large income from his business or assets. When he gets US residency, he is subject to Federal tax (currently at 28 per cent + 5 per cent surcharge) on his worldwide income. There is also a 12 per cent California income tax. Some cities, like New York add a third tax. To live in California with a US passport might cost him 45 per cent of his worldwide income even before he began to enjoy the benefits of the location.

A better way to move to California would be to get a Canadian passport. A Canadian may come and go and stay in the US without a visa for up to six months. He can rent or own property with fewer restrictions than an American. An American cannot enjoy tax-free rent from a vacation home, but a foreigner can. A Canadian citizen who spends the winter in California will pay no US income taxes and no Canadian taxes either, if he is a non-resident of Canada. Another, more exotic option is to become a citizen of an American tax haven like Palau, Guam or Samoa. More on this in another section we call Oddball Passports.

Now, suppose our South African, or you, should prefer the Riviera. France also has high income taxes. **Rather than becoming a French national, the South African would be better off with an Italian or South American passport**. His home could be in Monte Carlo for up to 12 months a year, all tax-free! **A Frenchman in Monte Carlo would pay a huge amount of income tax. With a non-French passport, however, there would be no French taxes, no currency restrictions, and complete freedom** to commute from Monte Carlo to California, following the sun.

The passport of a banana republic in Central or South America may seem a strange choice against the French or American passport – but second and third rate countries do not seek to collect taxes from their subjects abroad. Regardless of political changes at home, they will normally renew passports indefinitely.

The point is, the best choice in a passport will probably be from a nation in which you will seldom, if ever, choose to live or own a home or business. The passport you want is one from a country whose citizens need no visas to visit the places you like.

A passport from any European Community (EC) country you don't live in would be excellent, but the drawback is that normally a minimum of five years residence is required – yet there are a few exceptions. There are instant or short residence required passports to be had in Europe for those who know how to get them. One EC country requires only a three year residence. Oddball passports giving full ingress and egress rights to France (and Europe) with tax haven advantages include those issued at Monaco, Martinique or St. Pierre and Micquelon.

Any passport that allows you to move abroad freely and legally transfer and keep your assets in safe havens without taxation is a good one. But some passports are better than others. Deciding upon your personal course of action will take careful planning. Whilst considering your preliminary plan, you must ask yourself:

1.   Where do I want to spend my time physically? Remember, generally over six months in any one place (except for tax havens) makes you a resident for tax purposes, and subject to tax on your worldwide income.

2.   Where do I want to keep my personal assets? Generally for safety and tax advantages, liquid assets should **never** be held in or near the country where you are resident or have substantial business operations. No country can tax or confiscate foreign assets they don't know about.

3.   What do I want as my place of refuge and escape from wars, revolution, etc.? In other words, what do you fear most and wish to get away from?

Generally, your domicile-fiscal-address-legal-residence (if any) should be in a different place from the nation of your passport. The reason is that most countries cater to foreigners more than they do their own citizens. For tourists and most "foreign visitors", taxes are nil. In a political upheaval, foreigners are protected. Police brutality for political mis-steps is not generally applied to "visitors" with the same vigor as to natives.

You too can be a Perpetual Traveler with no fixed place of residence. But you must start with goals and develop a plan to meet those goals.

In this report we cover many of the options currently available. The world is constantly changing. Political changes mean new immigration and citizenship laws. But here are your options as of 1993.

Comments, questions, additions and constructive criticism should be sent to:
Scope International, 62 Murray Road, Waterlooville, Hampshire PO8 9JL, Great Britain.

Part III

THE EASY BUT USEFUL
SECOND PASSPORT

HOW TO OBTAIN TWO OR MORE PASSPORTS FROM YOUR HOME COUNTRY

Countries generally do not like issuing more than one passport to their citizens. They want each of us to possess only one travel document so that they can keep tabs on our whereabouts at all times. For this reason, if not any other, it is essential to secure a second travel document. Often, a duplicate passport from your home country is the best place to start.

A country with hostile relations with another country often will not admit anyone with a visa or entry/exit stamp from its enemy. Many Black African countries have a restriction of this sort for individuals who have visited South Africa. Although Congo, Benin, Kenya and Senegal have recently "theoretically" lifted such restrictions, they are still often arbitrarily enforced. Iran and Iraw have similar restrictions.

So how does this relate to getting a second passport? It's simple. Tell your local passport office that you are making a trip to country A which will not admit you because you have a visa or stamp in your passport from country B. Another ploy is to say your passport it as the Japanese Embassy for visa processing and you have to make an emergency trip to France.

The other method which some people use, and which we emphatically do not recommend because it involves making a fraudulent statement, is the lost passport ploy. "My pocket was picked at the airport." To obtain a new passport you will usually be obliged to file a police report of the loss or theft and obtain a copy of the police report to append to your duplicate passport application.

It is not a bad idea to obtain a duplicate set of all ID documents (driver's licence, voting card, birth certificate, etc.) You never know when they will come in handy, if your documents are really lost or stolen, for example.

TWO PASSPORTS FROM THE SAME COUNTRY?

US TIGHTENS SCREWS ON THOSE DESIRING TWO OR MORE US PASSPORTS.

Recently, the United States tightened up on applicants for second American passports. Together with the application for a second passport they now want a signed statement showing your itinerary. For a second US passport to be obtained, you must:

1) Submit an itinerary showing **immediate** travel to destinations, where one passport will be tied up at a consulate or otherwise unavailable while you are required to be travelling elsewhere, and

2) File a 2nd DSP-II.

The form requires you to be very specific, but one reader (a personal friend) countered the official treatment succesfully by replying:

> *"I hereby certify that a second passport is necessary for my travel to various areas, see below, for the following reasons: I expect to be travelling extensively in countries where the US permits its nationals to go, during the next four years or so. This includes the continents of North and Latin America*

and Europe, nations of the Caribbean, the Pacific Basin, the Mediterranean and Indian Ocean rims, Africa, the Middle East and possibly Antarctica. Inquiries made to several consulates and embassies recently about excluding travelers with various stamps on their passports indicate that 'the question is sensitive', that travelers are 'sometimes' excluded on such a basis, that 'it is true' and 'the matter is handled by issuing a second passport', but policies appear to change from week to week. Specific problems as of this date arise both in Africa and in the Middle East. South Africa, Kenya, Iran, Iraq, Israel, Egypt, Jordan and Nigeria all appear to be sensitive now. Greece, Turkey, the two Cyprusses, many African nations and some Middle Eastern nations are also threatening to refuse admission to travellers who have passport stamps from their enemies.

If some limitations must appear on my second passport, it would appear that these should be a time rather than an area limitation. However, as you know, most countries insist that visitors have at least six months of remaining validity on their passports. Any expiry date is therefore effectively six months earlier than any date stamped on the passport itself.

In the event of the loss of either passport, I will report that loss immediately to the Passport Office or to the nearest American Embassy or Consulate.

(SIGNATURE OF APPLICANT)

Although the US used to mark second passports for travel to specific countries, it now only imposes time restrictions. A similar letter to the one above submitted with two pictures should be successful for obtaining a second passport almost completely free from restrictions.

LOST PASSPORT? IT'S EASY TO GET A REPLACEMENT

This US form of application for a replacement passport is quite typical. Normally you are expected to have reported to the police any loss or theft. A copy of any loss or theft report filed with police is routinely available to the "injured party" and will be needed by the Passport Office. The government will of course give your application for a replacement extra scrutiny if you are a habitual passport loser. Why? Because they may well suspect that you are selling your own passports on the black market for $5,000 or $10,000 a pop.

Finally, if your replacement passport is issued abroad by almost any country these days, it will NOT have the standard full (5 or 10 year) maximum life. Normally, a **replacement passport** is only going to be valid for a short period, typically three months. At the end of this time, the holder must report to the passport office nearest his residence (domicile) and certify in writing that the old passport has not yet turned up. The passport office then does a computer check to see if your old passport has been used to enter the country or whether it has been turned

UNITED STATES DEPARTMENT OF STATE
STATEMENT REGARDING
LOST OR STOLEN PASSPORT

INSTRUCTIONS It is necessary to submit a statement with an application for a new passport when a previous valid or potentially valid passport cannot be presented. The statement must be set forth in detail why the previous passport cannot be presented.

TYPE OR PRINT IN INK IN WHITE AREAS ONLY

IDENTIFYING INFORMATION

NAME

FIRST/MIDDLE

LAST

| PASSPORT NUMBER | | | | | | | | |

ISSUE DATE

| Month | Day | Year |

PLACE OF ISSUE

SEX   PLACE OF BIRTH (City, State or Province, Country)

Male   Female

DATE OF BIRTH

| Month | Day | Year |

DOCUMENT CODE

L

For Official Use Only

ADDRESS (Street, City, State, ZIP Code)

LOST/STOLEN PASSPORT INFORMATION (Please answer all questions. Be specific.)

HOW WAS PASSPORT LOST OR STOLEN?

WHEN WAS LOSS DISCOVERED?

WHERE DID LOSS TAKE PLACE?

IF STOLEN, WERE POLICE AUTHORITIES NOTIFIED?
Yes   No

IF YES, STATE WHERE AND WHEN:

WHAT EFFORTS HAVE YOU MADE TO RECOVER THE PASSPORT?

HAVE YOU HAD PREVIOUS PASSPORTS LOST OR STOLEN?
Yes   No

IF YES, GIVE DATE AND PARTICULARS, INCLUDING NUMBER OF PASSPORTS LOST OR STOLEN.

CERTIFICATION I, the undersigned, certify that the information furnished herein is correct and complete to the best of my knowledge and belief and that I have not given my passport to another person or disposed of it in an unauthorized manner. If I subsequently find or recover it, I will immediately return it to Passport Services (Attention: Correspondence Branch), Department of State, Washington, D.C. 20524 or to the nearest Passport Agency.

Date   X   Signature

FORM DSP-64
12-84

Form approved OMB No. 1405-0014 (Exp. 10/31/87)

33

```
-THIS PASSPORT IS ISSUED AS REPLACEMENT
FOR A LOST/STOLEN PASSPORT AND IS LIMITED
TO EXPIRE ON APRIL 21, 1990. EXTENSION OF
VALIDITY MUST BE APPROVED BY THE
DEPARTMENT OF STATE.
```

in at a consulate. As of date, only a few countries have the ability to do these computer checks extensively. Singapore and the United States are the foremost in the field.

Assuming that your government has no unsatisfied questions, at the end of its validity period the replacement passport you received will be extended to its full life – usually by means of a simple rubber stamp.

HOW TO FILE A POLICE REPORT OF LOST PASSPORT

As mentioned, if you need to get a replacement passport for one you have lost, you'll need to file a police report, even if there was no theft.

Here is a sample:

Start off by stating your name and address after a "Filed By;". Also indicate the date filed.

Sample working:

"On 14 November 1991, at Paris Air Terminal No. 1, after clearing passport control, but before customs, I found it necessary to use the bathroom at around 9.30am. A leather money pouch that attached to my belt mut have, at that time, slipped off my belt onto the toilet floor. I did not notice the loss at the time because my rucksack was also in the stall. However, shortly after departing the airport, I noticed that this pouch was missing. I returned to the airport and asked and found an official to check the toilet I had just left. [I was not allowed to go because it was in the restricted area]. He reported back that it was not there and had not been turned in. Later that day, I filed a loss of property report at the airport, and have checked back several times. My belt and contents were not turned in. I believe that in my belt was about 500 French francs in cash, various identity cards, air tickets and most importantly, my CANADIAN PASSPORT, number unknown, issued about 2 or 3 years ago in London in the name of DONALD DUCK. Inside the money belt was an offer for the return of the belt and contents. I had hoped that it would be mailed back, but after

one week it has not been returned. I do not believe the belt and my passport was stolen, but I could be wrong. This report is being filed with the Paris police because an official at the Canadian Embassy in Paris has told me that filing such a statement is a pre-requisite for obtaining a duplicate or replacement passport.

POLICE REPORT NUMBER: 78/5643/91, STATION: WEST CENTRAL.''

Comments, questions, additions and constructive criticism should be sent to:
Scope International, 62 Murray Road, Waterlooville, Hampshire PO8 9JL, Great Britain.

Part IV

VITAL STATISTICS

INSTANT PASSPORTS – 50 COUNTRIES
RESIDENCE/MARRIAGE REQUIREMENTS FOR CITIZENSHIP

Country	Years of Residence before Foreign Spouse may apply for Citizenship & Passport	Normal Residency Years Required	Citizen. to Child born in Country with Foreign Parents
ANDORRA	Immediate if male marries an "only child". None if female marries Andorran male.	Foreigners can only become citizens by marriage to an Andorran. Passports for Andorrans are also issued by France and Spain.	N
ARGENTINA	2. Immediate if foreign woman marries an Argentinian.	2	Y
AUSTRALIA	2	2	Y
AUSTRIA	2. Or after 5 years of marriage, even if residency outside Austria.	10. Immediate, if with investment.	Y
BARBADOS	7. Immediate if foreign woman marries a Barbadian.	7	Y
BELGIUM	½	5. Immediate if with investment.	N
BELIZE	5	5	Y
BERMUDA	5	10	N
BOLIVIA	1	2. Immediate if with investment	N
BRAZIL	5	5	Y
CANADA	3	3	Y
CHANNEL IS.	3	5	N
CHILE	5	5	Y
COLOMBIA	2	5	Y
COSTA RICA	5	5	Y
CYPRUS	After 4 years of marriage, even if residency outside Cyprus. 1 if foreign woman marries Cypriot.	4	N
DENMARK	4	7	N
DOMINICAN REPUBLIC	½. Immediate if foreign man marries a Dominican	2	Y
ECUADOR	2	2	Y
FINLAND	5	10	N
FRANCE	After 6 months of marriage, even if residency outside France.	5	N
GERMANY	3. Plus 2 years concurrent marriage.	10. Shorter period for ethnic Germans, investors, public benefactors, or descendants of Nazi victims.	N
GREECE	5	5	Y
HONDURAS	5	5	Y
IRELAND	After 3 years of marriage, even if residency outside Ireland.	5. Immediate for ethnic Irish.	Y
ISRAEL	Immediate.	Immediate if Jewish.	Y
ITALY	Immediate, or after 3 years of marriage if residency outside of Italy.	Immediate for ethnic Italians. Otherwise 3 or 10.	N
JAMAICA	7	7. Immediate if with investment.	Y
LEBANON	Immediate.	7. Special arrangements possible.	Y
LIECHTENSTEIN	Female 6 if former residence in country, otherwise 12. Male – rarely granted.	Male foreigner cannot generally acquire citizenship.	N
LUXEMBOURG	3	10	N
MALTA	½. Immediate if foreign woman marries a Maltese.	6	Y
MAURITIUS	5	5	Y
MEXICO	5	5	Y
MONACO	Female - immediate. Male - 12 years.	12. Few applications successful.	N
NETHERLANDS	After 3 years of marriage, even if residency outside Netherlands.	5	N
NEW ZEALAND	Immediate.	3	Y
NORWAY	6	7	N
PANAMA	Immediate.	5	Y
PARAGUAY	3	5	Y
PERU	2	5	Y
PORTUGAL	Immediate.	6	N
SPAIN	1	10. Shorter for ethnic Spanish.	N
ST. KITTS	Immediate.	Immediate if with investment.	Y
SWEDEN	5	5	N
SWITZERLAND	6. Immediate if foreign woman marries a Swiss.	12. Each year counts double for children.	N
THAILAND	Female - Immediate. Male - 7.	5. Immediate for Buddhist monks.	Y
TRINIDAD	5	5	Y
TURKEY	Immediate.	5. Immediate for ethnic Turks.	Y
UNITED KINGDOM	3	5	N
USA	3	5	Y. Must choose by age 25.
URUGUAY	5	5	Y
VENEZUELA	3	4	Y

1993 NATIONALITY SURVEY

	Are children born in your country automatically and by operation of law CITIZENS of that country? Assume foreign, non-citizen parents. (See notes below)[1,2]	Can a newborn child (upon application by parent/s) get his or her own PASSPORT?	If a FOREIGN PARENT has a child in your country, does it give the foreign parent any special rights to residency or citizenship?
Austria	YES	YES	NO
Belgium	NO	NO	NO
Belize	YES	YES	NO
Brazil	YES	YES	NO (Freedom from extradiction till child 18)
Cameroun	YES (If applied for within 6 months of birth)	NO	YES (Permanent Residency)
Colombia	YES	YES	NO
Costa Rica	YES (If registered before age 25)	YES	YES (Permanent Residency)
Cyprus	NO	YES	NO
Denmark	NO	YES	NO
Djibouti	NO	NO	NO
El Salvador3	YES	YES	NO
FinlandNO	YES	NO	
France	NO	YES	NO
Germany	NO	NO	NO
Greece	NO	YES (both parents)	NO
HondurasYES	YES	NO	
Hungary[3]	NO	YES	NO
Ireland	YES	YES	YES ("strong tie", right of residence)
Israel	YES	YES (Israeli parent)	NO
Ivory Coast	NO	YES	YES (Official's discretion)

CONTINUED ON NEXT PAGES

*Note 1: Almost all countries, children of diplomats stationed there do NOT gain citizenship by birthright.
*Note 2: If a child is born stateless most countries of birth will grant the child citizenship even though other children born in that same country to foreign parents may not be entitled to citizenship. Observe: Not only children of refugees or stateless persons may be born stateless. Laws of Mexico state that child born to Mexican citizens living outside of Mexico doesn't get Mexican citizenship. In some cases, such a child could be born stateless even though its parents are not. Honduras, and other countries, have similar rules.
*Note 3: In Colombia, only a Cedula (national ID card) and 3 photos are needed to apply for passport. In El Salvador, the same applies, although you must also present your Birth Certificate as well. In Hungary, one photo and a short coupon ("Utiokmnay") stating your birth date, name and address is enough.

Does marriage to one of your citizens give the spouse right to citizenship/passport even if his or her residency is outside of your country?	If the individual has a PARENT who is a citizen of your country, does that entitle him or her to a passport of your country if he/she is born abroad?	Who or what office or officials are in charge of issuing passports to babies or other citizens? (See note 4 below)[4]
YES (after 5 yrs of marriage)	YES	Nearest embassy
YES (after 6 months of marriage	YES	Moniteur Belge, Bruxelles, Belgium
NO	YES	Passport Off., POB 1200, Belize City
NO	YES (Until age 21)	Ministerio das Relacoes Exteriores
NO	YES	Nearest embassy or consulate
NO	YES	Passport Off, Carrera 13#31-95, Bogota
NO	YES	Dir. Migracion, San Jose, Costa Rica
YES (after 4 yrs of marriage)	YES (Only if father is Cypriot)	Migration Dept, Nicosia, Cyprus
NO	YES (Until age 21)	Nearest embassy
NO	YES	Nearest embassy or consulate
NO	YES	Dir. Migracion, San Salvador
NO	YES	Nearest embassy
YES (after 6 months of marriage)	YES	Nearest embassy or consulate
NO	YES	Nearest embassy
NO	YES (If registered with Greek Consul when born)	Nearest embassy or consulate
NO	NO	Nearest embassy or consulate
NO	YES	Embassy/consulate of your residence
YES (after 3 yrs of marriage)	YES	Passport Off, Maleworth St, Dublin 2
NO	YES	Interior Office, Jerusalem, Israel
NO	YES	Dir. Naturiale, Cote d'Ivoire

*Note 4: Almost all countries require that you appear in person when applying for and/or picking up a passport, especially if the passport applied for is the first to be issued to you from that country. If you are below the age of consent (usually 18 or 21) or if you have previously applied for a passport, national provisions in most countries may allow all procedures to be handled by mail.

ADDITIONS, QUESTIONS, CORRECTIONS OR COMMENTS?
SEND TO SCOPE INTERNATIONAL, 62 MURRAY ROAD, WATERLOOVILLE, HAMPSHIRE, PO8 9JL, GREAT BRITAIN

1993 NATIONALITY SURVEY

	Are children born in your country automatically and by operation of law CITIZENS of that country? Assume foreign, non-citizen parents. (See notes below)[5,6]	Can a newborn child (upon application by parent/s) get his or her own PASSPORT?	If a FOREIGN PARENT has a child in your country, does it give the foreign parent any special rights to residency or citizenship?
Italy	NO	YES	NO
Japan	NO	YES	YES (Permanent residency)
Kenya	YES (Only if application is made)	NO (ID can be issued)	YES Permanent residency)
Luxembourg	NO	NO (some exceptions)	NO
Mexico	YES	YES (both parents)	NO
Monaco	YES(Only if parents are unknown)	YES	NO
Netherlands	NO	YES (both parents)	NO
Nicaragua	YES	YES	NO
Norway	NO	YES	NO
Oman	NO	YES	NO
Peru	YES	YES	NO
Philippines	NO	YES	NO
Portugal	NO	YES	NO
Seychelles	NO	NO	NO
Spain	NO	YES	NO
SyriaNO	YES	NO	
Togo	NO	NO	NO
Trinidad & Tobago	YES	YES	NO
Turkey	NO	YES	NO
United Kingdom	NO	YES	NO ("strong tie", right of residency)
USA	YES	YES	NO (unless child is adult or wage earner)
Zambia	YES	NO	YES (if married to a local)

*Note 5: Almost all countries, children of diplomats stationed there do NOT gain citizenship by birthright.
*Note 6: If a child is born stateless most countries of birth will grant the child citizenship even though other children born in that same country to foreign parents may not be entitled to citizenship. Observe: Not only children of refugees or stateless persons may be born stateless. Laws of Mexico state that child born to Mexican citizens living outside of Mexico doesn't get Mexican citizenship. In some cases, such a child could be born stateless even though its parents are not. Honduras, and other countries, have similar rules.

Does marriage to one of your citizens give the spouse right to citizenship/passport even if his or her residency is outside of your country?	If the individual has a PARENT who is a citizen of your country, does that entitle him or her to a passport of your country if he/she is born abroad?	Who or what office or officials are in charge of issuing passports to babies or other citizens? (See note 7 below)[7]
YES (After 3 years of marriage)	YES	Nearest embassy
NO	YES	Nearest embassy
NO	YES (only if father is Kenyan)	Imm Off, box 30191, Nairobi, Kenya.
NO	YES	Ministère des Aff. Estrangères, Lux.
NO	NO	Nearest embassy or consulate
NO	YES	The Prince, Monte Carlo, Monaco
YES (After 3 years of marriage)	YES	Nearest embassy or consulate
NO	YES	Migration Authorities, Managua
NO	YES (if other citizenships are renounced)	Nearest embassy or consulate
YES (After 10 years of marriage)	YES	Royal Oman Police, Mutrah, Oman
NO	YES (If registered within 30 days)	Min. d. Interior, Av 28 de Juli, Lima
NO	YES	Passport Off., Manila, Philippines
NO	YES	Any local Governo Civil in Portugal
NO	YES	Nearest embassy or consulate
NO	YES	Nearest embassy or consulate
YES (After 5 years of marriage	YES	Nearest embassy
NO	YES	Ministry of Justice, Togolaise
NO	YES	Imm. Dept. 119 Duke St, Pt of Spain
NO	YES	Nearest embassy or consulate
NO	YES	Nearest embassy or consulate
NO	YES (Many exceptions)	Nearest embassy or consulate
NO	YES	D.-Cit., Box 30104, Lusaka, Zambia

*Note 7: Almost all countries require that you appear in person when applying for and/or picking up a passport, especially if the passport applied for is the first to be issued you from that country. If you are below age of consent (usually 18 or 21) or if you have previously applied for a passport, national provisions in most countries may allow all procedures to be handled by mail.

ADDITIONS, QUESTIONS, CORRECTIONS OR COMMENTS?
SEND TO SCOPE INTERNATIONAL, 62 MURRAY ROAD, WATERLOOVILLE, HAMPSHIRE, PO8 9JL, GREAT BRITAIN

VISA REQUIREMENTS FOR SOME COUNTRIES
OFFERING INSTANT PASSPORTS

TYPE OF PASSPORT HELD:	ARGENTINA	BOLIVIA	BRAZIL	COSTA RICA	DOM. REP.	ECUADOR	HONDURAS	PANAMA	PARAGUAY	VENEZUELA
VISA REQUIRED TO VISIT:										
ARGENTINA	–	NO	NO	NO	NO	NO	NO	YES	NO	YES
AUSTRIA	NO	NO	NO	NO	NO	NO	YES	NO	NO	NO
BAHAMAS	NO*	NO*	NO*	NO*	NO*	NO*	NO*	NO*	NO*	NO*
BAHRAIN	YES, BUT CAN OBTAIN TRANSIT VISA ON ARRIVAL FOR STAY NOT EXCEEDING 3 DAYS									
BARBADOS	NO*	NO*	NO*	NO*	NO*	NO*	NO*	NO*	NO*	NO*
BELGIUM	NO	NO	NO	NO	YES	NO	NO	NO	NO	NO
BERMUDA	YES	NO	NO	NO	NO	NO	NO	NO	YES	NO
BRAZIL	NO	YES	NO	YES	YES	NO	YES	YES	NO	YES
CANADA	NO	YES	YES	NO	YES	YES	YES	YES	NO	NO
CAYMAN ISLANDS	YES	YES	NO	NO	NO	NO	YES	NO	YES	NO
COSTA RICA	NO	YES	NO - 30 days	-	YES	NO - 30 days	NO - 30 days	NO	YES	NO - 30 days
CYPRUS	YES	YES	YES	YES	YES	YES	YES	YES	YES	YES
DENMARK	NO	NO	NO	NO	NO	NO	NO	NO	NO	NO
FRANCE	YES	YES	YES	YES	YES	YES	YES	YES	YES	YES
GERMANY	NO	NO	NO	NO	YES	NO	NO	NO	NO	NO
GIBRALTAR	YES	NO	NO	NO	NO	NO	NO	NO	NO	NO
GREECE	NO	YES	YES	YES	YES	YES	YES	YES	YES	YES
HONG KONG	YES	NO - 30 days	NO	NO - 30 days	NO - 30 days	NO	NO - 30 days	NO - 30 days	NO - 30 days	NO - 30 days
IRELAND	NO	YES	NO	NO	YES	NO	NO	NO	NO	NO
ISRAEL	NO	NO	NO	NO	NO	NO	NO	YES	NO	YES
ITALY	NO	NO	NO	NO	NO	NO	NO	YES	NO	NO
JAMAICA	NO - 30 days	YES	NO - 30 days	NO - 30 days	YES	NO - 30 days	YES	YES	YES	YES
JAPAN	NO	YES	YES	NO	NO	YES	NO - 30 days	YES	YES	YES
KOREA	NO*	NO*	NO*	NO	NO	NO*	NO*	NO*	NO*	NO*
LUXEMBOURG	NO	NO	NO	NO	YES	NO	NO	NO	NO	NO
MALAWI	YES	YES	YES	YES	YES	YES	YES	YES	YES	YES
MALAYSIA	NO*	NO*	NO*	NO*	NO*	NO*	NO*	NO*	NO*	NO*
MALTA	YES	YES	YES	YES	YES	YES	YES	YES	YES	YES
MEXICO	NO - 30 days	YES	YES	YES	YES	YES	NO - 30 days	YES	YES	NO - 30 days
MOROCCO	NO	YES	NO	YES	YES	YES	YES	YES	YES	NO
NETHERLANDS	NO	NO	NO	NO	YES	NO	NO	NO	NO	NO
NORWAY	NO	NO	NO	NO	NO	NO	NO	NO	NO	NO
PANAMA	T/C	T/C	T/C	NO	YES	T/C	NP	-	YES	T/C
PHILIPPINES	NO**	NO**	NO	NO**	NO**	NO**	NO**	YES	NO**	NO**
PORTUGAL	NO	YES	NO	NO	YES	NO	YES	YES	YES	YES
SEYCHELLES	NO	NO	NO	NO	NO	NO	NO	NO	NO	NO
SINGAPORE	NO*	NO*	NO*	NO*	NO*	NO*	NO*	NO*	NO*	NO*
SOUTH AFRICA	YES	YES	YES	YES	YES	YES	YES	YES	YES	YES
SPAIN	NO	NO	NO	NO	NO	NO	NO	NO	NO	NO
SWEDEN	NO	NO	NO	NO	NO	NO	NO	NO	NO	NO
SWITZERLAND	NO	NO	NO	NO	NO	NO	NO	NO	NO	NO
THAILAND	NO*	NO*	NO*	NO*	NO*	NO*	NO*	NO*	NO*	NO*
UNITED KINGDOM	NO	NO	NO	NO	NO	NO	NO	NO	NO	NO
USA	YES	YES	YES	YES	YES	YES	YES	YES	YES	YES
VENEZUELA	T/C	YES	T/C	T/C	YES	YES	YES	T/C	T/C	-
YUGOSLAVIA	NO	NO	YES	NO	YES	YES	YES	YES	YES	YES

*   NO VISA PROVIDING STAY DOES NOT EXCEED 2 WEEKS
**   NO VISA PROVIDING STAY DOES NOT EXCEED 3 WEEKS
T/C   TOURIST CARD ISSUED BY AIRLINE

VISA REQUIREMENTS FOR AFRICANS WISHING TO TRAVEL

Country of Passport Holder	Visa required by				
	UK	AUS	NZ	CDA	USA
ALGERIA	Yes	Yes	Yes	Yes	Yes
ANGOLA	Yes	Yes	Yes	Yes	Yes
BENIN	Yes	Yes	Yes	Yes	Yes
BOTSWANA	No	No	No	No	No
BURKINA FASO	Yes	Yes	Yes	Yes	Yes
BURUNDI	Yes	Yes	Yes	Yes	Yes
CAMEROON	Yes	Yes	Yes	Yes	Yes
C.A.R.	Yes	Yes	Yes	Yes	Yes
CHAD	Yes	Yes	Yes	Yes	Yes
COMOROS	Yes	Yes	Yes	Yes	Yes
CONGO	Yes	Yes	Yes	Yes	Yes
COTE D'IVOIRE	No	Yes	Yes	Yes	Yes
DJBOUTI	Yes	Yes	Yes	Yes	Yes
EGYPT	Yes	Yes	Yes	Yes	Yes
EQU GUINEA	Yes	Yes	Yes	Yes	Yes
ETHIOPIA	Yes	Yes	Yes	Yes	Yes
GABON	Yes	Yes	Yes	Yes	Yes
GAMBIA	No	No	No	No	Yes
GHANA	Yes	Yes	Yes	Yes	Yes
GUINEA-BISSAU	Yes	Yes	Yes	Yes	Yes
GUINEA REPUBLIC	Yes	Yes	Yes	Yes	Yes
KENYA	No	Yes	Yes	Yes	Yes
LESOTHO	No	No	No	No	No
LIBERIA	Yes	Yes	Yes	Yes	Yes
LIBYA	Yes	Yes	Yes	Yes	Yes
MADAGASCAR	Yes	Yes	Yes	Yes	Yes
MAURITANIA	Yes	Yes	Yes	Yes	Yes
MALAWI	No	No	No	No	No
MALI	Yes	Yes	Yes	Yes	Yes
MAURITIUS	No	No	No	No	No
MOROCCO	No	No	No	No	No
MOZAMBIQUE	Yes	Yes	Yes	Yes	Yes
NAMIBIA	No	Yes	Yes	Yes	Yes
NIGER	No	Yes	Yes	Yes	Yes
NIGERIA	Yes	Yes	Yes	Yes	Yes
RWANDA	Yes	Yes	Yes	Yes	Yes
SAO TOME	Yes	Yes	Yes	Yes	Yes
SENEGAL	Yes	Yes	Yes	Yes	Yes
SEYCHELLES	No	No	No	No	No
SIERRA LEONE	Yes	Yes	Yes	Yes	Yes
SOMALIA	Yes	Yes	Yes	Yes	Yes
SOUTH AFRICA	No	Yes	Yes	Yes	Yes
SUDAN	Yes	Yes	Yes	Yes	Yes
SWAZILAND	No	No	No	No	No
TANZANIA	No	No	No	No	Yes
TOGO	No	Yes	Yes	Yes	No
TUNISIA	No	Yes	Yes	No	No
UGANDA	No	Yes	No	Yes	Yes
WESTERN SAHARA	Please enquire				
ZAIRE	Yes	Yes	Yes	Yes	Yes
ZAMBIA	No	No	No	No	Yes
ZIMBABWE	No	No	No	No	No

NOTE: Most nationalities that do not require a visa for Tanzania require a Visitor's Pass.

ALL THE FACTS IN ONE LITTLE BOOK

No, we're not talking about *The Passport Report,* although we can understand your confusion. The *Travel Information Manual,* also known more simply as TIM, is put together in conjunction with IATA, the International Association of Travel Agents. This little book is issued monthly and explains in detail not only which countries require visas from which, but also all you need to know about the geographical features, health precautions (such as necessary vaccinations), customs, currency, and embarkation and landing taxes of over 150 countries.

Best of all, you can normally arrange to get your own copy absolutely free. Stop by your local travel agent and make arrangements to pick up their current copy next month when they have received a new one, assuming of course that they don't have any old ones lying around already. For PTs, this information doesn't change so often that one absolutely must have the most recent edition. However, if you would like to buy your own current copy, you can. The price per copy is 42.50 Dutch Guilders (approximately US $20). Contact: The Travel Information Manual, PO Box 902, NL-2130EA Hoofddorp, The Netherlands.

DEPENDENCIES, COLONIES AND AREAS OF SPECIAL SOVEREIGNTY

Listed below are the principal political dependencies of the world. Several geographic entities have been included in the list either for the sake of total area coverage or to group smaller, less significant territories. These geographic entities are enclosed in brackets ([]).

American Samoa TERRITORY OF AMERICAN SAMOA
Sovereignty: US unincorporated territory. *Capital:* Pago Pago (on the island of Tutuila). *Population:* 41,000. *Area:* 199 sq km.
Comment: American Samoa also includes Manua, Rose, and Swains Islands.

Anguilla (No long-form name).
Sovereignty: Dependent territory of the United Kingdom. *Capital:* The Valley. *Population:* 7,000. *Area:* 91 sq km.
Comment: On December 16, 1980, Anguilla was officially separated from the then British-associated states of Saint Christopher-Nevis (Now Saint Kitts and Nevis).

[Antarctica] (No long-form name).
Sovereignty: The United Nations recognizes no claims to Antarctica. *Capital:* None. *Population:* No permanent habitation. *Area:* 14,000,000 sq km.
Comment: Antarctica consists of the territory south of 60 degrees south latitude. This area includes claims by Argentina, Australia, Chile, France, New Zealand, Norway and the United Kingdom, the legal status of which remains in suspense under the terms of the Antarctic Treaty of 1959.

Aruba (No long-form name).
Sovereignty: Self-governing part of Netherlands realm. *Capital:* Oranjestad. *Population:* 63,000. *Area:* 193 sq km.

Ashmore and Cartier Islands TERRITORY OF ASHMORE AND CARTIER ISLANDS.
Sovereignty: Australian external territory. *Capital:* Administered from Darwin, Australia. *Population:* No permanent habitation. *Area:* 5 sq km.

Bermuda (No long-form name).
Sovereignty: Dependent territory of the United Kingdom. *Capital:* Hamilton. *Population:* 58,000. *Area;* 50 sq km.

Bouvet Island (No long-form name).
Sovereignty: Norwegian territory. *Capital:* Administered from Oslo, Norway. *Population:* Uninhabited. *Area:* 58 sq km.

British Indian Ocean Territory BRITISH INDIAN OCEAN TERRITORY.
Sovereignty: Dependent territory of the United Kingdom. *Capital:* None. *Population:* No permanent civilian population; formerly about 3,000 islanders. *Area:* 60 sq km.
Comment: The British Indian Ocean Territory consists of the Chagos Archipelago.

Cayman Islands (No long-form name).
Sovereignty: Dependent territory of the United Kingdom. *Capital:* George Town. *Population:* 24,000. *Area:* 266 sq km.

Christmas Island TERRITORY OF CHRISTMAS ISLAND.
Sovereignty: Australian external territory. *Capital:* The Settlement (Flying Fish Cove). *Population:* 2,000. *Area:* 135 sq km.

Clipperton Island (No long-form name).
Sovereignty: French possession. *Capital:* Administered from French Polynesia. *Population:* Uninhabited. *Area:* Undetermined.

Cocos (Keeling) Islands TERRITORY OF COCOS (KEELING) ISLANDS.
Sovereignty: Australian territory. *Capital:* West Island. *Population:* 616. *Area:* 14 sq km.

Cook Islands (No long-form name).
Sovereignty: Self-governing in free association with New Zealand. *Capital:* Avarua (on the Island of Rarotonga). *Population:* 18,000. *Area:* 240 sq km.
Comment: Under the ''Treaty of Friendship and Delimitation of the Maritime Boundary Between the United States of America and the Cook Islands'', which entered into force on September 8, 1983, the United States relinquished its claims to Danger, Manihiki, Penrhyn and Rakahanga Atolls.

Coral Sea Islands CORAL SEA ISLANDS TERRITORY.
Sovereignty: Australian external territory. *Capital:* Administered from Kingston, Norfolk Island. *Population:* 3 meteorologists. *Area:* Less than 3 sq km.

Falkland Islands (Islas Malvinas) COLONY OF THE FALKLAND ISLANDS.
Sovereignty: Dependent territory of the United Kingdom (also claimed by Argentina). *Capital:* Stanley (on East Falkland Island). *Population:* 2,000. *Area:* 12,170 sq km.

Faroe Islands (No long-form name).
Sovereignty: Self-governing part of Danish realm. *Capital:* Torshavn. *Population:* 47,000. *Area:* 1,400 sq km.

French Guiana DEPARTMENT OF GUIANA.
Sovereignty: French overseas department. *Capital:* Cayenne. *Population:* 95,000. *Area:* 91,000 sq km.

French Polynesia TERRITORY OF FRENCH POLYNESIA.
Sovereignty: French overseas territory. *Capital:* Papeete (on Tahiti Island). *Population:* 196,000. *Area:* 3,941 sq km.
Comment: French Polynesia comprises the Îles de la Société, Îles Tuamotu, Îles Marquises and Îles Tubuai.

French Southern and Antarctic Lands TERRITORY OF THE FRENCH SOUTHERN AND ANTARCTIC LANDS.
Sovereignty: French overseas territory. *Capital:* Administered from Paris. *Population:* 210 (mostly research personnel). *Area:* 7,781 sq km (excluding Antarctic portion).

Comment: "French Southern and Antarctic Lands" includes Île Amsterdam, Île Saint-Paul, Îles Crozet and Îles Kerguelen in the southern Indian Ocean, along with the French-claimed sector of Antarctica, "Terre Adélie". The United Nations does not recognize the French claim to "Terre Adélie".

Gibraltar (No long-form name).
Sovereignty: Dependent territory of the United Kingdom. *Capital:* Gibraltar. *Population:* 30,000. *Area:* 6.5 sq km.

Greenland (No long-form name).
Sovereignty: Self-governing part of Danish realm. *Capital:* Nuuk (Godthab). *Population:* 55,000. *Area:* 2,175,600 sq km.

Guadeloupe DEPARTMENT OF GUADELOUPE.
Sovereignty: French overseas department. *Capital:* Basse-Terre. *Population:* 341,000. *Area:* 1,780 sq km.
Comment: The Department of Guadeloupe includes the nearby islands of Marie-Galante, La Désirade and Îles des Saintes, as well as Saint Barthélemy and the northern three-fifths of Saint Martin (the rest of which belongs to the Netherlands Antilles), 240 kilometers to the northwest.

Guam TERRITORY OF GUAM.
Sovereignty: US unincorporated territory. *Capital:* Agana. *Population:* 138,000. *Area:* 541 sq km.

Guernsey BAILIWICK OF GUERNSEY.
Sovereignty: British Crown dependency. *Capital:* Saint Peter Port. *Population:* 57,000. *Area:* 194 sq km.

Heard Island and McDonald Islands TERRITORY OF HEARD ISLAND AND McDONALD ISLANDS.
Sovereignty: Australian external territory. *Capital:* Administered from Canberra, Australia. *Population:* Uninhabited. *Area:* 412 sq km.

Hong Kong (No long-form name).
Sovereignty: Dependent territory of the United Kingdom. *Capital:* Victoria. *Population:* 5,709,000. *Area:* 1,040 sq km.
Comment: Under a Sino-British declaration of September 1984, Hong Kong will revert to China upon expiration of Britain's 99-year lease on the New Territories on July 1, 1997.

[Iraq-Saudi Arabia Neutral Zone] (No long-form name).
Sovereignty: Jointly administered by Iran and Saudi Arabia. *Capital:* None. *Population:* No permanent habitation. *Area:* 3,520 sq km.
Comment: In July 1975, Iraq and Saudi Arabia signed an agreement to divide the zone between them. The agreement must be ratified, however, before it becomes effective.

Jan Mayen (No long-form name).
Sovereignty: Norwegian territory. *Capital:* Administered from Oslo, Norway. *Population:* No permanent habitation. *Area:* 373 sq km.

Jersey BAILIWICK OF JERSEY.
Sovereignty: British Crown dependency. *Capital:* Saint Helier. *Population:* 83,000. *Area:* 117 sq km.

Johnston Atoll (No long-form name).
Sovereignty: US unincorporated territory. *Capital:* Administered from Washington, DC. *Population:* 1,000. *Area:* 2.8 sq km.

Macau (No long-form name).
Sovereignty: Portuguese overseas territory. *Capital:* Macau. *Population:* 436,000. *Area:* 16 sq km.
Comment: Under a Sino-Portuguese declaration of April 1987, Macau will revert to China on December 20, 1999.

Man, Isle of (No long-form name).
Sovereignty: British Crown dependency. *Capital:* Douglas. *Population:* 65,000. *Area:* 588 sq km.

Martinique DEPARTMENT OF MARTINIQUE.
Sovereignty: French overseas department. *Capital:* Fort-de-France. *Population:* 332,000. *Area:* 1,100 sq km.

Mayotte TERRITORIAL COLLECTIVITY OF MAYOTTE.
Sovereignty: Territorial collectivity of France (claimed by Comoros). *Capital:* Dzaoudzi. *Population:* 69,000. *Area:* 375 sq km.

Midway Islands (No long-form name).
Sovereignty: US unincorporated territory. *Capital:* Administered from Washington, DC. *Population:* 13 US military personnel. *Area:* 5.2 sq km.

Montserrat (No long-form name).
Sovereignty: Dependent territory of the United Kingdom. *Capital:* Plymouth. *Population:* 12,000. *Area:* 100 sq km.

Netherlands Antilles (No long-form name).
Sovereignty: Self-governing part of Netherlands realm. *Capital:* Willemstad (on Curaçao Island). *Population:* 183,00. *Area:* 960 sq km.
Comment: The Netherland Antilles comprises two groupings of islands: Curaçao and Bonaire are located off the coast of Venezuela; Saba, Sint Eustatius, and Sint Maarten (the Dutch two-fifths of the island of Saint Martin) lie 800 km to the north.

Navassa Island (No long-form name).
Sovereignty: US unincorporated territory. *Capital:* Administered from Washington, DC. *Population:* Uninhabited. *Area:* 5.2 sq km.

New Caledonia TERRITORY OF NEW CALEDONIA AND DEPENDENCIES.
Sovereignty: French overseas territory. *Capital:* Nouméa. *Population:* 152,000. *Area:* 19,060 sq km.
Comment: New Caledonia includes Îles Loyauté, Île des Pins, Île Huon, Îles Belép, Îles Chesterfield and Île Walpole.

Niue (No long-form name).
Sovereignty: Self-governing territory in free association with New Zealand. *Capital:* Alofi. *Population:* 2,000. *Area:* 260 sq km.

Norfolk Island TERRITORY OF NORFOLK ISLAND.
Sovereignty: Australian external territory. *Capital:* Kingston. *Population:* 2,000. *Area:* 34.6 sq km.

Northern Mariana Islands COMMONWEALTH OF THE NORTHERN MARIANA ISLANDS.
Sovereignty: Commonwealth in political union with the United States. *Capital:* Saipan. *Population:* 21,000. *Area:* 477 sq km.
Comment: The Covenant by which the Northern Mariana Islands became a commonwealth of the United States entered into force on November 3, 1986.

Pacific Islands (Palau), Trust Territory of the TRUST TERRITORY OF THE PACIFIC ISLANDS (PALAU).
Sovereignty: UN trusteeship administered by the United States. *Capital:* Koror. *Population:* 14,000. *Area:* 458 sq km.
Comment: The government of Palau signed a Compact of Free Association with the United States on January 10, 1986, but the implementing legislation has not yet been passed by the US Congress.

[Paracel Islands] (No long-form name).
Sovereignty: South China Sea islands occupied by China but claimed by Vietnam. *Capital:* None. *Population:* No permanent habitation. *Area:* Undetermined.

Pitcairn Islands PITCAIRN, HENDERSON, DUCIE AND OENO ISLANDS.
Sovereignty: Dependent territory of the United Kingdom. *Capital:* Adamstown (on Pitcairn Island). *Population:* 68. *Area:* 47 sq km.

Puerto Rico COMMONWEALTH OF PUERTO RICO.
Sovereignty: Commonwealth associated with the United States. *Capital:* San Juan. *Population:* 3,301,000. *Area:* 9,104 sq km.

Reunion DEPARTMENT OF REUNION.
Sovereignty: French overseas department. *Capital:* Saint-Denis. *Population:* 566,000. *Area:* 2,510 sq km.
Comment: Europa Island, Juan de Nova Island, Glorioso Islands, Tromelin Island and Bassas da India are controlled by France and are administered from Reunion. (These islands are claimed by Madagascar. Tromelin Island is also claimed by Mauritius and Seychelles).

Saint Helena (No long-form name).
Sovereignty: Dependent territory of the United Kingdom. *Capital:* Jamestown. *Population:* 7,000. *Area:* 410 sq km.
Comment: The territory of Saint Helena includes the island group of Tristan da Cunha. Saint Helena also administers Ascension Island.

Saint Pierre and Miquelon TERRITORIAL COLLECTIVITY OF SAINT PIERRE AND MIQUELON.
Sovereignty: Territorial collectivity of France. *Capital:* Saint-Pierre. *Population:* 6,000. *Area:* 242 sq km.

South Georgia and the South Sandwich Islands SOUTH GEORGIA AND THE SOUTH SANDWICH ISLANDS.
Sovereignty: Dependent territory of the United Kingdom (also claimed by Argentina). *Capital:* None. *Population:* No permanent habitation. *Area:* 4,066 sq km.

[Spanish North Africa] (No long-form name).
Sovereignty: Spanish territory. *Capital:* None. *Population:* 118,000. *Area:* 36 sq km.
Comment: Spanish North Africa comprises the five Spanish plazas de soberania: the enclaves of Ceuta, Melilla and the islands of Peñón de Alhucemas, Peñón de Vélez de la Gomera and Islas Chafarinas.

[Spratly Islands] (No long-form name).
Sovereignty: South China Sea islands claimed in entirety by China and Vietnam and in part by the Philippines and Malaysia; each of these nations occupies some part of the islands. *Capital:* None. *Population:* Undetermined. *Area:* Less than 5 sq km.

Svalbard (No long-form name).
Sovereignty: Norwegian territory. *Capital:* Longyearbyen. *Population:* 4,000. *Area:* 62,049 sq km.

Tokelau (No long-form name).
Sovereignty: New Zealand territory. *Capital:* Administered from Apia, Western Samoa. *Population:* 2,000. *Area:* 10 sq km.
Comment: The Governments of the United States and New Zealand signed a treaty on the 'Delimitation of the Maritime Boundary Between Tokelau and the United States of America' on December 2, 1980. In Article V of the treaty, the United States relinquished its claim to the Atagu, Nukunonu and Fakaofo Atolls. The treaty entered into force on September 3, 1983.

Turks and Caicos Islands (No long-form name).
Sovereignty: Dependent territory of the United Kingdom. *Capital:* Grand Turk (Cockburn Town). *Population:* 10,000. *Area:* 430 sq km.

[United States Miscellaneous Pacific Islands] (No long-form name).
Sovereignty: US unincorporated territories. *Capital:* Administered from Washington, DC. *Population:* Uninhabited. *Area:* 13 sq km.
Comment: Comprises Kingman Reef; Baker, Howland and Jarvis Islands; and Palmyra Atoll.

Virgin Islands VIRGIN ISLANDS OF THE UNITED STATES.
Sovereignty: US unincorporated territory. *Capital:* Charlotte Amalie (on the island of Saint Thomas). *Population:* 109,000. *Area:* 352 sq km.
Comment: Also includes the islands of Saint Croix and Saint John.

Virgin Islands, British (No long-form name).

Sovereignty: Dependent territory of the United Kingdom. *Capital:* Road Town (on the island of Tortola). *Population:* 12,000. *Area:* 150 sq km.

Comment: Also includes the islands of Anegada, Jost Van Dyke, Virgin Gorda, and numerous smaller islands.

Wake Island (No long-form name).

Sovereignty: US unincorporated territory. *Capital:* Administered from Washington, DC. *Population:* 302. *Area:* 6.5 sq km.

Wallis and Futuna TERRITORY OF THE WALLIS AND FUTUNA ISLANDS.

Sovereignty: French overseas territory. *Capital:* Mata-Utu (on Île Uvéa (Wallis), Île Futna and Île Alofi.

Western Sahara (No long-form name).

Sovereignty: Status of sovereignty unresolved. *Capital:* None. *Population:* 186,000. *Area:* 266,000 sq km.

COMPLETE LIST OF RECOGNIZED COUNTRIES, (MEMBERS OF THE UNITED NATIONS)

Abu Dhabi, see United Arab
  Emirates
Abyssinia, see Ethiopia
Aden, see Yemen (People's
  Democratic Rep.)
Afghanistan
Ajman, see United Arab
  Emirates
Albania
Algeria
American Samoa, see Samoa
  (American)
Andorra, see Spain
Angola
Anguilla, see Leeward Islands
Antigua and Barbuda
Antilles, French, see French
  West Indies
Antilles, Netherlands, see
  Netherlands Antilles
Arabia, see Saudi Arabia
Arab Republic of Egypt, see
  Egypt
Arab. Rep. (Syrian) see Syria
Aruba, see Netherlands Antilles
Argentina
Armenia
Australia
Austria
Azerbaijan
Azores, see Portugal
Bahamas
Bahrain
Bangladesh
Barbados
Barbuda, see Antigua and
  Barbuda
Basutoland, see Lesotho
Bechuanaland, see Botswana
Belarus (Byelorussia)
Belgium
Belize
Benin (People's Rep.)
Bermuda

Bhutan
Bolivia
Bophuthatswana, see South
  Africa (Rep.)
Botswana
Brazil
British Guiana, see Guyana
British Honduras, see Belize
British Virgin Islands, see
  Leeward Islands
British Windward Islands, see
  St. Lucia
British West Indies, see
  Barbados or Jamaica or
  Leeward Islands or Trinidad
  & Tobago
Brunei
(Negara Brunei Darussalam)
Bulgaria
Burkina Faso [Burma], see
  Myanmar
Burundi
Caledonia, New, see New
  Caledonia
Cameroon
Canada
Canary Islands, see Spain
Cape Verde Islands
Caroline Islands, see USA
Cayman Islands, see United
  Kingdom
Central African Republic
Ceylon, see Sri Lanka
Chad
Channel Islands, see United
  Kingdom
Chile
China (People's Republic), see
  also Taiwan (Formosa)*
Colombia
Comoros Islands
Congo People's Rep.
Congo (Dem. Rep.) see Zaire
Congo (Kinshasa), see Zaire

Cook Islands
Costa Rica
Cote d'Ivoire
Cuba
Cyprus
Czechoslovakia
Dahomey, see Benin (People's
  Rep.)
DDR, see Germany
Denmark
Djibouti (Rep.)
Dominica
Dominican Republic
Dubai, see United Arab Emirates
Ecuador
Egypt
Eire, see Ireland, Rep.
El Salvador
Ellice Islands (see Tuvalu)
England, see United Kingdom
  (Great Britain)
Equatorial Guinea
Estonia
Ethiopia
Federal Republic of Germany,
  see Germany Federal
  Republic
Federation of Malaya, see
  Malaysia
Fiji
Finland
Formosa, see Taiwan
  (Formosa)*
France
French Antilles, see French
  West Indies
French Guiana
French Polynesia
French Somaliland, see Djibouti
  (Rep.)
French Territory of Afars and
  Issas, see Djibouti (Rep.)
French West Indies
Fujairah, see United Arab
  Emirates

Gabon
Gambia
Germany
Ghana
Gibraltar, see United Kingdom
Gilbert Islands, see Kiribati
Great Britain & Northern
    Ireland, see United Kingdom
    (Great Britain)
Greece
Greenland, see Denmark
Grenada
Grenadines, see St. Vincent and
    the Grenadines
Guadeloupe, see French West
    Indies
Guam (Mariana Island)
Guatemala
Guernsey, see United Kingdom
Guiana, British, see Guyana
Guiana, French, see French
    Guiana
Guiana, Netherlands, see
    Suriname
Guinea, Australian, see Papua
    New Guinea
Guinea
Guinea-Bissau
Guinea, Portuguese, see Guinea-
    Bissau
Guinea, Rep. of
Guinea Equatorial, see
    Equatorial Guinea
Guyana
Haiti
Hawaiian Islands, see USA
Holland, see Netherlands
Honduras
Hong Kong, see United
    Kingdom
Hungary
Iceland
India
Indonesia
Iran (Islamic Rep. of)
Iraq
Ireland (Rep.)
Irian Jaya, see Indonesia
Israel
Italy

Jamaica
Japan
Jersey, see United Kingdom
Johnston Islands, see USA
Jordan
Kazakhstan
Kenya
Kiribati
Korea (Democratic People's
    Rep.) (North Korea)
Korea (Republic) (South Korea)
Kuwait
Kyrgyzstan
Lao People's Dem. Rep.
Latvia
Lebanon
Leeward Islands
Lesotho
Liberia
Libya
Liechtenstein
Lithuania
Luxembourg
Macao, see Portugal
Madagascar (Dem. Rep.)
Madeira, see Portugal
Malagasy Republic, see
    Madagascar (Dem. Rep.)
Malawi
Malaysia
Maldives
Mali
Malta
Mariana Islands, see Northern
    Mariana Islands
Marshall Islands
Martinique, see French West
    Indies
Mauritania
Mauritius
Mayotte, for 1. Passport, 2. Visa
    see French Polynesia; for 3.
    Health, 4. Customs, 5.
    Currency see Reunion
Mexico
Micronesia Federated States of
Midway Islands, see USA
Moldora
Monaco
Mongolia (People's Rep.)

Montserrat
Morocco
Mozambique
Muscat, see Oman
Myanmar (formerly Upper
    Volta)
Namibia
Nauru
Negara Brunei Darussalam, see
    Brunei
Nepal
Netherlands
Netherlands Antilles
Netherlands Guiana, see
    Suriname
Nevis, see St. Kitts-Nevis
New Caledonia
New Guinea, see Papua New
    Guinea
New Hebrides, see Vanuatu
New Zealand
Nicaragua
Niger
Nigeria
Niue
Norfolk Island
Northern Mariana Islands
Northern Rhodesia, see Zambia
North Vietnam, see Vietnam
    (Soc. Rep.)
Norway
Nyassaland, see Malawi
Okinawa, see Japan
Oman
Pakistan
Palau Islands, see USA
Panama
Papua New Guinea
Paraguay
Persia, see Iran (Islamic Rep. of)
Peru
Philippines
Poland
Polynesia, French, see French
    Polynesia
Portugal
Portuguese Guinea, see Guinea-
    Bissau
Portuguese East Africa, see
    Mozambique

Portuguese West Africa, see
    Angola
Principe, see São Tomé &
    Principe
Puerto Rico
Qatar
Ras Al Khaimah, see United
    Arab Emirates
Reunion
Rhodesia, see Zimbabwe
Romania
Russian Federation and
    Commonwealth of
    Independent States
Rwanda
Ryukyu Islands, see Japan
Salvador, El, see El Salvador
Samoa (American)
Samoa (Western)
San Marino
São Tomé & Principe
Saudi Arabia
Senegal
Seychelles
Sharjah, see United Arab
    Emirates
Sierra Leone
Siam, see Thailand
Singapore
Solomon Islands
Somalia
Somaliland (French), see
    Djibouti (Rep.)
South Africa (Rep.)
South Korea, see Korea
    (Republic)
South West Africa, see Namibia
Southern Yemen, see Yemen
    (People's Democratic Rep.)
Spain
Sri Lanka
St. Christopher-Nevis, see St.
    Kitts-Nevis
St. Kitts-Nevis
St. Lucia
St. Vincent and the Grenadines
Sudan
Suriname
Swains Islands, see USA
Swaziland

Sweden
Switzerland
Syria (Syrian Arab Republic)
Tahiti, see French Polynesia
Taiwan (Formosa)*
Tajikstan
Tanzania
Tangier, see Morocco
Thailand
Togo
Tonga
Transkei, see South Africa
    (Rep.)
Trinidad & Tobago
Trucial States, see United Arab
    Emirates
Trust Territory of the Pacific
    Islands, see Northern Mariana
    Islands
Tunisia
Turkey
Turkmenistan
Tuvalu
Uganda
Ukraine
Umm Al Qawain, see United
    Arab Emirates
United Arab Emirates
United Kingdom (Great Britain)
Upper Volta, see Burkina Faso
USA
US Virgin Islands, see Virgin
    Islands (USA)
Uruguay
Uzbekistan
Vanuatu
Vatican
Venda, see South Africa (Rep.)
Venezuela
Vietnam
Virgin Islands (USA)
Wake Island, see USA
Wallis and Futuna, see New
    Caledonia
Western Germany, see Germany
West Indies (British), see
    Barbados or Jamaica or
    Trinidad & Tobago
West Indies (French), see
    French West Indies

Windward Islands, see St. Lucia
    or St. Vincent and the
    Grenadines
Yemen Republic
Yugoslavia**
Zaire
Zambia
Zanzibar, same regulations as
    Tanzania
Zimbabwe

*Expelled from UN when
    ''Red'' China was admitted

**Croatia and Slovenia have
    been recommended for
    admission to the UN. The
    remaining republics of the
    former Yugoslavia have not
    yet resolved their position.

COUNTRIES ESTABLISHED AFTER 1943 (MEMBERS OF THE UNITED NATIONS)

Country	Chronology of Sovereignty	Date of Sovereignty
Algeria	47	July 5, 1962
Angola	80	November 11, 1975
Antigua and Barbuda	94	November 1, 1981
Bahamas, The	73	July 10, 1973
Bahrain	69	August 14, 1971
Bangladesh	72	April 4, 1972
Barbados	61	November 30, 1966
Belize	93	September 21, 1981
Benin	28	August 1, 1960
Botswana	59	September 30, 1966
Brunei	96	January 1, 1984
Burkina	30	August 5, 1960
Burma	8	January 4, 1948
Burundi	45	July 1, 1962
Cambodia	14	November 8, 1949
Cameroon	23	January 1, 1960
Cape Verde	77	July 5, 1975
Central African Republic	33	August 13, 1960
Chad	32	Auigust 11, 1960
Comoros	82	December 31, 1975
Congo	34	August 15, 1960
Côte d'Ivoire (Ivory Coast)	31	August 7, 1960
Cyprus	35	August 16, 1960
Djibouti	84	June 27, 1977
Dominica	87	November 3, 1978
Equatorial Guinea	66	October 12, 1968
Fiji	68	October 10, 1970
Gabon	36	August 17, 1960
Gambia, The	55	February 18, 1965
Ghana	20	March 6, 1957
Grenada	74	February 7, 1974
Guinea	22	October 2, 1958
Guinea-Bissau	75	September 10, 1974
Guyana	58	May 26, 1966
Iceland	3	June 17, 1944
India	7	August 15, 1947
Indonesia	15	December 28, 1949
Israel	10	May 15, 1948
Jamaica	48	August 6, 1962
Jordan	4	March 22, 1946
Kenya	51	December 12, 1963
Kiribati	89	July 12, 1979
Korea	11	August 15, 1948

Kuwait	42	June 19, 1961
Laos	13	July 19, 1949
Lebanon	1	November 22, 1943
Lesotho	60	October 4, 1966
Libya	16	December 24, 1951
Madagascar	25	June 27, 1960
Malawi	52	July 6, 1964
Malaysai	21	August 31, 1957
Maldives	56	July 26, 1965
Mali	38	September 22, 1960
Malta	53	September 21, 1964
Marshall Islands	97	October 21, 1986
Mauritania	40	November 28, 1960
Mauritius	64	March 12, 1968
Micronesia, Federated States of	98	November 3, 1986
Morocco	18	March 2, 1956
Mozambique	76	June 25, 1975
Namibia	99	March 21, 1990
Nauru	63	January 31, 1968
Niger	29	August 3, 1960
Nigeria	39	October 1, 1960
Pakistan	6	August 14, 1947
Papua New Guinea	79	September 16, 1975
Philippines	5	July 4, 1946
Qatar	70	September 3, 1971
Rwanda	46	July 1, 1962
Saint Kitts and Nevis	95	September 19, 1983
Saint Lucia	88	February 22, 1979
Saint Vincent and the Grendines	90	October 27, 1979
Sao Tome and Principe	78	July 12, 1975
Senegal	37	August 20, 1960
Seychelles	83	June 28, 1976
Sierra Leone	41	April 27, 1961
Singapore	57	August 9, 1965
Solomon Islands	85	July 7, 1978
Somalia	27	July 1, 1960
Sri Lanka	9	February 4, 1948
Sudan	17	January 1, 1956
Suriname	81	November 25, 1975
Swaziland	65	September 6, 1968
Syria	2	January 1, 1944
Tanzania	43	December 9, 1961
Togo	24	April 27, 1960
Tonga	67	June 4, 1970
Trinidad and Tobago	49	August 31, 1962
Tunisia	19	March 20, 1956
Tuvalu	86	October 1, 1978
Uganda	50	October 9, 1962
United Arab Emirates	71	December 2, 1971
Vanuatu	92	July 30, 1980

Vietnam	12	March 8, 1949
Western Samoa	44	January 1, 1962
Yemen (South)	62	November 30, 1967
Zaire	26	June 30, 1960
Zambia	54	October 24, 1964
Zimbabwe	91	April 18, 1980

Comments, questions, additions and constructive criticism should be sent to:
Scope International, 62 Murray Road, Waterlooville, Hampshire PO8 9JL, Great Britain.

Part V

SPECIFIC COUNTRIES EXAMINED IN DETAIL

SPECIFIC COUNTRIES EXAMINED IN DETAIL

ARGENTINA – COMRADES WELCOME

The Argentine Republic is the second largest country in Latin America and occupies most of the southern part of South America. It is bordered by five countries; Chile to the east, Bolivia and Paraguay to the north and Brazil and Uruguay to the northeast. The Rio Colorado which runs from west to east cuts the country in two. Argentina is home to a wide variety of terrains, including, jungle, pampas, infertile plain and South America's highest mountain, Mount Aconcagua.

Like most of South America, Argentina is a former Spanish colony. It declared its independence from Spain in 1816 and became a republic in 1852. Politically the country has followed an uncertain course in much of the 20th century – to the detriment of its great economic potential. However, since 1983, Argentina has had a democratically elected president as head of government.

Argentina is a cosmopolitan country with a population of 33 million, mostly of Spanish, German, Italian and English descent. Buenos Aires, its capital, is one of the largest cities in the world, population 11 million. The country is one of the more highly developed nations in the western hemisphere. Its people are amongst the most educated in South America, with a literacy rate of 90 per cent. Its economy has gradually shifted from an exclusive dependence on large scale livestock and agriculture production to one in which service and industrial sectors are dominant. Since the 1950's it has been one of the 20 largest trading nations in the world. However, economic growth has been much hampered by excessive inflation.

As Argentina had one of the highest standards of living at the turn of the century, it is anxious to regain its past glory. It plans to accept up to 100,000 migrants a year and is particularly interested in immigrants from Eastern Europe and the former Soviet Union.

Also, Argentina at one time granted permanent residency with a minimum investment of US $30,000. However, at least US $50,000 was recommended. Agency fees were US $20,000. After two years of actual residency, citizenship was granted. If the investment is larger (in excess of US $150,000) one could apply for citizenship earlier although there was no guarantee. This program closed in 1992, but it seems likely that with Argentina's current desire to attract new immigrants, a new program (undoubtedly with a more substantial minimum investment) will emerge.

An Argentinian passport is valid for a period of five years. As a travel document, it does not fare badly, allowing for visa-free travel to 32 countries, including many countries in Europe and South America.

AUSTRALIA – THREE YEARS OF PART TIME RESIDENCE

Australia is one of the dozen or so countries in the world actively courting new immigrants. How easy or hard it will be to get in at any given time relates to unemployment levels in Australia. The population of Australia more than doubled immediately after World War Two, when the former "all white, all English" flavor was replaced by a more cosmopolitan group of six million immigrants. The largest new nationality is Italian, with many Greeks, Slavs and a large number of Russians (mostly Jewish) residing in the major cities.

If you have a job skill currently needed by Australia (list supplied at any Consulate), your immigration application is speeded along by Consular officials. The process takes several months. A few years ago Australia would pay for all or most of the costs of transportation, assist with housing and provide free English language training if needed. Citizenship and a passport was granted one year after arrival!

Now it is a bit tougher to qualify as an immigrant, but the above benefits still come free. Only the financial assistance for immigrant passage has been temporarily discontinued. Also, these days it takes a minimum of two years (but in practice closer to three years) to get full citizenship and a passport. This is one of the world's shortest residence periods. No fees or investments are required of job-qualified immigrants.

Other ways to qualify as an immigrant are through the "Business Migration Program", marriage to an Australian or by having a close relative in Australia.

In July of 1991, the Australian government radically changed its "Business Migration Program". Before all one had to do was show assets of A$500,000 (US $350,000) which can be transferred into any Australian investment (including a bank account). After meeting these fairly simple requirements, one was granted permanent residency, the freedom to leave and enter Australia as one felt necessary and Australian citizenship after a period of two years of (non-continuous) residence. However, this program was criticized because of its reliance on private sector consultants and the ability of' would be immigrants to bring in ready cash.

In February of 1991, a new scheme was introduced which concentrates more on actual business and English language skills than wealth. A point system, similar to those of Canada and New Zealand, has been introduced. Applicants must score a certain number of points to gain approval. Points are awarded on the basis of size and sector of existing business, age (applicants aged 30 to 45 score highest), English-language skills and cash and non-cash assets. An applicant with no money can still qualify for admittance solely on the basis of experience, age and English-language ability.

Applications are now also reviewed by the Department of Immigration rather than private-sector consultants. The government claimed that the old program didn't work because, "Consultants were always under duress from their clients, who could say, 'If you don't approve me I'll go to somebody else who will." Monitoring procedures have also become more stringent, and business-skills visas can now be cancelled if holders have not attempted to start a business within three years.

Basically, the Australian government is no longer simply interested in an influx of capital. They want the natural resource that governments most love to exploit, people. People who seriously want to invest and belong in Australia should not have a problem. PTs may fare worse.

These changes have dramatically affected the number of applicants for the "Business Migration Program". During the 10 years that the former program ran, about 10,000 immigrants and 30,000 dependents were admitted to Australia. In the first six months after the introduction of the new program, only 100-150 applications have been received. What does all this mean if you also are no longer quite so keen on becoming Australian? If you are interested in applying for a passport somewhere and qualify now . . . apply now! Programs change every day, and there is simply no way of knowing whether you will still qualify tomorrow or not.

However, if the image of incessant shrimp barbecues lures you on, Australian citizenship is still possible through this program. Preferred industries are what one would expect, such as non-polluting high-tech and/or export oriented industrial production. Real estate investors are definitely unwelcome, as there is already a general feeling that "speculators" have pushed land prices too high. Agriculture is Australia's major industry. It is currently in a bad state with historically low commodity rates caused by the erosion of traditional European markets and high interest rates. Any product or service you could supply that would help local farmers compete more effectively might get faster consideration and approval.

The application procedure involves an interview and a background check. However, these are only intended to ward off major criminals, and a conviction for something not considered a crime in Australia will not necessarily be held against you.

Once residency is obtained, the path to citizenship is still fairly simple and straightforward. You are still free to leave and enter Australia as you see fit. After at least two years actual residence in Australia (these two years need not be continuous, but must have been accumulated in the past five years, one year of which must fall in the past two years) you are allowed to apply for a passport. This application procedure also involves a brief interview and a few other minor considerations, such as proof of basic knowledge of the English language and good character.

Australia has many tax-holiday programmes for entrepreneurs, exporters and investors in favored industries. They are liberal about allowing offshore trusts to be set up before immigration, which accumulate abroad and shelter the income of the wealthy migrants. Importantly for tax exiles, unlike in the US, **you can't be sent to jail for tax evasion in Australia since tax evasion, as opposed to tax fraud, is not a crime**. The worst punishment is a fine. By this, I do not mean to say that it is impossible to go to jail in Australia for a tax-related offense. Many Australians have received jail sentences, and a few, including those who made millions in the "Bottom of the Harbor Scandals" are even pursued and extradited back to Australia. If an Australian merely doesn't report some interest, dividend or profits on his personal tax return, he has not committed a crime. It may be tax evasion, but an Australian prosecutor must do more than just show that a taxpayer didn't report all his receipts. There must be an active fraud, such as submitting totally false and forged bills and receipts to justify deductions and losses that never happened. Switzerland has similar rules. But the US and Canada are quite different. Not filing a tax return, not reporting all bank accounts where one has any financial interest (regardless of what name they are held in), not reporting every last dime – these are criminal offenses for which people do serve long jail terms. The American prosecutors have gone so far as to claim that ANY ACTION TO REDUCE ONE'S TAXES BY ANY MEANS MAY BE, AT THE OPTION OF THE IRS, CONSIDERED A CRIMINAL OFFENSE. And *that* cannot happen in Australia (at least for the moment). The "Bottom of the Harbor Schemes" of a few years ago became a scandal because promoters openly advertised a plan whereby businesses could divert **all** their profits to "shell companies" whose only purpose was to receive merchandise or bogus "expense" checks. Kickbacks were made to the owners of the businesses in cash, under the table. The corporate taxes that were saved were then divided up between the promoter and the company owner. A non-resident withholding tax system has since been introduced.

There had never been many criminal tax fraud prosecutions in Australia before 1980 when Brian Maher, a used car salesman who ran these operations for hundreds of businessmen, became something of a folk hero and regularly appeared on television and magazine covers to tell exactly what he was doing and why. (He simply didn't like taxes). He drove a gold Rolls Royce and passed out hundred dollar bills to newsboys when he bought a paper. This high profile brought the obvious, predictable government reaction – criminal indictment and prosecution. In 1985 Maher received a five year jail sentence for diverting over $1 billion in tax revenues to the "Bottom of the Harbor". The expression was used because the financial records of the shell companies run by Maher could never be found, and he had suggested that they were probably deep-sixed (i.e. submerged in the depths of Australia's many harbors). Had Brian Maher been less flamboyant he could probably, to this day, be making a good living by dispatching files to the bottom of the harbor. Instead, he created a flood of righteous indignation, a vastly increased bureaucracy of tax collectors and investigators and left a legacy of greatly increased penalties. The easy going attitude of Australia on tax matters was changed forever – so much so that a proposal to give everyone a mandatory identity card and tax number that had to be recorded and reported to the government with every financial transaction was almost implemented in 1987. Many Australians believe that their country is only a step behind Moscow in Big Brotherism. But few realize that compared to the USA, where the tax ID number has been in place for years and there is no right of privacy at all in financial matters, Australia is still something of a tax-evader's paradise.

Australia has a reputation for being somewhat corrupt. This reputation seems to be borne out by local news stories continually reporting cases of bribery among public servants. Officials of the Passport Office were supposedly selling Australian passports to newcomers at about $1,000 each. These were legal passports, but backup files with applications and photographs didn't exist – though the passports were properly registered on the computer system.

The result was that any inquiry about individuals using these passports was met with a positive response from the Passport Office. Any in-depth inquiry by police officials was met with a "missing file" notation. The ring came to light when a convicted drug dealer revealed how he got his non-registered passport with a false name on it. For exposing the passport fraud he got a lighter sentence on the drug trafficking charges. This happened recently and the Australian passport procedure was then tightened up.

Our advice is to steer clear of any schemes proffered by bartenders, cab drivers or the like. Be guided by reputable lawyers who can generally give good advice on the propriety of "short cuts" to obtaining the documents you want. In general, if you have the two years to wait, an Australian passport can be obtained without paying any legal fees, gratuities, or under-the-table money.

All the details of Australian Immigration Law and Practice are spelled out quite clearly, with annual supplements to bring it up-to-date, in *Obtaining Permanent Residence in Australia* by Adrian Joel (publisher: Legal Books Prop. Ltd., Sydney, Australia).

Another book that is more technical and aimed at immigration lawyers is *Australian Citizenship Law* by Michael Pryles (publisher: Law Book Co. Ltd – 1981).

Both are available from Australia's major law book distributor, Law Book Co. Ltd., 44-50 Waterloo Road, North Ryde, New South Wales 2113, Australia. You can order books from this company by describing the book you want and providing a credit card number. Most major book retailers worldwide, by the way, will send your order by return air-mail with a charge to your Visa, Master, Amex, Bankcard, Eurocard or Diners Club account.

For Australia, a visit to the Australian Consulate near you is the best first move. Pick up their brochures and "Job Preference List". There is a do-it-yourself rating scale to figure out if you score enough points to qualify. After just two years of residence, a passport is obtainable.

See also *The Tax Exile Report,* published by Scope International.

AUSTRIA – AN ALMOST INSTANT PASSPORT FOR REFUGEES

One hundred years ago, the Austro Hungarian Empire, presided over by the immensely rich and powerful Hapsburg royal family, was a super-power in company with France and England. The Hapsburgs dominated Spain, the Low Countries (Belgium and Holland), major portions of Germany and Prussia (now Poland). Vienna splendidly reflects monuments of these past glories.

After the ravages of two world wars, this once mighty Empire is now a small neutral state buffering Eastern Europe to the east, Switzerland to the west and Italy and what was Yugoslavia to the south. Austria was occupied by the Russians at the end of World War Two and was saved as an independent neutral through post-war negotiations. As a neutral, Austria is not a member of either the European Common Market or of NATO.

Vienna is highly civilized, has fine local wines, the world's most beautiful opera house and boasts sophisticated entertainment at all levels. This historic city is the center of the Austrian Socialist Democracy, replete with an active stock exchange and a decidedly entrepreneurial class. In all, Vienna is diverse, cosmopolitan, wealthy and interesting.

Austria's climate is slightly warmer than Switzerland's. The atmosphere is sparkingly clean. Austrians are far more tolerant of eccentric behaviour than are the Swiss. Austrians speak German as their official language, but English and French are widely understood.

What makes Austria particularly interesting in our context is that it is perhaps the world's biggest center for processing the resettlement of refugees. Large grants from the United Nations support a huge bureaucracy of "re-location experts". Temporary decent housing is provided by the UN for stateless people, who arrive (often without papers) at the rate of hundreds per day. As can be imagined, most arrivals are from the neighbouring former communist countries.

Many Russian-Jews with visas for Israel stop in Vienna where two-thirds choose to change course for the US or Australia. Individuals and families from oriental countries show up in Vienna after bribing their way to Austria.

This country has a worldwide reputation as a safe haven for individuals without a passport or country. Essentially, Austria offers a good stopping-off place to get one's bearings, plus the free services of an international staff of knowledgeable and helpful people who will match up your need and abilities with those countries willing or able to accept you under special refugee quotas. Many countries are actively recruiting settlers in Vienna.

If you are running from persecution of any sort and wind up in Austria without a passport, it is likely that after very sympathetic questioning, you will be issued an Austrian Refugee Passport. If you are broke, you'll be given assistance in obtaining temporary food, shelter and medical treatment.

Because of its small size, Austria cannot accept huge numbers of new alien residents. Yet their law provides unusual flexibility in deciding citizenship on a case by case basis. Those with substantial assets who can provide export stimulation or employment for the locals will receive preference.

Representation by a knowledgeable Austrian lawyer is essential. The minimum cost is said to be US $250,000, although it may be possible to negotiate a better arrangement. The bulk of this amount will be for investment and not fees which you ultimately lose.

The idea is to present an acceptable business or investment proposal to the Office of Economic Development. This process takes between six months and one year and is conducted in an open and above-board manner. On approval of the plan, residence and passport documents are issued.

THE BAHAMAS – SUN AND NO TAXES

Not only do the Bahamas offer an excellent climate, but they also do not have income, gifts, value added, capital gains, wealth, inheritance nor corporate profit taxes.

The Bahamas Investment Promotion Programme, started in December 1990, allows foreigners to obtain instant permanent residency under three categories. Although one can obtain an alien passport, citizenship is out of the question, unless by marriage to a Bahamian national. As mentioned throughout this Special Report, the last place in the world one wants to be a citizen is where one actually lives, and we believe that there is little to be gained through citizenship in the Bahamas that cannot be gained through permanent residency. Anyway, the categories are:

Category I: For the Individual Investor. One must prove a personal net worth of US $2 million, reside in the country and make a minimum investment of at least US $500,000 which must stay in the country for at least 10 years.

Category II: For the Group Investor. One may invest a minimum of US $150,000 in a government approved programme (similar to Canada). The actual amount will depend upon the individual programme which is usually a tourist development, such as condos, town houses and the likes.

Category III: For the Entrepreneur. One must invest in a government approved programme for a period of at least 10 years.

Obviously, the category which is the most suitable and easiest is number II.

One such programme was recently brought to the attention of Scope International. It involves the Sandyport Marina Beach Club, a timeshare development on New Providence, not far from Nassau and only a 10 minute drive from the international airport. It allows for permanent residency for the investor, spouse and children under 18 years of age through a one time investment of US $250,000 in redeemable 9 per cent preference shares in the development for five years, after which time they can be bought back. The project claims an anticipated return to investor of 12 to 19 per cent per annum. You will have to reside in the Bahamas for at least one month a year which should not prove to be difficult as the investment includes five weeks of accommodation at the resort. You do not need to buy a house. However, if spending one month a year in the sun is too horrible for you to bear, the requirement can be waived for up to five years through an annual payment of US $5,000 to the Bahamian government. Write: The

Sandyport Marina Beach Club & Resort Ltd., PO Box N-8585, Nassau, Bahamas. Alternatively, contact the nearest embassy or consulate of the Bahamas for details on this and other existing programs.

We have no direct knowledge of this scheme other than that a salesman rang and wrote constantly touting the resort which tells us that they employ commission only salesmen on big profits (paid for by you) and that the resort is hard sold. *Caveat emptor*.

The agency fees for any of the other categories are US $20,000. Scope can offer you a personal recommendation to another development on request.

BELIZE – CAN'T MAKE UP THEIR MINDS

Belize is an independent English speaking Commonwealth country (formerly known as British Honduras until the name of the country was changed in 1973). It lies on the Caribbean coast of Central America bounded by Mexico to the north and Guatemala to the west and south. The climate is unbearably hot and humid, tempered only by trade winds.

The total population of Belize is only 200,000 of which 24 per cent live in Belize City, the main commercial center and largest city. Belmopan which has a population of 5,000 is the capital and is located practically in the geographic center of the country. The Phillip S.W. Goldston International Airport is situated 16 kilometers (10 miles) from Belize city and is two hours flying time from Miami, New Orleans and Houston. Belize is also a short boat ride from the many nations and islands of the Caribbean.

The main ethnic groups are Creole (African descent), Mestizo (Spanish-Maya) and Garifuna (Caribs). There are also a number of people of Spanish and East Indian descent. Caucasians are a definite minority of less than one percent. These groups, however, are heavily intermixed and the multi-racial makeup of Belizian society includes Chinese, Arabs and other ethnic groups.

The official language is English, although Spanish is also widely spoken. The majority of the population is unquestionably poor, much like those in Haiti.

Belize has an ancient history dating back to Mayan times which experienced its peak between AD 300 and 900 (not much of importance appears to have happened since). In the 17th and 18th centuries Belize was subject to British influence and in 1871 British Honduras was formally declared a British colony. The country did not achieve its independence until the 21st of September, 1981. It is currently a parliamentary democracy based on the Westminster model.

The government passed an amnesty in 1984 granting citizenship to all illegal resident aliens choosing to identify themselves. This opened the door to citizenship for a flood of Mayans and others who had fled the continuous wars in neighboring El Salvador, Nicaragua and Guatemala. Belize is relatively unpopulated. Free land suitable for coconut palms and sugar cane is still available to homesteaders.

A genuine Belize passport used to be quite easy to obtain by fraud. Citizenship could have been bought as recently as 1983 for about US $300. The US $300 passport was not entirely legal, of course, since it involved a local police officer or lawyer filing a certification that the applicant had been physically resident in Belize for at least five years. The residence could have been with or without proper documentation such as visas or residence permits. Another variation was for a delayed birth certificate to be filed. This was called the Belize "born again" or "rebirth" procedure. The US $300 passport has unfortunately disappeared along with 5 cent cigars.

Due to floods and a general absence of vital statistics, many persons actually born in Belize and thus Belizean by birth, must still obtain police or lawyer affidavits in lieu of birth certificates. Obviously if the documentation supporting a passport application is false, the passport can later be invalidated. These fraudulent passport deals were far more costly when the government itself sold passports for $35,000 each.

Belize is not our first choice as a place to live. It would be near the bottom of the list. The government and many local professionals such as lawyers we spoke to seem to be hostile towards whites. Yet Belize is a good domicile for English-speaking black people from Africa or the Arab world. A black person with a Belize passport can easily blend into the communities in Belize and travel more freely in the US than on an African or Arab passport. Of course a PT never lives in the country that issues him a passport in any case.

Indians (from India) control most of the retail trade, and Mennonites, the legitimate agriculture. The wealth and influence of these groups is out of proportion to their tiny numbers. Natives grow quite a bit of marijuana or ganja for local consumption and export to the US.

ECONOMIC CITIZENSHIP PROGRAM
Since 1987, the government of Belize has opened and then closed two different programs offering instant citizenship.

The first ran from 1987 to 1989. This program worked much like many of the others described in this report. For US $30,000 passports were issued, as long as other documentation such as a birth certificate, certificate of medical health and background check were satisfactorily provided. In 1989, due to a change of government, the program was closed and passports already issued were rendered unusable.

The second program ran from February of 1992 to March of 1993. This program worked much like its predecessor. However, the fee was raised to US $44,000 for a single applicant and US $54,000 for a family application. This program also differed in that applicants not able to supply a certificate of no criminal conviction could instead supply signed and sworn affidavits from the legal, medical or accountancy professions. Also, the required photocopy of a passport could be replaced by an alternative travel or identity document. Apparently this program closed when a quota was attained, and the passports issued through it are still valid.

After March of 1993, individual applications may be submitted to the government of Belize. We have heard that the minimum contribution will be raised again and full payment will be required in advance. However, as we go to print this information has not been confirmed by the government of Belize.

Is Belize the country for you? The cancellation and revocation of passports under its first Economic Citizenship Program provides little confidence for any future programs. Belize appears to have little to offer, except that it is English-speaking and a member of the Commonwealth. It has a terrible reputation of selling enormous quantities of illegal passports through – what we consider – perhaps the most corrupt government offices and officials in Latin America. Canada has recently placed a ban on entry and special visa requirements on Belizean passports for this reason. Other countries are likely to follow. Visa are required for almost all countries.

BLACK AFRICA

An intelligent and highly educated black African diplomat once said to me, "I received my appointment due to the political good fortune of a close relative. Because I am not a rich man and the job may only last a few years, this is the only opportunity I will ever have to secure my financial future. Anything, and I mean anything, that I can do for you, any service I can render . . . please just ask." That is the way of life in Africa. **Passports are sold by most diplomats for whatever the traffic will bear**. Also for sale: Honorary Consulates, medals and decorations, permits to do business, smuggle or exploit natural resources.

Many Europeans, Arabs and especially Indians and mixed-race people have dual citizenship with second African passports. **There is not a single country of Black Africa that has what we would rate as a good passport, permitting visa-free travel or work in the white, Arab or Asian world**. Even if they can be obtained cheaply, African passports are only good as identification. You can never be sure that there will be proper back-up registration with the Ministry of Foreign Affairs of the issuing country. Records are in such a poor state in most African countries that they cannot usually respond to any request to confirm passport validity. **Worst yet, an African citizen must get an "exit visa" to leave most countries, as well as an entry visa before he can get in anywhere**.

If you are offered any favors from Black African countries be aware that the documents involved may be totally fraudulent or stolen blanks – even if you get them from a high official. If you are lucky enough to get valid documents, be aware that exit visas and renewal fees could be higher than the issue price. Summary: Aside from Senegal, Kenya and Ivory Coast (fairly respectable countries), stay away from Black African passports unless you need one to own local property or a business or are simply interested in a Banking Passport. As a citizen you might need to pay a bribe for permission to leave the country. It is better also to keep the passport of a Western country for international travel. **African citizenship, in our opinion, is generally more of a burden than a benefit**. But if you have the need to travel in Black Africa or are in need of an inexpensive Banking Passport, see the entry on Chad in this part of the report.

BOLIVIA – AN FAIRLY RESPECTABLE PASSPORT AT A BARGAIN PRICE

Bolivia is a totally landlocked country in South America. The major activity is farming with about two-thirds of the population engaged in subsistence agriculture. Sugar, rice, coffee, rubber and forest products are exported to a minor degree. Spanish is the national language.

Bolivia's total population is about 6 million, 60 per cent of whom are Aymara Indian, 30 per cent Mestizo (an Indian/Spanish/Portuguese mixture) and 10 per cent predominantly Spanish Europeans. La Paz is the administration capital and has about 1 million inhabitants. It is also the world's highest capital with an elevation of 11,900 feet. It has a constant cool temperature of 50°F the year round.

There are no monetary or exchange controls. Political stability is quite good. A popular civilian government is in power and it maintains a fairly progressive human rights posture.

The Bolivian constitution provides that any foreigner may apply for naturalization and citizenship after two years of residence. Immigration is wide open. An elimination of the residence requirement is possible for those who retain a local lawyer. The law also provides for special dispensation and earlier citizenship for persons "with exceptional skills, or for those who have rendered meritorious service". This is the "loophole" by which an instant passport may be obtained.

Although this program was closed "temporarily" in May of 1991 (the officials formerly in charge are said to be in jail), it is likely to reopen at some point, undoubtedly with a higher contribution requirement. The program involved financial contributions to government approved development projects. Quasi-government companies sought private grants from individuals of approximately US $25,000. These led to recognition as a benefactor to Bolivia and rapid conferral of citizenship and a passport. The attorney generally received $7,500 and the remainder may have actually been applied to some national development program. There were several variations of these programs, and the prices quoted were as low as $10,000. For $25,000, the package included a cedula (identity card), driver's licence and several other useful documents. The beauty of this benefactor arrangement was that a single contribution would cover the applicant, his spouse and all dependent children under 18. *No visit to Bolivia was necessary.*

As with most South American passports, Bolivian passports are good for five years and must be revalidated every two years, technically by visiting Bolivia. In practice they are renewable at nominal cost, with the right connections. They are excellent and allow travel to Europe without visas. Unfortunately, recent publicity about huge US military anti-cocaine operations has led some customs officials to be more than usually attentive to Bolivians. Americans will find it difficult or impossible to become Bolivian citizens.

BRAZIL – A FIRST CLASS COUNTRY. A PASSPORT IN 3 WEEKS?

Brazil will unquestionably be a super-power in the 21st century. It is self-sufficient in food and everything else, including jet aircraft, computers and all of the most sophisticated manufactured products. It is in fact the fifth largest country in the world in land area. With 130 million people Brazil has a formidable population as well. The national language is Portuguese, but various communities speak mainly German, English, Japanese, Korean or even an African language. The country is multi-racial, and though the majority are Roman Catholic, almost every religion on earth including voodoo would have a following here.

As in all of South America, special arrangements can be made for those who have problems in their own country and might like to immigrate to Brazil or travel on her passport. We understand the same is true in neighbouring Argentina, Chile and Venezuela, but we have actually been visited by a Brazilian lawyer who has proven to be reputable and effective. He was able to help readers of earlier editions of *The Passport Report* obtain Brazilian passports very quickly. The price has been high (around $50,000) but we have learned that the gentleman who makes these arrangements is a man of high ideals, willing to listen to worthy individuals who cannot afford this relatively high price. Our clients have paid $27,000 per person or $45,000 per couple. If this still sounds to high, and you have some time to spare, Scope International also has a contact that can arrange Brazilian residency, which will lead to citizenship and a passport in one to five years. See the PERMANENT RESIDENCY PROGRAM entry below.

Due to high taxes, currency controls and a government that has had an ambivalent attitude towards capitalistic enterprises, Brazil has been an economic graveyard for many wealthy foreigners who started but were never allowed to finish large development projects. One of our

66

personal acquaintances lost 90 per cent of his fortune (of nearly a billion dollars) on a pulp and paper making facility he built near Manaus. Any reader who moves to Brazil is advised to look long and carefully at any business venture before investing. Like America in 1880, Brazil is a land of opportunity, but in the Brazilian Wild West there are also many outlaws. The political realities take some understanding. To operate effectively in Brazil, Portuguese must be learned.

A Brazilian passport is one of the best travel documents in the world, with visa-free travel possible to 66 countries. The fact that a holder does not speak good Portuguese is not fatal – many Italians, Arabs, Africans, Germans, Americans, Mennonites and Asians are Brazilian citizens. They do not necessarily speak the language. Any race can fit in here. There is a large black population and a larger number of Lebanese and Armenians than in Lebanon or Armenia. Brazil has been a popular destination for Americans since the Civil War of 1865 when over a million Americans, mostly from the defeated Confederacy, sought refuge here. At various times it was the favored destination of 98 per cent of the Jews of Spain, escaping black slaves, Arabs, Fascists from Germany and Argentina and leftists from elsewhere in South America. Brazil as a result is a melting pot of races, religions and persecuted people. Because of its large size, all climates and terrains are present from Alpine mountains to tropical rainforests.

Brazil may also prove to be useful as a back door, both to the US and the EC. For people with either a Brazilian passport or resident visa, a B-1, B-2 visa can be obtained for entry into the US. A similar process can be used to gain entry into Canada. As for the EC, the special relationship between Spain and its former colonies allows one to first gain residency (in Spain) and then citizenship and a passport after a period of two years.

A unique feature to Brazil is that it has few extradition treaties. In fact, there is an existing law that the father of a Brazilian child cannot be extradited, even if he is not Brazilian himself. Fathering a child also grants one the right to residence, which will lead to a passport in five years. See the entry on Brazil in the BACK DOORS section of this Special Report.

We would rate Brazil as a top place for a passport as well as a top place to live. The nation itself offers all earthly delights. It is on our list as one of the top sex havens of the world, see our forthcoming report, *Sex Havens*. However, high taxes, excessive corruption and a socialistic government make it a less than desirable place for investment in spite of the obvious opportunities. Also on the negative side, it should be noted that the larger cities (Rio and Sao Paulo) have excessively high rates of pollution, violence and petty crime.

PERMANENT RESIDENCY PROGRAM

Scope International can refer you to a reliable contact that can arrange residency for almost anyone. The visa is obtained through a joint venture between an existing company in your country and one in Brazil, arranged by our contact. Basically, a request will be made that you come to Brazil to work in the capacity of a Director on a company's Commercial Board. In Hong Kong and many other Asian countries, an invitation is required to enter the Brazilian Consulate. In this case, two Brazilian attorneys will visit you, preventing such a problem.

The cost of the program is US $20,000 per person. If the application is for a family, an additional US $3,000 is charged for a spouse and US $1,000 per child under 18 years of age. (There may be an additional fee of US $3,000 to US $7,000 if Brazilian attorneys must visit you, as explained above.) All fees are held in escrow which means they will remain safe until

SOUTH AMERICA
WHERE INSTANT PASSPORTS
GOOD FOR VISA FREE
TRAVEL TO EUROPE AND ASIA
ARE EASILY OBTAINED
IN ALMOST ALL
COUNTRIES

you receive your Permanent Resident Visa. Processing time takes approximately 120 days. If an application is unsuccessful, for reasons other than undisclosed problems of health or character, the applicant will receive a full refund.

You may apply for citizenship and passport after living permanently in Brazil for one year.

If you are interested in receiving more information about this program or applying for it, ask Scope International for the appropriate referral. Scope International, 62 Murray Road, Waterlooville, Hants PO8 9JL.

CANADA – IT'S FREE, BUT TAKES THREE YEARS

Canada has no "instant passport" program but is a relatively "wide open" place for immigration. After three years of strictly defined residence, one can apply for a passport. With a huge land mass and a rather small population of about 20 million, Canada is looking for immigrants. They have broken their selection system down into three classes:

1) The family class – you must have a relative living in Canada who has legally promised to give you financial help.
2) The refugee class – applicants in this class are admitted under special refugee rules.
3) The independent and other applicants class (the PT one) – you can apply on your own, with or without the financial help of relatives in Canada.

The Canadian government at least claims that everyone who applies is judged and chosen by the same standards. Race is not a factor. Independent applicants are assessed on a point system. Although the factors used in this point system change with great regularity, as we go to print they were listed as education, vocational training, experience, chances of finding a job, having a job already arranged, age, knowledge of English and French, personal suitability and having relatives in Canada.

Investors of over C$250,000 and entrepreneurs with a proven track record will receive preferential treatment. If you do not wish to start a business you can be a passive investor in what amounts to a government trust fund. Extra points are scored if one wishes to establish a business in depressed areas. Once admitted as a "landed immigrant", there is no restriction on where you go or what you do.

Canada will also require an interview as well as legal and background checks of which some of the necessary documents will include: medical examination report, chest x-rays, police certification of clean record, references, financial statements and birth and marriage certificates.

Contact a Canadian consulate to receive a list of current requirements and a self scoring questionnaire. If you have the necessary points, you can ask for an application to immigrate. This application can only be submitted *from outside of Canada*. (They are strict about this one!)

The expected processing time of a visa application seems to be increasing annually. As we go to print, the current estimates seem to hover around 12 to 15 months and may be worse in backlogged countries such as Hong Kong and the Philippines. Priority is given to family and refugee class applications. Immigration visas come unexpectedly, giving you only a few weeks to make your move.

Canada advises applicants not to hire attorneys or others to assist with applications. Consular officials are generally very honest. Attempting to bribe one of them would surely result in a serious problem for you.

Once in Canada, immigrants may leave for business or vacation trips for up to 183 days per year – just under six months. An absence of more than six months is considered an interruption in legal residence. One must have permission in the form of a "re-entry permit" to take foreign trips of over six months. Otherwise, an immigrant may lose the right to re-enter Canada.

Hong Kong immigrants have discovered one way around this required residence problem which used to allow only 90 days absence per year. Before immigrating they "lose" their original Hong Kong passports containing their visa and use the new duplicate one for returning home to Hong Kong via the US. If challenged when re-entering Canada, they claim they were shopping in the US for the day. Relatives in Canada back up the story. No permit is now needed for trips or vacations of up to six months. The old "three month maximum stay abroad" was a difficult rule for Hong Kong immigrants to live with. It was even more difficult for the Canadians to enforce because of the ability to travel between Canada and the US on just a driving licence. The Canadian restriction on the right to travel abroad was of course an unjust deprival of liberty. The new rule is much more reasonable. In the US, a legal US resident may be temporarily absent abroad for up to one year without any re-entry permit.

A new Canadian super visa, incorporating an invisible ink, is being introduced to dissuade illegal immigrants from entering the country with fake documents and increase the efficiency of immigration officials. The super visa will replace about 10 different documents, ranging from a student visa to a work authorization permit, which currently allow non-Canadians to enter. The manufacture of phoney documents is a lucrative business in Asia, with Hong Kong or Sri Lankan nationals paying between C$2,000 and C$10,000 for fake papers in a bid to move to Canada.

Canadian income taxes are similar to those in the US. Immigrants are often required to show three years income tax returns prior to being granted citizenship and a passport. Worldwide income of residents is taxed, so applicants should be careful how they fill in their forms. Mismatches between income and assets could result in a tax audit which would cloud any citizenship application.

The Canadian passport is one of the best – but only if you don't expect to live there after you get it.

SPECIAL UPDATE FROM OUR CANADIAN IMMIGRATION CONSULTANTS
Finzer & Richardson, Immigration Lawyers, specialize in Canada. They note that Quebec (French Canada) no longer grants immigrants any special admissions treatment. From 1991, any non-French speaking prospective immigrants are simply refused by Quebec.

Investors may now be admitted upon arranging to make an investment of C$250,000 locked in for three years in the Provinces of Ontario, Quebec, British Columbia and Alberta. As an option, one is allowed to make a smaller investment of C$150,000 locked in for three years in the underpopulated provinces of Newfoundland, Nova Scotia, New Brunswick, Prince Edward Island, Manitoba or Saskatchewan. In either case, a **net worth** or personal means of C$500,000 is required to be shown by investor-immigrants.

One caveat to all our readers is that Canada wants entrepreneurs – ACTIVE business people, hence "persons who may have the requisite net worth but lack business background will not qualify under the investor program".

Another firm of Canadian immigration specialists is Canatrade International, 1200 Avenue McGill College, 11th Floor, Montreal H3B 4GY, Canada. We have no knowledge of this firm, but if you use them we would like to know if you have found them helpful and fairly priced. In our next edition of this special report, we would like to pass on your experiences with Canada as a case history (without divulging your name) for the benefit of future readers.

CANADA: THE FORMS

The next 3 pages reproduce the standard bilingual (English/French) Canadian passport application form with instructions.

In Canada, your passport can be issued in any name you choose. As long as you tell the Canadian authorities on your passport application of your desired "name change" and your previous names.

Most of the information required is standard. Yet, note that here you will need a "Declaration of Guarantor" on your photo. This is standard in the Commonwealth (ex-British Empire).

Your "guarantor" must have known you personally for at least 2 years and swear that he is confident that the statements you have made in your application are true. For applicants emanating from within Canada, he must also be a Canadian citizen residing in Canada. Furthermore, he must be included in one of the following groups: minister of religion authorized under provincial law to perform marriages, signing officer of bank or trust company, full-time manager of a credit union, judge, magistrate, police officer (Royal Canadian Mountain Police, provincial or municipal), person occupying a senior university administrative position or teaching appointment in a university, person occupying a senior administrative position in a community college, principal of secondary or primary school, professional recognized or chartered accountant, mayor, lawyer (member of a provincial bar association), notary public, medical doctor, dentist, postmaster, vetenarian or chiropractor.

The guarantor will have to co-sign your passport application where it says "Declaration of Guarantor" and will also have to certify on the back of two photos that they are a true and current likeness.

See also *The Tax Exile Report,* published by Scope International.

CAPE VERDE – INSTANT PASSPORT

The republic of Cape Verde is a group of ten islands lying in the Atlantic off the west coast of Africa, or, more precisely, 385 miles west of Senegal. It is a stable, democratic nation which has enjoyed a rich and interesting history. It is a member of the United Nations (where it has a seat on the Security Council this year), the World Bank and the International Monetary Fund. Cape Verde was, until 1975, a colony of Portugal.

The government of Cape Verde recently established what is referred to as an Economic Citizenship Program by publicly amending its constitution. This program works basically along the lines of those instituted by other countries. For a donation of US $35,000 to the Cape Verde Development Foundation, citizenship and passport are granted. The donation may even be tax-deductible as the government of Cape Verde claims that the money donated to this fund will

Department of the Secretary of State of Canada

Secrétariat d'État du Canada

APPLICATION FOR A CERTIFICATE OF PROOF OF CANADIAN CITIZENSHIP

GENERAL INFORMATION

If you are applying on behalf of another person (for example, a minor child), wherever the word 'you' appears, understand it to mean 'the person for whom the application is made'.

You can get FREE help to complete this form at any Court of Canadian Citizenship, Canadian Embassy, Canadian High Commission, or Consulate. If none of these are convenient, write to the Registrar of Canadian Citizenship, P.O. Box 7000, Sydney, N.S., B1P 6V6. You are strongly advised not to accept help from people who charge for this service.

After you have completed this form, you must sign it in front of an **authorized** person swearing or affirming that the information provided is true and correct. An **authorized** person is:

(a) in Canada; a Citizenship Officer, a Citizenship Judge, a Commissioner for Oaths, a Notary Public or a Justice of the Peace; or

(b) outside Canada; a Foreign Service Officer, Judge, Magistrate, an Officer of a Court of Justice or a Commissioner authorized to administer oaths in that country.

If you have this application attested by a Citizenship Officer, a Citizenship Judge or a Foreign Service Officer, only the application fee is payable. A Commissioner for Oaths, Notary Public or Justice of the Peace, etc., might charge a fee for attestation.

If this application is made for a child under 14 years, one parent should sign the form.

You can mail the completed form to the nearest Citizenship Court or to the Registrar of Canadian Citizenship, P.O. Box 7000, Sydney, N.S., B1P 6V6.

The information contained in your completed application form is kept in Personal Information Bank SSC/P-PU-050. The information is used to determine eligibility for the grant of Canadian citizenship and to maintain a record of persons to whom citizenship certificates were issued. Under the Privacy Act, you have a right to access, request correction of or have a notation attached to the information concerning yourself. For access procedures and further information, please consult the Personal Information Index which is normally available in public libraries, post offices in rural areas where there is no public library and federal government information offices.

NOTE: If you change your address before you receive your certificate, it is important to notify the office where you applied.

FEE

— $20.00 (Canadian) for an application by a person 18 years of age or older.

— $5.00 (Canadian) for an application by a person under 18 years of age.

NOTE: The fee for filing this application is not refundable.

Money orders or cheques must be made payable to the "RECEIVER GENERAL FOR CANADA".

CASH is acceptable if paid to an officer of a Court of Canadian Citizenship or to a Foreign Service Officer. A receipt will be issued.

DO NOT SEND CASH THROUGH THE MAIL.

PHOTOGRAPHS

You must provide two identical, unmounted photographs. These photographs must be taken within the last 12 months showing a full front view of head and shoulders without head covering. The photographs must be 43mm (1 11/16") by 35mm (1 3/8") plus a 10mm (3/8") white signature strip at the bottom. Please note that these photographs are not the size used for passports. The photographs must be signed on the signature strip if you are 14 years of age or more at the time the application is attested. A mark, or signature in another alphabet, is acceptable. If this application is for a person who is physically unable to sign, the signature strip must be left blank.

INSTRUCTIONS

WHEN COMPLETING THIS APPLICATION FORM, PRINT IN **BLOCK** LETTERS USING A BLACK OR BLUE BALL POINT PEN OR TYPE.

DO NOT PRINT IN THE SHADED AREA.

If you need more space to answer any question, please use an extra sheet. The information given on the extra sheet must also be attested by an authorized person.

Only your CORRECT, FULL NAME should be shown in Question #1.

The CORRECT, FULL NAME is generally the name shown on a birth or baptismal certificate or on a certificate of citizenship unless the name has since been changed LEGALLY (e.g. by marriage, adoption or court order, in which case, the appropriate document must be provided)

Please underline the given name usually used.

If you have used a name other then the names shown in Question #1, show this name in Question #2(a). This name will not appear on the certificate.

If you are now using a name other than the names shown in Questions #1 and 2(a), and wish this name to also appear on the citizenship certificate, it should be shown in Question #2(b). At least TWO satisfactory documents must be submitted to support the use of this name.

Since Citizenship Regulations do not allow a person to hold more than one certificate of citizenship or naturalization at any one time, all certificates of citizenship or naturalization and any pink transmission copy of a certificate currently in the possession of the person for whom the application is made MUST be surrendered. Loss or destruction must be fully explained and/or documented in Question #3.

GUIDE

This guide is to help establish your claim to Canadian citizenship and to decide what information and/or documents are required. In some cases, additional documents may be needed.

WERE YOU:
A. BORN IN CANADA?

Provide your birth certificate. A baptismal certificate stating the date and place of birth may be accepted.

B. BORN OUTSIDE CANADA TO A CANADIAN PARENT?

Provide your birth certificate showing parentage; proof that one or both of your parents were Canadian citizens at the time of your birth, and their marriage certificate.

C. NATURALIZED IN CANADA?

If so, full details are required.

D. (i) A BRITISH SUBJECT AND A LANDED IMMIGRANT BEFORE JANUARY 1, 1942?

Provide your birth certificate or British passport used on original entry and, if available, proof of landed immigrant status.

(ii) A BRITISH SUBJECT DOMICILED IN CANADA FOR AT LEAST 20 YEARS IMMEDIATELY BEFORE JANUARY 1, 1947?

Provide your birth certificate or British passport used on original entry.

E. A WOMAN WHO WAS MARRIED TO A CANADIAN AND WAS A LANDED IMMIGRANT PRIOR TO JANUARY 1, 1947?

Provide your birth certificate; proof of your husband's Canadian status at the time of your marriage and, if available, proof of your landed immigrant status.

F. A WOMAN, CANADIAN-BORN OR BRITISH SUBJECT, WHO LOST HER BRITISH SUBJECT STATUS BY MARRIAGE PRIOR TO JANUARY 1, 1947?

If you elect to be a Canadian, check the box in Question #9 beside "I elect to be a Canadian citizen." Provide your marriage certificate and birth certificate or your baptismal certificate showing date and place of birth.

NOTE
THE PERSON FOR WHOM THE APPLICATION IS MADE MUST PROVIDE AT LEAST TWO OTHER DOCUMENTS (OR CERTIFIED COPIES OF SAME) TO PROVE THEIR IDENTITY.

Canada

8. A PERSON WHO ACQUIRED CANADIAN CITIZENSHIP THROUGH NATURALIZATION <u>AS AN ADULT</u> NEED NOT ANSWER THIS QUESTION.
UNE PERSONNE QUI A OBTENU LA CITOYENNETÉ CANADIENNE PAR NATURALISATION <u>EN TANT QU'ADULTE</u> N'EST PAS REQUIS DE RÉPONDRE À CETTE QUESTION.
PARENTS OF THE PERSON DESCRIBED IN QUESTION 1 — LES PARENTS DE LA PERSONNE MENTIONNÉE DANS LA QUESTION 1

		Father — Père	Mother (Maiden Name) — Mère (Nom de jeune fille)
Full Names — Noms au complet			
Date and place of birth	Date et lieu de naissance		
Date and place of marriage	Date et lieu du marriage		
Claim to Canadian citizenship	Droit à la citoyenneté canadienne		
Date and place of entry to Canada	Date et lieu d'entrée au Canada		
Details of absences from Canada for more than six months	Renseignements sur les absences du Canada de plus de six mois		
Is/Was either parent a citizen or national of a country other than Canada?	Est-ce que l'un ou l'autre de vos parents est/était citoyen ou national d'un pays autre que le Canada?	☐ No Non ☐ Yes Oui ▶ Give details of country, date and manner of acquisition Indiquez le nom du pays, la date et le moyen d'acquisition	☐ No Non ☐ Yes Oui ▶ Give details of country, date and manner of acquisition Indiquez le nom du pays, la date et le moyen d'acquisition
Relationship to the person described in Question #1	Filiation avec la personne décrite à la question n° 1	☐ Natural father — Père naturel ☐ Adoptive father — Père adoptif	☐ Natural mother — mère naturelle ☐ Adoptive mother — mère adoptive

9. ☐ "I elect to be a Canadian citizen" (applies to women who ceased to be British Subjects by reason of marriage to an alien prior to January 1, 1947).
"Je choisis la citoyenneté canadienne" (s'applique à une femme qui, du fait de son mariage à un étranger avant le 1ᵉʳ janvier 1947, a cessé d'être sujet britannique)

10. ☐ I am applying for delayed Registration of Birth Abroad (applies to persons born outside Canada between January 1, 1947 and February 14, 1977 inclusive in wedlock to a Canadian father or, if born out of wedlock, to a Canadian mother). Give reasons for delay.
Je demande l'enregistrement tardif d'une naissance à l'étranger (s'applique aux personnes nées à l'étranger entre le 1er janvier 1947 et le 14 février 1977 inclusivement, dans les liens du mariage d'un père canadien ou, si nées hors du mariage, d'une mère canadienne). Donnez la (les) raison(s) du délai

11. Are you a citizen of one or more countries other than Canada? — Êtes-vous citoyen(ne) d'un ou de pays autre que le Canada?

☐ No Non   ☐ Yes Oui ▶ Indicate name of country, date and manner of acquisition Indiquer le nom du pays, date et le moyen d'acquisition

12. Name on immigration document at time of original entry to Canada — Nom figurant sur le document d'immigration lors de la première entrée au Canada

Surname — Nom de famille	Given Name(s) — Prénom(s)	Entry — date — de l'entrée Y A M D J
Place of entry — Lieu d'entrée	Name of airline, ship or other transportation / Nom de la ligne aérienne, du navire ou autre moyen de transport	
Accompanied by — Accompagné(e) de	Relationship — Lien	Destination

13. Are you now or have you ever been under, or included in an order of deportation from Canada?
Êtes-vous actuellement ou avez-vous été directement ou indirectement frappé d'un ordonnance d'expulsion du Canada?

☐ No Non   ☐ Yes Oui ▶ Give details and provide any related documents Veuillez préciser et fournir tout document pertinent

14. Have you ever served in the Canadian Armed Forces? — Avez-vous déjà servi dans les forces armées canadiennes?

☐ No Non   ☐ Yes Oui ▶ Give details Veuillez préciser

From — De (Dates)	To — A (Dates)	Theatres of Service — Endroits où vous avez servi	Service N° No matricule

15. Have you ever been absent from Canada for more than six months — Vous êtes-vous déjà absenté(e) du Canada pour plus de six mois?

☐ No Non   ☐ Yes Oui ▶ Give details Veuillez donner les renseignements

From — De (Dates)	To — A (Dates)	Destination	Reason(s) for absence(s) - Motif(s) de la ou des absence(s)

WARNING
A certificate of citizenship may be declared invalid if it was obtained by false representation, fraud, or by knowingly concealing material circumstances.

IMPORTANT
Un certificat de citoyenneté peut être annulé en cas de fausse déclaration, de fraude, ou de dissimulation délibérée de faits essentiels.

ATTESTATION — ASSERMENTATION

The statements made in this application are true and correct.

Les déclarations faites dans la présente demande sont vraies et exactes.

_____
Applicant's — Signature — Requérant(e)

Sworn/Affirmed before me at:
Assermentée devant moi à: _____   this ce _____ day of jour de _____ 19___

_____
Authorized Person — Agent autorisé

_____
Title — Titre (Affix seal or stamp — Apposez le sceau ou l'étampe)

Documentation — Documents

Receipt Date / Date du reçu	Court — Cour	Index	NR-AD	Micro	Ver.
		I			
	☐ $5.00 ☐ $20.00 ☐ $ .00	II	PR-DA		
	Receipt Nº de / No. reçu	Return — Documents — a retourner:
	Section — Article Former Act - Ancienne loi	1. _____
		2. _____
		3. _____
	Language — Cert. — Langue	To/À
	☐ Eng. — Ang. ☐ Fr. — Franç.	
	☐ L.I. — I.R. ☐ N.R.D. — A.D.E.	
	Approved — Approuvée	Certificate No — Nº du certificat
	_____ Sig	
	Date _____	
	Send Cert. to — Envoyer cert. à	Notify — Aviser
		Eff. — Date — Eff.

If you are completing this form for a minor, all questions relate to the minor. — Si vous complétez ce formulaire au nom d'une personne mineure, toutes les questions concernent la personne mineure.

1. ☐ Mr./M. ☐ Mrs./Mme. ☐ Miss/Mlle ☐ Ms/Mdle

Surname(s) — Nom de famille   Given name(s) — Prénom(s)

Place and country of birth — Lieu et pays de naissance	Birth — date — de naissance			Sex — Sexe	Height — Taille	Colour of eyes — Couleur des yeux
	Y-A	M	D-J			
					CM	

Present address in full (Postal Code) — Adresse actuelle au complet (Code postal)

Telephone No. — Nº de téléphone
Area — Région Residence — Domicile
Area — Région Business — Bureau

2. Give details of any name change, maiden name or aliases. — Veuillez indiquer tout changement de nom, de nom de jeune fille, ou de nom d'emprunt.

Name — Nom	Change — Date — du changement	Place of residence at time of change	Lieu de résidence au moment du changement
a-			
b-			

3. If you ever had a certificate of citizenship or naturalization, give details below.
NOTE: All these certificates and any pink transmission copy of a certificate in your possession must be surrendered.
— Si vous avez déjà eu un certificat de citoyenneté ou de naturalisation, veuillez fournir les renseignements pertinents.
NOTA: Tous ces certificats et toutes les copies de transmission roses en votre possession doivent être remis.

| Name on citizenship or naturalization certificate — Nom indiqué sur le certificat de citoyenneté ou de naturalisation | Certificate No. — Nº du certificat | Dated — Date | | |
| | | Y-A | M | D-J |

Are you applying for the replacement of a certificate? — Faites-vous une demande de renouvellement de certificat?

☐ No / Non   This is for my first certificate / C'est ma première demande de certificat

☐ Yes / Oui   This application is for replacement of my certificate. [Give reason(s) below.] / Il s'agit d'une demande de renouvellement de mon certificat. [Indiquez ci-dessous la ou les raison(s).]

☐ CHANGE OF PARTICULARS (The certificate being replaced must be surrendered) / CHANGEMENT DANS LES RENSEIGNEMENTS QUI FIGURENT (le certificat a être remplacé doit être remis)

☐ UPDATE CERTIFICATE (The certificate being updated must be surrendered) / MISE À JOUR DU CERTIFICAT (le certificat à être mis à jour doit être remis)

☐ LOSS or DESTRUCTION (Give details of date and place below). / PERTE ou DESTRUCTION (Veuillez préciser ci-dessous la date et l'endroit).

Was the loss reported to the Police? / La perte a-t-elle été signalée à la police?   ☐ No / Non   ☐ Yes / Oui

NOTE: ANY LOST CERTIFICATES FOUND AFTER RECEIPT OF A REPLACEMENT CERTIFICATE MUST BE SURRENDERED TO THE REGISTRAR OF CANADIAN CITIZENSHIP OR TO THE NEAREST CITIZENSHIP COURT — TOUS LES CERTIFICATS DECLARES PERDUS ET RETROUVES APRÈS QU'UN AUTRE CERTIFICAT AIT ÉTÉ ÉMIS POUR LE REMPLACER DOIVENT ÊTRES RETOURNES AU GREFFIER DE LA CITOYENNETÉ OU A LA COUR DE LA CITOYENNETÉ LA PLUS RAPPROCHEE

4. In which official language do you wish to have your Citizenship certificate prepared? — Dans quelle langue officielle désirez-vous que soit préparé votre certificat de citoyenneté?

☐ English — Anglais   ☐ French — Français

5. Marital Status — État civil:

☐ Single / Célibataire   ☐ Married / Marié(e)   ☐ Widower / Veuf(ve)
☐ Divorced / Divorcé(e)   ☐ Separated / Séparé(e)

Place and country of marriage(s) — Lieu et pays du (des) mariage(s)

| Marriage(s) — date(s) — du (des) mariage(s) | | |
| Y-A | M | D-J |

SPOUSE - CONJOINT (If married more than once, give details of all spouses — Si marié plus d'une fois, donnez les particularités de chacun des conjoints)

6. Surname (Maiden name) — Nom de famille (Nom de jeune fille)   Given name(s) — Prénom(s)

| Place and country of birth — Lieu et pays de naissance | Birth — date — de naissance | | | Name on entry to Canada — Nom lors de l'entrée au Canada | Entry — date — de l'entrée | | |
| | Y-A | M | D-J | | Y-A | M | D-J |

Is the spouse a Canadian Citizen? — Le conjoint est-il citoyen canadien?

☐ No — Non
☐ Yes — Oui ► ☐ By Naturalization / Par naturalisation ► or/ou ☐ By Birth / De naissance

| Name on Citizenship or Naturalization certificate | Nom sur le certificat de citoyenneté ou de naturalisation | Certificate No. — Nº du certificat | Dated — Date | | |
| | | | Y-A | M | D-J |

PARENTS

7. If you were born in Canada on or after January 1, 1947, was one of your parents employed by a foreign government or an international governmental agency at the time of your birth? — Si vous êtes né(e) au Canada après le 1er janvier 1947, est-ce-qu'un de vos parents était employé par un gouvernement étranger ou une agence gouvernementale-internationale au moment de votre naissance?

☐ No / Non   ☐ Yes / Oui ► Give details / Veuillez préciser form a public charity used ''to build schools, hospitals, libraries or other for other good public purposes'' rather than disappear into ''improper pockets''.

Through this program, one deals directly with the government as a whole rather than one or two ''open-minded'' officials. The fact that the country's constitution has been ''publicly'' amended means that the details of this program have been elaborately spelled out, in both Portuguese and English, and can be verified by any immigration attorney. However, there is no guarantee that the constitution will not be changed again and all rights granted under this program revoked, although Cape Verde does claim that once you are a citizen, you are so for life.

In addition to the actual donation, Cape Verde also requires that applicants prove that they are ''solvent, of good moral character and free of diseases which could imperil the public welfare of Cape Verde''. Applicants who have been convicted of a crime or are under investigation for a crime, unless it did not involve violent or reprehensible behaviour, must disclose all related facts and will normally not be favourably considered. If such information is not disclosed and later found out, citizenship will be annulled, no refund will be given, and international law enforcement and other authorities will be notified.

For the single donation of US $35,000, the applicant, his/her spouse and all their children under the age of 18 are included. A future spouse or child will also be eligible for citizenship without a further contribution. Although applicants are encouraged to visit Cape Verde, there is no requirement to ever actually do so, purchase a residence or spend any time there on a compulsory basis. If you do decide to live there, taxes are only payable on local source income. Gift, inheritance or estate taxes are only payable on property actually located in Cape Verde. There is no compulsory military service.

The passports issued are valid for a period of five years and are renewable at any Consulate for a nominal cost. Dual (or multiple) citizenship is not a problem. However, a major drawback to this passport is that visa-free travel is only possible to 17 countries, all located in West Africa. Other identification, such as a driver's license, are currently not included in the actual package, but can be applied for on the same basis as any other Cape Verdean citizen.

All money received will be held in escrow by a reputable bank, i.e. they won't get their money until you get your passport. If your application is rejected for reasons other than nondisclosure, you will receive a full refund less a small wire transfer fee. Complete confidentiality is assured.

If you are interested in this program, contact Scope International for a referral. Scope International, 62 Murray Road, Waterlooville, Hants PO8 9JL.

CHAD – THE BARGAIN OF THE PASSPORT WORLD

Official, government issued Chadian passports are available for only US $6,000. They come complete with an exit visa stamp and are valid for a period of ten years and you can arrange for passports to be issued in any name and with any date of birth. The price is the best we have seen – £4,000. As explained in the entry titled BLACK AFRICA in this section, a Chadian passport is neither good nor recommended for travel. However, if you do any banking that you do not want everyone to know about, then this just might be an easy way of arranging that. (See section on BANKING PASSPORTS at the beginning of this Special Report.) Furthermore, if you are from an Anglo-Saxon, Hispanic or Asian background, or otherwise worry about being scrutinised for not fitting the typical Chadian profile, you are also automatically granted a minor diplomatic appointment to allay any questions that may arise. You can choose from one of four titles which will appear in your passport: Counsellor for Humanitarian Affairs, Counsellor for Health and Welfare, Counsellor for International Development or Counsellor for International Business and Industry, name changes are permitted.

These passports are properly registered in Chad and may be verified at Chadian embassies around the world within a few months of issue. They are *not* stolen or forged blanks.

Details from: David Milton, Suite 1, 281 City Road, London EC1V 1WA, England.

CHILE – EXTENDED WELCOME FOR SOME

Chile can boast the most prosperous economy of Latin America. It is also in the habit of importing skilled workers from South Korea and Peru, which have been devastated by socialist experiments and Maoist guerrillas. However, Chile appears to be less anxious to accept immigrants from other areas of the world, such as the former Soviet Union and Eastern Europe.

We have heard reports that one can easily "buy" citizenship, simply by depositing US $20,000 in the country's National Bank. We have no firm information on this program and welcome input on your experiences with it. Let us know how you get on.

EX-COMMUNIST COUNTRIES

It seems that countries are sprouting up everywhere as a result of the anti-communist uprisings of 1989-91. Eastern Europe and the former Soviet Union remain volatile areas of the world where little is stable. Basic issues have yet to be decided, such as UN status, national borders and national currency (inflation was reported at 2,000 per cent in Russia for 1992). The familiar Poland, Hungary, Romania, Bulgaria, Albania and Mongolia have become new democracies while Estonia, Latvia, Lithuania, Kaliningrad, Belorussia, the Ukraine, Moldavia, Azerbaijan, Georgia, Armenia, Czech Lands, Slovakia, Slovenia, Croatia, Bosnia-Herzegovina, Serbia and Macedonia have emerged as new countries. Little seems to be less stable than the laws and policies of these countries.

In short, the passport situation in this part of the world is far from understandable. In some situations individuals who happen to fall inside territorial lines drawn by politicians do not qualify for citizenship of the newly formed country. In Estonia, for example, where almost half the residents are Russian colonists, Estonian citizenship was only granted to those of Estonian ancestry, including thousands of Estonian emigrants not actually resident. Residence periods vary tremendously, most rallying to the absurd side, i.e. 16 years in Latvia (Switzerland only requires 12).

Most of these new countries, nevertheless, do seem to be implementing programs whereby former nationals and their children/grandchildren can reclaim their nationality. If this situation applies to you, it is probably a good idea to take advantage of this opportunity while it lasts. Who knows what will happen in this part of the world tomorrow? Also, like in Morocco, special arrangements abound and can probably be arranged if you're willing to pay a visit and do a little snooping.

However, these passports are not particularly desirable at the moment. Most seem to still require the annoying "exit stamp" to be valid for international travel and require visas for most places. Also, the flood of immigrants from these countries to the West means that visa-free relations will probably not be established for some time to come. There are, however, some exceptions. Hungarians have the right to visa-free travel to France, the Polish to Germany and Lithuanians to the UK and Denmark.

These passports may someday be worth something. Some countries, such as Hungary, are interested in joining the EC. Even though such a union will probably not take place on this side of the year 2000, it may still be worth acquiring Hungarian citizenship in the long run. Once again, things change on a daily basis in this part of the world. We're not trying to predict the future. If Harry Schultz is right there will be a return to something like Stalinesque repression. We disagree, but who really knows what will happen.

Please write us and let us know how you get on with these newly established countries. If your information is useful, we're more than willing to reciprocate with a swell gift.

See also the entry on LITHUANIA.

COSTA RICA – PROVISIONAL PASSPORT AVAILABLE, BUT THEY MIGHT TAKE IT BACK!

Costa Rica is an exceptionally beautiful country. Although the population is 95 per cent Spanish speaking, English is also widely spoken.

Costa Rica was once considered the most stable democracy in all of Central and South America. The cost of living was cheap, and on US $750 a month one could live the life of the expatriate in a modern studio apartment complete with a splendid view and a swimming pool. A perfect spring-time climate year-round, the lack of restrictions on the ownership of real estate and excellent airline connections made Costa Rica an excellent place to spend part of the year. Taxes on local income was around 17 per cent and there was (and still is to the best of our knowledge) no taxes on foreign source income. Additionally, there was no army and an open door was maintained for all immigrants.

In 1984, a program offering what was referred to as a *pensionado* visa was established. The rules were fairly simple. If one purchased a home in Costa Rica as well as US $30,000 of government bonds, one more or less qualified for permanent residence. All that was asked was that one theoretically reside for at least six months a year in Costa Rica. However, this requirement was rarely enforced. After a period of five years, one qualified for citizenship and passport. This passport was renewable and allowed for visa-free travel to most countries.

If one hated waiting, an instant passport could be obtained for approximately US $60,000 through the auspices of a district police supervisor.

Sound too good to be true? It was. The influence of the Marxist revolution in nearby Nicaragua did much to diminish attitudes towards the *pensionados*. Unemployed Costa Rican youth started to blame the "foreigners" for everything wrong in their own country and the world.

Then too, several extremely wealthy American fugitives, including Robert Vesco, had taken advantage of the *pensionado* program. Costa Rica's lack of extradition treaties protected criminals like bugs in a rug. These renegades lived blatantly, like nineteenth century capitalists in the midst of food shortages and general misery. As a result, the provisional passport program was closed down and has only falteringly opened since.

President Regan of the US waged his "War on Drugs" which included serious negotiations with the Costa Rican government. The end result was that extradition treaties were signed between the two countries, and the Vesco-type fugitives are no longer protected.

A new *pensionado* program was introduced in 1988, designed by politicians to squeeze what they could from foreign property owners. Under this program one was required to import US $1,000 a month to stay longer than six months. One was also required to exchange this money at the official exchange rate, which, of course, bore little resemblance to the real or black market rate. Provisional passports were altered to look different from normal passports, and it is doubtful that this new passport was accepted by most countries for visa-free travel. The real doozy was that this provisional passport had to be renewed every two years for which one must bring an additional investment of US $50,000 into the country, at the official exchange rate again.

It is obvious that the Costa Rican politicians were in need of a scapegoat, and as history shows time and time again, foreigners are always a good one. They essentially told the *pensionados* to get out, which many did, abandoning the farms and homes they had invested in. As they left, their places were looted and ransacked almost immediately. Most lost a bundle.

The situation has changed little since 1988. Current attitude varies from time to time at the whim of local politicians. It oscillates between an open hostility towards "lazy, rich foreigners" to an eagerness to milk them for all their worth. In short, although Costa Rica used to be a paradise for expatriates, because of incredible mismanagement by socialist reformers, the prosperity has gone and with it everyone that can afford to leave.

However, if for some insane reason you are still interested in Costa Rican citizenship. The current *pensionado* program, if it even is still in existence, is simply not workable and therefore not an option we would recommend.

As a result, many "extra-legal" programs have sprung up, but as a lawyer friend of ours based in Costa Rica puts it, "because of political instability and competing power groups, the best cops that money can buy have short life spans in office, and passports granted by one group may be revoked by the next". If you still insist on taking your chances, our latest information indicates that passports are being sold to all comers at quoted prices between US $18,000 to US $22,000.

One also should consider that Costa Rica requires one to surrender all other passports upon naturalization, i.e. when and if they give you their passport. This is the letter of the law, but many Costa Ricans are known to hold dual citizenship and more than one passport, needless to say somewhat secretly.

The political upheaval seems to have little affected some aspects of Costa Rican life, and although one may not want citizenship, a visit is probably still not a bad idea for the PT. Even in the face of such extreme anti-foreigner sentiment, one particular Costa Rican social custom, which may be of interest to single or separated men, remains. Young Tica girls often move up the social ladder by becoming the mistress or wife of a wealthy foreigner. They are thus provided with the support and means of pursuing their education. These girls understand, better than their politicians and neighbours, how to get ahead in the world. The only country where it is easier to make such arrangements is Thailand. Our forthcoming *Sex Havens* will cover this topic in great depth.

DENMARK – BACK DOOR FOR NORDICS

In Denmark, although the normal required residence period for citizenship is seven years, people of Nordic citizenship or ancestry get a five year discount and can obtain citizenship in two years. This also works for Danes in the other Nordic countries (Sweden, Norway, Finland and Iceland). The Danish passport is the most attractive Scandinavian passport since Denmark (at present) is the only Nordic country also a member of the European Community.

This little known Danish ''Back Door to The EC'' is described this way by one of our Swedish readers:

''If a Swede, a Finn or a Norwegian wishes to live and work freely in any EC country, he just needs a two year quarantine in Denmark. Right now, any Nordic citizen can come to Denmark, live there and take any job without visa or permit – and vice versa. A person with Danish citizenship can also do the same in any EC country. I recommend that everybody with Scandinavian citizenship or Nordic parents or grandparents get a Danish passport. I do not know of any disadvantages to holding a Danish passport as compared to any other Nordic country (visas, safety, etc).''

Good thinking! But remember, you DO have to live two years in Denmark – on paper at least – and during that period you DO have to pay your ''dues to society'' (taxes). Danish taxes are skyhigh with a top marginal tax rate of some 78 per cent currently.

After your two years are up, to get off the Danish tax rolls, you can only move to a country having a tax of at least 50 per cent of the Danish rate. A Dane who moves to any other place, all considered tax havens, will have to pay Danish taxes as a sort of ''penalty'' for another four years. If he does not do that, he will be considered a tax evader and may have a problem renewing his passport. An even worse possibility is that he would be classed as a criminal fugitive and brought back to Denmark to serve the standard year in jail for tax evasion. Of course, Danish jails are more like hotels. You only sleep there (for free) and you can have overnight sex visitors (either sex). The food (also free) is said to be very tasty. So even the worst case scenario isn't too bad for Danish passport holders.

DOMINICAN REPUBLIC – BUY A HOME AND HURRICANE BONDS

This Spanish-speaking, democratic country shares the Caribbean Island of Hispaniola with Haiti. Despite sharing the same island, the two countries are very different. With a fortified frontier and populated by completely different races, there is little cross-migration between them. With flights from Miami, New York and Madrid, communication out of Santo Domingo is not bad.

A bit over a decade ago, the DR was run by the military dictator, Trujillo. This gentleman was overthrown by locals with the help of American Marines. The country has been in the American orbit ever since. Of course Dominican politicians make the mandatory anti-American noises, but there is no talk of removing US military bases, or of severing close economic ties.

The country is very prosperous by Caribbean standards. It is 90 per cent Spanish-speaking and 80 per cent mixed race – mulatto is the largest group. About 10 per cent of the people are ''pure white'' and 50 per cent are Chinese. There is a cultured and prosperous upper middle class. There is also a very large resort colony with the best beaches in the world, attractive young ladies and many luxury tourist condominiums on the coast. The capital and largest city, Santo Domingo, is sophisticated and "Spanish colonial" in flavor with many Las Vegas style gambling casinos. The DR is a pleasant, relatively safe place to live. There are burglaries, but violent crime is rare.

The Dominican Republic follows the old Spanish rule that any property owner is entitled to vote, ergo, is a citizen and entitled to a passport. This is the "theory". In practice, a substantial payment is necessary for a foreign home owner to get the passport he is legally entitled to. With the payment, officials don't care if you own a home or not! A decent home can be purchased here for as little as US $40,000. A pleasant condominium in a beach location would be at least $80,000. A first class home with pool might be had for $150,000.

Ten year financing is usually available on homes or condo apartments so only about 20 per cent of the price needs to be put up in cash. Loan payments usually can be covered out of short-term holiday lettings handled by a local agent. Some real estate developers have "package deals" offering property, citizenship and passports for the entire family for about US $75,000. This includes purchase of a US $10,000 Dominican Government Hurricane Bond, yielding market rate interest and redeemable in ten years.

The bond may be sold immediately after citizenship is obtained. At current market prices, the discount is around $3,000. This brings the net cost of citizenship (assuming the house is also sold at a discount) to slightly over $25,000 net. My personal opinion is that unless a person wants to spend his life there, the personal visits and bureaucratic hassles one must go through, make the official Dominican Republic's passport for aliens program too costly in terms of both time and the $75,000 cash outlay. I visited the DR in early 1990 and personally investigated the scene. It was relatively easy to find lawyers who could deliver legal passports for $15,000 to $20,000 cash.

However, if you would rather not travel to the Dominican Republic to do your own snooping, Scope International can refer you to a reputable lawyer who can arrange for both citizenship and passport at a very reasonable price. See the entry on INSTANT CITIZENSHIP at the end of this section.

Of course many individuals might wish to own and keep Dominican beach-front property. It probably is a good investment and a source of rental income – not to mention the fact that a little love-nest is nice to have in an area that is probably safe from nuclear fallout (as long as nearby Cuba is not a target). Part of the sales pitch by those who arrange for passports is that the profit on the property will more than pay for citizenship. The standard Dominican Republic passport is good for four years and may be renewed without difficulty at any consulate abroad.

Diplomatic passports, honorary consulates and standard Dominican Republic passports are available easily and quickly, the average time being 4-8 weeks. Diplomatic passports cost US $60,000 and the bearer is appointed either attaché to one of the country's foreign embassies through the Ministry of Foreign Affairs or as an extraordinary presidential advisor ad-honorem through the presidency for a period of two years. The passports, which grant diplomatic immunity and full diplomatic privileges worldwide, are renewable. An honorary consulate costs US $80,000.

There is also a Commercial Investment Scheme available, little known inside of the country, as it is rather complex and expensive. It involves the purchase of a property, or business, government bonds, altogether of a minimum of US $150,000 for instant residency. Naturalization is then granted approximately 6 months later. The applicant however must travel to the country on several occasions. We do not recommend this alternative unless an applicant has a true interest in the country for personal or business reasons.

The country offers largely visa free travel to most countries of the world. See table on page 42. Where visas are required, they may be obtained within a very short period of time. The country has had over 30 years of absolute political and economic stability, NO MILITARY DICTATORSHIP. It does not suffer the bad reputation of living on the drug trade and money laundering as most of its Latin American counterparts. It is known internationally that the main income of the country is derived from tourism. This makes travelling with this document easy and eliminates harrassment at borders. Instant citizenship is inexpensive and quick. However, many Dominican passports are sold internationally, and its reputation as a country for "selling" passports will grow with time.

INSTANT CITIZENSHIP

As mentioned earlier, Scope International can refer you to a reputable lawyer who can arrange for instant citizenship and passport of the Dominican Republic.

Single Applicant: US $35,000

Family Application: US $40,000

If you are interested you need to submit a copy of the form overleaf for each applicant (a photocopy is more than sufficient) duly filled out and signed, a clear photocopy of your current passport or birth certificate and four colour passport size photos, then contact Scope who will refer you to a lawyer.

IS THE DOMINICAN REPUBLIC A GOOD PLACE TO LIVE?

Even though you do not have to live in the Dominican Republic to get their passport, consider this: that it is one of the most beautiful places in the world. The physical geography is stunning. Columbus said it was the loveliest place he had ever seen. Columbus found the Dominican Republic on his third voyage to the New World. By this time he had visited practically all of the Caribbean. The Dominican Republic was chosen by Christopher as his personal home.

The north coast is where the interesting developments are these days. Until 1983, when a major international airport was opened in Puerto Plata, there had been no quick way to get to the north coast. For that reason, this region remained virtually undiscovered by foreigners. But they are definitely making up for lost time now. The north coast is booming. There are thousands of hotels, apartment buildings and condos under construction. Thousands of mainly Canadian and German tourists visit this resort area which begins at Puerto Plata and continues westward along the coast through the towns of Sosua, Cabarete, Rio San Juan and beyond. This stretch of beach reminds us of Pacific Coast Highway as it passes through the countless little beach towns south of LA. European readers compare it to the Riviera, starting in Italian Liguria and going into France and Spain. However, in the Dominican Republic, this excellent new coast road has very little traffic on it.

APPLICATION FORM FOR DOMINICAN REPUBLIC PASSPORT

Please fill out in block letters or type and answer EACH AND EVERY QUESTION. Avoid mistakes! Incorrect information delays processing of this application. Photocopy this form and use a separate form for each family member.

1. LAST NAME(S): . . . . 2. FIRST NAME(S): . . . .

3. PRESENT NATIONALITY/NATIONALITIES: . . . .

4. BEARER OF PASSPORT OF THE FOLLOWING COUNTRY(IES): . . . .

5. DATE OF BIRTH: DAY . . . .   MONTH: . . . .   YEAR: . . . .

6. PLACE OF BIRTH: . . . .

7. CIVIL STATUS (MARRIED/SINGLE/DIVORCED/WIDOWED): . . . .

8. PROFESSION: . . . .

9. COLOUR OF HAIR: . . . .   10. COLOUR OF EYES: . . . .

11. COLOUR OF SKIN: . . . .   12. HEIGHT IN CENTIMETRES: . . . .

13. WEIGHT IN KILOGRAMS: . . . .   14. SEX (MALE/FEMALE): . . . .

15. PARTICULAR SIGNS (SCARS): . . . .

I hereby declare that the foregoing information is complete, true and correct, without omissions, and that I have not been convicted of any criminal offence (except traffic violations) in the past in any country of the world.

Signed this . . . . day of the month of . . . . 1993.

SIGNATURE: . . . .
(signature must correspond to signature in passport).

SWORN DECLARATION

THIS DECLARATION MUST BE SIGNED BY EVERY APPLICANT AND INCLUDED IN THE SUBMISSION OF ALL DOCUMENTS.

I, the undersigned, person with the aforegoing particulars, hereby swear that the submission of the underlying and accompanying information for the purpose of obtaining a second citizenship/passport is correct and complete and intended solely for my personal use and that I am not employed by or in the services of any government, governmental agency, law enforcement agency or other official or semi-official institution or member of the press of any country of the world and that I am not related in any shape, fashion or form to any government, government agency or public institution or press/media/agency of any country of the world and that I will not divulge any of this information or any information or correspondence that I shall receive in conjunction with this application and its entire process to any government, governmental agency, press/media or similar, now or any time in the future.

Signed this . . . . day of the month of . . . . 1993.   SIGNATURE: . . . .
(signature must correspond to signature in passport).

IN ORDER FOR YOUR APPLICATION TO BE COMPLETE, MAKE SURE YOU HAVE INCLUDED THE FOLLOWING:

1. **This underlying Sworn Declaration, and the accompanying Application Form, properly filled out.**
2. **A legible copy of your current passport or birth certificate.**
3. **4 colour passport pictures taken from the front, approx. 2 inches by 2 inches (5cm x 5cm). No sunglasses, hats, wigs or veils.**

CONTACT SCOPE INTERNATIONAL FOR A REFERRAL TO A LAWYER

YOUR NAME . . . .

STREET (NOT PO BOX) ADDRESS . . . .

. . . .

. . . . TEL: . . . . FAX: . . . .

The beaches in the Dominican Republic are dark volcanic sand in the south and white sand with many bays and lagoons in the north. In many places, particularly on the south side of the island, rugged volcanic cliffs overlook the ocean. Small pocket beaches lie below. Outlying reefs and rock islets along the coast provide happy hunting grounds for spearing fresh fish and lobster.

The east-west north coast highway runs along mile after mile of sugar cane fields, with roadside stands that sell everything from native art to hot dogs. There are conspicious numbers of new developments in various stages of construction. Just beyond the cane fields to the south lie the lush green foothills of the major east-west mountain range which runs practically the entire length of the island. The foothills are liberally forested in coconut palms, towering royal palms and other trees. The further east along the shore one travels, the more dense becomes the vegetation. About 25 miles east of Sosua, we looked at some quasi-cultivated oceanfront property. Many areas had a striking resemblance to a rain forest. Everywhere were palms and fruit trees of all descriptions and a great variety of tropical plants and flowers. Mango trees, heavy with fruit, grow wild. The abundance and richness of the land is such that even fence posts sprout branches and soon turn into trees!

Beyond the mountain range to the south lies a high plateau stretching as far as the eye can see. Imagine a typical Swiss pastoral scene, but with palm trees! That's the picture. You will see mile after mile of pineapples, fruit orchards, dairy and cattle farms. At higher elevations there are coffee plantations. The natives here may seem poor, but none are starving. Given the richness of the land and the vast scores of fish which practically jump into nets, food is no problem. There are four sugar cane crops a year! This goes far to explain why the Dominican Republic is such a peaceful place. There is no radical agitation among the poor people. To feed themselves, the poor simply squat on a piece of vacant land and grow or raise all they need to live.

Land in the underpopulated Dominican Republic is incredibly cheap. One personal friend bought a 60-acre farm for US $350 an acre. Usually, land can be had from $500 per acre upwards. We saw one piece of land – 17 acres in a resort area, sitting right on a mountain road with electricity already on the property and with a river running through it – for $1,500 an acre.

Living in the best hotels will not set you back much either. At the newest 4-star oceanfront hotel in Sosua by the Sea, you will pay $80 a night, in high season, for a grand penthouse suite with an ocean view.

Sosua was settled in the early 1940s by Jewish refugees from Germany who became dairy farmers. It is still a major dairy region. Many of those original settlers and their children are still in Sosua. The village is comprised of the native quarter, called Charamicos, and the resort area, called Batey. In both, there are dozens of excellent restaurants and cafes, many serving ethnic specialities. Everything is cheap (except for wine, which must be imported). You have to be creative to spend $10 on dinner. Except for some obnoxious red-neck German tourists, the ambience is quite polite and peaceful. In towns it can get honky-tonk with hundreds of tourists speaking five or six languages, crowding into T-shirt shops and other tourist traps. There are always hundreds of noisy rented motor bikes frantically zooming through the streets filled with mulatto shoe shine boys, guides, touts and pimps hustling at every corner. It sounds terrible, but it isn't. All in all, even the shanty towns are quaint and delightful. The friendly young girls all seem to have beautiful smiles and ''come hither'' looks.

Entertainment is a bit provincial once you get outside the capital of Santo Domingo. Most cities have legitimate theatres, opera houses and movies. The Spanish dubbed movies are advertised in the local Spanish language press. There is skin diving, snorkelling and, at many locations along the coast, some sport fishing operations. There are a lot of tennis courts and a pretty good golf course at Playa Dorada. Then, of course, there are the exciting cock fights, popular all over the Caribbean.

The native population is a racial mix of Spanish, Indian and Negro, with skin tones ranging from jet black to *cafe au lait*. The people are not nearly so handsome as the Costa Ricans, whose Spanish ancestors never bred with the native Indians. But you will not find more friendly and happy people anywhere. Practically every local you pass will smile, wave and greet you with Hola! or Buenas Dias! Native waiters fall all over themselves to be helpful and filling station attendants will want to spit shine your car with every fill-up. If you stop along the road to ask directions, the person you ask is likely to just pile in the car and TAKE you to your destination.

Education is supposed to be compulsory to the eighth grade, but you will see a great many kids hanging out on the streets. Literacy is said to be 65 per cent. Outside of the resort areas, little English is spoken. Spanish, however, is very easy to learn. You could easily pick up an essential vocabulary in less than a month.

In the Dominican Republic, there is virtually no violent crime, although there seem to be many incidents of burglary if property is left vacant. All hotels, condominiums and stores have armed guards on duty at night, but there is no feeling of fear and insecurity such as one could expect in other places at the mere sound of a strange footstep in the night. Most foreign property owners arrange for a housekeeper or watchman to stay at their homes full time to guard against burglary.

Communications are pretty good. The phone company is owned by GTE and service is excellent. Good phones are somewhat slow coming to smaller towns of the north coast.

There is cable TV with HBO, Showtime, ESPN, CNN, Disney, Arts & Entertainment and several other familiar US cable channels. There are usually satellite dishes at condos. There are several local English language papers like the Puerto Plata News, as well as several English language papers in Santo Domingo. According to local "gringos", international airmail to the US will take anything between 10 days and 3 weeks. Retrieving merchandise shipped into the country means going from office to office for customs clearance and is avoided by the locals as much as possible. Normally imports should be brought in as personal property, in person. Once when in the Dominican Republic, we had our mail shipped down from Bermuda by Federal Express. It arrived in 48 hours and cost us $63 for 7lbs.

Transportation is fine, too. The airport at Puerto Plata has a 10,000 foot runway which will accomodate anything flying. Chartered flights arrive every day from every corner of the globe – Montreal, Toronto, Frankfurt and, of course, New York, Atlanta and Miami, just to name a few.

Automobiles carry an import duty of 27 per cent based on their value. The customs department arbitrarily determines what that value is, meaning that the duty could be even higher. Hiring a customs broker with good connections is necessary. Otherwise cars can be quite expensive to buy.

At Budget Rent-a-Car, a compact car rents for $59 a day. Motorbikes are the principal mode of transportation for the locals. They can also be rented. There are thousands of unusual things to be seen on the highways. An entire family of four on a motorbike is not uncommon. We have seen more cargo hauled on some of these home made contraptions than we could fit into our pickup truck.

Public electricity is unreliable. All developments and many private homes are equipped with backup generators. If you do not have a backup, be prepared for daily poweroutages and flooding in the rainy season. Why? Electronic pumps are sometimes needed to keep water out of the houses.

Economically, the Dominican peso, identified as RD$, is exchanged at the rate of ten for a US dollar. Yet, all evidence shows that inflation is about 20-30 per cent per annum, so it's only a matter of time before the peso is devalued again.

As you can imagine, locally grown meats and produce could only be cheaper if given away. But consumer goods imported from the US or Europe are probably a third more expensive than stateside prices. Local workers are paid very little. Thirty to forty dollars a week is the going rate for a night watchman, maid or gardener. Fifty to sixty dollars gets you an educated, bi-lingual hotel or shop clerk.

Contracts, such as for rent, must be written in RD$. Some landlords get around this by tying the RD$ rent to its US$ equivalent at the time due. Buying or building in RD$ and selling or renting in US$ is obviously a road to riches.

The major local industry here, if you don't count separating the touristas from their money, is construction. Most construction is concrete block. Top quality work is quoted at $35-$40 per square foot.

There is no zoning here, so much of the construction is extremely dense and targeted at the bottom of the market, e.g. Canadian tourists to whom densely packed cracker boxes are sold on a modified time share basis. An estimated 10,000 hotel or condo rooms are under construction along the coast within 50 miles of Puerto Plata. There is so much new construction that there is said to be a chronic shortage of cement. Very little speculative construction seems to be targeted at the top end of the market. This absence appears to be one of the voids in the local market and one which might represent an investment opportunity.

What is required for residency? Officially this appears to be pretty cut and dried, involving a big quota of bureaucratic red-tape. Most "gringos", however, never bother to obtain residency. They are PTs, coming in for three months at a time on a tourist visa which can then be extended almost indefinitely. Or, if one doesn't care to extend and be legal, he just overstays his visa and when he gets ready to leave the country pays a fine of a few dollars.

If you choose to obtain legal residency, you can import your automobile without the customary 27 per cent duty. Also, residents can purchase developed or agricultural property without prior government permission or operate businesses without some of the restrictions applying to foreigners, etc. But by far, the major advantage of obtaining legal residency is that, for property owners, after only six months, you can *theoretically* get Dominican Republic citizenship. The six months can be waived if you motivate the right officials. Even the property ownership requirement can be circumvented.

The Dominican Republic is a big, rich and beautiful country. The north coast needs, and needs badly, virtually every service you can think of. There is almost unlimited opportunity here for entrepreneurs. A close friend earns over $200,000 per year from a popcorn and take-away taco stand in a shopping center. Both of these foods were totally unknown in the Dominican Republic before he came along. We haven't seen any of the usual franchises here yet, but based upon the success of tacos, McDonald's and Kentucky Fried Chicken would do well.

Prices, as we said, are still cheap here, although ocean front land has multiplied several times in the past few years. You want a retreat where it is cheap to live, where there is little or no violent crime, where there is some infrastructure in place, where you can be virtually self-sufficient and where, if you decide to work, there are ample opportunities for various kinds of development. This place has all that. We would be hard pressed to think of any other place in the Caribbean that offers as much as the Dominican Republic.

Finally, the author adds that the Dominican Republic is one of the top five sex-havens in the world. Local young friendly girls love foreigners, even if they are old and pot-bellied. See our forthcoming *Sex Havens* report for details on this topic.

EUROPEAN COMMUNITY

PASSPORT, VISA, RETURN TICKET AND VACCINATION REQUIREMENTS FOR TRAVEL ON AN EC (EUROPEAN COMMUNITY) PASSPORT

For travel between European countries, all that is needed is a National Identity Card, not a passport. Since the UK has no such card, UK citizens can get by with a "British Visitor's Passport". This document looks like a cardboard bus pass with stapled on photo and is issued informally and on-the-spot in British Post Offices.

To travel with an EC passport to *non*-European countries, one must be aware of a constantly changing myriad of rules. For instance, prior to 1985, a French passport could get you across many more borders without any visa or return ticket. However "to combat terrorism" France began requiring visas of almost every non-EC visitor. This resulted in the usual tit-for-tat diplomatic games. Now visa-free travel for the French is limited to a few former French colonies. As of 1990, France withdrew its visa requirement, and for the time being reciprocity is back again. This uncertainty is why everyone needs at least two passports.

Charts similar to the one preceding (courtesy of Charterama Travel, Paris) are generally available from the larger travel agents in any major city. Before going on a trip with any passport, it is a good idea to check the latest requirements and obtain visas in advance.

If any reader sends us an up-to-date chart from any major country, we will probably use it in our next edition and send that reader a little token of our gratitude. Please help us to help you! We welcome all updated forms, copies of correspondence with consulates, corrections and comments.

Typically, the holder of a European passport can go, without a visa, to former colonies. This means in effect that UK citizens can go to most English speaking (Commonwealth) countries (except South Africa and Australia) with just a passport. Spanish citizens can go to most of Central and South America and Portuguese passport holders get special consideration in Brazil, Macau and Angola. The same is usually true in the opposite direction. Thus holders of a Honduras passport, by treaty, can become Spanish citizens in about one year, and enter and work there without a visa.

PASSPORT, VISA & VACCINATION REQUIREMENTS FOR FRENCH CITIZENS

PAYS	CONSULATS ÉTRANGERS À PARIS	FORMALITÉS			VACCINATIONS					MONNAIES 1 FFR égal environ:
		passeport	visa	billet retour ou autres	paludisme	variole	fièvre jaune	choléra	typhoïde	
AFRIQUE DU SUD	59, Quai d'Orsay, 75007 PARIS, Tél. : 45.55.92.37	•	•	•						Rand = 0,29
ARGENTINE	62, Impasse Kléber, 75016 PARIS, Tél. : 45.53.22.25	•								Austral = 0,11
AUSTRALIE	4, rue Jean Rey, 75015 PARIS, Tél. : 45.75.62.00	•	•	•						Dollar australien = 0,21
BOLIVIE	12, Av. du Présid. Kennedy, 75016 PARIS, Tél. : 45.25.47.14	•	•	•		o	o			Peso bolivien = 273115,84
BRESIL	12, Av. des Ch. Élysées, 75008 PARIS, Tél. : 43.59.89.30	•	•	•						Cruzeiro = 2021,43
CAMEROUN	73, rue d'Auteuil, 75016 PARIS, Tél. : 46.51.89.00	•	•	•	R		O			Franc CFA = 50
CANADA	37, Av. Montaigne, 75008 PARIS, Tél. : 47.23.01.01	•		•						Dollar canadien = 0,21
CHINE	9, Av. V. Cresson, 92130 ISSY-LES-MOULINEAUX, Tél. : 47.36.77.90	•	•	•						Renminbi Yuan = 0,46
COLOMBIE	11, rue Chr. Colomb, 75008 PARIS, Tél. : 47.23.36.05	•	•	•		R				Peso colombien = 26,20
CÔTE-D'IVOIRE	8, rue Dumont d'Urville, 75016 PARIS, Tél. : 47.20.35.09	•		•	R		O			Franc CFA = 50,00
ÉQUATEUR	34, Av. de Messine, 75008 PARIS, Tél. : 45.61.10.04	•			R				R	Sucre = 15,99
ÉGYPTE	58, Av. Foch, 75016 PARIS, Tél. : 45.00.77.10	•	•	•					R	Livre égyptienne = 0,10
ÉTATS-UNIS	2, rue St-Florentin, 75008 PARIS, Tél. : 42.96.12.02	•	•	•						Dollar = 0,15
GRÈCE*	23, Rue Galilée, 75016 PARIS, Tél. : 47.23.72.23	•								Drachme = 20,20
ÉTHIOPIE	35, Av. Charles Floquet, 75007 PARIS, Tél. : 47.83.83.95	•	•		R		O			Birr = 0,30
GUINÉE BISSAU	24, Rue E. Meunier, 75016 PARIS, Tél. : 45.53.72.25	•	•	•	R		O			Peso = 24,70
BURKINA FASSO (HAUTE-VOLTA)	159, Bd Haussmann, 75008 PARIS, Tél. : 43.59.90.63	•		•	R		O	O		Franc CFA = 50,00
HONDURAS	6, Place Vendôme, 75001 PARIS, Tél. : 42.61.34.75	•	•	•	R			O		Lempira = 0,29
INDE	15, Rue Alfred de Hodencq, 75016 PARIS, Tél. : 45.20.39.30	•	•	•	R				R	Roupie indienne = 1,73
INDONÉSIE	49, Rue Cortambert, 75016 PARIS, Tél. : 45.03.07.60	•		•	R					Rupiah = 160,29
JAMAÏQUE	60, Av. Foch, 75016 PARIS, Tél. : 45.00.62.25	•		•						Dollar jamaïcain = 0,79
JAPON	7, Av. Hoche, 75008 PARIS, Tél. : 47.66.02.22	•		•						Yen = 26,30
JORDANIE	80, Bd Maurice Barres, 92200 NEUILLY/SEINE, Tél. : 46.24.52.38	•	•							Dinar jordanien =
KENYA	3, Rue Cimarosa, 75016 PARIS, Tél. : 45.53.35.00	•	•	•	R	R	R		R	Shilling du Kenya = 2,26
MADAGASCAR	4, Av. Raphaël, 75016 PARIS, Tél. : 45.04.62.11	•	•	•	R					Franc Malgache = 88,14
MALAISIE	2 bis, Rue Bénouville, 75016 PARIS, Tél. : 45.53.11.85	•	•	•	R			R		Ringgit = 0,36
MALI	89, Rue du Cherche-Midi, 75006 PARIS, Tél. : 45.48.58.43	•		•	R		O	R		Franc CFA = 50,00
MAROC (1)	19, Rue Saulnier, 75009 PARIS, Tél. : 45.23.37.40	•								Dirham = 1,32
MAURICE (ÎLE)	68, Bd de Courcelles, 75017 PARIS, Tél. : 42.27.30.19	•								Roupie de Maurice = 1,93
MEXIQUE (2)	16, Rue Hamelin, 75016 PARIS, Tél. : 42.27.30.19	•	carte touristiqu							Peso mexicain = 64,38
NÉPAL	7, Rue Washington, 75008 PARIS, Tél. : 43.59.28.61	•	•					R	R	Roupie népalaise = 2,91
NIGER	154, Rue Longchamp, 75016 PARIS, Tél. : 45.04.80.60	•		•	R		O	R		Franc CFA = 50,00
PAKISTAN (3)	18, Rue Lord Byron, 75008 PARIS, Tél. : 45.62.23.32	•	•		R				R	Roupie pakistan. = 2,26
PÉROU	50, Av. Kléber, 75016 PARIS, Tél. : 47.04.35.97	•		•				R	R	Sol = 2,4
PHILIPPINES	39, Av. G. Mandel, 75016 PARIS, Tél. : 47.04.65.50	•	•	•						Peso philippin = 3,13
SALVADOR (El)	12, Rue Galilée, 75016 PARIS, Tél. : 47.20.42.02	•	•	•	R					Colon = 0,57
SÉNÉGAL	22, Rue Hamelin, 75016 PARIS, Tél. : 45.53.75.86	•		•	R	O	O	R		Franc CFA = 50,00
SIERRA LEONE	6, Rue Médéric, 75017 PARIS, Tél. : 42.56.14.73	•	•		R		O			Léone = 0,71
SINGAPOUR (4)	12, Square de l'Avenue Foch, 75016 PARIS, Tél. : 45.00.33.61	•		•						Dollar de Singapour = 0,31
SOUDAN	56, Av. Montaigne, 75008 PARIS, Tél. : 47.20.07.86	•	•	•	R	R	R			Livre soudanaise = 0,37
SRI LANKA (3)	15, rue d'Astorg, 75008 PARIS, Tél. : 42.66.35.01	•	•	•	R					Roupie cinghalaise = 3,91
SYRIE	20, rue Vaneau, 75007 PARIS, Tél. : 45.51.82.35	•	•		R			R		Livre syrienne = 0,57
TAIWAN	9, Av. Matignon, 75008 PARIS, Tél. : 42.99.16.80	•	•	•						Nouveau dollar de Taïwan = 5,56
TANZANIE	70, Bd Péreire Nord, 75017 PARIS, Tél. : 47.66.21.77	•	•	•	R		O	R	R	Shilling tanzanien = 2,26
THAÏLANDE (4)	8, rue Greuze, 75016 PARIS, Tél. : 47.04.32.22	•	•	•	R			O		Baht = 3,85
TOGO	8, rue Alfred Roll, 75017 PARIS, Tél. : 43.80.12.13	•		•	R		O			Franc CFA = 50,00
TUNISIE (1)	17/19, rue de Lübeck, 75016 PARIS, Tél. : 45.53.50.94	•								Dinar Tunisien = 0,10
TURQUIE*	184, Bd Malesherbes, 75017 PARIS, Tél. : 42.27.32.72	•			R					Livre turque = 84,09
URSS	8, Rue de Prony, 75017 PARIS, Tél. : 47.42.47.40	•	•							Nouveau rouble = 0,10
VENEZUELA (2)	42, Av. du Président Wilson, 75016 PARIS, Tél. 45.53.00.88	•		•	R		R			Bolivar = 0,63
YÉMEN NORD	21, Av. Charles FLoquet, 75007 PARIS, Tél. : 43.06.66.22	•	•	•	R			R		Ryal = 0,99
YÉMEN SUD	25, rue G. Bizet, 75016 PARIS, Tél. : 47.23.61.76	•	•	•	R					Dinar = 0,05

EXPLICATIONS DES SIGNES UTILISÉS :
(1) Carte d'identité en cas de voyages organisés. — (2) Carte de tourisme délivrée gratuitement par le Consulat. — (3) Visas obligatoires pour des séjours supérieurs à 21 jours. — (4) Visas obligatoires pour des séjours supérieurs à 14 jours. — * Carte d'identité en cours de validité obligatoire. — O : Obligatoire. — R : Recommandé.
Les formalités ci-dessus sont valables pour les ressortissants français. Les ressortissants étrangers sont invités à se renseigner auprès des consulats des pays où ils désirent se rendre. Nous vous conseillons de vérifier les renseignements mentionnés auprès des Consulats des pays concernés car des modifications peuvent intervenir pendant la validité de notre brochure.

EC: ELIMINATION OF BORDER CONTROLS WITHIN EUROPE

As of January 1, 1993, all border controls within the EC have more or less been eliminated. By more or less, we mean that the UK has vowed to maintain checks at British frontiers and will still require passports from non-EC citizens. As for EC citizens, most report that they merely have to wave their passport at the immigration officers standing sleepily by the special blue channels for EC citizens. (Regular readers of this report will realise that borders between countries on mainland Europe have been down for some time now.)

Most countries, however, still reserve the **right** to check visitor's ID. Germany, for one, insists that *random sample* border checking is an effective weapon against crime. German officials arrest 100,000 people each year at frontiers! Half of these arrests result from the on-the-spot instincts of the officials, the rest from recognizing those on "wanted" lists. Internally papers are routinely checked in connection with traffic law violations or emergency assistance requests. Don't assume you can get away with having no passport, ID card, driving license or insurance even after 1993.

As the national borders within Europe are lifted, the anticipated consequences will include:

1) Harmonised VISA POLICIES. For instance – France's questionable unilateral decision in 1987 to "fight terrorism" by requiring visas of most non-EC foreign visitors will be unavailable to any EC country.

2) All EC countries will adopt similar rules on ASYLUM and IMMIGRATION. While national rules could, in theory, be policed with residence permits, in practice immigrants will always exploit the softest regime. In the EC, Spanish, Italian and Portuguese immigration laws are lax. Many immigrants otherwise unable to enter the EC have used the Italian back door. Once inside, they can go anywhere and work "without paper" as do about 25 per cent of all workers in Europe.

3) A common DRUGS POLICY. Our view – legalize drugs and thus reduce street crime. This is not the view in Brussels. In the EC, only the Dutch are permissive about soft drugs. Dutch tolerated drugs already flow freely across the open frontier into Germany, where they are prohibited.

4) A common GUN LAW. Problematic because France and Italy will not toughen laws on gun possession because of a right to go hunting that dates back to before the Napoleanic era.

5) Greater rights of HOT PURSUIT. If criminals cannot be stopped at borders, they must be pursuable across them. That means German police cars zooming into France on high speed chases. There will be rapid, routine EXTRADITION and return of fugitives, with minimum paper work required.

6) Harmonisation of laws on STOLEN PROPERTY. Otherwise, loot will make its way to the jurisdictions where it is least recoverable, by law.

7) Binding agreement on ARRESTS at the external frontiers. Germany must be able to tell Spain to make a pinch when a known German criminal is spotted boarding a ferry to Morocco.

8) A powerful INFORMATION SYSTEM for exchanging "wanted" lists. A computer network called the Schengen Information System is being set up. The French are worried about acting on this exchange of data. They want the right to vet the lists for accuracy before using them.

9) Tighter CHECKS ON FOREIGNERS entering the EC. The only way of compensating for the lack of frontier checks, both to catch criminals and to enforce immigration laws, is to get tougher on identity checks, residence papers and the like. The solution – be a PT, a Perpetual Tourist. If you have not yet read *PT* be sure to get a copy from our publisher, Scope International. If you want to be free to visit and roam within the new United States of Europe, now is the time to start the process of getting at least one EC passport or residence permit. Wait two or three years and the door may be closed.

We can recommend consultants who can assist you to obtain EC passports. We do not "sell" passports, but we can show individuals certain LEGAL ways to obtain EC residence and passports. See back pages of this report for consultation details and charges.

ECUADOR – A POLICY OPEN TO WIDE INTERPRETATION

Most of what was said about Bolivia also applies to its neighbor, Ecuador. Diplomatic representatives of Ecuador around the world have been instructed to bring in as much hard currency as possible. Further, they have been directed to give favorable consideration to all proposals from investors that would bring in new skills and capital. For the time being, Ecuador has no exchange or currency controls.

Consulates will issue an immigrant visa (10 III) and possibly a provisional passport to any investor/entrepreneur who deposits US $1,000 upon application and agrees to invest another US $24,000 within 90 days of entering Ecuador. The capital may be invested in any industry, farming or export-oriented business. Citizenship can then be granted at the discretion of the Ministerio de Relaciones Exteriores. A visit to Ecuador and a genuine business operation there is required. See our section on Brazil for an analysis that applies to all South American countries.

Like Bolivia, Ecuador is a poor, Third World country with unmanageable debts. Its passports have not been distributed as extensively as Bolivia's. This probably means very low prices for do-it-yourselfers who are willing to contact consular officials or work with an attorney in Quito, the capital.

One interpretation of the present situation is that a person who agrees to make the US $1,000 deposit with a consulate can possibly get a provisional (non-citizen) five year passport and then by *not* entering Ecuador, forfeit the deposit and keep the passport. One problem is that the passport must be renewed every year at a consulate. This will involve another gratuity. Your success will depend upon how much the consul is motivated to assist you. After five years, a visit to Quito is normally required to get a new passport.

Of course, a definite option is to go to Ecuador, start a business or buy a small farm and get citizenship in a reasonably short time. Ecuador is not a place where most people would care to settle down, even for just a year or two – unless one has the pioneering spirit and an excellent command of Spanish.

In our opinion, time would be well spent in calling upon Ecuadorian Consular officials and explaining your need for a second passport and asking what it would take for them to help you. Legally, Ecuadorian diplomats have wide discretion. If you have plenty of time, an Ecuador do-it-yourself project could yield interesting dividends. Let us know how you make out (anonymously, if you wish). We must share helpful information with fellow PTs for our own survival.

FRANCE – BUREAUCRATS STILL BUSY

Despite the official relaxation of barriers between EC countries, bureaucrats are still busy chasing pieces of paper around desks all over Europe to make sure everyone is documented. For example, if a UK national wants to enter France, he still needs a valid identity card or passport but may then stay for three months without a residence permit if looking for work. If he does find a job, he must apply for a five-year residence permit which can be renewed automatically for a further ten years. As long as he has a residence permit, the worker is entitled to all the social benefits available to a French national.

If you are working, you do not need to worry too much about income tax levels at a maximum of 56.8 per cent as only one-fifth of inland revenue is funded by income tax because of an inordinate number of exemptions including home purchase, certain bank savings accounts and allowances for children. An individual's liability to French tax depends on his Tax Domicile. If his family home, economic or professional interests are France-based, he will be liable to French taxes on his worldwide income. Non-residents are liable to French tax only on their French source income, subject to double taxation relief which prevents them from being taxed both by France and their country of domicile.

GERMANY: REFUGEES AND NATIONAL GUILT

Most of what was said about Austria also applies to West Germany. A huge bureaucracy in Berlin exists for no other purpose than the processing and resettlement of refugees. Most are fleeing from communism. Many have religious reasons or simply seek economic opportunities in the West.

Millions have been processed. Despite the removal of the Berlin Wall and the partial lifting of the Iron Curtain, they still pour in – lately many from Asia and Africa. Germany feels a national guilt about its treatment of minorities during the Nazi era and is helping people who say they are fleeing oppression. Admission to Germany to refugees used to be automatic, even without a passport (in West Berlin only). The German government formerly supplied housing, medical attention and relocation assistance.

Since 1981, high unemployment in the country has made foreign workers in Germany unpopular with the local workers and voters. This problem has become significantly worse, as unemployment figures rise and refugees continue to flood in. Thus Germany is giving out fewer work permits and is trying to export refugees to other countries. Germany actually pays non-ethnic Germans in Germany large sums to give up their residence permits and move back home. This applies mainly to Greeks, Turks and Portuguese, who came to work in German factories but are no longer needed. There is talk of closing Germany to further refugees, but so far it is still "legally" open. However the flood of poor Bangladeshis and others from the Indian sub-continent was stemmed by fining airlines who used to transport them to Berlin without proper visas.

We have not received a formal statement about entrepreneur or business immigration, but have been told that Germany has a program of economic development zones. The prompt assistance of all branches of government will be given (along with loans, tax concessions and subsidies) for setting up businesses that will provide jobs or stimulate the local economy. Particular preference is given to investors who will create jobs in former East Germany.

Artists, creative people, self-employed people and those who will not compete for jobs are apparently welcomed and given residence permits and identity cards (good for travel throughout the Common Market). For those who have given up their old passports or have renounced prior citizenships and wish to travel, German refugee passports are immediately available. These are good for transit through all countries, but only with visas.

Citizenship and regular German passports may be applied for after ten years of residence. The German ten year residence requirement can be reduced or waived in individual cases, such as descendants of persons who were forced to flee their country due to Nazi persecution or invasion or ethnic Germans (if you speak good German, you will probably qualify). Ethnic Germans from East Germany were and still are granted *immediate Federal Republic citizenship and passports*. As of today, in spite of *glaznost* many people are still trying to leave the socialist paradise. Germany is now actively discouraging most immigration until the East German situation settles down.

Still, desirable artists, creative persons or entrepreneurs may get special consideration, especially if persecuted in their own home countries. Check with your local German consulate for a sympathetic interview and review of your chances for a fast German passport.

Applications for German passports are processed **after arrival** in Germany. The **paperwork always takes at least a year even for ethnic Germans**. No bribery should be attempted in Germany, but an experienced immigration lawyer will possibly be able to speed things along.

Taxes in Germany are quite high. We hear that Germany is considering imitation of the US policy, i.e. taxing German citizens on their worldwide income, regardless of where they reside. As a result, many more Germans would acquire a second nationality, which the German government says will result in the loss of their German citizenship. So far, this is just rumor.

Although the German passport is generally well accepted, there is a certain international residue of ill feeling towards Germany due to Nazi excesses. This, coupled with an uncertain tax situation and the long wait for naturalization, causes me personally to relegate Germany to a less than top place on my list of passport targets. Also, Germany is a very authoritarian country where bureaucrats have much power. This fact makes Germans one of our largest group of clients seeking other passports! Is it a good passport for you?

For those with German language skills, this is a country offering culture, high technology, very high standards of living and perhaps the least corrupt government and most efficient civil service in the world. Most people find that the ''German mentality'' is very close to the ''American way of thinking''. English is spoken by all educated Germans and most businessmen. One ''strange freedom'' in Germany is the complete lack of any speed limits on their highways or autobahns.

For those who are willing to actually work, live and do business in a favored economic zone (such as Berlin), the government is flexible enough to make concessions. These could include reducing required residence time and giving an investor considerable tax freedom for a period of years. Whenever we write about Germany we think of that old definition of paradise on earth: a French cook, an Italian girlfriend and British cops. Germans run the trains and utilities. Hell is having an English cook, Italian engineers, German cops and a French girlfriend. Pssst! Don't be offended. It's only a joke.

GUATEMALA – A NEWLY OPENED DOOR

Guatemala has not yet caught on to the benefits of selling passports officially, but a new civilian government has expressed a willingness to receive as emigrants and new citizens any persons who could "contribute to the country". As you can see, the definition is vague and allows local bureaucrats a great deal of leeway.

The Guatemala plan involves making a personal visit to Guatemala and, in Guatemala, finding two responsible guarantors or sponsors within the country who will vouch for the fact that you are an OK upstanding kind of person. Generally, no visa is required to get into Guatemala, but border officials can ask to see onward tickets or enough money to buy at least a bus ticket to Mexico or Belize. With a visa, or prosperous looking appearance, one would no doubt be admitted to Guatemala without question. Guatemala City was described to this author as a "terrible place", but expecting the worst, we were pleasantly surprised by a relatively unpolluted city of eternal spring, reminding us much of Mexico City in 1935 when it had a far smaller population than it has today.

Guatemala is the Spanish-colonial Mexico City of an earlier era. The Zona Rosa (European Quarter) of Guatemala City is chic, ultra-modern and full of European-style coffee shops, boutiques, beautiful apartment high-rises and the sort of people you'd expect to find in London's Mayfair or Palm Beach, Florida. The town is surrounded by four towering and slightly smoking volcanoes. Very picturesque. The volcanoes never erupt, but there are earthquakes every hundred years or so.

We discovered that in the nearby resort town of Antigua, one can live, have rent and full board, and take four hours per day of Spanish lessons from a private tutor (in our case a beautiful seventeen year old single girl with long black hair down to her knees and a sensuous way of walking that takes your breath away). All this for about $300 per month – for everything! Why not go there and discover this wonderful place for yourself? There is much to see in this country with a magnificent climate, cheap, cheap everything and a most attractive native Indian population who dress in colorful wool garments. Almost immediately upon my arrival in Guatemala, I was set upon by adorable street urchins and a brother-sister team about six and seven years old. They became my mascots, guides and go-fers for the duration of my stay, and they felt they were overpaid at fifty cents per day, plus an occasional ice-cream cone.

The Guatemala passport is theoretically issued to anyone who has been around for two years or more and isn't a communist or black person. However, American citizen blacks are considered not to be black. The reasoning seems to be that Guatemalans don't like the neighboring (black) Belizians very much. The blatant discrimination (like signs at the border saying "No Blacks admitted to Guatemala") is aimed at Belizians rather than negroes in general. The two year residence requirement can be waived locally if you get a lawyer who can convince a police official. This is accomplished in the usual South and Central American way.

The cost shouldn't be over a few thousand dollars if one makes personal contacts and fiddles around with the project for six months or so. We have no personal contacts down there for passports, but if you stumble upon a reliable immigration lawyer, let us know.

Life in Guatemala is *sweet for the elite*. In Guatemala this means European or white people. I saw almost no blacks in Guatemala. There are quite a few different tribes of local Indians. They actually make up the majority of the population. It seems that Spanish speaking, European looking people (5 to 10 per cent of the population) have all the good jobs, land, fancy cars, major businesses and political offices. During the past twenty years, there have been periodic rebellions by Marxists financed by Cuba and the Soviet Union, but most of those rebels have either been killed or exiled to neighboring countries. Those who went (or were forced to go) abroad to actually see how things worked in Marxist Nicaragua decided it wasn't any improvement and have lately been drifting back.

Today there seems to be more of a spirit of accommodation and a willingness to spread the wealth around. In the papers one reads about the occasional ambush, but military activity has now died down to almost nothing. The only people who get shot are government officials and the individuals they describe as "major troublemakers". Foreigners are rarely, if ever, caught in the crossfire.

Guatemela is still a Third World country. It has the heavy population density of say, Italy. However, no one seems to be going hungry, and people have a happy-go-lucky, open and friendly attitude something like that in Thailand.

The Mayan people in particular are very serene and beautiful. All are very friendly. The Indian children especially try to sell tourists everything from chicklets to hand woven bracelets and dolls, but they do it in an irresistable and charming way.

Bottom line: If you want to get away from it all to a place that is charming, off the beaten track, yet surprisingly sophisticated, try Guatemala. It is highly recommended as a port in a storm. A Guatemalan passport is good for travel to most countries in Europe without a visa, and dual citizenship is common. Most upper-class Guatemalans hold US and Spanish passports. Spain gives special consideration to Guatemalans, who by treaty need only one year of residence in Spain to acquire Spanish citizenship or vice-versa.

HONDURAS

Mid-1987 saw the opening up of a new entrant on the instant passport scene. As Costa Rica closed down, Honduras opened up. This Central American nation could be described as a typical banana republic, controlled by a landowning, military aristocracy. Somewhat less advanced politically and economically than Costa Rica, it enjoys frontage on both the Pacific and Caribbean sea coasts. The population is about 4½ million, with the capital, Tegucigalpa well served by many international airlines. The population speaks Spanish as well as the native indigenous tongues. The élite speak English and generally hold dual-citizenship in the US. Nicaraguan "Contra" or anti-communist forces, backed by the US, used to occupy the southern border areas. They have all gone home. The Pan American Highway which runs from California to Panama via Honduras is now getting back to normal after years of war. Internally, Honduras is peaceful as of 1992. Normal civilian airline traffic flows in and out of the airport. Civil wars going on in bordering El Salvador and Nicaragua have been bad for tourism and have also caused internal strains due to the influx of thousands of refugees. In the process of opening its doors to political refugees, certain influential officials let it be known that wealthy individuals from outside the immediate area would also find a refuge in Honduras, with passports made available, for a price.

Honduras might not be an appealing destination for you. However, this small country has always had a vast array of Honorary Diplomats abroad and has, as a result, superb diplomatic relations. We have discovered to our pleasant surprise that Hondurans enjoy visa-free travel to the same extent as the holder of a Swiss or Canadian passport. A Honduras passport gets you to all countries of Europe (excluding France), as well as Central and South America, Canada, Asia and even Romania! The cost of an instant passport would be around US $20,000 for the head of a family. A discount is available for spouses and dependent children. Honduras is accommodating in providing supporting documents like driving licences, voting cards, tax clearances, etc. All the documents would be available at nominal cost if you went to Honduras personally and were able to push the paperwork through the bureaucracy. We are also informed that the services of a top lawyer shortens the process by several years. We have located an agent who says he will operate on a contingent fee basis and complete the process in about sixty days. Write to Scope International, if interested. Several clients have expressed great satisfaction with their Honduran travel documents.

Generally a statement of goals and what you hope to accomplish can help us decide if your plans will work out for you. A Honduran passport would probably be best for someone who wanted to live far away from Central America, yet was willing to learn Spanish. It is a good "back-door" for Spain because as it was a former colony, Hondurans can easily get Spanish residency. After a one year residence a Spanish passport may be obtained. Honduras is one of our top choices for "instant passports".

Alternatively, an investment in the country (purchase of a house) of at least US $50,000 will provide instant permanent residency status. According to the existing laws, after 5 years, the applicant may apply for citizenship, which is usually granted.

Additional investments of approximately US $100,000 are deemed as "meritorious services" to the country (provided the right people in the government are contacted) and instant citizenship is more than likely.

IRELAND – FIND AN IRISH ANCESTOR!

Ireland is a member of the European Community and an altogether delightful island country located next to Great Britain. Irish citizens can, as a result, live and work without visas or permits in all EC countries. Ireland permits dual citizenship.

In all of Ireland and Northern Ireland (under UK Jurisdiction) there are roughly 4 million people qualified for Irish passports.

What is most interesting about the Irish situation is that with this population of 4 million, Ireland has about 14 million current passports outstanding! Like England, Canada and many countries who follow the old Roman Law, they believe that "once a Roman, always a Roman – down to the last descendant". Even if one turns in an Irish passport for cancellation and takes oaths of allegiance to another country because it is required in order to obtain a new passport, it is always possible to get the Irish nationality back again, normally with minimum formality and red tape. Unfortunately, in 1987 the Irish tightened up a little by saying that mere ancestry (grandparent) wasn't enough, and one's immediate parent had either to hold an Irish passport or at least be registered (during their lifetime) at a consulate or embassy as an Irish citizen. The moral of the story is, if you can qualify anywhere for a second passport *now,* by all means get it *now* because next year your rights may be terminated. As the PT option becomes more popular, the doors will start slamming shut.

Ireland's application form requires proof of Irish descent by birth and marriage certificates. In some countries, if you admit to holding another local passport, you may be required to turn it in for cancellation. The policy varies from country to country. Thus it is always better to apply for Irish travel documents in a country outside of your home country. When you go abroad on a visit you can do such things with greater ease and confidentiality.

Ireland does not, as a matter of policy, require an oath of allegiance nor does it notify the host country or the country of original citizenship of its passport issuances. Thus, because the Irish passport is acquired as a birthright, nations like Australia recognize that their citizens may legally hold dual-nationality with Ireland.

To avoid border crossing problems, a holder of an Irish or any foreign passport who was born in Australia or the US, for instance, should only enter or leave his home country (i.e. birth place) with the local passport. A native born American entering the US on a foreign passport would always be subjected to suspicion and questioning. Since US laws mandate that US citizens enter and leave the US only with a US passport, a US border official who discovered a second passport in your luggage would probably confiscate both passports and let you sue in court to sort out your status. It is a simple matter to mail your second passport on ahead or to leave it in a safe-deposit box. A good rule for all seasons – do not cross borders with two passports!

The US Immigration and Naturalization Service might say that they do not contest the fact that you legitimately are a citizen of more than one country. However, after confiscating your US passport and your Irish passport they might try to stop you from getting a new US passport on the grounds that the US government has the right to know where their citizens travel by means of passport stamps, and that a person who holds two passports is probably a dope dealer, currency smuggler or another type of "bad guy".

The US would then notify Ireland. Upon learning that you are accused of some naughty activities you could find yourself without the right to a new Irish passport. A second passport, as mentioned earlier in this report, should be kept for emergencies and used with discretion!

With three photographs, proper proof of Irish ancestry and the legal right to be in the country from which you make the application, an Irish passport is normally issued within 48 hours. The cost is currently about US $110 for a ten year maroon passport that is issued under the heading "European Community".

How do you find an Irish ancestor? Sometimes, this can be a bit tricky. Many churches and court records were destroyed in the "troubles", the long running Irish independence struggle against the British. Fires consumed many public buildings all over the island and anarchists once even blew up Cork county's public records.

Without proper records, it could be difficult to firmly establish that your ancestors DID come from Ireland. Fortunately, some Irish consulates and embassies abroad will understand your plight and can be satisfied with affidavits and research papers procured from a certified genealogist or other expert in Ireland. If you do not know your ancestors' exact name and birth place, you will need a genealogist to look up the facts for you.

If you know the full facts, names, places and dates of birth, marriages and deaths and other details of your Irish ancestors, then there is no need to use the services of any genealogist. Just fill out the Irish Citizenship Application form for foreign births registration (reproduced on the next few pages) and file it with your local Irish consulate.

You may only have one shot at obtaining Irish citizenship and a passport. Thus, it is vital that you get it right the first time.

Without Irish ancestry, it is also possible to get citizenship and a passport after a seven year period of residence. Irish residence is not generally sought after because of exceedingly high income taxes of 60 per cent on all income over subsistence. There are a few unique Irish exceptions to the confiscatory income taxes:

1. Artists, writers and composers can get an exemption of tax on royalty income.
2. Retirees over 65 years old are exempt.
3. Entrepreneurs or self-employed persons who start a new business in Ireland are exempt, with certain time limits.

In the last case, the Irish Industrial Development Authority has been authorized to dangle many incentives, including 100 per cent loans, cash grants, tax holidays, free land and possibly shortened residency requirements for passports. Business proposals are handled on a case by case basis, but *Ireland reportedly puts out the red carpet to attract investors or those who create local employment opportunities*.

Contact the nearest Irish Consulate for a friendly chat on the possibilities for you!

(Note: Persons with ancestors or themselves born in Northern Ireland qualify for Irish passports. Most of the Northern Ireland Catholics have them but so do many farsighted Protestants who realize that if Northern Ireland is ever ceded to the "Free Irish Republic" they may be protected from deportation and expropriation of their property by their Irish citizenship).

See also *The Tax Exile Report,* published by Scope International.

IRELAND: THE FORMS

On the following pages, we have reprinted some of the forms and letters similar to those you may receive from officials when you seek to get Irish citizenship and an Irish passport.

Your first step would normally be to secure a certified copy of your own birth certificate. To get an Irish issued birth certificate, all you have to do is fill in the short form (A) and return it to the Registrar General with the fee. The Dublin address is on the form.

Under Irish laws, the spouse of a person who is Irish by virtue of Irish birth or descent may become an Irish citizen if they make a simple declaration accepting Irish citizenship after 3 years of marriage. Such "post-nuptial acquisition" of Irish citizenship by declaration used to be immediate, but after 1989, the law was changed so that the declaration cannot be made earlier than 3 years after the marriage took place or after the Irish spouse became Irish (whichever is the later). The marriage must be intact at the time of the application and grant of citizenship.

We have reprinted the necessary forms here. Return these signed forms or any later

CONSULATE GENERAL OF IRELAND

655 MONTGOMERY STREET, SUITE 930

SAN FRANCISCO, CA 94111

A chara,

Thank you for your recent enquiry about acquisition of Irish citizenship through the process of registration in the Foreign Births Entry Book of this Consulate. I am enclosing the relevant application form in connection with your application.

The regulations governing applications from people who have Irish born grandparents are explained in Section A. on Page 2 of this letter : the procedure governing applications from people with Irish born great-grandparents are explained in Section B on Page 3.

Applicants who fall into either of these categories should read this letter carefully, in order to establish the documents which they will need to submit to make a successful application for Irish citizenship.

An application for citizenship consists of the application form and ALL relevant documents required to support the application. Applications received lacking any relevant documentation, do not qualify as valid applications and Cannot be accepted for the purposes of registration.

Having read this letter and enclosures if you have any queries, do not hesitate to contact either myself, or my colleagues.

Mise le Meas

Barbara Jones
Vice-Consul

SECTION A
(Irish born grandparent)

If you are claiming Irish citizenship on the basis of an Irish born grandparent* please note that all relevant documents in connection with your application must be the official version (certified copies) bearing the seal of the the Bureau of Vital Statistics or the relevant issuing authority.(i.e photopcipies or notarised copies are not acceptable) Birth certificates should be in the long format clearly indicating the details of lineage. Accordingly please submit certified copies of the documents listed below in order to apply for Foreign Births Registration.

(1) A completed application form

(2) Your birth certificate; this should be in the long format showing your parents names/ages/places of birth

(3) The birth certificate of the parent through whom you are claiming Irish citizenship (long format also)

(4) The birth certificate of the grandparent who was born in Ireland. If this is not available, please submit documentation which will give evidence of the Irish birth of your grandparent e.g marriage certificate; foreign immigration or naturalisation papers; death certificate.

(5) A fee of US$155.00 if you are over 18 years of age or US$53.00 if you are under 18 years.

If you are claiming descent through the maternal line e.g. through your mother and/or your grandmother you are also required to submit civil marriage certificate(s) showing the relevant changes from the maiden names to the married names.

Please also enclose a complete set of photocopies of the documents which support your application. We will return all originals or certified copies to you.

---

*The regulations for acquisition of citizenship through Irish born great-grandparents are explained in Section B on Page 3.

SECTION B
(Great-grandchild of Irish born great-grandparent)

Please be advised that the regulations of the Irish
Nationality and Citizenship Act 1956 were amended by Act of
the Oireachtas in 1986. As a consequence of this amendment
eligibility for applications for Irish citizenship on the
basis of an Irish born great-grandparent is regulated on the
basis of the following criteria.

Great-grandchildren of Irish-born great-grandparents are
eligible to apply for Irish citizenship
    (a) if the applicant was born after 17 July 1956
            and
    (b) if one of the applicant's parent's was registered
as an Irish citizen at the time of the applicant's
 birth.(or had registered as an Irish citizen on or
before 1 July 1986)

Accordingly applicants who satisfy both conditions (a) and
(b) above should submit submit the following documentation
in order to apply for Irish citizenship:
    (1) A completed application form

    (2) Applicant's birth certificate; this should be in
the long format showing parents names/ages/places of
birth

    (3) Evidence of parent's Irish citizenship i.e a copy
of their certificate of registration in the Foreign
Births Register or in the Foreign Births Entry Book
of an Irish Diplomatic Mission

    (4) A fee of US$155.00 if you are over 18 years of age
or US$53.00 if you are under 18 years.

    (5) A large Stamped Addressed 9x12 Envelope with
appropriate postage for First Class Mail

All relevant documents submitted in support of your
application must be the official version issued by the
Bureau of Vital Statistics and be in the long format. Please
also enclose a complete set of photocopies of the documents
which support your application. We will return all originals
or certified copies to you.

Ambasáid na hÉireann

Embassy of Ireland

20 Arkana Street,
Yarralumla, A.C.T. 2600
Telephone: (06) 273 3022
Facsimile: (06) 273 3741

C.1.5.

Dear

I refer to your recent enquiry about acquiring Irish citizenship
by means of Post-Nuptial Declaration.

Anyone married to a person who is an Irish citizen by birth or
descent may become an Irish citizen by making, on a special form,
a declaration of acceptance of Irish citizenship not earliler
than three years after the marriage or after the Irish partner
became Irish, whichever is the later.

The following documentation is required:-

1.   Form 3 to be completed by the non-Irish spouse and must be
     declared and subscribed in the presence of the witness
     (enclosed).

2.   Affidavit by Irish spouse stating that the couple are living
     together as husband and wife and that their marriage is
     subsisting and duly witnessed as above (enclosed).

3.   2 passport-sized photographs of the alien spouse, which have
     been signed and dated on the reverse side by the witness to
     the declaration on Form 3 and which are securely attached to
     that declaration.

4.   2 passport-sized photographs of the Irish spouse, which have
     been signed and dated on the reverse by the witness to the
     affidavit and which are securely attached to that affidavit.

5.   Copy of the civil marriage certificate. This should show the
     civil status of each party before marriage, age of each party
     at date of marriage, and names of one of the parents of each
     party.

6.   Long form birth certificates for both spouses.

                                                        .../2

7. 3-5 <u>proofs of identity</u> for the declarer e.g. <u>passport</u>, identity card with photograph, driver's licence, utility account statements, bank account statements, bank cards, credit cards, etc.

8. 3-5 <u>proofs of identity</u> for Irish spouse e.g. <u>Irish passport</u>, identity card with photograph, (as above). (Three to five of either of these sets of proofs of identity at 7 and 8 must include proof that the couple are residing at same address).

9. Proof of entitlement to <u>Irish citizenship</u> for the Irish spouse if other than by birth in Ireland, such as parent's long form birth and marriage certificates, foreign births registration certificate, and where the latter is concerned all the documents submitted to acquire that certificate.

10. If the Irish spouse was born in Northern Ireland, please state date and place of birth of <u>parent</u> and a <u>grandparent</u> born in any part of Ireland before 6 December 1922.

11. If one of the parties to the marriage has been previously married, evidence that that party was free to contract a second marriage must be provided, such as, (a) petition and final decree for the divorce which dissolved the previous marriage or (b) death certificate of previous spouse, whichever is applicable.

12. The PNC fee: A$92.00.

13. Passport application if required (enclosed).

Kindly note that <u>all</u> documentation must be originals and where in a language other than Irish or English, must be accompanied by a certified translation.

Yours sincerely

Dr Seán Ó Riain
Second Secretary

<u>N.B.</u> Please note that it takes a minimum of 12 months for processing of Post Nuptial Citizenships as all applications are referred to Dublin.

<u>IRISH NATIONALITY AND CITIZENSHIP ACTS 1956 AND 1986</u>

Affidavit by Irish citizen who is the spouse of an alien seeking post-nuptial citizenship

I...formerly.................................
  (full name of Irish citizen)   (family name at birth, if different)

of..
                (current address in full)

(born on the.....day of.................19...at........................
                            (name of town/district)

in......................holder of Irish Passport No...................)
    (name of country)

hereby affirm, declare and swear that I married........................
                         (full name of alien)

(who was born on the....day of...............,19...at...................
                            (name of town/district)

in......................a national of.....................) on
    (name of country)

the.....day of.............19...at.................in.................
    (date of marriage)   (town/city)   (name of country)

and I further affirm, declare and swear that we are <u>LIVING TOGETHER</u> as husband and wife; that our marriage is subsisting; and that no proceedings for divorce or annulment of this marriage have been commenced or are about to be commenced in any court of law.

                    Signature................................

                    Date....................................

Sworn this.....day of.................19...by the said................

................................whom I personally know for.......years,

(or who has been identified to me by.................................

whom I personally know for.....years, and who has personally known

....for.....years)++
        (full name of Irish citizen)

at..
        (full address where affidavit is being sworn)

before me...................., a................................
    (full name in block letters)   (insert qualification)*

        Affix
        Stamp   Signature........................

++delete whichever is not applicable, otherwise affidavit is defective.

*This affidavit must be made before a person who is authorised to administer oaths by the law of the country where it is made e.g. a notary public or a commissioner for oaths. If it is being made outside Ireland, it may be made before an Irish diplomatic officer (not below the rank of First Secretary) or an Irish consular officer accredited to the country in which it is made.

IRISH NATIONALITY AND CITIZENSHIP ACT, 1956

Declaration of acceptance of Irish citizenship as post-nuptial citizenship
by alien who has married a person who is an Irish citizen
otherwise than by naturalisation or under section 8 or 12
of the above Act (inserted by the Irish Nationality
and Citizenship Act, 1986).

I ....
(name in full)

of ....

a ....national, was married at

....on ....
(place of marriage)   (date of marriage)

to ....

of (address) ....

who was born at ....

....on ....

and is an Irish citizen otherwise than by naturalisation.

  I hereby declare that the marriage is subsisting and that I accept Irish citizenship as my post-nuptial citizenship.

        Signature ....

        Date ....

Declared and subscribed before me a ....
(insert qualification)
by the person named above who is personally known to me (or, who is identified

to me by ....

....who is personally known to me).

        Signature ....

        Address ....

        ....

        Date ....

Except in the case of a woman who is an alien and is making a declaration prior to the 1st day of January, 1987, this declaration must be supported by an affidavit by the spouse who is an Irish citizen to the effect that the couple are living together as husband and wife. The declaration and the affidavit should be made:-

  If made in Ireland before a notary public or a commissioner for oaths or a peace commissioner, and if made elsewhere, before a diplomatic or consular officer of Ireland, a notary public, or any person who is by the law of the country in which the declaration is made a commissioner for oaths or other person authorised to take affidavits and for that purpose to administer oaths.

Oifig an Ard-Chláraitheora

Joyce House,
8-11 Lombard Street East, Dublin 2

Oifig an Ard-Chláraitheora

Teach Sheoighe,
8-11 Sráid Lombaird Thoir, Baile Átha Cliath 2.

TEL. (01) 711000 EXTN...........
TELEX: 33451 HLT E1

Our Ref: 26B
Your Ref:

..................................19...............

A Chara

With reference to your application for a birth certificate the information requested below should be provided as accurately as possible and the form returned to this Office with the necessary fee. All Cheques, Postal or Money Orders should be made payable to "The Registrar General".

Mise le meas,

Ard-Chláraitheoir

FEES

Full Birth Certificate (including search fee)..US$9.00

Short Birth Certificate (including search fee)...US$6.00

If more than one certificate relating to the birth of the same person is required an additional fee of US$6.00 should be forwarded for each extra full certificate or US$3 for each extra short certificate.

SURNAME of PERSON whose Birth Certificate is required

FIRST NAME(S) in full

Date of Birth

Place of Birth
(If in a town, name of street to be given) .

Father's Name

Father's Occupation

Mother's First Name(s) and Maiden Surname

Has the Person whose Birth record is required been legally adopted? Yes/No

Signature of Applicant...

Address ....

....

Date ....19............

ÉIRE IRELAND PAS 2

FOIRM IARRATAIS AR PHAS

PASSPORT APPLICATION FORM

Ní mór an fhoirm seo agus Foirm M (más cuí) a chur chuig Oifig na bPasanna laistigh de 6 mhí ó dháta a sínithe.

This form and Form M (where appropriate) must be submitted within 6 months of signature.

Lena úsáid den Stát. Sa Stát ní mór foirm Pas 1, atá ar fáil ó na Gardaí, a úsáid.

Only for applications from outside the State. In the state use form Pas 1, obtainable from the Gardaí.

1. Cuir an t-iarratas chuig Oifig na bPasanna, Sráid Theach Laighean, Baile Átha Cliath 2, nó tar lear, chuig an Ambasáid/Consalacht Éireannach.

   Breithnímid gach iarratas chomh tapa agus is féidir. Baintear moill as sin, áfach, nuair nach mbíonn na doiciméid in ord. Chun nach mbeidh díomá ort, is cóir duit d'iarratas a chur isteach <u>ceithre seachtaine</u> roimh dháta d'imeachta.

1. Send applications to the Passport Office, Molesworth Street, Dublin 2, or, overseas, to the Irish Embassy or Consulate.

   We process all applications as quickly as possible. However, delays will arise if documentation is not in order. To avoid disappointment you should apply at least <u>four weeks</u> before your departure date.

2. **Más in Éirinn a rugadh tú,** seol:

   (a) **grianghraif** — dhá phas-ghriangraf díreach mar a chéile (4cm x 5cm); a tógadh laistigh de thrí mhí roimh dháta an iarratais.

   (b) **táille** — trí ordú poist, ordú airgid, dréacht bainc nó seic (iníoctha le hOifig na bPasanna);

   (c) **deimhniú breithe** (ní leor fótachóip ná deimhniú baiste) más é do chéad iarratas ar phas é nó **an pas Éireannach is deireanaí atá agat** má eisíodh pas chugat roimhe (féach Roinn D. Uimh. 7 lastall).

   (d) **deimhniú pósta,** (ní leor fótachóip), más bean phósta tú atá ag cur iarratais isteach faoi do shloinne pósta den chéad uair.

2. **If born in Ireland** send:

   (a) **photographs** — two recent identical passport photographs (4cm x 5cm); taken within three months before date of application.

   (b) **fee** by postal order, money order, bank draft or cheque (payable to Passport Office);

   (c) **birth certificate** (not photocopy and not baptismal certificate) if you are applying for the first time or **your most recent Irish passport** if you have previously been issued with a passport (see Section D. No. 7 overleaf).

   (d) **marriage certificate,** (not photocopy), if you are a married woman applying for the first time in your married name.

3. **Má tá tú faoi bhun 18 mbliana d'aois,** cuir isteach toiliú scríofa fianaithe ó do bheirt thuismitheoirí nó do chaomhnóirí ar fhoirm bhreise (PAS M) agus **an fhoirm fhada de do dheimhniú breithe ar a bhfuil ainmneacha na dtuismitheoir.**

3. **If you are under 18 years of age,** send in written witnessed consent of both parents or guardians on an additional form (PAS M) and **the long form of your birth certificate showing names of parents.**

4. **Más thar lear a rugadh tú,** agus gan pas Éireannach agat cheana, seol (a) agus (b) mar atá thuas agus (d), más cuí, i dteannta le:

   (a) Más in Éirinn a rugadh tuismitheoir duit, **deimhniú breithe an tuismitheora sin** agus **do dheimhniú breithe féin** i leagan a luann ainm an tuismitheora sin agus **deimhniú pósta do thuismitheoirí;**

   (b) Más rud é go bhfuil saoránacht Éireannach bainte amach agat trí Eadóirseacht, tríd an gClár de Bheireatais Choigríche nó trí Dhearbú Iarphósta, **fianaise dhoiciméadach ar shaoránacht** agus **do dheimhniú breithe** (ní leor fótachóip). Féadfar aistriú údaraithe de do dheimhniú breithe a lorg freisin.

4. **If born outside Ireland** and applying for your first Irish passport, send (a) and (b) as above and (d) if appropriate with:

   (a) if you are Irish because one of your parents was born in Ireland, **birth certificate of that parent** and **your birth certificate** showing the name of that parent and **your parents' marriage certificate;**

   (b) If you have acquired Irish citizenship by Naturalisation, Foreign Births Registration or Post Nuptial Declaration **documentary evidence of citizenship** and **your birth certificate** (not photocopy). An authenticated translation of your birth certificate may also be required.

COINNÍOLLACHA DO PHAS-GHRIANGHRAIF:

— Dhá ghrianghraf, 4cm x 5cm
  Líne dhubh: an méid ceart
  Líne Bhriste: an méid is lú

— aghaidh iomlán, ceann agus guaillí amháin, gan hata, ar chúlra geal

— páipéar grianghraif tanaí

— cúl an ghrianghraif bán agus neamhghlónraithe

PASSPORT PHOTOGRAPH REQUIREMENTS:

— Two photographs, 4cm x 5cm
  Black line shows correct size
  Broken line shows smallest size accepted

— full face without hat, head and shoulders only against light background.

— photographic paper thin

— reverse of photograph should be white and unglazed

RABHADH: Féadfar an dlí a chur ar aon duine a bhéarfas eolas bréagach chun pas a fháil nó chun cabhrú le duine eile pas a fháil.

WARNING: A person who gives false information to get a passport or to help another person to get a passport may be prosecuted.

1

ROINN A AN PAS A IARRTAR	**PASSPORT REQUIRED** SECTION A

Cuir √ sa bhosca cuí

Put √ in box required

GNÁTHPHAS   IR£45.00
32 leathanach, bailí go cionn 10 mbliana. (Ní féidir é a athnuachan thar 10 mbliana: ní mór pas nua a fháil.)

STANDARD PASSPORT   IR£45.00
32 pages, valid for 10 years. (Cannot be extended beyond 10 years: a new passport must then be got.)

PAS BLIANA   IR£5.00 sa bhliain
Tig le duine faoi 18 nó thar 65 bliana d'aois, pas bliana a fháil. Is féidir blianta eile a fháil anois nó níos déanaí ar na táillí bliana ag an am. I gcás duine óig, caithfidh an bhliain dheireanach tosú roimh an 18ú lá breithe.

YEARLY PASSPORT   IR£5.00 per year
If under 18 or over 65 years of age you may get a one-year passport. Extra years of validity may be got at time of issue or later, for the yearly fees at the time. For young people, the last year of validity must begin before the 18th birthday.

Cé mhéad blianta?

How many years?

PAS MÓR   IR£90.00
Tá pas 96 leathanach ar fáil. Moltar é do dhaoine a bheas ag taisteal go minic in áiteanna ina gcuirfear a lán víosaí nó stampaí air. (Ní féidir é a athnuachan thar 10 mbliana: ní mór pas nua a fháil.)

LARGE PASSPORT   IR£90.00
A 96 page passport is available. It is recommended if you travel frequently in areas where many visas or stamps will be put in it. (Cannot be extended beyond 10 years: a new passport must then be got.)

MALAIRT PHAS   IR£15 i gcás gnáthphas
Is féidir pas nua a fháil don tréimhse neamhchaite de bhailíocht seanphas (a thugtar ar ais dúinn). **Is gá toiliú tuismitheoirí le haghaidh aon leanaí breise atá le háireamh ar phas nua.**

EXCHANGE OF PASSPORT   IR£15.00 in the case of Standard Passport
A new passport booklet can be got for the unexpire period of validity of an existing one (but not if lost, **Parent's consent is needed for any extra children to be included on new passport.**

ROINN B   COMHPHAS

JOINT PASSPORT   SECTION B

Más Éireannach do chéile, is féidir é/í a chur ar do phas ag am a eisiúna saor in aisce. Cuir isteach foirm iarratais eile dó/dí (mar aon le doiciméid agus grianghraif) agus deimhniú pósta (nó, roimh an mbainis, nóta ón sagart/cláraitheoir.) **Rabhadh: Ní thig leis an gcéile an pas a úsáid chun taisteal ach amháin i gcuideachta an tsealbhóra.**

Your spouse, if Irish, may be included on your passport at time of issue free of charge. Send in his/her separate application form (including documents and photographs) and marriage certificate (or, before the wedding, a letter from the clergyman/registrar). **Warning: A spouse can use the passport to travel only in the company of the holder.**

Más comhphas, cuir √ sa bhosca

If joint passport, put √ in box.

agus abair cé acu tusa nó do chéile an 'sealbhóir'

and say whether you or your spouse is to be the 'holder'

ROINN C

SECTION

Do dhaoine a rugadh i dTuaisceart Éireann i ndiaidh 6 Nollaig 1922:

Only for people born in Northern Ireland since 6 December 1922:

Má thugann tú freagra deimhneach (√ sa bhosca) ar cheist amháin acu seo, is leor sin.

If you answer 'YES' (√ in box) to any one of the following questions, this is sufficient.

1. An raibh pas Éireannach agat cheana, nó ag tuismitheoir nó seanathair nó seanmháthair agat a rugadh in Éirinn?

1. Have you (or a parent or grandparent of yours, born in Ireland) ever had an Irish passport?

2. Ar rugadh d'athair nó do mháthair, nó aon seanathair nó seanmháthair agat in áit ar bith in Éirinn roimh 6 Nollaig 1922 nó sa Stát (26 Chontae) ón dáta sin i leith?

2. Was any one of your parents or grandparents born in any part of Ireland before 6 December 1922, or in the State (26 counties) on or after that date?

3. An dtiocfadh le tuismitheoir nó le seanathair nó seanmháthair agat a rugadh i dTuaisceart Éireann, 'Rugadh' a thabhairt mar fhreagra ar cheist 2?

3. Could any parent or grandparent of yours, born in Northern Ireland, have answered 'Yes' to question 2?

Mura dtig leat freagra deimhneach a thabhairt ar cheist amháin thuas, iarr foirm ar leith: tig leat a rá ar an bhfoirm sin gur saoránach d'Éirinn tú.

If you cannot answer 'Yes' to any of the above questions you should ask for a separate form on which you can state that you are an Irish citizen.

2

FEE	CH	Pas Uimh PP No.		Comhad File
CRT	CE	Dáta eisiúna Issue Date		Táille Fee
CT	Q			
PH	W	Bailí go dtí Valid until		Táille, tag Fee ref.
MSC	CR			

ROINN D   SONRAÍ AN IARRATASÓRA   **DETAILS OF APPLICANT**   **SECTION D**

Sloinne
1. **Surname** [ ]
     (BLOCLITREACHA)   (BLOCK LETTERS)

Sloinne ar dheimhniú breithe (murab ionann)
Surname on birth certificate (if different) ....   Sa chás seo conas agus cathain a   In this case how and when did you

thosaigh tú ag úsáid do shloinne nua mar ghnáthshloinne?
begin to use your present name as your main name? ....

Sloinne eile agat (tabhair míniú)
Any other surnames (also state circumstances) ....

Ainmneacha
Forenames [ ]   **Dhá ainm de ghnath** Normally two forenames
     (BLOCLITREACHA)   (BLOCK LETTERS)

Ainmneacha iomlána ar an deimhniú breithe (murab ionann)
Full forenames on birth certificate (if different) ....

Dáta Breithe   [_____]   Gnéas   fireann   [ ]   baineann   [ ]
3. **Date of Birth**   4. **Sex**   male   female

Contae do bhreithe (nó tír más thar lear a rugadh)
5. **County of birth (or country if born abroad)** ....

Airde
6. **Height** ....

7. An raibh Pas Éireannach agat riamh roimhe?   Bhí [ ]   Ní raibh [ ]
    Were you ever issued with an Irish Passport?   Yes   No

Más "Bhí", cuir chugainn an pas Éireannach is deireanaí a bhí agat lena chealú. Mura dtig leat déanamh amhlaidh cuir chugainn míniú mionsonraithe agus ráiteas faoi chailliúint mar aon leis na doiciméid go léir a luaitear i míreanna 2, 3 agus 4 ar leathanach 1 den fhoirm seo.

If yes, submit your most recent Irish passport for cancellation. If you are not in a position to do so submit a detailed explanation and statement of loss together with full documentation mentioned at paragraphs 2, 3 and 4 in page 1 of this form.

ROINN E   LEANAÍ   **CHILDREN**   **SECTION E**

Tá feidhm ag an méid seo a leanas cibé acu a bhí nó nach raibh na leanaí ar áireamh i bpas roimhe seo:

Tig le do leanaí faoi bhun 16 bliana d'aois atá ainmnithe ar do phas taisteal leat de ghnáth gan pasanna dá gcuid féin.
Chun leanaí a bheith ar an bpas cuir isteach:

— Foirm M (maidir le toiliú fianaithe an tuismitheora eile);

— deimhnithe breithe (ní leor fótachóip) na leanaí, ar a mbeidh ainmneacha na dtuismitheoirí.

The following applies whether or not the children were included on a previous passport:
Children under 16 years of age named on your passport can normally travel with you without separate passports.
To include children on the passport enclose:

— Form M (concerning witnessed consent of the other parent);

— birth certificates (not photocopies) of children showing the names of the parents.

NA LEANAÍ: CHILDREN:	Sloinne Surname	Ainmneacha Forenames	Dáta Breithe Date of Birth	Gnéas Sex	Tír Bhreithe Country of Birth
1.					
2.					
3.					
4.					
5.					

Ní fhéadfar leanaí a chur ar phas an tuismitheora ach amháin ag tráth eisiúna pas nua nó pas ionaid.

Children may be added to parent's passport only at time of issue of either a new or a replacement passport.

3

107

Seoladh baile
Home address ....

Ainm
Name

....

Seoladh

Teileafón
Telephone ....

Address

{ **Seoladh faoi láthair;** chuige seo a chuirfear an pas.
{ **Present address;** to which passport will be sent.

Teileafón sa lá (má tá sin agat.)
Daytime telephone (if any) ....

1.

2.

{ **Do ghnáth-shíniú** faoi dhó (taobh istigh de na línte) ag 1
agus 2 os a choinne seo.
{ Your **normal signature** twice (within the lines) at 1 and 2
across.

ROINN G   DEARBHÚ AN IARRATASÓRA

Le síniú í láthair an fhinné ag Roinn H thíos.

Dearbhaím go bhfuil na sonraí san iarratas seo ceart, gur
liomsa (agus le mo chuid leanaí) a bhaineann na deimhnithe atá leis, agus gur díomsa na grianghraif atá leis.

Síniú an iarratasóra
Signature of applicant ....

Mura dtig le hiarratasóir síniú, síníodh tuismitheoir/caomhnóir anseo
If applicant unable to sign, a parent/guardian should sign here ....

DECLARATION BY APPLICANT   SECTION G

To be signed in the presence of the witness at Section H below

I declare that the particulars in this application are correct,
that the accompanying certificates relate to me (and my
children) and that the accompanying photographs are of
me.

ROINN H   DEIMHNIÚ AITHEANTAIS

Síníodh duine acu seo (nach gaol) an deimhniú seo:

| Ná sínigh gan a bheith cinnte cé hé/hí an t-iarratasóir. Féadfar fiafraí díot an tusa a shínigh agus conas a d'aithin tú é/í. | **Duine den Chléir**
Dochtúir Leighis
Príomhóide
(Leas) Bhainisteoir Bainc
Dlíodóir (ag cleachtadh dlí)
Póilín
Breitheamh/Giúistís |

| Na Gardaí amháin dheimhníonn iarratais sa Stát, ar fhoirm PAS 1. |

Deimhním go bhfuil aithne agam ar an iarratasóir nó gur
chuir duine a bhfuil aithne agam air/uirthi an t-iarratasóir,
in aithne dom agus go bhfuil Roinn G sínithe aige/aici i mo
láthair. Deimhním, freisin, gur samhail dhílis den iarratasóir na grianghraif a chuir sé/sí isteach leis an iarratas
seo (agus a bhfuil m'ainm sínithe ar a gcúl agam.)

CERTIFICATE OF IDENTITY   SECTION H

One of these (who is not a relative) must sign this certificate:

| **Clergyman**
Medical Doctor
School Principal
(Assistant) Bank Manager
Practising Lawyer
Policeman
Magistrate/Judge | Do not certify unless satisfied as to the applicant's identity. You may be contacted to con-firm your signature and your basis for signing. |

| In the State, only Gardaí may certify applications, on form PAS 1. |

I certify that the applicant is personally known to me, or
he/she has been identified to me by someone personally
known to me and has signed Section G in my presence. I
also certify that the photographs (on the back of which I
have signed my name) supplied with this application are a
true likeness of the applicant.

Síniú
Signature ....

Gairm
Profession ....

Dáta
Date ....

Ainm (bloclitreacha)
Name (in block letters) ....

Seoladh Gnó
Business address ....

....

Uimhir Theileafóin sa lá (riachtanach)
Daytime Telephone number (essential) ....

Seoladh ag a bhfuil tú murab ionann
Address where you can be contacted if different ....

....

Stampa oifigiúil
(Nó nóta do
pháipéar litreach gnó)

Official Stamp
(Or a note on your
headed notepaper)

Guthán
Telephone ....

versions promulgated by the Irish government to the nearest Irish consulate or embassy within 30 days of filling them out. Ensure that your declarations and affidavits are sworn to before a Notary Public or similar local official who is personally known to you or who personally knows a third party who can identify you to the notary.

Lastly, we reprint a letter from the Irish Vice-Consul in San Francisco regarding the acquisition of Irish citizenship on the basis that either a grandparent or one of your great-grandparents was Irish born.

Once you have established your right to Irish citizenship via either Irish descent or via marriage, you can apply for a passport. Also included is the actual Irish passport application.

ISRAEL – NO INVESTMENT OR FEES!

Why is an Israeli passport so desirable? Mainly because it is the only non-EC passport that is a near equivalent to an EC passport. That is, an Israeli can visit most of Europe (not France) without a visa.

As a stepping stone to still another passport, Israel is very good since Israelis get special consideration and reduced residence periods in Spain and Germany. These countries are atoning for past injuries and forced exile inflicted upon Jews. Also, many other countries, such as the US, have in the past welcomed large quotas of immigrants from Israel. Israelis have reputations as hard working, ambitious and generally non-disruptive citizens.

Israel also gives a tax holiday from its horrendous income taxes to new immigrants for up to thirty years! There is a special tax concession for wealthy people who choose to make Israel the headquarters of their business empires.

What are the drawbacks? If you are of military age (which in Israel is 18 to 39), check carefully with the Israeli Consulate on whether you would have to serve in the Army. Israel has a good military service, one of the best in the world. If you want excellent training and combat experience, fine! But if military service is something you seek to avoid, get a written guarantee that you won't be drafted.

Israel's official government policy is to gather the scattered Jews of the world (they call it Diaspora) and give them a homeland. Herein lies your opportunity. This welcome mat and an instant passport are available, not to anyone, but to Jews and their spouses, children and grandchildren, as well as the spouses of such children and grandchildren, even if they are not Jews themselves.

What is a Jew? The Law of Return defines a Jew as anyone who was born of a Jewish mother or has been converted to Judaism and has not yet embraced another faith. Documentary certification of the circumcision ceremony (Briss) or other important Jewish ceremonies (Bar Mitzvah, marriage) or perhaps most simply, membership in a Jewish Congregation are all adequate proof of your Jewishness.

How does one convert to Judaism if not Jewish already? Well, the process seems to vary greatly from place to place. In Israel, conversion procedures are standardized by government paid rabbis. This course takes ten months, while the transformation process from gentile to Jew takes almost two years. No knowledge of Hebrew is required, as courses, interviews and tests can be given in English upon request. Outside of Israel practices and procedures run the gamut.

We have heard rumors that in the US, some liberal rabbis will perform a five minute conversion ceremony for around US $5,000.

However, you can convert just as easily and at less expense by simply walking into a local reform synagogue and joining. Again, conditions vary from place to place and synagogue to synagogue. After being a member for a respectable time, contact the local Israeli Consulate or Aliyah (Immigration Aid) group for information on Israeli immigration and citizenship. Some zealots in Israel have pressured the government to deny citizenship to ''non-orthodox'' converts, but as yet have not succeeded in their demands.

Read up on Jewish history and culture, Jewish humor books may provide a good start. If the fact that you don't appear Jewish comes up, don't worry. Explain that you were not raised Jewish and never attended a schule or yeshiva. Your desire to study Jewish culture and customs will be well received and encouraged.

If you have an obviously non-Jewish name, this is not a fatal situation. You could be the offspring of a mixed marriage. The Jewish tradition is the mother's heritage in any event.

If your mother has a non-Jewish name, you should consider adopting an obvious Jewish middle name such as Cohen, Levy or Israel. Ben-Israel (son of Israel) is utterly smashing. You can always make a vague reference to a family name adjustment due to events in the late 1930s and then proclaim a return to your heritage and true family name. You might consider legally changing your name before you go to Israel, particularly if it is something like ''Christian St. James'' or ''Mohammed D'Arabia''.

An Israeli custom is for new immigrants (and veteran Israelis who have non-Hebrew names) to choose a Hebrew name. This involves a legal change of name which is carried out by means of a simple procedure at the local office of the Ministry of Interior. Once the name is thus officially changed, it is used in all official documents, including your Israeli passport. Abe, for example, might become Avrom. If your father's name is David Jones, you may elect to become Avrom Ben-David. You are not limited to translating your old name – you may choose any new Hebrew name.

You will be required to prove your Jewishness when you apply for immigration. You will present a certificate from the Rabbi of your congregation attesting to your membership. Even if you were born and raised a Jew, you should make certain that you obtain this critical document.

One obvious, yet sometimes overlooked point. The Covenant of Abraham mandates that Jewish males be circumcised as a mark for all eternity. Nobody will purposely check, but if someone does notice that you are uncircumcised, you will lose whatever gains you have made towards an Israeli passport. **There is no such thing as an uncircumcised male Jew**.

Once your Jewishness is safely established, you may arrange to move to Israel through the Consulate or Aliyah group nearest your present home. If you cannot afford the passage, the Government of Israel may pay and arrange for you to attend the three month long ''Ulpan'' language and orientation school. If you work part-time, your classes will be free. Otherwise, you will be required to pay nominal tuition.

As an immigrant in virtue of the Law of Return, you will automatically become an Israeli citizen 90 days after having entered Israel as an immigrant, unless, during that period, you opt not to become a citizen. Once a citizen, you are entitled to apply for, and obtain, an Israeli passport. It is the practice of the Ministry of Interior, however, not to grant a passport during the first year, but only a *laissez-passer* which is valid for a year at the end of which a regular passport will be granted routinely. You should also be aware that if you receive any government loans or grants as an immigrant, your application for a passport will trigger a demand that you repay these or, at least, that you produce sufficient guarantees to assure such repayment before you will be allowed to leave the country. Israel requires a written pledge that a new citizen intends to make Israel his permanent home.

Israel permits dual citizenship. Hence you will not be obliged to surrender your present passport on being granted one by Israel. They also maintain a policy of not reporting your acquisition of citizenship to your parent country. You will not be required to take an oath of allegiance. Your allegiance and loyalty is taken for granted.

Israel does not tax its non-residents or new immigrants, the latter for a period of thirty years, on passive income earned outside of Israel and not remitted directly to Israel. Moreover, new immigrants are also entitled, for more limited periods, to certain tax benefits on income earned inside of Israel, but these are not of great significance. Israel is liberal in renewing passports abroad every five years without belaboring tax questions. However, in order to leave Israel, males of military age must obtain an exit permit which is stamped in their passport and is valid for multiple exits as long as the passport is valid. This exit permit is routinely granted, except in unusual circumstances.

If you are interested in immigrating to Israel, Scope International can refer you to a respectable firm of attorneys located in Israel and completely conversant in Israeli immigration policy. At least one member of this firm is fluent in Hebrew, English, French and German and therefore correspondence can be carried out in any of these languages. Scope International, 62 Murray Road, Horndean, Waterlooville, Hants PO8 9JL.

See also *The Tax Exile Report,* published by Scope International.

ITALY – RECLAIM YOUR ETHNICITY

Italy radically changed its immigration and passport policies in January of 1992. Now, the children of Italian nationals are automatically recognized as Italian citizens. Dual nationality has also been officially recognized and is thus no longer a problem. This change of policy is retroactive, meaning that those Italian nationals who lost Italian citizenship as a result of acquiring a different nationality are once again Italian. Likewise, their children and their grandchildren may qualify for Italian citizenship.

For those that lost Italian nationality as a result of acquiring nationality in another country, citizenship can be regained, within two years from January of 1992, by simply providing a declaration to do so. After January of 1994, one year of legal residency in Italy will be required.

The rules for the children and grandchildren of former Italian nationals are fairly complicated. You qualify if any of the following apply:
1) Your father was an Italian citizen at the time of your birth.
2) Your mother was an Italian citizen at the time of your birth, and you were born after January 1, 1948.
3) Your father was not born in Italy, and your paternal grandfather was an Italian citizen at the time of his birth.

4)   Your mother was not born in Italy, you were born after January 1, 1948, and your maternal grandfather was an Italian citizen at the time of her birth.

This program is obviously favors the paternal line of the family (strange when one considers all that one hears about the notorious Italian mother). However, if you do not qualify under these somewhat stringent stipulations, you can receive Italian nationality after only three years legal residence in Italy. See the entry on Italian residency in this section.

Citizenship can also be acquired through marriage to an Italian national (male or female). Nationality is granted after either six months residence in Italy or after three years of marriage if residency is outside of Italy.

As for individuals interested in becoming naturalized Italians (those that are not "ethnic Italians") the required residence period has now been raised to ten years, far too long in our opinion.

Another route to Italian citizenship is through the passing of a private bill in parliament. We have heard that this can be done by any politician who can be motivated to act on your behalf. Providing such motivation is said to cost around US $250,000.

The Italian passport is a good document for visa-free travel. It is now the standard maroon EC document. Italy alone in Europe requires annual validation (tax) stamps to keep its passport current during its five year life. The Italian passport is highly recommended for "ethnic Italians" and those who have an Italian *affianzata* (lover) willing to marry.

ITALIAN RESIDENCY

Tourist (non-working, residence) visas are easy to get and can be renewed indefinitely for persons who are self-supporting or can show means of support. Unemployment is very high, particularly in Southern Italy, but a foreigner who manages to get a job or job offer reportedly has little trouble getting a work permit (with the assistance of his employer). Foreigners opening a new business or investing are generally given a red carpet welcome. There are many tax-concession programs. Italians have never enforced their tax laws against resident foreigners who derive their income from sources outside Italy. Thus the whole country is a *de facto* tax haven. Once inside Italy, registering as a resident or domiciliary is a simple matter involving two visits to the local police station. Registration is renewed at three month intervals, but the local police will generally give six month and year long permits once a person is established and known in the community. There are government subsidized Italian language and culture courses at the University for Foreigners in Perugia, Siena, Rome, Milan, etc. Passable Italian can be learned at these institutions, in the company of exceptionally beautiful young females from Germany and Scandinavia, in about two to three months. Italians are exceptionally friendly to foreigners, and their emotionality and warmth is legendary. Although the power of organized crime (The Sicilian Mafia and the Neopolitan Camorra) has been well documented, the average tourist will not have any unpleasant experiences aside from pocket picking, purse-snatching and car radio thefts. Such thefts can be avoided by taking the same precautions one would take in any big city. Italy is an altogether civilized place of unparalleled man-made scenery blending with natural landscapes. It would rate among our top five places in the world to live. It is another place where it is much better to live as the holder of a foreign (non-Italian) passport. Why? Because Italian citizens resident in Italy are among the most highly taxed people in the world. Foreigners resident in Italy usually don't pay Italian taxes unless they have a visible Italian business.

JAMAICA – A NEW PROGRAM THAT'S A FLOP

We include the outline of the following program merely for historical perspective, or perhaps more importantly as a warning to countries interested in setting up a similar program. According to our information, this Jamaican scheme died for lack of a single applicant.

Hoping to attract new capital, Jamaica initiated a program to give "instant passports" to persons who had lived in any British Commonwealth country during five of the previous seven years and whose financial and moral characteristics were deemed appropriate. Special arrangements were possible for non-Commonwealth residents. Neither an oath of allegiance nor travel to Jamaica was required. Dual nationality was specifically allowed. So far so good!

The financial requirements involved:

1. The purchase of a US $100,000 zero interest Bank of Jamaica bond for US $30,000. This bond was to be repaid (one hoped) in ten years at full face value. This translated into providing a ten year loan to the government of Jamaica at approximately 13 per cent per year. The bond could probably have been sold at a discount after one obtained his passport.

2. The long-term investment of US $50,000 or the purchase of an approved real estate development project. One could look for his own deal or invest in a ten year syndicated package already approved by the government. This was handled by American entrepreneurs.

3. Fees of US $20,000 were quoted as necessary to get through the bureaucracy.

Summary: This $100,000 up-front cash scheme was overpriced by $80,000, in our opinion. Even though the country's travel documents are good for visa-free travel in most of Europe.

Jamaica's major industry is tourism. Exports have been bauxite ore (aluminium), sugar, bananas and coffee. Because of low commodity prices and a flirtation with leftist anti-American policies, conditions deteriorated after independence from Great Britain. These policies have been reversed. Now foreign investors are being actively courted.

This program may or may not resurface in the future, hopefully with a lower up-front cash requirement. However, be warned about the misleading impression created by glossy brochures. This poor, overpopulated island is no paradise!

JAPAN - EQUALITY BUT A FIVE-YEAR WAIT

Equality of treatment for women arrived in Japan in 1984 with the introduction of a new Nationality Law which allowed the children of a Japanese mother and foreign father to become naturalized Japanese. Previously in mixed marriages, only children of a Japanese father and foreign mother became Japanese at birth. This led to some stateless children, particularly in Okinawa where US Servicemen had children by Japanese women and then abandoned them, preventing them from obtaining American citizenship.

Under the new law, children with dual nationality must choose by the age of 22 which citizenship they wish to take, either Japanese or foreign. Children born of Japanese mothers before the law was introduced who are still under 20 qualify as well. Contact the Regional Legal Affairs Bureaux and District Legal Affairs Bureaux in Japan, or overseas Japanese embassy and consulate, for application forms. When filled in these forms are all that is needed to acquire Japanese nationality if one's mother is still a Japanese national.

Foreigners who want to become Japanese must apply to the Minister of Justice and receive his approval. Five years' residence and good behavior are among the requirements for applicants. It is advisable to consult a Legal Affairs Bureau. Foreign husbands and wives of Japanese nationals now are treated equally under the law. Three years' residence in Japan is required before nationality can be taken. Where couples have been married continuously for three years, the requirement is reduced to one year. Another anti-sex discrimination move has been the definition of a livelihood requirement before naturalization. The ''ability to maintain an independent livelihood'' now applies to the family unit, not just one individual member.

Japan will grant nationality to someone who is unable to renounce his original citizenship because the laws of their natural country forbid such renunciation, but only if there are special reasons arising from kinship with a Japanese national (such as spouse or parent) or due to special circumstances, such as refugee status. A child made stateless in Japan because both its parents are unknown or stateless can become naturalized if he or she has lived continuously for three or more years in Japan.

Since November 1991, resident Koreans and Taiwanese and their descendants became exempt from immigration control laws concerning deportation and re-entry. Other nationalities are not so favored.

LEBANON – A PASSPORT FOR DISPLACED ARABS
The *Wall Street Journal* reported in July 1986, that the Palestine Liberation Organization had made a large financial contribution to Lebanon in return for the right to obtain Lebanese passports for all members of the PLO.

For Palestinians who don't know of the current arrangements, your nearest PLO Legation should be able to assist in gaining a Lebanese passport. With all such deals being fluid and temporary, applying while they are available would seem appropriate.

Other prospective Lebanese should contact the nearest Lebanon Consulate, or work with an attorney in Beirut. The passport is definitely available. However, there is a major cost – you will be treated as a potential terrorist and given the third degree by some border officials, particularly in the US and at any major European airport where you are attempting to board a flight. If you don't mind extra attention and have nothing to hide in your luggage or your past, Lebanon (quoted price US $16,000) may be your cup of tea.

LITHUANIA – NEW COUNTRY, NEW PASSPORT
In 1992, Lithuania achieved its independence. It is located slightly north of Poland which it borders along with the newly formed Belorussia, Kaliningrad and Latvia. As a government in exile, the pre-Russian administration had been quietly issuing passports from both Vatican City and Washington DC for over fifty years. It seems that any person who was willing to donate US $25 and had some sort of Lithuanian connection qualified for such a passport. Indeed, this passport was accepted by most countries in the free world, but, of course, not by former communist states.

Now that independence has been achieved. The new government is issuing its own passport. These passports were printed up by a Norwegian bank and are actually quite impressive for this one year old country. (Apparently, the former passports issued by the government in exile can be exchanged for this new passport.)

These new passports were issued to every resident of Lithuania. In fact, they double as national identification and are therefore mandatory. Citizenship can also be granted to former Lithuanian nationals and to individuals of "Lithuanian origin". The categories include:

1) Persons who had citizenship of the Republic of Lithuania until 15 June 1940 and are at the present time residing in other states.

2) Children of persons who had citizenship of the Republic of Lithuania until 15 June 1940 who were born in Lithuania or refugee camps, but are at the present time residing in other states.

3) Other persons of Lithuanian origin who are residing in foreign states or on the territories governed by said states.

Who exactly is a person if "Lithuanian origin"? Basically, the rules are not spelled out in black and white, and the outcome of one's eligibility ultimately rests at the discretion of an Honorary Consul. Personal representation and sensitivity cannot be overemphasized. One naturally should be a strong supporter of Lithuania's struggle for freedom. Influential friends at the local Lithuanian community can be of great help, especially if you do not speak Lithuanian or your name does not sound Lithuanian. Most Lithuanian Honorary Consulates are not very prosperous and a few do accept donations from members of the Lithuanian community and general benefactors.

If you qualify as a person of "Lithuanian origin" you can receive a "Certificate of Lithuanian Citizenship" *("Piliecio Pazymejimas")* which is a plain green card with photo. It basically says that your are a citizen of Lithuania, nothing more, nothing less. To receive a passport, you must take this card to Vilnius, the old capital of Lithuania, where your application will be handled by a special passport division for foreign residents. Of course, this should be done as soon as possible, as there is nothing less permanent than East European laws.

People of definitely non-Lithuanian origin may also be eligible for Lithuanian citizenship. Anyone who has been "of Merit to the State of Lithuania" qualifies through a special arrangement. Who exactly they mean is at the discretion of a small group of Lithuanian MPs. At present, the full potential of this sort of arrangement has yet to be realized, but we're working on it.

One can also achieve nationality through naturalization, which requires a residence period of ten years (definitely for the strong in spirit), and through marriage to a Lithuanian national, which requires a more reasonable residence period of three years.

We have also heard rumors that quasi-legal passports can be obtained from corrupt officials at the Passport Office. No back files exist for these passports, but they may be registered on the computer. Such passports are, of course, only of limited value. Scope International strongly advises against the use of such documents, as it is obviously illegal. We only mention them here to inform readers of fraudulent documents so that they will not be cheated by unlawful operators.

Technically, one is required to renounce all other citizenship before acquiring Lithuanian nationality, but this requirement is almost never enforced. An oath of allegiance is, however, required.

As a new country, Lithuania has few agreements for visa-free travel. In September 1992, the list included only two EC countries, the UK and Denmark. Most East European countries and former Soviet States along with Singapore, Malaysia and South Korea also do not require visas. As a former communist country, Lithuania also does not enjoy a great deal of international prestige. However, most Western countries do not fear a flood of illegal immigrants from Lithuania due to its small population of 3.7 million.

A passport must be renewed when its holder reaches the ages of 25 and 45, meaning that if the timing is right, it will be valid for twenty years. Passports do still require an exit stamp, but these can be obtained on a routine basis, free of charge, and are valid for five years. However, foreign immigration officials are rarely concerned with an exit stamp, making one absolutely necessary only if the you're interested in living in Lithuania.

Although this passport has its obvious limitations, it may become quite valuable in the future. If nothing else, it will provide an excellent insurance policy. Therefore, if you qualify and can easily receive a passport today, apply today. The rules, especially those of Eastern Europe, change constantly, and what's here today will probably be gone tomorrow.

MARSHALL ISLAND – ANOTHER FLOP

The Marshall Islands hoped to make a bundle when it began selling its citizenship to foreigners early in 1989 at $200,000 a shot.

There were no takers – so the Pacific island nation slashed the price in half and held a bargain sale. There were inquiries from Hong Kong, Taiwan, Canada and Japan, but there are still no customers in sight.

The Marshall Islands had hoped that it could offer foreigners who bought passports the same unrestricted entry to the United States that islanders enjoyed. It did not work out that way. When the Marshall Islands approved legislation to sell the passports, Washington said naturalized Marshall Island citizens seeking to enter the United States would first have to estabish five-year residency in the Pacific nation and prove they had not bought the passports just to get to the US.

MAURITIUS – INDIAN OCEAN PEARL OF THE COMMONWEALTH
FOR US $50,000

Mauritius is the Hawaii of the British Empire. It is an exceptionally beautiful independent island republic between Africa and India. The population is mixed Asian, Indian and white. There are virtually no Americans in a total population of over 1 million. The island is a member of the Commonwealth and is very prosperous. Like Hawaii it is a favorite tourist destination for European sun and sea lovers. Because it was a French colony before becoming British, both French and English are official languages. The government is relatively sane and easy to deal with, especially when one is engaged in projects to encourage commerce and tourism.

Passport arrangements are straightforward and completely legal. Investors or potential employers who establish a business can get an immediate passport. Of course "immediate" means "allow at least six months for processing". The required passive investment is about US $50,000 minimum. Allow about US $25,000 more for legal expenses and one required visit. There is no extra charge for spouse and dependent passports. The government is said to be anxious to consider any business proposals, and a good lawyer in Mauritius will know how to prepare a business proposal that stands a reasonable chance of gaining you an investor-entrepreneur passport.

Mauritius is a nuclear-free, fairy-tale tropical island in the middle of the Pacific Ocean. It offers a good environment for business in general and a ten year tax holiday for new businesses. After ten years a 15 per cent corporate profits tax will apply. Numerous restaurants, entertainment and medical care of high standard are available and there is plenty to do in one's leisure time. The Mauritian passport is an excellent travel document with visa free travel to most of Europe. A total of sixty good countries worldwide do not require visas of Mauritians.

The disadvantage is the relatively high cost of about US $75,000. Since US $50,000 is for a minimum **investment** (with a wide range of possibilities), those who have the cash and want to diversify might find Mauritius an attractive option. Communication is very good with an excellent phone system. There are daily flights to Europe and South Africa. Mauritius is a little-known island outside of the Commonwealth, but we would rate it among our top ten choices for passport/investment/place to spend time.

You can contact the nearest Embassy of Mauritius, the Minister of Foreign Affairs, Port Lewis, Mauritius for the latest news, if Mauritius appeals to you.

When contacting a Mauritian ambassador, or any governmental agency for that matter, don't ask for the procedures involved in **buying** a passport. The proper way to ask is first to express interest in making investments and then, "by the way, what about citizenship".

No country will officially admit to "selling passports" since they all support the fiction that citizenship must be earned and *can never be purchased.*

MOROCCO – INSTANT AND CHEAP, BUT NOT DEFINITE
Morocco is mentioned only because it is one of the few "moderates" of the Arab world. Holders of other Arab or Muslim passports tend to be regarded as terrorists. Morocco has not yet been accused of being a militant country or a nation of fanatics.

This North African country lies directly across the Mediterranean from Spain and Gibraltar. It is a constitutional monarchy. Morocco has succeeded in remaining at a distance from most of the turmoil and strife so common throughout the remainder of the Arab world.

There are many ferry boats to Morocco running back and forth from Gibraltar and also from Spain. Morocco's hills can be seen from southern Spain, across from the Straits of Gibraltar, where the Mediterranean sea meets the Atlantic Ocean.

There are many exceptional resorts and hotels in Morocco, including a popular Club Med. The resort area on the coast is a favorite destination, especially for the French since it was once a French colony. French is the second language, Arabic is first. Vacationers enjoy five star restaurants, exceptional beaches and entertainment second to none. Professional locals you will encounter are likely to be cosmopolitan, charming and fluent in Arabic, English, Spanish and French.

The city of Casablanca was, until the mid-1950s, a tax haven and playground for wealthy Europeans. In an outburst of "Africa for the Africans" fervor, legislation removed Casablanca from the jet-set itinerary. The once exclusive European expatriate quarter soon fell into disrepair and squalor. Vestiges of hostility towards wealthy Europeans persist, although government policy now is to encourage tourism.

Morocco is hot, dry, dusty and poor (outside of tourist areas). It is not a place most people would choose to live permanently.

Official information regarding Moroccan passports is difficult to obtain. However, we are reliably informed that several lawyers in Casablanca will exercise "Levantine flexibility" and can obtain genuine passports for US $3,000.

Morocco thrives on fraud and bribery at every level. Therefore, be warned – pay for nothing in advance or expect to be swindled!

Contact with professionals and government officials in Morocco should be conducted while acting humble and polite. Avoid displays of wealth, jewelry and expensive clothing. Be prepared to drink endless cups of sweet tea while patiently pursuing your objectives. Patience and subtle behavior will be the important ingredient in your successful pursuit of Moroccan nationality. The author at this time (1993) has **no** personal connections nor contacts for passports in Morocco or the Arab world. We welcome any offers from governments or lawyers in a position to assist our many Arab readers.

NEW ZEALAND – AN UNUSUAL OPPORTUNITY

This country has so many positive attributes that it should be a finalist on anybody's list for a second passport. It would also make a good part-time residence. Its passport is one of the best in the world. Politically, New Zealand is neutral and enjoys normal diplomatic relations worldwide. As a result, travelers bearing its passports are welcome, usually without visas, throughout the world.

New Zealand's controlled and regulated economy proved to be restrictive to many entrepreneurs. However, excessively high tax rates have since been reduced, and libertarian ideas implemented to create a better environment for capitalists and entrepreneurs. There are substantial inducements to encourage maintaining a part-time residence. They have to do with the natural beauty and the healthy, safe and sane lifestyles to be enjoyed there.

New Zealand is an island the size of Great Britain lying southeast across the Tasman Sea from Australia. It is a very different country from that mini-continent, with its own very distinctive accents and customs. New Zealand enjoys a year-round growing season and is about as far south from the Equator as San Francisco is to the north. Rainfall is regular. The climate ranges from mild in summer to somewhat cold in winter.

Locals call their country "En-Zed", which is the way an Englishman would pronounce the letters "N" and "Z".

The scenery is amazing, including fine beaches, fjords, mountains, waterfalls, glaciers, volcanos, hundreds of fresh water lakes, geysers and thermal pools. In the two islands comprising NZ, one can enjoy a sampling of the world's most spectacular natural settings, from endless seashores to Alpine mountain ranges that will make you think you are in Switzerland.

As in Ireland, there are no snakes or dangerous animals. Fishing is the best in the world, and the locals have more boats per capita than in any other nation.

Population is about 3 million, principally of UK descent. Fifty-five million sheep and ten million head of cattle both outnumber humans. Gold and jade from local mines/quarries are exported, but the economy is principally agriculture-based. Wool, mutton, dairy products and beef are exported in great quantities. International trade considerations have led to a quest for new exports. The kiwi fruit is a relatively new and increasingly successful cash crop. Aluminium ingots made with Australian ore are refined and processed locally, then exported.

Geothermal and hydro-electric power is plentiful and very inexpensive. Large natural gas deposits are being developed into sources of synthetic gasoline. The tiny population grows enough food to feed itself twenty times over, and unique weather permits year round crop growing.

There are five television stations, each delivering a steady diet of second hand soap operas and American movies. Auckland, Dunedin and Wellington (the capital) as well as a number of smaller cities have both live theatre productions and music. Quite a few of the world class acts visit NZ via Europe from time to time. As a general rule, although NZ is not a wellspring of culture, there is plenty to occupy even the most easily bored of minds, if you know where to go or the right people.

New Zealand, for all its splendor and resources, has not been prosperous. In fact, after years of having the highest tax rates in the world, economic conditions bordered near governmental bankruptcy. The central core of this society aimed to abolish the class distinctions from which their ancestors fled in England a generation ago. By and large, they were successful in creating a Utopia, but overspending on a welfare state plus low commodity prices brought on the fiscal crisis. No one starved, but inflation, unemployment and large scale *emigration* were common.

As a result, major changes were implemented. Not the least of which was the Employment Contracts Act which effectively did away with unions. People now work on performance based contracts, thus creating a land of small businessmen and self employed individuals. Large scale emigration has been brought to a halt, inflation has been reduced to less than one per cent (the lowest of all OECD countries), and property prices have been rendered static.

Major efforts were also expended to attract new foreign investments, entrepreneurs and talent. As a first step, confiscatory income taxes were reduced, making them lower than any European country and roughly equal to those in the US. These were followed by a dramatic turnaround in immigration laws. This country, which once strictly limited immigration, is now one of the easiest countries to immigrate to. In fact, NZ even goes to the trouble of printing up elaborate full color "advertising" material to entice you to come and stay for a while.

The new program involved the introduction of a point system, much like that used by Canada. Applications can be submitted under one of four categories, general, family, humanitarian and business investment.

GENERAL CATEGORY
This category seems to have been established with the aim of luring young hopefuls to NZ. Applicants are awarded points based on a number of criteria, including employability (education, work experience), age (those aged 25-29 score highest) and settlement factors (assets, sponsorship by NZ family member or community organization, offer of skilled employment). Applicants must also have at least a basic knowledge of the English language.

This program is obviously designed with the young in mind. Anyone over 55 is not eligible, but there are circumstances under which this requirement may be lifted. Each applicant is scaled and then either accepted, declined or assigned to a pool, a process that currently takes six to eight weeks (rather impressive compared with the one year wait Canada now imposes). As for the applications not accepted but relegated to the pool, those with the highest scores will be drawn periodically and approved. If an application does not succeed in either of two draws, it will be declined.

FAMILY CATEGORY

This category is broken into two sub-sections, family reunion and partnership. The family reunion section extends to parents, children, brothers and sisters. For each sort of applicant there are many qualifying criteria. A partnership with a New Zealand citizen or resident is recognized and includes a legally married husband or wife, or a *de facto* or homosexual partner. For a partner to be admitted, you must prove that the relationship is genuine and stable and of at least two years duration if heterosexual, four years if homosexual.

HUMANITARIAN CATEGORY

To qualify under this category you must have a sponsor or close family member in NZ willing and able to support your application, be able to provide evidence of who or what is causing the physical or emotional harm and be able to provide evidence of why you think the granting of residence in NZ will resolve the situation.

BUSINESS INVESTMENT

New Zealand is a land of innovative people and projects, but the lack of existing capital does much to hinder progress. As a result, NZ is anxious to attract investors and entrepreneurs to develop this enormous potential.

This category is a little more tricky than just plonking down a wad of cash and walking away with a passport, or at least residency. An applicant must demonstrate that the investment funds have been lawfully earned and are the direct result of his or her own business or professional skills and experience (or are consistent with income and earnings) over a period of at least three years. Applicants must also prove what is termed skill (basically a minimum of education or business/work experience) and at least a basic knowledge of the English language.

There are three investment options:
1) A minimum of NZ$750,000 (US $407,000) into a "passive" investment, such as bank accounts, trust funds or listed stocks.
2) A minimum of NZ$625,000 (US $340,000) in a commercial venture in either the Auckland or Wellington urban areas.
3) A minimum of NZ$500,000 (US $270,000) in a commercial venture outside of the Auckland or Wellington urban areas.

All investments must be maintained for a period of at least two years, but if an original business plan does not work out, one can switch to any other legal economic activity.

For a free objective book on investing in NZ, write: Westpac Bank, Business Advisory Service, PO Box 691, Wellington, New Zealand.

Under each of the resident categories, applicants must also submit a police and health certificate (including a chest x-ray). Most applicants will also be interviewed. Suspected terrorists and those known to have criminal associations need not apply. However, this does not seem to extend to tax-evaders, except those who have also been unfortunate enough to have been resident in the pokey for either five years, or one year of the past ten years.

After three years of residence, one is eligible for citizenship and a passport. Foreign travel during these three years is unrestricted. Obviously, a genuine home should be rented or purchased, and some time should be spent there. Usual evidence of legal residence should be accumulated, including a drivers license and church or club memberships. Business contacts, hired attorneys and accountants will provide extra evidence of bona fide residence.

If you are interested in NZ, contact its nearest consulate or embassy for a big information pack.

WEDDING BELLS ARE RINGING

Instant citizenship can be obtained by marriage to a New Zealander. Processing normally takes about six months, and the new spouse must show "an association with New Zealand in addition to the marriage". Practically, this means having a home, business or job in New Zealand when applying for a passport.

Marriages are not hard to arrange. There is a shortage of eligible men. Many local boys have emigrated for better opportunities and lower taxes abroad. It is also common to see exceptionally beautiful young Asian wives with grandfatherly New Zealand husbands. There are loads of classified ads seeking wives and husbands, particularly in the Saturday Auckland Herald. Everyone reads them.

NEW ZEALAND TAXATION

To legally avoid taxes, steps must be taken before immigration. Worldwide assets can be placed in offshore trusts or corporations, however, it is advisable to do so several years in advance as a relatively new section of NZ tax law makes any arrangement entered into to avoid taxes illegal. There are also tough new laws on shareholdings in foreign companies or financial entities. One is now taxed on income derived from such shareholdings.

Owning a home in NZ can also make you liable for taxation on your worldwide income, regardless of whether you actually live in NZ or not. In order to not be taxed, you must rent out your house while not using it, so that it is not immediately available, and not stay in NZ for more than 6 months a year. (All the gritty details of this policy are explained in IRD Public Information Bulletin 180.)

The good news about NZ taxes is that there are no capital gains taxes and estate duties have been done away with.

PANAMA – IF YOU HAVE AN OFFSHORE INCOME OF $1000/MONTH, IT'S YOURS

In spite of the US invasion, immigration policies are still very favorable for the wealthy or even the moderately rich. Anyone who has a job offer from an international corporation in an executive capacity, or who will invest US $35,000 in Panama or who comes to Panama with a proven income of over US $1,000 per month from outside sources, is welcome as a resident.

Law no. 9 from the 24th June 1987 has been approved by the Panamanian Legislative Assembly, whereby a foreigner may obtain the status of pensioner in the country, if he can prove a steady and guaranteed income of at least US $1,000 a month.

For this purpose, the sum of approximately US $120,000 is deposited with the National Bank of Panama (which pays a very high monthly interest in the form of a fixed 5 year C.D. The immigration authorities will then issue immediate permanent residency and an alien passport. Time frame here is anywhere between 30 and 90 days. It is preferable if the applicant can travel personally to Panama. Agents fees range from US $20,000 to US $30,000 depending on urgency and client background. A five year residence is generally required, but this can be shortened to about five weeks for meritorious contributions to worthy causes.

Land and property ownership by a foreigner is encouraged in the desirable resort areas, but is restricted to within 10 miles of most borders. Although some real estate promoters will tell you otherwise, property *ownership* is *not* required and does not score extra points towards citizenship and a passport.

Besides granting ordinary passports, Panama is also known to be liberal in appointing Honorary Consuls. For those interested in the social life and partial diplomatic immunity provided outside of Panama by such an appointment, further inquiry is warranted. Your nearest Panamanian Consul is the best place to start. Alternatively we can refer you to an agent who can help you get a diplomatic appointment if you don't want to campaign for the job on your own and get it free.

The national language is Spanish, but all business people speak English. Society is multi-racial with substantial groups of Asians, Indians, Africans and Europeans to be found.

WARNING ON INSTANT PASSPORTS

Deposed dictator Manuel Antonio Noriega turned Panama's immigration service into a corrupt cash machine that made tens of millions of dollars each year peddling visas and passports, states the agency's new civilian chief.

Documents recovered from the militarized service reveal a vast network of sales deals and while-you-wait processing that brought a flood of refugees to Pawnama's shores along with the badly needed cash.

By the tens of thousands, Cubans desperate to leave their island and Chinese anxious over recent repression paid high prices for the chance to move here: US $2,500 for entry visas and US $12,000 for Panamanian passports.

Eight former agency officials were prosecuted for immigration abuses.

Over the five years before the US invasion, at least 30,756 Cubans, 11,687 Chinese and 2,585 Libyans have moved to Panama. In the last year alone, 11,931 Cubans and 8,850 Chinese entered the country.

The exposure of the files after the US invasion may be the only time that figures on the size of the passport market have been accurately revealed by any government. But the legitimacy of all these passports and visas in Panama is now open to question, and it would not be impossible for a purchaser to become charged with a crime in relation to the purchase, although simple revocation of the documents is more likely.

The affair highlights the importance of either being part of an officially sponsored citizenship program legislated into existence or paying officials to expedite an application within an existing legal framework – such as waiving a residence requirement – when a statute provides that a residence requirement can be waived. Documents purchased "over-the-counter" without legal backing in the country of issue can be worthless upon the next change of government. There are many legitimate loopholes in citizenship laws that can be exploited by the properly connected agent.

PANAMA IS UNLIKE ALL OTHER CENTRAL AND SOUTH AMERICAN COUNTRIES FOR ONE MAJOR REASON – THE PANAMA CANAL

The US considers the Canal vital to its strategic interests. Even after the Canal reverts to Panama at the end of this century, US efforts to prevent Panama from becoming another (communist controlled) Cuba are likely.

Thus Panama is an unwilling US protectorate. Its leaders are bullied, or more often co-opted into following US policies on matters of strategic importance. In return, individual Panamanians are permitted to feather their own financial nests. Panama is to the US a client state with a love-hate relationship with its master.

Panamanian politicians must verbalize anti-American sentiments in order to stay in office, but Uncle Sam provides too many economic benefits along with a clear threat of military intervention to be seriously challenged on vested matters. Although the US invaded and kidnapped leading lights of the Noriega regime and then claimed to leave the country to be governed by its own elected politicians, the two countries affairs remain inextricably entangled.

Panama, along with Hong Kong, is probably the most unregulated commercial center of the world. There are more than 100 international banks here, and before the Noriega affair the volume of transactions was said to rival London or New York. The latest electronic office toys are available at tax-free discount prices. Favorable incorporation laws and a lack of taxes make Panama the headquarters for many major international corporations. There are no currency controls and US dollars are used as the medium of exchange.

The climate is hot, humid and tropical, but air conditioned first class hotels, homes and white limousines make it bearable. Life is pleasant for the many rich expatriates who live here, usually to avoid their own laws and taxes.

Panama received a lot of bad press in 1989 and 1991, but it is still a superb place to make money. Communications by air (40 airlines), telephone, mail and telex are first rate. Local laws and customs encourage free trade. There are minimal import or export duties if the Colon Free Trade Zone is used. Most taxes in Panama are nominal. Ship registration is cheap and lacks rigor. As a result, the growing Panamanian Merchant Marine (registered cargo ships) is now second only to Liberia's. Liberia's lead is due to its much earlier entry in the tax haven ship registry game. Every bank in the world has a branch or representative office in Panama City, as do most international law firms and major public accountants.

In summary, although there are currently big problems relating to excessive corruption and political instability, we would rate Panama very high for:
1.   Ease of obtaining a second passport or diplomatic appointment as an Honorary Consul General.

2. Visa free travel to most countries.
3. Use of passport by a person of any race who can speak Spanish or English.
4. Political stability as pro-business, banking and tax haven operations are concerned.

One serious drawback is that any Panamanian traveling to or from the US will be searched in the US and treated as a suspected drug dealer, "money launderer" or currency smuggler. Harrassment and delays at border checkpoints are to be expected worldwide.

PARAGUAY – PROTECTION AND NO INCOME TAX

Paraguay is very much an underrated country. Its government was a one man show, run until recently by an elderly individual, Alberto Stroessner, who was half German and half Guarni Indian. Stroessner maintained close friendships with Franco of Spain, Peron of Argentina and Mussolini of Italy during their lifetimes. His administration tended to reflect the same political attitudes. To call a spade a spade, Paraguay is a fascist police state, but for those who like stability, "law and order", and knowing exactly where they stand, a police state is not so bad.

The government is extremely stable. The same Colorado party runs the show even after the enforced retirement of General Stroessner. Contrary to what an outsider might expect, it enjoys popular acceptance. The strength of this government is derived from genuine popularity with an overwhelming majority of the residents who are more prosperous than their neighbors in the rest of South America. The current dictator is General Andres Rodriguez.

Government revenues are derived principally from tariffs and the sale of hydroelectric power to neighboring countries. There is little tax burden for the citizens to shoulder, but for young men a period of military service is compulsory.

As a consequence of longstanding feuds and wars which ended in 1938, Bolivia took control of the prime portion of the Chaco region, leaving Paraguay with an absolutely barren desert area which is now called the Chaco. Approximately two-thirds of the Paraguayan population emigrated to Bolivia and Chile after the 1938 loss of the river bottom lands. The climate and temperature is much like that of Arizonain the US but with the seasons reversed. It has hot, dry and comfortable weather from April to November, becoming hotter and nearly unbearable during the summers – which occur during Northern Hemisphere winters.

There is no personal income tax in Paraguay. Yet it is not particularly known as a tax haven, principally because of its geographic remoteness. Paraguay is landlocked between Argentina, Brazil and Bolivia. It does have an international airport with daily flights to Europe.

Paraguay welcomes immigrants and provides them with free land. It has allowed autonomous self government for many groups seeking refuge from religious or other persecutions. For example, a large group of German speaking religious fundamentalists have established an autonomous state in the Chaco. These Mennonites are similar to the Amish and the pacifist Quakers of Pennsylvania in the US. They originated in Germany, spent a generation in Canada, returned briefly to Europe and then moved to Belize and Paraguay. There are also autonomous colonies of Koreans, Japanese and Germans. A sophisticated cosmopolitan group is found in Asuncion. Paraguay has always been a place for the persecuted to find refuge. Asuncion however is no Buenos Aires or Rio. It is a relatively small provincial backwater where few international newspapers and magazines of current date can be found.

Deposed South American dictators almost always fled to Paraguay for sanctuary until the emergence of Miami in the 1970s as the Spanish-speaking exile capital. Anastasio Somoza of

Nicaragua was one of the last Latin American dictators to flee to Paraguay. He was subsequently assassinated there in a rare incident of political retribution.

There are a few Hitler-era German Nazis still living in Paraguay, along with other ageing folks with blood on their hands. They remain out of sight, avoid trouble and eschew local politics. The government opposes any discrimination against racial or religious groups.

Paraguay's relatively small Jewish population, for instance, has equal legal rights and is subject to less discrimination than in Argentina. Absolute freedom of religion is a favorable reflection upon Stroessner and his Colorado party. The regime is quite popular for its laissez faire, free trade policies which have kept Paraguay neutral and prosperous. It is one of the few countries in South America where the native Indian population is not exploited by a white ruling class. They are at the bottom of the economic strata, but this is more because of their non-materialistic instincts rather than laws or discrimination practices. The government actually promotes Guarni culture and language in all schools. The population is 95 per cent mixed race (native Indian and European) or *Mestizo*.

Requirements for Paraguayan residence permits center about your ability to purchase a home and support yourself and family. Decent housing can be obtained for as little as US $30,000. Residence of three years qualifies one for a passport. However, this requirement may be waived by the local Judge provided you can motivate him to do so. In such instances, passports have been obtained in about ninety days. Legal fees and gratuities are cheap in Paraguay.

Paraguay prides itself upon its relative independence from foreign powers. Extradition demands are commonly ignored if they involve a resident who has managed to carry favor with Paraguay's "establishment". Paraguay does not recognize tax or currency crimes, nor does it frown upon civilian henchmen and military personnel who "did their duty" under a deposed dictator. Thus, financial, tax and political criminals in the eyes of their homelands often find refuge in Paraguay. The only unwelcome categories appear to be communists and what the government calls "leftist agitators".

The smuggling of cigarettes, liquor and appliances between other South American countries appears to be a major industry. The prevailing attitude towards immigrants is that as long as they stay out of local politics, they are quite welcome to do anything else. Along with Uruguay and Ecuador, Paraguay is the only other country in South America with no currency controls.

The standard, maroon colored Paraguayan passport is good for only two years and must be renewed in Paraguay personally, not at a Consulate. Young males are theoretically liable for military service, if born in Paraguay. There is also a special green cover passport only issued to naturalized Paraguayans, i.e. foreigners. The expiration date on this passport is determined in negotiations with the chief of police. We understand that five or ten year periods are possible. This passport costs $35,000 or $40,000 for a family.

Paraguayan passports are also available easily and quickly by mail without a visit for US $35,000, in an average time of four to eight weeks. Diplomatic passports cost US $60,000, and the bearer is appointed either attaché to one of the country's foreign embassies through the Ministry of Foreign Affairs or as an extraordinary presidential advisor ad-honorem through the presidency for a period of two years. The passports, which grant diplomatic immunity and full diplomatic privileges worldwide, are renewable.

An honorary consulate costs US $60,000 but this also includes a diplomatic pass as attaché, an appointment deed as attaché and CD car license plate and international driver's license for diplomats. Documents needed by applicants include a bank reference, police clearance, residence permit from your home country and birth and marriage certificates. For US $15,000, a standard Paraguayan passport is available, including citizenship and has the advantage of offering "visa-free" travel to Canada, Germany, the Netherlands, Belgium, Luxembourg and most of western Europe. Please request a referral to an agent. Processing time is 45 to 60 days.

Paraguay is the country that almost "invented" the instant passport scheme as a source for foreign income. Many passports have been sold illegally over the years and the country has gained a reputation for "selling" passports on a large scale (which of course is the truth). Border officials tend to look very closely at Europeans that do not speak any Spanish travelling with a Paraguay passport. It is an open secret that criminals will obtain Paraguayan passports to flee their country, which has happened and is happening all too often.

THE PHILIPPINES

As of now, the Republic of the Philippines (RP) has no investor programs leading to instant passports. Citizenship can be obtained only by birth in the Philippines, by having a Filipino parent or by physically and legally living in the Philippines for the required residence period of five years. The Philippine passport has many serious disadvantages and only one advantage that we have been able to discover. Yet these facts do not seem to stop a number of promoters from selling valid, government issued instant passports to all comers at prices from $5,000 to whatever the traffic will bear. These passports are issued on the basis of sworn statements attesting to the Philippine parentage or birthplace of the applicant. The "facts" stated give rise to the legal right to a passport. These documents have been particularly popular with Chinese who wish to settle in the Philippines. Unfortunately for these new Filipinos, when they achieve a degree of wealth or political influence, someone in the police always seems to investigate their background. Blackmail is the name of the game. A person whose citizenship was based upon fraudulent affidavits who does not yield to extortion can be and sometimes is deported. The threat of deportation is used to extract protection payments. Thus while this passport may be suitable for getting out of a tight spot, for long-term usage we do not recommend them – with one exception, as the back door to Spain and the EC. For a person of "Spanish blood" (i.e. White race, Spanish surname, speaking Spanish) the Filipino passport provides a back door to Spain and the Common Market. A Filipino moving to Spain can acquire a Spanish passport in an abbreviated period. See section on Spain.

In Europe it is unlikely that anyone would ever bother to investigate records back in Manila.

DISADVANTAGES OF AN RP PASSPORT
1. The RP does not allow dual nationality (except with Spain). It obliges its citizens to take an oath of allegiance renouncing all other citizenships. But Spain allows dual citizenship with RP.

2. The RP taxes worldwide income of its citizens even if they do not reside in the RP. It is the only country in the world following US practices in this regard. As a practical matter it means that when renewing a passport (5 year validity) at a Consulate, Filipinos will have to make a negotiated cash settlement with the Consul. In practice, this amounts to about $2,500 unless one is visibly wealthy and able to bear a higher exaction.

3. As a member of an economically depressed country and exporter of "cheap labor", the Filipino citizen needs a visa to go almost everywhere and is always suspected of wanting to illegally immigrate. Thus, visas are hard to get except for executives of companies or those able to prove they have very substantial assets. The only places a Filipino can go without a visa are Brazil, Hong Kong, Thailand and a few "Fourth World" places. Even Switzerland and Spain recently imposed visa requirements.

4. Filipino young women and men (who are certainly among the most physically attractive people in the world) have a reputation with police all over the world for seeking tourist visas and then engaging in prostitution or working illegally at the destination. As a result, many legitimate entertainers, singers and musicians who fit the "young and beautiful" profile are given the third degree and subjected to a thorough search for drugs and pornography at borders, even when all their papers are in order. An "onward ticket" and adequate funds for the visa period are usually requested by border officials.

Since Filipinos are suspected of being into some sort of smuggling or illicit activity, the passport is not particularly attractive to someone who wants to avoid close government scrutiny. These comments are not made to denigrate the Philippines – potentially a great country, with intelligent, hard working, basically honest people. Unfortunately, a corrupt and exploitive regime has made economic survival there a matter of grabbing what you can, when you can. Petty crime is a major annoyance with burglary, purse snatching and hold-ups all very common in tourist areas.

ADVANTAGE OF AN RP PASSPORT

1. The RP actually is a beautiful country and a good place to live particularly for one who has an income from abroad. Taxes are very high, but, as in Italy, few people pay them.

2. The climate is tropical but high altitude regions like Bagio City offer "Paris in Springtime" temperatures all year round.

3. The RP is an excellent place for a single man or woman to find passionate lovers of either sex.

4. The common language is English. The other languages include Tagalog, Visaya and Ilocano. Five per cent of the population are Arabic speaking Muslims. Catholicism is the predominant religion.

Of course one may live in the Philippines without being a citizen. *But in order to work, own 100 per cent of a business or even to own any real estate, one must be a citizen.* While these rules are often circumvented by using friends as nominee partners, many nominal owners have been known to assert their "ownership" and oust the foreigner from his comfortable home or business.

SUMMARY

The RP passport can be obtained cheaply by visiting lawyers in any major city of the RP and possibly from Consular employees abroad. While issued by the government, these passports are issued either without back-up papers or on the basis of a fraudulent rebirth. If any serious investigation is ever made, the questionable basis of these documents may be discovered. In the RP itself, blackmail would be a considerable risk for residents and property owners. They could be classed as illegal immigrants, subject to imprisonment and deportation. For travelling, the RP passport is relatively undesirable because most countries do not welcome Filipinos without visas.

RECOMMENDATION

Better than nothing! Easy availability, cheap. Free with five year residence. Low utility value. Good backdoor to Spain.

PORTUGAL – EASY ENTRY TO THE COMMON MARKET

Portugal lies at the south western tip of the European continent on the west coast of the Iberian peninsula. Its population numbers in the tens of millions of whom approximately one million reside in the capital, Lisbon. It is governed by a democratically elected parliamentary government. Portugal is an enthusiastic member of the European Community (EC) which it joined in 1986, thus citizens of Portugal may live and work in any other West European country (except Switzerland).

In recent times Portugal has been the poor relation of Western Europe. Even today its living and labour costs are the lowest of the area. However, the growth of tourism in the Algarve and in the greater Lisbon area has steadily brought foreign wealth into the country over the last two decades. This influx is supplemented by the benefits of Community membership which is helping the country to develop fast. In a nutshell, this country offers a wealth of opportunity for the individual that is willing to find a need and fill it.

English is widely spoken and there are large British expatriate communities around Lisbon and in the Algarve. Beaches and golf courses are amongst the best in the world. Health and sanitation are at European levels. The finest merchandise, wines and foods are available in every city and resort. Prices are typically very low, on almost everything. In less popular areas, adequate condominium apartments start at US $25,000 while some farms with good houses are still under US $50,000. Magnificent mansions with grounds, pools, golf and club memberships and a sea view are in the US $1,000,000 range. Bargains in the Algarve region are more difficult to come by. Honest, competent household help is available at reasonable cost.

Portugal enjoys low crime rates and minimal political unrest. The communist party was very strong for a while, but now the social democrats rule. As wealthy foreigners are a recognized major source of income, the expatriate community and home ownership by foreigners have always been carefully protected by the government. In 1992, the government adopted a Reagan-Thatcher approach and embarked on a massive privatization program.

Travel is inexpensive to most European destinations, particularly to London. There are also government subsidized routes to the sunny and beautiful Azores and Madeira islands in the Atlantic Ocean, which are autonomous regions. We have heard rumors that individuals who spend some time on these islands can cultivate local officials and gain Portuguese nationality and passports in one or two years. We have no personal contacts, but welcome input from readers who are able to exploit such options in either Ponta Delgada or Funchal.

Otherwise, citizenship requirements are currently quite liberal. Marrying a citizen is one way, which provides "instant citizenship" although processing can take as long as two years. For the purpose of obtaining a right of abode leading to the issue of a European passport (in six years), Portugal is the easiest and least expensive country in the EC. It also compares well with other destinations. An investment of US $100,000 will support a business migration to Portugal whereas Canada would require a minimum of C $250,000 and the UK an investment in excess of £200,000. These liberal passport laws could change at any time. If the Portuguese program suits you, it is wise to get in before the door is shut.

HOW TO APPLY FOR PORTUGUESE RESIDENCE

Basically, the Portuguese government requires that you are what they call "a person of means". Their main interests are that you prove that you will not become a burden on the State and that your application "adds up". Therefore, individuals with an off-shore income, including pensioners, will generally qualify with few, if any, problems. Applicants may also either buy into an existing or establish a new business in Portugal, as long as the profits likely to arise from this business are adequate to support the applicant and his dependents.

Another basic requirement is that you prove you have secured adequate accommodation. For most, this involves purchasing a property, but there is no requirement to do so, renting will suffice. Beware of firms more interested in selling real estate to than securing residence for their clients.

To prove such an application the Portuguese government requires that you submit:

1) A declaration of intent, basically a letter explaining your reasons and intentions for applying for a residence visa and your financial capacity to support yourself.
2) Certificate obtained locally to prove adequate housing conditions.
3) Documentation showing that an account has been opened in Escudos, the Portuguese currency, in a bank in Portugal and that sufficient monies have been deposited. (As a general rule this is a minimum of £2400 per person on the application.)
4) Certificate of good character.
5) Medical Certificate attesting to good health.
6) Copies of relevant pages from your current passport.
7) Three passport size photos.
8) Three copies of the official visa application form (V3) duly filled in. (This form has been reproduced here.)
9) Testimonials from acquaintances in Portugal. (This final requirement is optional.)

The processing of this application through a Portuguese Consulate can take from 6 to 24 months, however an average time can be regarded as 12 months. This time may possibly even be shortened to only a few months by a good lawyer. (Ask Scope International for the appropriate referral.) Given that the application is successful a residence visa will be issued which can be transformed into a residence card in Portugal.

Initially a "type A" residence card will be issued which is valid for one year and renewable annually. After five years of residence a "type B" residence card valid for five years is issued and after twenty years foreign residents may apply for a "type C" card which is valid for life. Although this card cannot currently be used for EC travel, it does ensure that visas can be obtained easily for most EC countries.

After six years of residence, one qualifies for naturalization and passport. As in most European countries there is no continuous presence requirement, thereby allowing an absentee renter/home owner to travel freely or sub-let his Portugal property for short periods of time. In fact, after applying for an initial residence card, the applicant may return to his country of origin to which the card can be mailed a number of weeks later.

If six years is too long to wait, one may apply for what is called a Portuguese Aliens Passport after receiving a residence card. Such a passport generally allows for visa free travel throughout Europe. However, this passport is only issued "under exceptional circumstances". Generally this means stateless persons, but we have also been told that a foreigner with good legal representation willing to make a productive investment may also qualify.

TAX CONSIDERATIONS

Exchange controls are in effect, but these are not major considerations for persons with income or assets abroad. Annual property taxes are on the order of one month's rental value, or one per cent of total value. Residents of Portugal are theoretically taxable on their worldwide income at a rate which varies from 16 to 40 per cent, but there is no attempt to collect taxes unless the income is **generated in Portugal**. The higher rate of tax in respect of capital gains is 20 per cent.

Competent English-speaking attorneys whose speciality is immigration law are readily available. Consulates and branches of your bank in Portugal can make recommendations.

OTHER WAYS OF BECOMING PORTUGUESE

Portugal is an ancient and respected country and a former colonial power in Africa (Angola), the East (Goa, India and Macau on the Chinese coast) and South America (Brazil).

Reciprocity of citizenship (after a three year residency period) exists with Brazil. Movement to and from this former colony requires no visa. A Brazilian can vote in Portuguese elections upon registration as a resident.

All citizens born in former Portuguese colonies in India (Goa, Daman and Diu) before 1961 are entitled to Portuguese citizenship. They should apply in the nearest Portuguese consulate outside of India.

All citizens born before 1974 in Timor, an ex-colony in Indonesia, are also entitled to Portuguese citizenship. Application should take place outside of Indonesia, preferably in Singapore.

All citizens born in former African colonies are entitled to Portuguese citizenship as well. These are: Cape Verde and Guinéa-Bissau before 1961. Angola, Mozambique and St. Tomé and Principe before 1974.

To live temporarily in Hong Kong, the Portuguese passport is second only to the British. Other nationals who are not permanent residents in Hong Kong cannot travel freely to China or Macau to renew their visas in Hong Kong. They will have to fly overseas. Portuguese and British citizens have an easier time. They can just walk across the border to China or take a short ferry-ride to the glittering casinos of Macau every three months to stay "PTs" – perpetual tourists – in Hong Kong. No need to waste money on expensive airfares.

The only limitation thus far placed on Portuguese immigrants by another EC country involves Macau. Great Britain was concerned that holders of Macau Portuguese passports obtained by citizens of Hong Kong would overrun London and thus placed a limit of 100,000 upon new Portuguese citizens of Chinese ancestry. Long term residents of Macau are not affected and can still attain Portuguese nationality and access to the EC.

If one obtains Portuguese citizenship, he or she must swear allegiance and renounce his prior nationality. After obtaining Portuguese nationality, one can have two or more nationalities. The rule is "once Portuguese, always Portuguese".

PORTUGAL: THE FORMS

On the next couple of pages is the V3 form required in triplicate by the Portuguese government with applications for residence.

Portugal's bureaucracy is still not computerized. Almost everything is entered into handwritten ledgers. Bureaucracy in Portugal, as a result, is a very slow moving monster. A residence permit can easily take the better part of one year to get. However, even without one, no officials will bother you if you live in Portugal. The local cops are the friendliest in Europe. If you behave well, you really don't need any papers. In the country with Europe's nicest people and Europe's lowest prices, even the "authorities" don't like authority. The Portuguese are also non-racist and thus have provided a refuge for hundreds of thousands of African and Asian stateless people who now call this little European country their home.

The Portuguese "Serviço de Estrangeiros" is nothing like the dreaded INS in the US. Portuguese officials are courteous and most of them want to help, but their red-tape is one hell of a maze to get through. It takes the patience of a saint with many weeks wasted standing in line at dinky little government offices furnished with pre-World War II office equipment. They are friendly, but nothing seems to get done.

Fortunately, many Portuguese officials are corrupt enough to make the creaking system spit up the papers you need. For a relatively small "tip" they are willing to bypass usual channels to backdate papers or speed things up for you. Friendly behavior, an understanding smile and small gifts to the right people can still get you a long way in this backwater of the EC.

The great Portuguese paper chase for a passport can be done by a good lawyer within a few months, not a few years, if he knows what officials to go to for expedited service. We may be able to help consulting clients select the right lawyer or "advogado".

One thing more about Portugal. This government has the lowest tax rates in Europe. They keep taxes down by simply not spending any money. In 1990, they told their diplomatic corps abroad that they would have to go without pay for a while. No funds were available to pay them. Nobody quit!

On a low level, too, every government office tries to save. They don't know what an electric typewriter is, much less a computer. There is very limited public sector spending. No waste of tax-payers money here. Nothing is free at government offices in Portugal. If you want to fill out a form, you pay the cost of that form. We feel that the "Portuguese way" is reasonable. Each man pays his own way. Very libertarian!

(a) .... *de Portugal em* ....

PEDIDO DE VISTO PARA FIXAÇÃO DE RESIDÊNCIA EM PORTUGAL

1 ....
   Apelidos — Noms — Surname

2 ....
   Nome — Prénom — Name

3 ....
   Outros nomes — autres noms — Other names (**de solteira** — de naissance — maiden name, etc.)

4 .... 5 ....
   Sexo — Sexe — Sex; Masculino ☐ Feminino ☐   **Data de nascimento** — Date de naissance — Date of birth

6 ....
   Lugar de nascimento — Lieu de naissance — Place of birth

7 .... 8 ....
   País de origem — Pays d'origine — Country of birth   **Estado civil** — Situation de famille — Marital status

9 .... 10 ....
   Nacionalidade — Nacionalité — Nationality   **Morada** — Addresse — Address

....

11 .... 12 ....
   Profissão — Profession — Profession   **Nome e endereço da entidade patronal**

....
   Nom et addresse complet de l'employeur — Name and full address of the employer

13 .... 14 ....
   Tipo de passaporte — Type du passeport — Passeport type   **Número do passaporte** — Número du passeport — Passeport number

15 .... 16 ....
   Autoridade que o emitiu — Autorité qui l'a delivré — Entity who delivered it   **Local de emissão** — Lieu de delivrance — Place of delivery

17 .... 18 ....
   Data de emissão — Date de delivrance — Date of delivery   **Data em que expira a validade** — Valable jusqu'au — Valid until

19

Nome ou designação das pessoas a contactar em Portugal — Nom ou designation des personnes à contacter au Portugal — Name or designation of the persons to contact in Portugal

20

Motivo porque escolheu Portugal para residir — Raison par laquelle vous avez choisi le Portugal pour vivre — Reasons why have chosen Portugal to live

21

Endereço completo — Adresse complet — Full address

22

Data prevista para chegada a Portugal — Date d'arrivée — Date of arrival

23

Morada em Portugal — Residence au Portugal — Residence in Portugal

24

Já alguma vez solicitou visto de entrada em Portugal? — Avez-vous demandé auparavant un visa pour le Portugal? — Have you applied for a visa to Portugal before?   **Sim** — Oui — Yes ☐   **Não** — Non — No ☐

25

Que tipo de visto? — Quelle espéce de visa — Which kind of visa
☐ **Trânsito** — Transit — Transit   ☐ **Turismo ou negócios** — Tourisme ou affaires — Tourism ou business
☐ **Para fixação de residência** — Residence — Residence

26

Consulado onde foi solicitado — Consulat ou il à eté demandé — Consulate where application was submitted

27

O visto foi :	concedido	**Recusado**	
Le visa a été :	Accordé ☐	Refusé ☐	
The visa was :	Granted	Refused	

Data — Date — Date

Assinatura do requerente — Signature du requérent — Applicant's signature

OPINIAO DO CONSUL

Data   **Assinatura**

(Sêlo do Posto)

SINGAPORE

In a nutshell, the new citizenship program of Singapore is called the "Scheme for Entrepreneurs". It is designed mainly for wealthy residents of Hong Kong who wish to secure a place for themselves and their families in a similar bustling economic environment, but persons other than Asians may apply.

Citizenship and passports are granted to the entrepreneur, his wife and his children (under age 21) after two years of residence. During the two years of residence one's comings and goings from Singapore are unrestricted. The applicant is however expected to maintain a "home" (i.e. at least a rented apartment and not just a mail-drop) during the two year residence period.

There is also the unfortunate requirement of an oath of allegiance and the surrender of prior passports upon the granting of a Singapore passport. As readers of the *Passport Report* know, if one takes an "Oath of Allegiance" and surrenders a passport, it is possible in many cases to simply reapply for a new passport from the "old" country which will be granted without any notification to Singapore. This is true for all Commonwealth and US citizens, except Australians.

The most important requirement of the Singapore program is an investment of (Singapore dollars) $1,000,000 in Singapore. As of this writing, a Singapore dollar is worth roughly 50 cents US. Fifty per cent of this may be in any type of real estate: industrial, commercial or residential property. In the case of the latter (a personal home or apartment), government approval should be obtained in advance of making any purchase as not all residential property is in the scheme. Thus, a rather nice apartment could be purchased with around US $250,000, and another US $250,000 could be invested in a local business – perhaps as a loan with a good interest return. The funds can be deposited with the Government Treasury at interest for two years, but must be invested in Singapore after those two years. The investment must be for a minimum of five years.

Close family relatives such as parents, in-laws and non-dependant children over age 21 will be "considered favorably" for citizenship. Additional deposits of $300,000 per person are required for extra adult family members or relatives.

Application forms for this program may be received without charge from: Immigration Unit, Singapore Economic Development Board, 250 North Bridge Road, Raffles City Tower #24-00, SINGAPORE 0617. Phone: 330-6686. Fax: (65) 33-6077.

A very nicely illustrated brochure called "Making Singapore Your Home" is available to interested parties from the Immigration Department, Ministry of Home Affairs, 95 South Bridge Road #08-26, South Bridge Centre, Singapore 0105.

The official language of Singapore is English. The vast majority of the population is Asian, with commerce being dominated by ethnic Chinese usually of Confucian religious background. Persons of Malay background who are predominantly Muslim make up 15 per cent of the population. The remainder of the population is in part composed of a large sprinkling of Indians, a moderate balance of Thais, Vietnamese, Jews and Laotians and a very small number of Europeans. The Europeans tend to be in very high positions and are generally well regarded. Singapore is a multi-racial, multi-religious society with little ethnic friction. The political administration has been accused of high handed dictatorship in such things as at one time making gum chewing or smoking in public a minor crime. Littering and not carrying a poop-scoop to clean up dog-mess is still a crime. To this sort of restriction, I give my wholehearted blessings.

The City State of Singapore is one of the cleanest and most un-polluted population centres in the world. Sanitation in restaurants is also regulated at a high standard. Building and zoning is at Swiss levels of modernity and quality. Although this writer is a "Libertarian" in favor of minimum government controls, the result I've observed, in places like Thailand where there is no long tradition of individual responsibility, can be a jerry-built, dirty and unsafe city. In Singapore, the regulations have created in the last thirty years something of a paradise, at least in our opinion. Those who don't like high-rise buildings and crass materialism should go elsewhere. In Singapore they have won the "War On Drugs" without imposing a myriad of laws and regulations that allow government officials unlimited power over citizens. Intrusions on innocent people are only felt necessary in the US. Yes, serious penalties are meted out in Singapore to addicts and pushers, but those in the banking and private enterprise sector cannot be jailed and bankrupted just because they transacted unrelated business with these people. The public transport systems are clean, fast and comfortable. Government officials are generally uncorrupted.

Singapore is not a tax haven. It supports a generous social program of free schools, low-fee universities, child-care, socialized medicine, subsidised housing, etc. Tax levels are considered low, by international standards – slightly above Hong Kong's 25 per cent yet below those of the US. The top income tax bracket is 33 per cent, on income over S $400,000. While any tax code is complicated, generally speaking, worldwide income is not taxed in Singapore. Non-resident Singapore citizens do not pay any taxes. Persons engaged in exporting can usually apply and get a "tax holiday" for about 15 years under various tax incentive programs.

There are no currency controls, reporting requirements or restrictions such as the "US Money Laundering Laws". The bureaucracy generally stays out of businessmen's hair except in connection with Singapore product quality and health controls. The author spent time in Singapore thirty years ago when much of it was an unsanitary slum. The transformation to the Switzerland of Asia has been a remarkable achievement. We feel that the government of Singapore has "got it right".

Real estate is taxed at a rate that works out to be about 15 per cent of the annual rental value of real property. The maximum estate/inheritance tax is 10 per cent with a big exemption of around S $500,000 to S $1,000,000, depending upon the nature of the deceased's assets. Import duties are very low or non-existent on almost everything except cars which have a 125 per cent duty on them. As a result, Singapore is a shopper's paradise.

International copyrights were not enforced until recently with the result that the latest pirated computer programs and instruction books were given away free with computer purchases or sold for nearly the price of blank discs. Copied Gucci bags, video-tapes, music cassettes, Encyclopaedia Britannica and Rolex watches are still available, from *under the counter* at 10 per cent of the cost of the "real thing" but Singapore Police will today confiscate counterfeits and enforce anti-piracy laws where complaints are filed.

Restaurants and hotel services are of very high standard and charge about half of European prices. Prices in nearby Thailand are half-again below Singapore rates. Singapore being primarily a port-city is modern and beautiful. The climate is generally hot and tropical (about 80°F or 30°C) on a typical day. There is a dry season during European winters and a monsoon (wet) season during European summers.

I would rate Singapore very high, with cities like San Francisco and Sydney, for quality of life and economic opportunity. Singapore is more "high-tech oriented" than any other city in the world with the exception perhaps of Sophia Antipolis, France; Tokyo, Japan and San Jose, California. It is a good place to live for those interested in business and commerce. As to the two year citizenship program, the only disadvantage is the relatively high investment required. However it should be remembered that persons with a long list of skills or professions deemed needed in Singapore do not have to make any investment at all to get Singapore Permanent Resident status. After 5 years as a resident, they can apply for citizenship. Children born in Singapore are automatically citizens, and the parents of Singapore citizens can expect some preference in obtaining residence status.

Should you do it? As in choosing a mate, we all have different needs, expectations and desires. A six month visit to Singapore with an investment-search could make some of our readers into multi-millionaires with a new nationality. Other countries may be cheaper. For those who prefer nature, hunting and fishing, New Zealand (with a three year program and a much lower investment) is a better bet. Singapore is a very small urbanized "city-state" with very little countryside – at least within its own borders. On the other hand, it is a quick (and cheap) flight away from anywhere in Asia and the most important transportation hub (shipping and air traffic) in the Pacific. For lovers of open space, there is always the sea. Many Singaporeans own boats used for fishing and recreation.

SOLOMON ISLANDS – A WAY TO A SECOND PASSPORT IF YOU'RE BLACK

If you are a "man of color" using the newest politically correct way of referring to one of the black race, you may be able to get a second foreign passport with relative ease from the Solomon Islands. You will have to demonstrate that your ancestors were one of the many Melanesian Pacific Islanders, mainly from the Solomon Islands and New Guinea, that Europeans hunted for slave duty in Australian coconut plantations in Fiji, Samoa and other places. During the days when England ruled the waves, "blackbirding" was the accepted practice of supplying slave labour for its possessions throughout the empire.

Recognizing this past history of the Solomon Islanders, the present prime minister wants his kinsmen to return to their ancestral home. He says, "Anyone wanting to take back his Solomon Island citizenship is very much welcome to do so." If you are a man of color with or without ancestry in the Solomon Islands (how is one to prove that you are not Solomon), we can bet that you will find no records in the court house and be able to obtain a passport.

The Solomon Island's may not be everyone's cup of tea. Jobs are hard to find, the birth rate is currently increasing by 3.5 per cent annually, malaria is common and schools are rudimentary . . . but remember that the last place a PT wants to actually reside is in a country where he is a citizen. As the Solomon Islands are part of the British Commonwealth, a visa is not required to visit the UK. This route could also prove to be a successful back door to British nationality. However, visas are required for most other European countries and the US.

SOUTH AFRICA – THEY'LL PAY YOU TO COME

South Africa is a strange place. Its government seems to be gradually getting in touch with reality yet civil strife seems to be erupting into more minor battles between the black population and white police. How long the white monopoly can be sustained is anyone's guess at this point. Once the whites are out the different black tribes will no doubt start many civil wars between themselves.

Although immigration is easy and subsidized, restrictions and the general difficulty in obtaining a South African passport would lead one to believe that the whole world is lining up to get one, rather than the other way around. If my passport was South African, I'd buy this report and find out how to obtain a different one!

Why, then, should we present information on South Africa? The direct answer is that there are a few short-term advantages to immigration that might prove to be useful to your particular situation. The passport they offer after a five year residence period is *not* one of these advantages.

South Africa, as stated, encourages white immigration and will provide economic assistance and pay passage for the able-bodied. Residence permits are relatively simple to obtain. Lifestyle for whites is quite good in the material sense, although revolution or a mass uprising of the blacks would obviously change things fast, but where there is crisis and uncertainty there is always opportunity!

South Africa is rich in minerals and cheap skilled labor. An income of US $20,000 would permit an equivalent South African standard of living of at least US $200,000 in New York. Food, housing and servants are inexpensive. Business opportunities are amazingly abundant, particularly since many foreign firms have been evacuating for years at fire-sale prices or on "no money down" terms.

The principal advantage of a sojourn in South Africa is that before the final curtain falls you could live like a millionaire for some years and amass a fortune at the same time. If there are unpalatable political changes you can always move on to more idyllic settings.

Taxes are high and evasion is a commonly played game. Exchange controls make exportation of your wealth illegal, but there are ways and alternatives. In particular, many residents simply take yachts or diamonds out with them on visits to other countries. There are hundreds, if not thousands of variations of schemes to transfer wealth abroad in circumvention of local currency laws.

The government also controls moral and sexual matters quite heavily, banning many books and movies. This makes criticism of the government a serious matter. Even telling an anti-government joke may be considered subversive in this country. The US and South Africa are now the world's top jailers on a per capita basis.

Thus, being non-political would be essential for a new immigrant. Having local black partners might be some insurance against confiscation in a revolution. However, my white South African readers say that having a black partner in most businesses is currently not a viable option.

United Nations data indicates that South African blacks have the highest standard of living, literacy, life span and employment rate and the lowest level of infant mortality in all of Black Africa. Every other government in Africa is far more oppressive. They are all police states – with the possible exceptions of Senegal and Kenya. To underscore this, note that a large proportion of the black workers in South Africa come from neighboring black countries in order to enjoy jobs and a standard of living they can't get at home.

The majority of South African blacks would none-the-less still prefer self rule, even if it meant greater oppression. At least it would be by their own kind instead of by whites. Of course, no sane person can condone the discrimination of apartheid with its separate bathrooms, segregated schools, and the many inhuman restrictions on where people can live due solely to race. We are happy to note that apartheid is being dismantled at last.

South African passports are obtainable after five years of residence. Being of draft age means military conscription. There are no tax exemptions for new citizens. Criminal penalties apply to having undeclared foreign assets. Possession of a secret second passport is a crime, only certain business people are exempt. Dual citizenship is only possible if the second citizenship is gained as a matter of right, rather than by an oath of allegiance. As to assets, a foreign trust will keep your offshore income tax free.

South Africa restricts foreign travel by limiting the funds one can take out. Most Moslem, Third World and other African countries bar entry to holders of South African passports. More and more countries are refusing to issue visas. This passport is becoming an increasingly heavy burden to South Africans. As a result, the government's Ministry of External Affairs will grant permits (for business people who need to travel) to acquire or hold second passports. Countries which refuse entry to people whose passport contains evidence of a visit to South Africa do not include Senegal, Congo or Kenya.

South Africa offers but one attraction – that of being able to build a nest egg quickly. This is aided by the special incentive of the "financial Rand". Simply stated, if a foreigner invests in South Africa, he can change money into Rands at a very favorable rate giving a 20-40 per cent bonus. Cultural activities, intellectual stimulation and freedom of expression are simply lacking. If you have another passport, it would not be a good idea to give it up for South Africa.

Several black ruled countries within South Africa issue their own passports. They are fast and easy to obtain but are almost useless for visa-free travel due to an exceptionally low international acceptance factor. These include Transkei, Venda, Lesotho and Basutoland. Swaziland is also liberal on appointing diplomats and honorary consuls.

SPAIN – COMMON MARKET COUNTRY WITH SPECIAL PROGRAMS

Post-Franco Spain is more attractive than ever. "The sun is always shining in Spain" are the words of the popular song. They are true! Winters are mild and snow-free along the south coast. Spain is a great place to live and offers fast passports to descendants of colonists with Spanish blood including Safardic Jews.

An individual of Spanish descent or one returning from a former Spanish colony "with the intention of taking up permanent residence" can apply for a passport in two years. Purchase of a home is not required and the legal right to work is normally granted instantly or after six months residency. Normal residency requirements for non-Spanish ancestry individuals to obtain citizenship is ten years. There is a special treaty with Honduras and Guatemala, granting automatic Spanish citizenship after one year of bona-fide residence in Spain.

Northern Europeans maintain large expatriate colonies in the major cities in southern Spain and on the islands in the Mediterranean and Atlantic. To become a citizen you will be expected to become a Spanish-speaking member of the community and maintain a real presence, but during the residency period travel is unrestricted. No one in Spain will be counting the days you are away.

Spanish lawyers are inexpensive. The paper work to obtain a passport currently costs under US $1,500. If you speak Spanish, have the time and are willing to pass out small gifts to some of the many officials who process your papers, it can be a do-it-yourself project.

While there are no travel restrictions during the required residence periods, token residence is not acceptable. Spain's distinctive La Guardia civil police maintain close tabs on foreigners and will actually visit your home and interview neighbors to make certain you *really live there* and are behaving yourself. While they are not so fearsome as under Franco, the La Guardia remains an effective and elite police force with the ability to find and expel any unwanted alien, literally in a matter of minutes.

Spain taxes permanent residents worldwide income at rates in excess of 50 per cent. Income is estimated by authorities based upon home, car and lifestyle. Many wealthy Spanish passport holders who do not want to keep a low profile establish legal residence in the tax haven of Andorra for this reason.

Wealthy foreigners are therefore advised to consider Spain as a fine place to spend some leisure time, but not as a place to live tax-free after acquiring a passport.

Major reform of Spanish taxation legislation became effective on January 1, 1992, and although the maximum percentage rate of tax payable is 53 per cent for residents and 35 per cent for non-residents, the changes mean one will be deemed resident if he stays in the country for more than 183 days annually or his main centre of professional or business activities or economic interest is in Spain. If the person's spouse or dependents remain resident, he will be deemed resident unless he can prove he was resident for more than 183 days in another country. Temporary absences will be included.

As a general rule, income obtained by non-residents is deemed to be earned on the date it became claimable or when effectively collected. Another new measure affecting non-residents is that unless they have a permanent establishment, they must appoint a fiscal representative resident in Spain and notify the tax authorities of the appointment.

A number of rules affect the purchase and sale of real estate by non-residents. Purchasers of private property from non-residents must withhold 10 per cent of the purchase price for vendor's tax on the gain realized. Non-resident companies owning real estate in Spain will be subject to an annual tax of 5 per cent on the rateable (cadastral) value of the property, but as this measure is aimed at companies based in tax havens which invest in Spanish property, there are several exempt categories. The new net worth tax also means the applicable value of real estate will be the highest out of the cadastral value, acquisition cost and the value proved by the administration in connection with other taxes.

Spanish passports are respected worldwide and are relatively easy, fast and cheap to acquire, particularly for those with a Spanish colonial citizenship or Spanish-Jewish ancestry. Renting an apartment and keeping it for about two years qualifies members of these lucky groups. No home purchase is needed.

Spain is the most popular tourist destination in the world and it has much to offer as a place in which to invest, vacation or live. Developers and speculators are reaping vast fortunes in real estate, property and building developments. Restaurants, transportation companies, brewers, hotel operators, golf and tennis clubs and purveyors to the tourist industry are all prospering.

Prime attractions are year-round sunshine, low prices and low rents. Spain is not so inexpensive as Portugal, but prices are still below prevailing European levels. Spain has an incredible variety of restaurants and entertainment. Domestic help is very inexpensive.

A grotty basement studio condominium in Fuengirola on the sea may be bought for as low as US $40,000, while a pleasant and proper two bedroom, two bath home with seaview will run between $80,000 and $150,000. Veritable castles and palaces built by Arab princes near Marbella sport gold plated plumbing and luxurious appointments. These sumptuous villas can be acquired from bored owners for $500,000 to $900,000. Real estate in Spain will probably be an excellent long-term investment. Thus, while home ownership is not required to become a resident, owning may be more economically desirable than renting. As of 1993, there is a real estate slump. Many bargains are available at 1986 prices.

Legal residents in Spain, whether citizens or not, enjoy protection from extradition for tax and currency offences, but are vulnerable to deportation for violent or terrorist offences, even if those crimes were committed abroad. Spanish police are notoriously political. They are inefficient in ordinary criminal cases but keep a close watch on anyone suspected of international intrigues. Annoying petty crime is one of the most negative features of Spain. Pornography and paid female companionship are openly advertised and touted in all cities and tourist centers, especially Barcelona. Drugs are so common it is hard to avoid stepping on used needles at most beaches.

For the rich, country club communities and private villas are protected from burglars by dogs, guards and high walls capped by broken glass set in cement. An unoccupied, unguarded home in Spain will probably be burglarized within a week. The consequences of *violent* criminal acts against tourists can be gruesome for the perpetrators. Nonetheless, armed robbery and crimes of violence are approaching New York City levels in some parts of Spain. Most crime seems to be drug related.

Tourism is Spain's major industry. As such it is fiercely protected by the entire governmental apparatus. A mild tourist complaint to the Minister of Tourism's office often unleashes a bureaucratic paper blizzard that results in businesses paying heavy fines over and above settling up with the wronged tourist.

In summary, the Spanish passport is a good one, relatively easy to obtain in one to ten years. If you want to actually live at least part-time in Spain it is best to hold a foreign passport and merely take long "vacations" in Spain. Tourists are (as usual) a more privileged class than citizens. Thus, a Spanish passport is good only if you don't intend to live there.

Want more reasons why *not* to become a citizen of Spain? Besides typical soak-the-rich taxes on residents, they require renunciation of existing citizenship and an oath of allegiance. They recognize dual-citizenship only with Spaniards in the Philippines and their ex-colonies in Latin America. They have eighteen months of compulsory military service for men of draft age (about 19-20). On the other side of the coin, if one doesn't plan on staying on to live (and pay

MODELO DE INSTANCIA SOLICITANDO DISPENSA DE RESIDENCIA ON ENPAÑA PARA AQUELLAS PERSONAS QUE DESEEN OPTAR POR LA NACIONALIDAD ESPAÑOLA Y TENGAN MAS DE 20 AÑOS

EXCMO. SR.:

Don (Doña) . . . . mayor de edad, de estado . . . ., de nacionalidad . . . . y con domicilio en . . . ., ante el Consulado General de España en Caracas,* presenta esta instancia dirigida a V.E. en el que EXPONE:

PRIMERO. — Que naci en . . . ., el día . . . . de . . . . de 19 . . . ., hijo de . . . . y de . . . ., constando inscrito mi nacimiento en el Registro Civil (consular o local) de . . . ., Tomo . . . ., página . . . ., número , siendo por nacimiento de nacionalidad venezolan,* y acompaño certificación de nacimiento a tal efecto.

SEGUNDO. — Que mi padre (o madre) (o mis padres) (señalar nombre y apellidos) era(n) español(es) de origen y nacido(s) en España, y acompaño certificado(s) de nacimiento a tal efecto.

TERCERO. — Que deseo acogerme a la disposición transitoria tercera de la Ley 18/1990, de 17 de diciembre, y optar por la nacionalidad española.

CUARTO — Y, por todo ello, SUPLICA:
Que en bas al art. 26, 1,a) del Código Civil, le sea concodida por V.E. la dispensa del requisito de residencia legal en España.

Caracas,   de   de 199

El(La) interesado(a) (Firma).

EXCMO. SEÑOR MINISTRO DE JUSTICIA. – MADRID

DOCUMENTACION A PRESENTAR POR EL ENTERESADO(A):
1.— Instancia por duplicado, senún modelo.
2.— Impreso "Información del solicitante".
3.— Acta de nacimiento del solicitante (original y fotocopia).
4.— Certificación(es) de nacimiento del padre (o madre) o (padres) que haya(n) sido originariamente español(es) y nacido(s) en España. (Dichas certificaciones deben ser LITERALES).

* Or wherever you are
** Or whatever nationality you are

taxes) in Spain after getting citizenship and a passport, it's a *very good* passport allowing visa-free travel almost everywhere, except a few communist countries. A Spaniard can go visa-free to a dozen *more* places than an American. Spain of course has superb relations with its former colonies (the Spanish-speaking world) in the same way that Great Britain has good relations with The Commonwealth. Spain does not tax non-resident citizens.

One little loophole we discovered is that a Spanish passport can be obtained by right of law if one has *ever* been married to a Spaniard, even if the marriage was dissolved! But a one year residence is required. The same rule applies if either *parent* was entitled to a Spanish passport or if one was born during certain periods in Spain or in any Spanish territory. The Spanish government was most co-operative in providing material for this section, and we thank Madrid for their assistance and promptness in responding to our inquiries.

If one of your parents was born in Spain, you are entitled to a Spanish passport. Use the form on the previous page to apply at any consulate. The old rules required taking up Spanish residence. The new rules dispense with this requirement.

ST KITTS AND NEVIS – INSTANT, BUT EXPENSIVE

A new island republic in the Caribbean, formerly a British Colony with a majority black population, St. Kitts had little going for it except natural beauty. To exploit this, the government agreed with various promoters to permit casino and hotel-condominium developments. The government further agreed that substantial investors in these projects would receive passports and residence permits within 45 days. Thus far the developments are proceeding according to schedule. Passports have in fact been issued under the program. Because it is a new country, visa-free travel on the St. Kitts passport is limited, but a prosperous looking traveler and his family will have no trouble getting visas. The main drawback of the plan is the fact that the required minimum passive investment is US $150,000 for a luxury condominium, a US $25,000 contribution to the government and US $10,000 for legal and processing fees. No visit is required, and the developers say they can lease out your condo apartment to produce rental income commensurate with the investment. It is probable that someone who would make a personal visit to the island might be able to work out a less expensive investment, but for a fast, absolutely legal deal with legally authorized passport, St. Kitts and Nevis is the real McCoy. St. Kitts is a fine place for those who enjoy beaches, deep-sea fishing and gambling at the new casino. Golf, tennis and all the usual resort activities are also present. Communication is adequate and getting better. Unlike the generally poor race relations at most Caribbean islands (outside of Bermuda) St. Kitts natives do not yet resent the rich foreigners.

Considering that many other passports are available for under US $25,000 net, this author's judgment is that the St. Kitt's document at US $185,000 net, is US $160,000 overpriced. For those who consider such sums mere pin money, just write: Director of Immigration, Saint Christopher and Nevis, Caribbean West Indies. Your letter will reach the officials who can make the necessary arrangements. Please let us know the results of your inquiries for reporting in future editions of the *Passport Report*. We will not use your name of course.

Alternatively, Scope International can refer you to a local lawyer specializing in this programme. Please send standard £200 consulting fee.

SAINT CHRISTOPHER AND NEVIS

PLEASE PRINT	SURNAME	CHRISTIAN NAME OR OTHER NAME

PHOTO

NOTES

1. Application must be completed in triplicate.
2. Include three (3) passport sized photographs with application.
3. Include a certified copy of your Birth Certificate.
4. Obtain and submit, as evidence of good character, a Standard Police Report.
5. Furnish a Credit Report, Bank or financial reference as evidence of Credit Standing and Credit History.

Application for Citizenship

1. SURNAME AT PRESENT:

2. SURNAME USED PREVIOUSLY:

3. FULL CHRISTIAN NAMES

4. PRESENT ADDRESS:

5. PERMANENT ADDRESS (if different from Present Address):

6. DATE OF BIRTH

Date   Month   Year

7. PLACE OF BIRTH:

8. PRESENT NATIONALITY:

9. NATIONALITY AT BIRTH
(List date of any change and place at which such change was recorded.

Nationality

Place   Date

Nationality

Place   Date

Nationality

Place   Date

143

10. DESCRIPTION:

Height: _____

Weight: _____

Colour of Eyes: _____

Colour of Hair: _____

Distinguishing Marks: _____

_____

11. LANGUAGES SPOKEN:

_____ _____

_____ _____

_____ _____

_____ _____

_____ _____

12. NAME, ADDRESS AND NATIONALITY OF THE FOLLOWING:

FATHER:

Name   Nationality

Address

WIFE/HUSBAND:

Name   Nationality

Address

BROTHERS:

Name   Nationality

Address

Name   Nationality

Address

Name   Nationality

Address

SISTERS:

Name   Nationality

Address

Name   Nationality

Address

Name   Nationality

Address

MOTHER:

Name   Nationality

Address

Name   Nationality

Address

CHILDREN:

Name   Nationality

Address

Name   Nationality

Address

Name   Nationality

Address

Name   Nationality

Address

Name   Nationality

Address

Name   Nationality

Address

— IF DECEASED, GIVE DATE OF DEATH —

13. DATE OF MARRIAGE:

Date   Month   Year

14. IF DIVORCED, GIVE DATE AND PLACE WHERE GRANTED

Date   Place

15. PRESENT OCCUPATION:	16. ADDRESS WHERE EMPLOYED:
17. PROPOSED SOURCE OF INCOME:	

18. APPROXIMATE ANNUAL INCOME:

19. LIST ALL COUNTRIES WHERE APPLICANT RESIDED WITH DATES OF ENTERING AND LEAVING:

ENTRY DATE	PLACE	DEPARTURE DATE

20. LIST THE FOLLOWING DETAILS OF APPLICANT'S PRESENT PASSPORT:

Passport #: _____   Date of Issue: _____

Place of Issue: _____   Date of Expiration: _____

21. LAST DATE OF ENTRY INTO ST. CHRISTOPHER & NEVIS:	22. INTENDED PLACE OF RESIDENCE:

23. LIST THE PERSONS OR COMPANIES WITH WHOM THE APPLICANT WILL BE CONDUCTING BUSINESS:

24. REASON FOR DESIRING CITIZENSHIP IN ST. CHRISTOPHER AND NEVIS:

_____
Signature of Applicant

_____
Notary Public

SWITZERLAND

In May, 1992, the Swiss government announced it was to apply for membership of the European Community, the World Bank and the International Monetary Fund. Previously, Switzerland was not the easiest place in the world to get a passport. Yet contrary to popular belief it is not "nearly impossible". As a general rule, an individual must actually live in Switzerland legally for twelve consecutive years. For children under high school age, this is reduced to six years. The application process involves an in-depth investigation, plus detailed personal questioning of neighbors. Citizenship has been denied for such things as "complaining about noisy cow-bells early in the morning". Every Swiss person or person worthy of becoming Swiss should be thrifty, LOVE cow-bells, yodelling and cleanliness. A person whose garage was untidy and who sometimes left his mess exposed to public view through open doors was denied a passport even after a lifetime of residence. A famous (reformed) hallucinatory drug guru, Tim Leary, was said to have been denied citizenship on the grounds of morality – neighbors reported that he lived in sin with two nymphets. The Swiss have many ideas about proper conservative behavior. They are well known for refusing to renew residence permits or grant citizenship to those who don't measure up. Coming to a citizenship hearing five minutes late was considered proof of irresponsibility to the punctual officer in charge. But Swiss rules *do* allow instant grants of citizenship for "Persons of International Stature" including poets, authors, deposed aristocrats, movie stars, heads of state and religious leaders. Also "Tax Exiles" can agree to pay a fixed sum or annual sums in lieu of taxes to a Swiss canton in return for residency. Citizenship comes later. The multi-million dollar amounts involved would seem stratospheric to ordinary mortals, but five million bucks might be chicken-feed to an Arab prince.

Birth in Switzerland does **not** qualify one for citizenship unless at least one parent is also Swiss. Marriage to a Swiss male will get a woman a passport, but marriage to a Swiss female will only get men a residence permit (subject to the 12 year wait for citizenship). The most important exception or loophole is that Swiss citizenship is determined on a Cantonal (Provincial/State) basis. Each Canton is free to establish its own rules. It is said that only a few years ago, someone who went to one of the poorer Cantons and became a public benefactor by building a hospital, school or providing employment with a new business could gain citizenship in about a year (by popular vote). Total cost? Around $250,000. In recent years, the Swiss are becoming xenophobic (anti-foreigner), and few public benefactor citizenships have been given. However, this may change with the end of the Cold War and Switzerland's membership of the EC, IMF and World Bank. A Swiss lawyer has contacted us claiming to be able to gain permits to buy property, get work and gain expedited citizenship. He notes in his letter, "Persons with a net worth of under US $2.5 million need not apply". This is not the cost of citizenship, but just the prerequisite for it. The required contribution he says, is negotiable, depending upon what the Canton thinks of you. The project is too "iffy" and too expensive for my taste, especially since I know several individuals who have been living as 'PTs' in Switzerland for over 20 years without the benefit of any official permits or registration.

Switzerland is of course a Utopia – clean, prosperous, beautiful, crime-free, neutral for hundreds of years and internationally respected. Drawbacks include the summer military camp required of all males, *from age 18 to age 50*. About the same draft laws as Israel – but with less likelihood of combat. Communication and financial services are AAAA-1. Personal freedom thrives in Switzerland (aside from National Service). Of course, we are talking about economic freedom (investing, trading, etc.). Outside of business and economic matters (where they are progressive and innovative), the Swiss are very conservative people. They are in fact less tolerant of eccentricities involving illicit sex, drugs, pornography, fraud and violence than most other places. See the SWITZERLAND: VIA THE ITALIAN (CAMPIONE) ROUTE in the Back Doors section of this special report or my *Campione Report* (see back of book for further details). One can have all the advantages of Switzerland, without the negative features, if one knows the PT secrets. For more detailed information on Switzerland, read Marshall Langer's *The Swiss Report*. See back pages of this report for details.

We have recently received tentative information about a new Swiss passport programme. Becoming a citizen of Geneva and receiving Swiss naturalization has possibly become much quicker and a lot less expensive, thanks to a new ruling (passed on 28th April 1992) by the Grand Council of Geneva.

Formerly a prospective citizen had to reside in the Canton for two years. This period has now been reduced to six months, after which you can make an application for residency.

But perhaps the greatest change is in the cost of an application which is down from a maximum SFr100,000 to a ceiling of SFr10,000.

We do not have any more detailed information on this legislation. If you find out more about this new program, please let us know.

THAILAND – PARADISE FOR MALES – OPPORTUNITY FOR AN ALMOST INSTANT PASSPORT

People in Thailand think differently from Europeans or Americans. Their culture, religion and morality are quite un-Western. Virtually every Thai is proud and happy to have been born a Thai. They believe that their nation is infinitely better than any other on Earth, and that their Royal Family is divinely inspired. Accordingly, any disparaging remark about the nation or the Royal Family will be taken very seriously and would probably have severe negative consequences for anyone seeking favors (like a passport). One local celebrity went to jail for a few weeks for merely saying, "I would like to have been born a Thai prince, then I wouldn't have to work so hard at being a comedian." The police thought the remark to be unfunny and an "illegal slur on the monarchy".

Thailand in fact is the only nation in Asia that was never colonized by European Powers. In its foreign relations it has always cultivated the logical "winner" in international power struggles. As a result it has stayed free. In World War Two, when the Japanese could have over-run Thailand militarily, they became reluctant allies of Japan thus sparing themselves from the destruction that befell their neighbors. After the war they became allies of the victorious Americans until the US defeat in Vietnam. Then Thailand asked the Americans to remove their big airbase, in order to cultivate better relations with communist neighbors. Thailand's own government is, in Western terms a constitutional monarchy. Army officers run things, but they are subject to the moral authority of the King and Buddhist monks. There are frequent coups and power changes, but the power of the King and the religious leaders is never challenged. For a more detailed picture of Thailand's ways, suggested reading would be *Culture Shock – Thailand,* a book found in the travel book section of most bookstores.

The old capital city of Thailand, Ayuthia, was a center of art, music and culture when Europe was in the Dark Ages. Thailand was a unified nation where people could engage in a lively commerce, travel freely on good roads, and where highly advanced metallurgy, chemistry, astronomy, rockets and canal building on a national scale were all commonplace. This at a time when in Europe (700 AD) every little hilltop was occupied by warlords in constant states of conflict. During this period individual Thai adventurers were "discovering" the world and, like Marco Polo, writing their memoirs. According to Thai folklore, Buddhist missionaries travelled all over Europe in post-Roman times where they established religious centers like Canterbury which still survive today. (The Thai word for town is *Buri,* and thus there may be some truth in these tales.)

There are very few non-Asians resident in Thailand. The white percentage of the total population is under 1 per cent. Off the beaten tourist track of Bangkok, Pattaya and Chaing Mai, most Thais have never seen a white person, except on television news programs. Thus an occidental will be something of a curiosity to be squeezed, touched and perhaps pinched in order to make him say something funny in his incomprehensible, silly sounding language. During the Vietnam era, Thailand was the site of a huge airforce base. The first foreigners ever seen by most Thais of the present generation were probably American airmen exploring the countryside in jeeps from this base. Many of these men fell in love with the country and one – or more – of its spectacularly beautiful women. Many GIs stayed or came back to live after their discharges. Individuals stayed behind when the US Government was asked to remove its military presence.

Thailand until recently was underpopulated and willing to absorb all immigrants. They were always quickly assimilated. There was no racial prejudice or discrimination. Chinese, Burmese, Cambodians, Laotians, Vietnamese, Indians and a few Whites settled and intermarried throughout Thailand. Their children (usually half Thai) spoke only Thai and typically became Thai in outlook and language.

Due to mass migrations as the result of nearby communist revolutions (whose ideology conflicted with a desire to practise their religion and own their own land) the population of Thailand tripled during the past 40 years. Native Thais felt squeezed by newcomers. Today, immigration has been restricted. For a European, there are only a few ways to get a residence permit. Citizenship and a passport comes after twelve years of legal residence. Marriage to a Thai woman by a male does not result in citizenship for the male – but causes *loss of Thai citizenship* for the woman. Any children ultimately born to the marriage are not Thai. A non-Thai female who marries a Thai man does get immediate citizenship and passport. Marriage to a Thai woman does result in "favorable consideration" for a permanent residence permit for a foreign man who wishes to stay in Thailand. Then in twelve years, both can apply for Thai passports. "Special arrangements", African or South American style (for money), seem difficult, if not impossible to make for unassimilated white people. Once an individual can speak and write Thai and has powerful sponsorship (i.e. Establishment friends who will vouch for him) "arrangements can be made" – not necessarily for cash. Aside from getting chummy with the Royal Family, the most powerful sponsorship one can get in Thailand is from a Buddhist teacher or monk.

Thailand in many ways is a Theocracy. Ninety-nine per cent of the population are devoutly Buddhist. It is customary for young Thai males between 14 and 22 to spend three months or more following the disciplined life of a Buddhist monk. Unlike Christian religious leaders, Buddhist teachers live incredibly austere lives, with no possessions other than a piece of cloth to wrap around their bodies and an iron "begging bowl". Christian ministers in Europe or America who come to visit their parishioners for donations may be mildly resented. *Buddhists never ask for anything,* but are always given food. They are appreciated for the opportunity to "make merit". The idea is that by supporting a worthy person, one will have better luck in the present and will be reincarnated into a good life form in the future. According to Buddha, the spirit or soul never dies, but keeps returning to Earth in different forms. Thus a Buddhist will often refuse to kill insects or eat animals killed for food. Like Italian Catholics, lay Thai Buddhists are very loose in their beliefs and do not necessarily interfere with or object to others who eat meat, get drunk, gamble, commit adultery or engage in un-Buddhist practices. They believe that the Buddha will judge and punish, and it is not the place of an individual to make moral judgments, unless perhaps that person is a very saintly monk. In that connection, a venerated monk with a following of disciples (students) is extremely important in Thailand and will be asked to decide such questions as fitness for promotions in the Army or even questions of Royal descent. The moral authority of the religious establishment is the greatest power in Thailand.

What does all this have to do with getting a Thai passport?

Simply this: The shortest path to Thai citizenship (and a passport) is by way of becoming a monk. Unlike his Christian equivalent, most Buddhist monks do not regard their vows of poverty and celibacy as lifelong. In fact, the vast majority of Buddhists take this path of enlightenment for only three months. *The Passport Report* has up to this point been entirely pragmatic – perhaps a bit cynical. In this context, you may find it strange that we now say that becoming a Buddhist monk will be *the most significant experience of your life!* Buddhism does not reject or conflict with any other religion. It is a search for enlightenment. Even after three or four months, your quest for a second passport, material success, sexual adventures and everything else you once regarded as important will be relegated to a lower level. After emerging from the monkhood, the odds are that you will be a different, much improved person – more effective at whatever you do as a result of improved powers of concentration.

You may not be willing to undergo the experience we describe here but if you can, you will have an inner peace and satisfaction of the sort claimed by "born again" Christians. Unfortunately, the Buddhist equivalent takes considerably more work. It is however, longer lasting than conversions that take place with less discomfort.

HOW DO YOU BECOME A THAI BUDDHIST MONK?

The first stop is the nearest Thai Buddhist temple or *Wat.* Go to any Thai Embassy, restaurant or grocery to make inquiry. Near London, for instance, in Hampstead, is *Wat Ba Pong.* You can begin your studies locally, or even by mail, and move to Thailand for the last three months. It's best to know the Thai langauge before you leave to enter the monastery.

Will the life of a monk appeal to you? You will sleep on a wooden plank and rise before dawn. There will be several hours of silent meditation and contemplation while you are sitting in somewhat painful, Yoga-like positions. The idea is to be able to transcend physical sensations such as pleasure, pain, heat and cold. The goals are:

> Harmony with Nature and the universe.
> Perfect peace.
> Contemplation of the true nature of things.
> The impermanence of life.
> Doing no harm to any living thing.

A bell signals the end of pre-dawn meditation. Monks assemble in a military-style single file to walk in silence to a point where villagers will place food in their iron bowls. The food is rice and vegetables, but monks are not supposed to notice or taste what is in the bowls. This is the only meal of the day.

Daily existence for a novice is strictly disciplined, involving 227 rules which must be memorized and chanted singly and as a group. These rules relate to the complete and sincere renunciation of all earthly pleasures, emotions, relationships, possessions and ambitions. It is not expected that a novice will be able successfully to follow even a small fraction of these rules, but one does try. At a public confession twice a month, transgressions are admitted. A sincere effort at purification is expected, and "faking" will be impossible under the circumstances. Some violations are considered serious enough to result in immediate expulsion from the Order, without second chance. One such violation is having any sexual relationships. A monk is expected to have no physical contact (touching) with his parents, children, wife, girlfriend or anyone else. The head is shaved to symbolize a renunciation of vanity.

After the morning walk and only meal of the day, monks return to their Wat where each is assigned a routine, monotonous and repetitive task. This is another form of meditation – a way to leave behind changing moods, memories of past life, lust, greed, hate, love and all other emotions. Extreme concentration is put on to the physical task with the idea of doing it automatically and emptying the mind of all thought. This is very difficult. To achieve it initially, the monk concentrates on his breathing, experiencing only the moment. The first month is always very difficult and thoughts of despair and suicide are common. These are banished by *Patimoka,* the group recital of the 227 rules as a monotone mantra. There is also prayer and singing of chants. The idea is to "let go of self" and thus separate from the physical body without trying.

Eventually there are results. The mind becomes as still and empty and pure as a forest pool. Strange and wondrous animals come to drink from the pool. The nature of reality and ultimate truth begin to unfold. The monk has the "religious experience". This is the reward for one, two or three months of sensual deprivation.

Discussions with the Spiritual Master follow. The teachings of the Buddha are studied. Inspiring and uplifting ancient chants are learned and sung. The monk is now able to show moral leadership to the laity and to new novices. His purpose in life is revealed to him. He finds great inner strength, peace and a complete release from all stress.

The period of training is at an end. The monk returns to the world, only to re-enter the monastery from time to time, as desired. The process can be as short as a few months, as long as a lifetime.

Since a foreigner is only allowed to stay in Thailand for three months, at which time he must leave the country and re-enter, it is necessary to inform the Spiritual Master of one's immigration status at the time training is initiated. As a monk is considered higher than a mere human being, one's immigration status will be worked out by the Master and the authorities so that no departure is needed. By the time three months have passed, the novice will have undergone a training that will give him physical and mental health and far more self-control. He will begin to understand why the typical Thai never shows anger or aggressiveness, but has vast reserves of strength to meet any adversity.

A good student who expresses the desire to stay on in Thailand for a period after his training and wishes for citizenship, will normally have his request granted. He will be considered the most desirable sort of citizen, son-in-law or employee. A former monk presumably will always be relatively free of avarice, sin or illicit desires. He who has trodden the path of Enlightenment sets a moral example to others and is greatly admired. If after a period as a monk, a young (or not-so-young) Western male becomes a teacher (of, for instance, European languages) in Bangkok, he achieves considerable status and is a welcome guest in most Thai homes. This stature does not accrue to a mere vacationing tourist or Western businessman on duty in Thailand. A foreigner's social contacts are normally only with the lower classes. Of course, about six months will have passed and by then you will have become a Thai and a Buddhist. You'll have left behind a lot of the ideas that caused you to read this book and become a Thai passport holder. You will no longer seek to avoid what you now perceive as legitimate "duties", like paying taxes, or submitting to authority. For this author, the Western Humanistic Libertarian idea of controlling my own destiny (not becoming part of a beautiful, harmonious pre-ordained Universe) was too strong to enable me to fully accept Buddhist teachings. However, I'm glad and will forever be nostalgic about the one time I tried it and came close, just for an instant, to Enlightenment.

As my Spiritual Master once said, "Every human being can create a new Universe. We see what we will. We create by our perceptions."

Your Thai passport will, however, not be philosophical abstract reality. It will be a little maroon booklet. It is a fair document for traveling with, but not good in Europe for visa-free travel. You will also need a tax clearance to leave Thailand each time you go. A Westerner with a Thai passport is likely to be asked more questions than an Asian.

Is a Thai passport something to try for? Yes, but only if you want to live mainly in Thailand and own property there (something foreigners can't do). Thailand's most appealing attraction, its serenely beautiful, accommodating women have not even been discussed here. For a full treatment, you will have to see my forthcoming Special Report – *Sex Havens,* the report that COULD NOT HAVE BEEN WRITTEN BY A MONK. Shortly available from Scope International.

THE NON-SECULAR WAY OF BECOMING A THAI

Official guidelines for establishing residence and, subsequently, citizenship in Thailand have been translated from the Thai language by Dr. Hill's Phuket girlfriend and are presented below.

As we have mentioned previously, with powerful sponsorship, anything can and will happen. Thai rules below are often waived on a personal basis by a wide variety of officials who will readily thump away with the necessary rubber stamps if properly motivated.

1. **Getting your Thai resident's permit (the "CI" card)**
   1.1. You must stay in Thailand continously for a period not less than 3 years with the entry stamp "non-immigrant" type in your passport (not the tourist visa). During your stay, you are allowed to travel abroad, but you must be back in Thailand prior to the date your visa expires. Before travelling, you must always register your intention to return with the Thai immigration office.
   1.2. Foreigners in Thailand must have a firm financial status or, if an employee, must be at least employed in a managerial position. If your moving to Thailand involves any investment on your part, be sure that you keep all forms and other evidence showing the amounts transferred from foreign country through the Bank of Thailand.
   1.3. When investing in a Thai limited company or a limited partnership, a registration certificate and the trade registration, issued by the Commercial Ministry, is required.
   1.4. Further, in all visa or citizenship matters you must submit evidence of corporate tax and personal tax payments for the last three years.
   1.5. When submitting the application, a 2,000 Baht fee is required. [Note: 2,500 Baht is approximately US $100.]
   1.6. It takes at least 6 months for the application to be processed. When approved, a further 5,000 Baht must be paid.
   1.7. Each year, Thailand will grant only 100 permanent residence permits for the nation. This quota is waived, however, if you invest more than ten million Baht in the country. Furthermore, it is also waived in "special cases".
   1.8. If the applicants are Taiwanese, the nationality must be transferred to Red Chinese (the People's Republic of China) prior to submitting the application. Thailand has no diplomatic connections with Taiwan.

2. **Getting Thai citizenship and passport**
   2.1. All applicants must have had residence in Thailand for at least 5 years and must hold a CI (permanent residence card).
   2.2. Usually, no one under 21 is considered.
   2.3. You must have no criminal record within Thailand.
   2.4. A basic knowledge of the Thai language is required – you must be able to communicate in Thai.
   2.5. When submitting the application, a 5,000 Baht fee is required. Upon approval, another 5,000 Baht is payable for the necessary papers to be completed.
   [Author's Note: The above fees do not include any tip or gifts to sponsors which might be a decisive factor in the success of your application.]

TURKEY – ALMOST ANYBODY CAN BE A TURK

Issuance of a Turkish passport is discretionary with Turkish diplomats abroad who are empowered to give them to any Turk. Can you be a Turk? Perhaps, but it takes slightly more than buying a fez and a scimitar.

One Turkish Ambassador told me that he could identify a Turk in two minutes of conversation, because only Turks spoke Turkish. I asked if anyone who spoke Turkish was a Turk and thus entitled to a passport, regardless of place of birth. He responded: "Over 100 million Turks have emigrated to all parts of the world; we regard them and all of their descendants as Turks. As a practical matter, anyone who ever came into this office who spoke Turkish and had a Turkish name or some evidence of Turkish ethnic associations would be considered a Turk. We are very liberal and flexible about extending the benefits of our passport to those in need of one."

In view of this situation, it is suggested that a crash course in Turkish or a friend in the Turkish diplomatic corps would be useful. There are Turks of many races and physical descriptions, although European and Asiatic types are dominant. Their religion is mainly Moslem, with a substantial Jewish minority.

Could you become a Turk? The answer seems to be, with a bit of study, effort and the cultivation of a few Turkish ethnic associations – yes!

Bottom Line: Since Turkey is an overpopulated, labour exporting country like Pakistan or Korea, most countries require visas of Turks. This makes a Turkish passport less desirable than one from more prosperous countries. Yet Turkey has applied for membership in the European Community, which is expected to be granted, eventually.

UNITED KINGDOM – A BANK DEPOSIT PLUS A FIVE YEAR WAIT

The British Isles are small, overpopulated islands in a very convenient location. Although public opinion has been anti-immigration for some considerable time, it is still relatively easy to immigrate to the UK and, after a five year residence, to get the coveted British passport. Although Britain had a color blind policy for many years, recent political backlash by the natives now makes it easier for white people to get residence permits than those of other races.

All usual means of gaining preference for a residence permit apply in England: marriage to a local, family re-unification, political asylum, veteran of the British Armed Services, various occupational classifications, etc.

There is a complex group of preferences and rules of maze-like quality only exceeded by those in the US, but with one important difference. British consular officials are knowledgeable, polite and efficient. They will try to help and generally give good advice. As a result, if your situation is not borderline you do not need a lawyer to represent you – if you can read and write English.

Once you are a legal resident of the United Kingdom, a passport can be obtained after five years, but a residence permit is obtainable at once. It should be remembered that except for certain categories of persons who have an absolute right to citizenship, obtaining residency and a passport is a matter of discretion for the bureaucrats or politicians.

To obtain competent advice, you might consider purchasing an excellent, detailed book entitled *Immigration Law* by Ian A. MacDonald, price £40 (publisher: Butterworth & Co., 88 Kingsway, London WC2 6BA, England). Although it is a lawbook, it is easy to understand. If you study the rules in this book, you are likely to pigeonhole yourself into a suitable category eligible for immigration. Then in five years, you can apply for the respected British passport.

As there is no passport stamp or record of arrivals and departures for British or other EC citizens within the EC, there is no conclusive check on how much time you actually spend in England. Non-EC passports are always date-stamped in and out, unless one arrives and departs the UK via Ireland. In this case the Irish may or may not stamp you.

The most interesting categories of immigration are:

PERSONS OF INDEPENDENT MEANS

A bank deposit of over £200,000 makes you, by definition, "a person of independent means", but just having the £200,000 is not enough. There must also be some "close connection" with the UK so that your admission is considered to be in the general interests of the UK. One such connection for anyone with £200,000 in assets is a membership in Lloyd's of London. For details on how to become a member of Lloyd's of London and generate a second income by underwriting insurance in the Lloyd's market, read *The Lloyd's Report*. See back of this report for further details.

A managed investment account in a London bank plus a Lloyd's membership would probably generate an income of over £30,000 per year. This would satisfy UK immigration requirements very nicely and assure the authorities that you are not about to steal the job of some poor coal miner or janitor. Ownership of real estate in the UK would satisfy both the substantial connection and the means test.

The Independent Means category would also permit anyone with a trust income or pension of over £20,000 a year to become a resident or retiree in the UK without an additional investment in the country.

SMALL BUSINESS ENTREPRENEUR

This category, until recently, permitted entry by anyone from any Third World country who could scrape up enough to open a small restaurant or laundromat. However, so many local tradespeople were hurt that business proposals submitted by an intending immigrant now have to be something that is "needed" and not competitive with existing enterprises. However, this still leaves a lot of room for an individual who will "find a need and fill it". These days a self employed person must invest at least £150,000 and provide full time paid employment for at least two persons already settled in the UK.

Unfortunately, with UK residence, it seems difficult, if not impossible, to avoid filing a return with the Inland Revenue and paying at least a token tax. Once a British passport is obtained, you can withdraw your capital, discontinue being a permanent resident of the UK and move your legal residence elsewhere. You never lose British subject status. Britain is one of the few countries that doesn't care how many other passports you hold. UK nationality laws are being tightened – for example, automatic British citizenship is no longer automatically granted to the child of foreigners that is born within the United Kingdom.

RESIDENT WRITER OR ARTIST

Another interesting category, showing just how enlightened the British are, is that of resident "Writer or Artist". This category does not include theatrical performers or musicians, who must obtain work permits. But it would include poets, composers, sculptors, painters and creative persons in unspecified categories, who may be admitted for an initial four years.

Before going to an interview at a Consulate claiming you are another Shakespeare, it would be wise to get a letter from a well recognized artist or University professor to the effect that you have some degree of talent. The British, who have a vibrant cultural life, are anxious to attract stimulating artists from anywhere in the world – the only requirement being that they must show assets or earning capacity to indicate that they can maintain themselves and their dependents purely from their art. They must convince immigration that they will not become a public charge or apply for "the dole" once they settle in the United Kingdom.

The financial or capital requirements for a writer or artist would be minimal, but an application would be helped if you could show that you owned an apartment or had a rich patron who would provide support plus free accommodation. Without this most artists would be hard put to demonstrate sufficient earning capacity to qualify in this capacity.

WORKING IN THE UK

Anyone who is subject to immigration control, unless they come from an EC country, will need a work permit to take employment in the UK. Special types of temporary work (see section below) and a few exceptional categories are exempt from this requirement. If a foreign worker remains for four years continuously, then he may apply for all restrictions on remaining and working in the UK to be lifted. A year after the restrictions are lifted, British naturalization may be sought.

Work permits have to be obtained at least at eight weeks (longer if the worker is from the Commonwealth or Pakistan) before the worker wishes to travel to the UK. The possession of a work permit does not absolve the holder from complying with visa requirements. The potential employer has to apply for the permit from the UK government's Department of Employment after satisfying a number of criteria. An overseas worker has to be aged between 23 and 54 years, except sportsmen or women, who may be younger.

Permits are issued only for workers who come within the following categories:
(a) Those with recognised professional qualifications.
(b) Administrative and executive staff.
(c) Highly-qualified technicians with specialized experience.
(d) Other key workers with a high or scarce qualification in an industry or occupation requiring expert knowledge or skills.
(e) Highly-skilled and experienced workers in the hotel or catering trade who have trained at least two years at an approved course or, exceptionally, have other special or unusual skills and experience.
(f) Established entertainers, including self-employed entertainers.
(g) Sportsmen and sportswomen who meet appropriate skills criteria. This does not apply to professionals attending international competitions.
(h) Others only if, in the opinion of the Employment Secretary, their employment is in the national interest.
(i) Those coming for a limited period of training or work experience, for whom there are other regulations.

If a potential worker qualifies, further rules apply to the definition of the job. A genuine vacancy has to exist, there has to be no suitable labour in the UK available, the employer has to have made adequate efforts to fill the vacancy from suitable labour in the UK or the EC, and the pay and conditions of employment have to be at least as good as those offered in the area for similar work. It is also expected that the foreign worker's qualifications, skills and experience were acquired outside the UK, and that he or she has an adequate knowledge of the English language.

The application for a work permit has to be for a named worker for a specific post. Applications (on form OW1, available at UK Jobcentres) have to be accompanied by documentary evidence of qualifications and experience. The potential employer also must send a job description, copies of any advertising material relating to the vacancy and proof of efforts to recruit from UK or EC residents. The completed forms should be returned to the Department of Employment, Overseas Labour Section, Caxton House, Tothill Street, London, SW1H 9NF, which deals with inquiries about work permits, as do Jobcentres in most large towns and cities.

If a work permit is granted, it will be sent to the employer for onward despatch to the worker abroad unless the worker lives in the Commonwealth or Pakistan in which case it is channelled through the UK government offices in that country. When the worker arrives in the UK, he must show immigration authorities the work permit, a valid passport and, if necessary, a visa – without these, entry to the UK may be refused. Leave to enter the country could be refused if fraud or misrepresentation in obtaining the permit is suspected. The worker can stay in the UK for as long as specified in the permit. It may be extended if the employer or employee applies to the Home Office Immigration and Nationality Department two to three months before the permit expires. The Employment Department has to give approval if the employer wishes to move the foreign worker to another job, but no permission is needed if the employer or employee want to end the employment. However, the worker would need approval to take another job, which would be expected to be similar to that for which the original work permit was issued.

If a foreign national already in the UK wants to obtain a work permit, the procedures are similar to those applying for pre-entry permits but permission to work may not be granted if the original reason for coming to the UK was other than for employment (such as staying for a holiday or study). The Home Office Immigration Department first has to decide if the person's conditions of stay allow the potential worker to take employment or, if not, whether the conditions can be changed. If the foreign worker already is in an approved job, the Employment Department will consider a permit application only if notice of termination in the existing job has been given by the employer or employee.

Overseas students studying in the UK who want to take part-time or holiday work will need to give evidence in writing that taking a job will not affect their studies. Permission will be given by the Employment Department only if there is no other suitable resident worker available and if the wages and conditions are comparable with similar work in the area. Applications should be made by the employer to a Jobcentre.

A dependent wife and/or children under the age of 18 may accompany the foreign worker at the time of entry or later but they will need prior entry clearance through the UK government office in their native country. Entry clearance normally will not be given to dependents until the overseas worker is in possession of a valid work permit. The worker must state in writing that he will be able and willing to maintain his dependents and provide a home for them in the UK without help from public funds.

All foreign nationals aged 16 and over who are given limited leave to enter the UK, such as those working for more than three months, have to register with the British police. The rule also applies to those allowed to stay temporarily for more than six months in the special categories such as "au pairs" and self-employed businessmen.

FOREIGN WORKERS TRAINING AND WORK EXPERIENCE SCHEME: The main purpose of the foreign workers training and work experience scheme is to help developing countries by allowing their nationals to come to the UK for a limited time of training which is not available in their own country and leads to an occupational skill or qualification. Young people from non-EC countries may be given permits to develop their industrial or commercial experience and to improve their knowledge of English.

A number of rules apply to the schemes which, although they are run separately, have a number of elements in common. The employer must offer training or work experience which will lead to an occupational skill or qualification (where appropriate), be of a type and standard approved by the Employment Department, not be easily available in the foreign worker's home country but will be of use there and be for a set period, fixed in advance. The overseas national must intend to return abroad at the end of the training period and a transfer to ordinary employment will not be allowed. The worker must have an adequate knowledge of English.

Specific regulations for training situations are that the worker, aged 18 to 54 years, must be suitable for and benefit from the training and must have educational or professional qualifications for the course. Any qualifications gained from the training must be clearly stated, set out and recognized in the worker's home country. On the employer's side, he must be capable of giving the proposed training, provide a detailed program and offer wages and training similar to those in the locality. Permission for the foreign worker to remain on the course will depend on whether he or she makes satisfactory progress or not, including satisfactory marks on examinations.

The maximum period for work experience is usually 12 months. If agreed in advance with the Employment Department, this period can be extended for up to two years. The worker, aged between 18 and 35 years and near the start of his career, must have educational or professional qualifications or experience to enable him to benefit from the UK scheme. He must be extra to normal staff needs and not be used to take a vacancy which could be filled by a British person, unless there is a one-for-one exchange between UK and overseas companies. The employer must be able to give the work experience, provide a detailed programme and clearly state objectives. Foreign workers may be paid only pocket money or a maintenance allowance (far less than an ordinary wage) unless a legal minimum wage is in force. Job exchangers may be paid full wages, as can those paid by their employer abroad and those on an inter-company transfer for a short period.

As with standard work permits, the potential employer must apply at least eight weeks before the foreign worker is due to arrive in the UK. The permit then will be sent to Commonwealth citizens via the UK government office in that country and to the potential employer for onward transmission to other foreign nationals. When the trainee arrives in the UK he must have the permit, a passport and, if necessary, a visa.

An employer must apply to the Employment Department if he wants to change the type of training or work experience offered, but does not need permission to end the arrangement with the trainee, who is also at liberty to leave the scheme, although he cannot move to another company without new permission.

Overseas students of agriculture and horticulture have a separate UK training scheme which is administered by The International Farm Experience Programme, YFC Centre, Kenilworth, Warwickshire, CV8 2LG, UK. Technical students can take part in the international student exchange programme organized by IAESTE, Seymour Mews House, Seymour Mews, London, W1H 9PE, UK, while students of commerce and economics are catered for through AIESEC, UKIN House, Phipp Street, London, EC2A 4NR, UK. More information is available from the Department of Employment, Overseas Labour Section, Caxton House, Tothill Street, London, SW1H 9NF.

WORKERS WHO DO NOT NEED PERMITS: European Community nationals (except Spaniards and Portuguese), Gibraltarians, and Commonwealth nationals who have one grandparent born in the UK may seek and take work without a permit. Also, Commonwealth citizens, aged 17 to 27 inclusive, can take an extended holiday in the UK which may involve incidental employment if the total length of their stay is not more than two years, they can pay for their return journey and will not have recourse to public funds.

Once employed, citizens of EC countries are subject to all laws and regulations covering UK nationals and are entitled to the same treatment with regards to pay, conditions, access to housing, training, social security and trade union rights. They can be joined by their family and immediate dependents, who themselves have the same rights as the worker. If EC nationals are incapable of work because of sickness or industrial accident or disease, or if they become unemployed, they can use the services of the Social Security Department and the Employment Department for obtaining benefits or help with seeking other jobs. They may set up in business or provide or receive services as specified in Community law. If coming to work or seek work they will be admitted for six months without restriction. A residence permit for up to five years is required for a longer stay. They are not required to register with the police.

TEMPORARY ADMISSION TO THE UK
Temporary admission to the UK is available in a number of categories but visitors rarely are able to gain permanent resident status unless a fresh application is made from abroad and the relevant criteria are satisfied. Visitors normally are prohibited from taking employment and admission is dependent on the person having sufficient funds to maintain himself during his stay, which is limited to six months.

Students must be able to support and accommodate themselves and pay for their studies without working in the UK, although relatives or friends in the UK may provide support with costs and accommodation. The foreign national must be able to follow the intended course and must have a place at a university, college of further education, polytechnic, independent school or other genuine private educational institution. The course of study should occupy at least 15 hours a week of organized day-time study of a single subject or related subjects. When the studies are completed, which will depend on the course undertaken, the student should intend to leave the UK. Foreign nationals requiring entry clearance must obtain a valid student visa, which entails applying to the nearest British Mission (form IM2A) with documents including relevant diplomas or educational certificates, a letter from the educational establishment confirming acceptance on a course of study and evidence of Government sponsorship (if any). Potential students also may be asked for proof of funds to pay for the stay and course in the UK or a letter from a host or sponsor in the UK. It is inadvisable to buy a travel ticket or pay for any part of course fees until entry clearance is confirmed. A student's wife or children can be admitted with him.

A Doctor or dentist may enter the UK for a year's post-graduate training if he is qualified under the regulations of the General Medical Council or General Dental Council. He has to intend to leave the UK at the end of the period, and, if he had spent time studying in the UK previously, his aggregate period in the country may not exceed four years.

Dependents may be admitted.

Au pairs (unmarried girls aged 17 to 27 without dependents who wish to learn English while living with a family) can be admitted from any western European country, as well as Malta, Cyprus and Turkey, for up to two years in total but cannot take any other employment. A girl coming for full-time domestic employment requires a work permit.

Ministers of religion and members of religious orders, if they are coming to work full-time as such and can maintain and accommodate themselves and their dependents, do not require work permits.

Representatives of overseas newspapers, news agencies and broadcasting organizations on long-term assignment in the UK do not need work permits.

If they hold appropriate entry documents, the following groups of people can be admitted for up to 12 months: private servants working in diplomatic or consular missions; employees of an overseas government, the United Nations Organization or similar international organization; teachers and language assistants on official exchange schemes; seamen joining a ship in British waters; operational ground staff of overseas airlines and seasonal workers at agricultural camps under approved schemes.

OPPORTUNITIES FOR BUSINESSMEN

Temporary work permits are available to businessmen or those of independent means in three categories.

A sole representative of an overseas company which has no branch, subsidiary or other representative in the UK may apply to establish a place of business with an attendant representative. Audited accounts are required to show the company is trading, solvent and not merely a sham to facilitate entry. One must also prove that representative office will be beneficial to the UK economy. After an initial period of 12 months, a three-year extension may be granted.

Someone seeking to enter the UK to establish himself in business or self-employment, whether on his own account or in partnership, must hold a current entry clearance issued for that purpose. To obtain the entry clearance, which is valid for a year, he must show he is bringing at least £200,000 of his own into the business, he will be able to bear his share of the liabilities, he will be occupied full-time in running the business, and that there is a genuine need for his services and investment. If intending to join a partnership, he must meet all the above requirements and show that his share of the profits will be sufficient to maintain him and his dependents. Audited accounts and statements of the business's position and evidence that full-time jobs will be created for UK nationals are necessary before entry clearance will be given.

A person of independent means, who must obtain entry clearance in such a definition, can be admitted for up to four years with a prohibition on taking employment. The applicant will need to show he has at least £200,000 under his control in the UK or an income of not less than £20,000 a year. He must be able and willing to support himself and his dependents without public funds. In addition, he must have a close connection with the UK, such as resident relatives or periods of previous residence, or prove that his admission would be in the general interests of the UK. If he qualifies for admission, but intends to establish himself in business, he must satisfy the regulations applying to entrepreneurs.

FAMILIES AND FIANCES/FIANCEES

People admitted temporarily to the UK may bring their wives/husbands and children under 18, if they have entry clearance. The original applicant must be able to maintin them. A child cannot enter unless accompanied by (or intending to join) both parents. This requirement does not apply if the applicant's spouse is deceased or there are compelling reasons for the child to accompany the foreign national.

Someone seeking entry to the UK intending to marry someone settled in the UK must hold an entry clearance which will be valid for six months. A visa may be refused unless it is certain:

(a)   The primary purpose of the marriage is not to obtain admission to the UK.

(b)   The parties intend to live together permanently as man and wife.

(c)   The parties to the proposed marriage have met.

(d)   That adequate maintenance and accomodation are available before the marriage.

(e)   After the marriage the parties will be able to maintain and house themselves without using public funds. The fiance/fiancee is not allowed to take a job and at the end of six months must apply to the Home Office for leave to remain in the UK.

STATELESS PEOPLE, ASYLUM AND REFUGEES

Every potential case of asylum is referred to the government's Home Office for consideration, regardless of other immigration rules which may justify refusal of entry. Asylum will not be refused if the only country to which the person could be removed is one to which he is unwilling to go owing to a well-founded fear of being persecutied for reasons of race, religion, nationality, membership of a particular social group or political opinion.

BEING REFUSED ENTRY

Even if immigration requirements are satisfied, a foreign national still may be refused leave to enter the UK if he fails a medical examination, has a criminal record, is subject to a deportation order, or if his exclusion would be for the public good.

APPEALS PROCEDURE

No appeal is available to someone who is refused admission to the UK on the grounds of exclusion for the public good, nor to someone claiming to have a right of abode who does not hold a British Citizen's passport, a CUKC passport with right of abode or a certificate issued by the British government certifying a right of abode.

A person who holds a current entry clearance or has a work permit can appeal before removal from the UK. He must be given access to friends, relatives, a legal adviser, the UK Immigrants Advisory Service or his High Commission or Consul. The immigration officer must provide the adjudicator and the appellant with a summary of the facts of the case and reasons for the decision.

In all other cases, rights of appeal only can be exercised outside the UK. Where a foreigner is admitted but is unhappy about a time limit or condition imposed, he can apply to the Home Office for variation of the limit or condition if he applies before his time limit expires.

Foreign nationals may be deported if conditions attached to the leave to enter have not been met, if the person is the wife or child of a deportee, if the person is convicted of a criminal offence and the court recommends deportation or if the Home Secretary deems the deportation is for the public good. In all cases of deportation, the deportee can appeal to be sent to a country specified by himself. An immigration consultant's advice on rights of appeal should be sought if deportation is likely.

ENTITLEMENT TO BRITISH CITIZENSHIP AS A MATTER OF RIGHT

Britain no longer rules the waves. Gone are the days when Crown subjects could travel freely to almost any country in the world without visas. These days, not even birth in the UK carries automatic entitlement to British citizenship as it did for almost a millennium.

The 1981 British Nationality Act links British Citizenship with the 1971 Immigration Act's concept of a UK "right of abode" held by persons who were Citizens of the UK and Colonies (CUKC). Only persons having a right of abode can live and work in the UK without restriction, and only British citizens have such right of abode. All others entering the UK are theoretically subject to rigorous immigration controls both before and after entry.

There are now three main groups of British subjects: British citizens, British Dependent Territories citizens and British Overseas Citizens. Only British citizens are free to come and go from the UK "without let or hindrance". The label "Commonwealth citizen" and residual classes of "British subjects" and "British protected persons" are today *only of symbolic value* when it comes to getting into the European Community.

Only BRITISH CITIZENS are free to live and work in the UK (and the EC) without restriction. They include those who as of 1 January 1973 were born, adopted, naturalised or registered in the United Kingdom. Formerly known as "patrials", these British citizens also included those who were descended from or adopted by patrial parents or married to a patrial spouse. Patrials also included those who under the 1971 Act had been "settled" and ordinarily resident in the UK for five years or more.

BRITISH DEPENDENT TERRITORY CITIZENS (BDTC's) include those who have a connection by birth, descent, naturalization or registration with a "dependent territory", i.e. Gibraltar and Hong Kong. The connection can be traced through parents or grandparents who were themselves CUKC's by birth, naturalization or registration in a dependent territory. Although viewed by many in Hong Kong as a means of escaping Chinese rule on 1 July 1997, BDTCs now have no automatic right of abode in the UK. Further, under the Hong Kong (British Nationality) Order of 1986, a person who, but for his connection with Hong Kong, would not be a BDTC will lose such citizenship on the 1st of July, 1997. The Order, however, creates a new citizenship for persons connected with Hong Kong – British Nationals (Overseas). Such citizenship, again, does not carry any automatic right of abode in the UK.

BRITISH OVERSEAS CITIZENS (BOC's) is a residual class of British citizenship which includes all CUKCs who are neither British citizens nor British Dependent Territory Citizens. **In general, it covers those who, when their Colony became independent, did not acquire the new citizenship.** As with BDTCs, there is no automatic right of abode in the UK. BOC status prevents former British subjects from being stateless. But the BOC passport is little better than a refugee passport for visa-free travel. The holder needs a special voucher, issued to him by a British government representative overseas, to present at immigration control for entry.

THERE ARE NOW ONLY FOUR WAYS TO ACQUIRE BRITISH CITIZENSHIP UNDER THE 1981 ACT:

> **By birth/legal adoption.**
> **By descent.**
> **By registration.**
> **By naturalization.**

BIRTH IN THE UNITED KINGDOM: Birth in the UK is no longer the automatic route to citizenship it used to be.

Only a child born in the UK to a parent who is a British citizen is automatically (after 1981) a British citizen. Legal adoption by such a parent will also confer British citizenship on the adopted child. If the parent is settled but not British, the child would probably take the parent's nationality (unless the rules of that country prevented it). A child born in the UK to parents who at no time satisfy these requirements no longer becomes a British citizen as of right, but such a child is entitled to be registered as a British citizen after the age of 10 if in each year of his life he has not been absent from the UK for more than 90 days.

A child born *outside* the UK may be a British citizen if at the time of birth one parent had acquired British citizenship otherwise than by descent. One major disadvantage of British citizenship by descent is that citizenship is not automatically conferred on a child born abroad although he may obtain British citizenship by registration.

Registration is the acquisition of citizenship by administrative grant, in most cases as a right. The Secretary of State has *discretion* to register a minor as a British citizen within 12 months of the date of birth (provided one parent is a British citizen by descent *and* one grandparent is or has become a British citizen otherwise than by descent). The child's parent must also have spent three years in the UK before the date of birth and must not have been absent during that period for more than 270 days. Residence and time limits for applications are sometimes extended at the discretion of officials involved.

CITIZENSHIP BY NATURALIZATION: Naturalization may be granted to persons of "full age and capacity" if they satisfy the following conditions:

– They must have a sufficient knowledge of English, Welsh or Scots Gaelic.
– They must be of good character.
– They must intend to live mainly in the UK or to enter or continue in Crown Service abroad or in some other international organization of which the UK is a member.
– They must have been registered and legally resident in the UK for five years prior to the application and absent for no more than 450 days in that period.
– They must not have been absent from the UK for more than 90 days in the 12 months immediately prior to the application nor in that period can they have been subject to any restrictions on their length of stay.
– In the five years prior to the application, they must not have been in breach of the immigration laws.

To become a naturalized citizen, the spouse of an existing British citizen gets a two year discount and need only be resident for three years with not more than 270 days absence.

Officials acting for the Secretary of State can, on a case-by-case basis, waive or modify all or any of the conditions except those relating to linguistic ability, good character and the intention to remain in the UK.

It should be remembered that **naturalization** is never a "legal right". Citizenship may be refused at an administrative level without publicly giving any reason. It is unfortunate, in our opinion, that bureaucrats are given such arbitrary powers, but that's the way it is. The bottom line is that naturalization candidates, if they can afford it, should obtain the best possible representation. Once naturalization has been refused, it is difficult, expensive and almost impossible to appeal that decision in court or win it.

If you plan on becoming British by "birthright", an American reader in Japan has the following good news for you. He writes:

"One week after I furnished the British Embassy, Consular Section, Tokyo, with an original of my parents marriage certificate, I got my British passport. A photocopy was not acceptable.

All that was needed was:
1) My birth certificate.
2) My father's birth certificate showing that he was born in Britain.
3) My parents' marriage certificate.
4) A simple form, duly filled in.

My passport was then obtained in two days.

There was also:
A) No need to surrender previous passports.
B) No need to give up former citizenship (dual nationality is recognized).
C) No need to make any pledge of allegiance.
D) No report of new British citizenship obtained as a matter of right was made to US authorities.

IM2A
(Revised 9/88)

Full Name | Post Ref.

APPLICATION FOR UNITED KINGDOM ENTRY CLEARANCE

This form must be accompanied by the appropriate fee and two passport sized photographs. Entry clearance fees are non-refundable.

A separate form should be completed by every person intending to travel. Please read the following notes carefully before you fill in this form: More information is contained in leaflets INF 1 - 6, available at your nearest British Mission.

This form is also to be used for an application for a certificate of entitlement confirming the right of abode.

A An entry clearance is a Visa, Entry Certificate or Letter of Consent.

B The holder of a valid entry clearance will not be refused leave to enter the UK unless the Immigration Officer is satisfied that:-

   (a) the entry clearance was obtained by false representations or by concealment of material facts, whether or not to the applicant's knowledge (if you are in doubt whether a particular matter or fact is relevant to your case you should ask the entry clearance officer when you apply); or

   (b) a change of circumstances since issue has removed the basis of the holder's claim to admission; or

   (c) refusal is justified on the grounds of restricted returnability, medical grounds, criminal record, because the holder is subject to a deportation order or because exclusion would be conducive to the public good

C If you intend to stay in the UK longer than 6 months you may be required to undergo a medical examination before an entry clearance is issued. The issue of an entry clearance does not exempt the holder from being medically examined at the port of entry to the United Kingdom, if this is considered necessary.

Please use black or blue ink and ✓ *where necessary.*

For Official Use Fee

The basis of my application is:

Short Stay (Visitor, business visitor, student)	☐ → Complete all questions on this form
Settlement, spouse, fiance(e), other relative	☐ → Complete questions 1 - 16 on this form, and also complete form IM2 B.
Permit free employment, work permit holder, businessman and self employed person, person of independent means	☐ → Complete questions 1 - 16 on this form, and also complete form IM2 C.
Certificate of Entitlement/ Confirming the Right of Abode, UK Ancestry	☐ → Complete questions 1 - 16 on this form, and also complete form IM2 D.
Returning resident	☐ → Complete questions 1 - 16 only on this form.

For Official Use Fee

Crown Copyright

164

All applicants must answer questions 1- 16

1. Full Name (exactly as in passport, and in both forms, if two scripts are used)

Title   Mr ☐   Mrs ☐   Miss ☐   Ms ☐   Other (specify) ☐

Attach
PHOTO
here

2. Former name(s) (where different from above)

3. Date of Birth

4. Place and country of birth

5. Passport Details:

Issuing Government:

Number:

Place and Date of Issue:

Expires on:

Citizenship / Nationality:

Former citizenship/nationality (if any)

Are you travelling on your own passport?   Yes ☐   No ☐

If 'No' give: Name of passport Holder

Relationship to you of holder

6. Are you: Married ☐   Single ☐   Divorced ☐   Widowed ☐   Separated ☐

7. If married, give details of husband or wife:

Full Name:

Place of birth:

Date of birth:

Citizenship/Nationality:

Present whereabouts:

8. Your present address

Telephone Number

9. Your permanent address (if different from 8)

10. Father's name:

11. Mother's name:

12. Particulars of any dependants included in your passport who are NOT accompanying you

Name	Date of birth	Sex	Relationship

13. What is your job / occupation?

State date you started in this employment

14. Name and address of employer (if any)

Telephone Number

State your annual income

Crown Copyright

165

15. Give dates of previous periods of stay in the UK

16. (a) Have you ever been refused a visa or entry clearance at a UK diplomatic mission or Post?   Yes ☐   No ☐   **If Yes complete form IM2E**

(b) Have you ever been refused leave to enter on arrival in the UK   Yes ☐   No ☐   **If Yes complete form IM2E**

(c) Have you ever been refused a visa for another country   Yes ☐   No ☐

(d) Have you ever been deported from the UK   Yes ☐   No ☐

ANSWER QUESTIONS 17-30 ONLY IF YOU ARE APPLYING FOR A SHORT TERM STAY

17. Is your visit   Official ☐   Private ☐   Business ☐   Student ☐   Other ☐

18. Which entry clearance do you require   Single ☐   Double ☐   Multiple ☐

19. If official, give name of sponsoring Ministry or Organisation

20. (a) Country of normal residence   **(b)** Residence Permit No. (if any): Issued on: Expires on:

21. Re-entry visa (if applicable)   Exit visa No: Issued on: Valid for:

22. How long do you intend to stay in the UK: **23.** What is your proposed date of: Departure for the UK   Arrival in the UK

24. If a private visit give details of host/sponsor in the UK. If staying in a hotel give the name and address (it is not enough to say c/o Embassy or High Commission)

Name	Nationality
Address	Telephone No:
	In UK since:
	Occupation:
	Relationship:

25. If your visit is for business, study, professional or official reasons give details of sponsors/contacts/school or university in the UK as appropriate.

Name	Telephone No.
Address	

26. How much money is available to you during your stay: (a) from your own resources

(b) from other resources

27. What kind of ticket (single, return confirmed, open dated) do you hold or intend to buy?

FOR STUDENTS ONLY

28. What technical or educational certificates do you hold?
Any relevant diplomas or cetificates should be submitted

29. Give full particulars of the course you wish to follow and submit evidence of acceptance for a course of study

30. Who will pay for the course

PLEASE NOTE DECLARATION OVERLEAF <u>MUST</u> BE SIGNED

166

I understand that failure to disclose to the Issuing Authority, Entry Clearance Officer or to an Immigration Officer any change of circumstances between the date of this application and my arrival in the United Kingdom may invalidate the Entry Clearance. I declare that the information given in this application is correct to the best of my knowledge and belief.

Signed

Date

For Official Use Only

INSTANT PASSPORT FOR CHILDREN OF BRITISH SUBJECTS

British nationality was easily obtainable to "those of British ancestry" a few years ago. Too much immigration has caused the laws to be drastically tightened up. Today a person with a British parent can usually get instant citizenship and a passport. Because the law is complex and subject to many ifs, ands and buts, you can get a free brochure entitled *British Citizenship*. It is available free of charge from any UK consulate or from The Home Office, Croydon CR9 2BY, Surrey, UK.

It is not necessary to renounce any other citizenship, swear allegiance nor give up other passports if British nationality is acquired by birthright. Not all British *subjects* will have the right of domicile in the British Isles, but the passport is still a useful document, giving the right to work or settle in many Commonwealth countries without further visas or permits. Essentially, if you were born before 1981 and have a British-born mother and father, all that is needed is *their* birth and marriage certificates, your birth certificate, a bank guarantee that you are whom you say you are and a simple passport application form which you can get from the Home Office or the The British Passport Office: Clive House, 70-78 Petty France, London SW1, Great Britain. Tel: 071-279-3434. (Open 9am to 4.30pm.)

APPLYING FOR ENTRY CLEARANCE

Some foreign nationals must have a valid entry clearance before arrival in the UK. Others who are not obliged to have it may find it helpful to get one anyway to ensure they are eligible to enter the UK. Applicants should fill in form IM2A, available from your nearest British Mission, and return it there with your passport, two photographs and the fee. The entry clearance officer may be able to decide your application without further inquiries but you may be asked to attend an interview or provide further documents.

See also *The Tax Exile Report,* published by Scope International.

UK IMMIGRATION/WORK PERMIT/VISA SPECIALIST

Needless to say, applications often proceed more quickly and produce a more favourable outcome if handled by a competent professional. Once an applicant is rejected, all subsequent applications are subjected to severe scrutiny, i.e. if you don't get through on the first try, you may never. As these rules are complicated and change frequently, it makes sense to hire a professional to save yourself time, money and the many headaches that are often the result of too much contact with a government agency. Scope International can refer you to a firm of leading immigration consultants for the UK. Amongst other services, they can assist you with:

*   Entry to the UK for work, marriage or study.
*   UK Passports and Citizenship through naturalization or ancestral entitlement.
*   Work Permits for businessmen, including treaty traders, investors and sole representatives.
*   Intra-company transfers.
*   Person of Independent Means entry.
*   Full Work Permits for those with specialized skills.
*   Trainee/Work Experience Permits.
*   Student Visas.

* Greencard and UK settlement through civil and common law marriage.
* Political asylum and refugee status.
* Working Holiday Visas
* Border Requirements.

Please contact Scope International and ask for the appropriate referral. All consultations are strictly confidential. Scope International, 62 Murray Road, Horndean, Waterlooville, Hants, PO8 9JL.

URUGUAY – THE SWITZERLAND OF SOUTH AMERICA

Uruguay, located on the East Coast of South America next door to Paraguay, has a good reputation as a resort area for rich South Americans. It is not a place of high level cultural activity, rather it's a place to rest, relax on beaches and watch the world go by. Uruguay – like Guatemala – can be your safe harbor in a stormy world.

The climate is mild with average temperatures ranging from 70 to 80 degrees Fahrenheit. As Uruguay is a former Spanish colony, the estimated population of 3 million inhabitants (1.3 million of which live in the country's capital, Montevideo) is mostly of European descent, and the official language is Spanish. With an economy that relies on cattle and agriculture, more than half of the national territory is devoted to pastures. Industrial activity is heavily related to these activities, manufacturing excellent by-products of beef, wool, leather, sugar cane and cotton. Uruguay is a stable Unitarian Republic, with a president elected every five years, a bi-cameral legislative branch and complete separation between Church and State.

Once assimilated in the relatively large expatriate community of Punta del Este (Uruguay's answer to Newport, Rhode Island or Puerto Banus, Spain), life in this "Switzerland of South America" could be quite pleasant. Bridge nights and cocktail parties are part of the daily routine. The international yachting set does their thing and special interest groups are so varied and numerous you might even walk into the Montevideo or Punta del Este yacht club on Scottish Folkdancing night. All you need to gain admission to any yacht club worldwide is A) a boat, or B) an ID card from any Yacht Club or C) a good gift of gab to talk your way in.

An added benefit is that holders of a Uruguay passport can easily acquire a residence and work permit in Spain. Two years and a few Spanish lessons later, an Uruguayan in Spain can become Spanish, with passport and all. In special cases, the waiting period can be as little as one year. With a Spanish passport, the holder is free to move and work anywhere in the EC. This "back door to the EC" is open now. As Europe continues to integrate, this opportunity – like all good things – could easily disappear. Act now to become a Uruguayan or South American citizen while you still have the chance to parlay it into European citizenship!

With no big fuss, officials in Uruguay embarked on an instant passport program in July of 1990. Local expatriate lawyers helped set up this program.

The principal requirement is that one invest a minimum of US $70,000 in certain programs approved by the Uruguayan government. Currently they include:
1) 10 year Reforestation Bonds issued by the Central Bank of Uruguay
2) 10 year Certificate of Deposit escrowed at Banco de la Republica (Bank of the Republic, Uruguay)

Both of these investments are US dollar denominated, and the interest thereof is tax-free in Uruguay. Additional passports for the investor's spouse or children under 21 years of age are possible by investing an additional US $10,000 per person.

Interested parties must demonstrate that they have no police record, provide health certificates and state their intention to invest in Uruguay and that they are free to leave and return to their country of residence.

Once this documentation has been submitted, it is studied by the Ministry of Uruguay which will ultimately recommend or deny the granting of a passport. If the recommendation is favorable and proof of investment is submitted, the passport will be granted within 90 days.

If you are interested in this program, ask Scope International for a referral to a lawyer with a one hundred per cent success rate.

See also *The Tax Exile Report,* published by Scope International.

US – THE MOST EXPENSIVE PASSPORT, BUT YOU GET IT FREE

The United States has been a large scale immigrant destination for over 200 years. Originally a British colony, it was founded in 1620 by those escaping religious oppression in England. The British colony gradually conquered, absorbed or purchased the Dutch colony at New York, the French of Louisiana and the Spanish of Florida, Texas and California. As a polyglot country of every race and language, the US continues to be a desired destination for the homeless, oppressed and persecuted, as well as for rich individuals who want to invest or live in the "last bastion of capitalism".

Ambition, drive and creativity can make anyone in the US financially comfortable, or even wealthy in a short time. America is still the most economically free country in the world. Because there are fewer regulations and restrictions upon starting or owning an enterprise, it is the easiest place in which to become an entrepreneur. Aside from agriculture, most elements of the economic system are allowed to function without undue government control. Privatization and deregulation has been a conscious and deliberate government policy for several years.

Rents, wages and prices are generally not controlled. Local voters can and do occasionally implement residential rent controls, especially in places with many students or high densities of non-whites such as Los Angeles and New York. Other prices are set by supply and demand.

Leveraged or geared trading in property and "going public" with privately-held businesses (making them into public corporations) accounts for many new American personal fortunes.

US tax laws are complex. Legal tax shelters exist, but the normal person would need a lawyer or accountant to understand how they work. A wealthy individual subject to US tax laws can expect to pay 33 per cent in federal income taxes, 15 per cent in state income taxes, 5 per cent in local income taxes and up to 20 per cent in indirect taxation. THE US IS THE ONLY MAJOR COUNTRY THAT TAXES THE WORLDWIDE INCOME OF NON-RESIDENT CITIZENS. THIS IS THE MAIN DRAWBACK OF HOLDING A US PASSPORT.

Despite an overwhelmingly complicated and burdensome tax structure, social and public services are astonishingly poor. Medical costs are the highest in the world. Poor police coverage and poverty/drug induced crimes make many major city streets dangerous during the day and absolutely unsafe at night. The public education system has produced a nation of functional illiterates woefully lacking in elementary mathematical skills.

The US is diplomatically and militarily active worldwide. The US also maintains extensive foreign aid programs. Because many unpopular foreign despots benefit from such policies, it is quite common for persons traveling on US passports to encounter hostility and even violence in places where foreign aid is most lavishly dispensed.

TERRORISM DIRECTED AT AMERICANS IS ANOTHER REASON WHY MORE AND MORE YANKS PREFER NOT TO TRAVEL ON A US PASSPORT.

No other country has so many activities defined as criminal acts, whether committed abroad or within its borders. The US now has the highest per-capita incarceration rates, surpassing even South Africa and the former Soviet Union. This reality is in direct conflict with the concepts of personal freedom and liberty upon which the country was founded.

In all, however, the US standard of living is in the "top ten" and the possibility of making one's fortune is still possible. The US, therefore, is attractive as a part-time residence and a place of financial opportunity. Legal residents (defined as spending at least six months and one day per year within the borders) may apply for a passport after five years. During the last three years before application, federal income taxes should have been paid. Investigations into applicants for citizenship vary in intensity. There are severe penalties for oral or written misrepresentations. Consequences usually include deportation and may involve incarceration prior to being deported.

The US Immigration and Naturalization Service (INS) is said to be notoriously arbitrary, offensive, high handed and rude. The prevailing attitude seems to be: "Find any way to say no".

One wrong response to INS questions at an entry point or during the naturalization process can result in exclusion as an undesirable alien. "Undesirables" have in the past included homosexuals, marijuana smokers, political activists, original thinkers and even artists. The process of immigration incorporates the application of regulations which are arbitrarily interpreted to suit the official involved. This, in turn, leads to frustrations and aggravations of unlimited proportion. While corruption in the immigration process is occasionally present, such is not the usual mode of operation. Bribery of US government officials, therefore, is not recommended as a fast path through the INS bramble.

It is definitely advisable to hire an American attorney who specializes in immigration matters. Cost of such services can run to US $20,000 or more. Not having a lawyer could result in permanent prejudice to your case. Aliens do not have the same rights as US citizens and cannot get judicial review of a negative INS administrative decision in most cases.

The US immigration system operates under two categories: Quota and Non-quota. Rules and procedures under one system are essentially not applicable under the other.

THE QUOTA SYSTEM

The quota system establishes formal annual quotas under which emigration from every country in the world is limited to a certain number of individuals who will be considered for entry into the US. Each applicant is assigned a number and then must wait until the year his/her name goes to the top of the list. Thus applicants from countries like the Philippines and Hong Kong (where millions seek entry with relatively small quotas) may wait for ten or twenty years. Conversely, applicants from low demand countries such as Belgium and Iceland enjoy walk-in status.

Priorities within the quota determine any applicant's place on the list. They are, in order of decreasing precedence:

1. Unmarried children of US citizens.
2. **Spouses** and children **of legal residents**.
3. **Persons with desirable occupational skills or who are sponsored by a particular employer**.
4. Married children of US citizens.
5. Brothers and sisters of US citizens.
6. Skilled and other workers deemed to be in short supply.
7. Investors, retirees and refugees not otherwise classified.

Each category has a certain number of guaranteed immigrants.

Under such latitude and guidelines, it is easy to see how INS officials can get away with arbitrary behavior, admitting some people while turning away others with identical qualifications.

For the US-bound immigrant, moving from a quota waiting-list place like the Philippines and then obtaining residence through "rebirth" in an intermediate country is a common ploy to shorten the wait dramatically.

NON-QUOTA PROGRAMS

Non-quota immigrants generally avoid INS brutality because of their special status. Immigration as a non-quota individual is relatively pleasant and swift. To qualify as a non-quota immigrant, one must be any of the following:

1. **The spouse of a US citizen**.
2. A child under 12 of a US citizen, including step-children, adoptees and orphans to be adopted.
3. Parents of US citizens – the citizen (child) must be over 20.
4. Aliens who have previously qualified for immigration.
5. Certain former US citizens.
6. Certain ministers of religion.
7. Certain employees of the US government and those who served in the US armed forces for over 15 years.

Although not specifically published by the INS, the US president can issue executive orders under humanitarian or other circumstances. Such orders are tantamount to creation of a top priority non-quota allocation.

For example, near the end of World War Two, German scientists were recruited by the US in "Operation Paperclip". They were admitted on a wholesale basis by order of President Truman. Presidents Nixon and Ford signed similar executive orders which allowed massive influxes of refugees from Vietnam and Korea. Other mass admissions of Haitian and Cuban refugees have also occurred in recent years.

Another class of residence granted by the US is the Non-Immigrant Visa. The more common categories include tourists, diplomats, employees of foreign governments, students and employees or trainees of corporations doing business in the US. There are 12 types of Non-Immigrant Visa.

NON-IMMIGRANT VISAS

In all categories of non-immigrant visa, the length of stay is at the discretion of the immigration officer at the port of entry, and the visitor must have no intention of abandoning his or her residence outside the US. Your passport should also have six months to run after the end of your stay, to ensure you will be allowed back into your own country. Certain types of visa are issued only on the basis of reciprocity, i.e. if your government issues similar visas to US citizens. If you are aiming eventually for permanent residence, starting with a non-immigrant visa may give you the opportunity to develop close family ties to a US citizen or an offer of permanent employment which would entitle you to a Green Card. This much sought after piece of paper allows foreign nationals to live and work in the US without time limitations.

All applicants for visas must satisfy certain conditions such as freedom from mental or physical disability, illiteracy, alcoholism and drug addiction. They also must not be involved with an organization seeking to overthrow the government of the United States.

Type A: For diplomats and certain accredited officials of foreign governments and their immediate families.

Type B1: Business visitors, usually for less than a three month stay, but can be issued for up to a year.

Type B2: Visitors for pleasure. Tourists automatically are given six months, but they cannot take employment and must leave the US at the end of their stay.

Type C: Transit visas for immediate and continuous transit through the US, including to the United Nations headquarters.

Type D: For the crew of ships and aircraft who will leave on another ship or aircraft after a short stay.

Type E1,2: The treaty trader or treaty investor category is for businesspeople seeking entry for a lengthy period to oversee or work in a business which has substantial trade between the US and a foreign country or where a major investment is made in the US. Spouses and unmarried children under 21 also are entitled to the visa and to work in the US.

Type F: Students, plus spouses and unmarried children, can enter on this visa for the length of a recognised course of study.

Type G: Another form of diplomatic visa for a ''designated principal resident representative'' of a recognized foreign government or international organization, including staff.

Type H1,2,2B,3: These are the principal visas available for foreigners who wish to work in the US and have certain desirable skills. (See heading THE ''H'' VISA).

Type I: For bona fide representatives of foreign newspapers and broadcasting organizations.

Type J1,2: For students or academics on short-term exchanges or training programs.

Type L: For managers or executives who are allowed to come to the US on a transfer basis within their company for up to five years, but their spouses or children cannot work without visas of their own.

Students are restricted in a number of ways. The place of study has to be defined and approved in advance, and no change of school is allowed without INS approval. Working is not allowed, unless the student can show that due to unforeseen circumstances, he must work to maintain himself as a student. Employment for practical training may be permitted if it is not available in the student's home country. A student's spouse or children may not have jobs.

Visas other than C, D or K categories may be extended if an application to stay is made before the visa expires. When you make a visa application you will be told of any additional documents needed, particularly evidence to show you intend to return to your home country such as a business letter or proof of property ownership. Type B visa can be applied for by letter or at a US Embassy. Visa types A, G, H2, H3, most I and L normally are applied for by the employer. With H1 visas, applicants or their employers have to prove their case. If you go to the US on a L Visa and want to change jobs or are self-employed and not eligible for an E visa, an immigrant visa may be needed. Admission to the US for non-immigrants chiefly depends on the immigration officer at the port of entry, if you have a return ticket to your home country and plenty of money (though not necessarily an American bank account), you should be able to stay for three or six months. It is easier to be admitted through East Coast ports or Canada than it is through California.

HOW TO GET YOUR VISA TO THE US: BECOME A PRIEST, RABBI OR PASTOR!
The United States Department of Labor has granted a blanket labor certification for members of certain professions. Referred to internally as ''Schedule A'', the certification is for the following groups:

GROUP I: A) Physical therapists, B) Medical doctors destined to an area in the US designated by the Department of Health and Human Services as a health manpower shortage area and C) Registered nurses who hold CGFNS (Commission on Graduate of Foreign Nurses) registration or a full and unrestricted license to practice nursing in that particular US state.

GROUP II: Aliens of exceptional merit and ability in the sciences or arts (except the performing arts) having international acclaim or recognition.

GROUP III: A) Religious workers proceeding to the US to teach or preach, B) Religious workers proceeding to the US to work for a non-profit organization. [W.G. Hill's Note: In most countries of the developed world, special provisions allow clergymen to circumvent official rules and restrictions on immigration. Thus, if you can connect yourself in any official way to any church, cult or sect, you will usually find it easier to gain right of entry to wherever you want to live and work.]

GROUP IV: Aliens who hold, or would qualify for, an L-1 non-immigrant visa which allows one to work in the US in a managerial or executive position with a company for whom they have been working outside the US for a period of one year immediately preceeding the job offer and application for labor certification.

To qualify for US immigration on the basis of your profession or occupation, you must get a permanent offer of employment in the United States and have your prospective employer initiate the immigrant visa application. **If your occupation is included in one of the four groups just mentioned, your prospective employer in the United States is not required to obtain an individual labor certification from the US Department of Labor – members of your profession have been granted certification in advance. The employer may immediately file an immigrant visa petition (US INS Form I-140) in your behalf with the INS. You can then apply for permanent residence status. If you do qualify for an immigrant** visa, you start the procedure by filling out a Preliminary Questionnaire from the US Embassy, then you are told which other documents – and fees – are needed. Later you will be called to the Embassy for an interview and medical examination.

IMMIGRANT VISAS

There are five categories of immigrant allowed into the US, three of these are straightforward: (a) refugees who do not have an automatic right of entry but for whom there is no quota; (b) "special immigrants", covering former citizens, non-citizen lawful immigrants returning from a temporary visit abroad, ministers of religion (plus spouses and children under 21), employees of the US Government and (exceptionally) retired ex-Government employees of at least 15 years' service and (c) immediate relatives, including the children, spouse and parents of a US citizen. There are regulations specifying the details of those who qualify.

Other immigrants are subject to quotas, both numerically in total and by country of origin. Further definitions for those in the "preference category" are as follows:

1. Children of US citizens over 21 and/or married, i.e. those not in the immediate relatives category (20 per cent of total).
2. Spouses and unmarried children of permanent resident aliens (26 per cent of total plus any not required for first preference).
3. Members of professions or those with exceptional ability in the sciences or arts who will substantially benefit the US economy, cultural interests or welfare and whose services are sought by a US employer (10 per cent of the total).
4. Married children of US citizens (10 per cent of the total, plus any not required for the first three preferences).
5. Brothers or sisters of US citizens who are over 21 (24 per cent of the total, plus any not required for the first four preferences).
6. Skilled or unskilled workers (not temporary or seasonal) who can fill vacancies which cannot be filled by US workers. Labor certification is required for this category (10 per cent of total).

Non-preference immigrants, after these six categories, will be admitted according to the chronological order in which they apply, but will only be allowed in if the preference categories are not filled. So, years may pass before you come to the top of the list. Of course, immigrants must also conform to US standards as applied to non-immigrant visas, such as mental and physical fitness. On the basis of filling in a preliminary questionnaire, Form 222, the would-be immigrant will be told by the US Embassy what other documents are needed, such as birth certificates and passports, and given a longer form to complete. Immigrants need to prove at least one of the following: (1) That they will have sufficient funds to maintain themselves and their families in the US. (2) That a waiting job will provide sufficient income. (3) That they are skilled in a profession which will enable then to get a job in the US and while they are seeking that job will be able to maintain themselves and their family. (4) That someone in the US will provide support.

Proving these circumstances will depend on individuals but ownership of real estate, investments or statements from a bank may be sufficient. Immigrants are interviewed by a consular official and will be examined medically. If the administrative process is not completed within a time limit, the immigrant may have to start again. Once a visa is obtained, the immigrant must go to the US within four months (less in some cases).

SPECIAL NOTE FOR PENSIONERS/RETIREES

One of the largest attractions to the US is its inexpensive property prices. If this fact makes this fabled land of opportunity sound like an ideal retirement spot, there is much to consider. Although there have been rumours that the US may loosen its laws and allow non-US retirees to stay year round, no new legislation has been introduced. However, it should not be difficult to receive a non-immigrant B2 visa, allowing one to stay for up to six months. (Bear in mind that a ·stay in excess of 122 nights, approximately four months, makes one liable for US income taxes.) If you are desperate to befriend the Internal Revenue Service and wish to retire permanently to the US, the most feasible current route is that of a non-immigrant E2 visa which would involve opening a small business. Under this program, one will never qualify for a US passport, but can enjoy permanent residence in the US.

There are also many considerations completely separate from the world of passports and visas. Although property itself may be inexpensive, the operating and maintenance costs will not stop when you leave, and arrangements to take care of things like mowing the lawn (Americans are quite particular about their lawns) will have to be made. If you are planning on subsidising the costs by letting your property while you're not using it, first make sure that there is no local legislation which will prevent you from doing so. (Such silly laws can be found in retirement spots such as Orange County, Florida.) Also, remember that rental homes are a family market, and there is little demand for one-bedroomed flats. As with most things in life, careful research is essential before action.

ONE US LOOPHOLE

An international **loophole** in US immigration law can become an indirect route to citizenship and a passport. **Certain businessmen and employees of domestic or foreign corporations or governments are allowed to use the time spent in the US to satisfy the five year residency rule.** This route neatly circumvents both the quota and the non-quota categories. **The standard operating procedure is for a wealthy foreigner to set up a US corporation. That corporation then employs him in an executive capacity on a "temporary basis". After five years of US residence the foreigner then obtains US citizenship.**

ANOTHER US LOOPHOLE THAT IS CLOSING DOWN: THE "H" VISA

Foreigners transferred to the United States by their multinational companies usually can come in on an L visa for five years. Most European companies that have American subsidiaries can bring in employees for even longer on E visas. This is a very desirable status, because applicants avoid the dreaded INS completely.

Not so with the H visa. This visa, nevertheless, is one to opt for as a second choice. It was designed to ease the skill shortage in the US by providing for a special category of foreign professionals and technicians who are in increasing demand not only by foreign companies operating in the United States, but by American concerns trying to compete internationally. See "Operation Paperclip", above.

Obtaining an H-2 visa and working papers can, however, take ages. The bottleneck in importing skilled foreign workers is partly due to a legal requirement deeply embedded in US public policy. *Employers must prove that they cannot find unemployed American workers who are able to fill the job.* A formal search for them to comply fully with Labor Department rules can drag on for 18 months. After this time, the job or its foreign candidate have often disappeared.

To circumvent this for "applicants of distinguished merit and ability", the United States in 1970 created an H-1 visa for artists, entertainers, scientists and others of top rank. It was really meant for Nobel Prize winners and similar luminaries. Ordinary folks were supposed to apply for H-2 visas, designed for "workers in short supply". This entailed the lengthy labor market search previously described.

Ingenious and highly paid American contingent-fee lawyers, always on the lookout, quickly discovered that lavishly worded lauditory letters could create a loophole to raise professionals and humble technicians to near-Nobel status, thus obtaining H-1 visas for them within six weeks. We learned how to do this as well. Two personal clients won quick approval: An Italian editor of interior decorating textbooks and a French plastics engineer specializing in molding perfume containers. These blokes were made to appear, on paper at least, "very distinguished".

In 1988, the INS issued 78,000 H-1 visas based on exceptional merit but only 33,000 based on worker shortage. This created a situation that the INS itself says "flies in the face of logic".

In practice, the INS these days looks for at least a bachelor's degree in the field or equivalent work experience to grant an H-1. That means making up a resume even more complex and self-serving than the one needed to get the job in the first place. This has spawned a whole cottage industry of Curriculum Vitae preparation experts. A new breed of immigration lawyer is earning handsome fees by gathering testimonials from professional societies and trade organizations.

The H-1 visa situation is being squeezed. A Connecticut Democrat, Rep. Bruce Morrison, got his "Family Unity and Employment Opportunity Immigration Act of 1990" through Congress. This act increased the number of visas for relatives of US citizens but limited to 25,000 per annum the number of H-1 visas that can now be granted.

YET ANOTHER US LOOPHOLE, BUT CLOSING FAST – ILLEGAL IMMIGRATION
Individuals of any race and nationality can blend into the background and acquire a new identity in the US with a legal name change or by simply using an American sounding name. It is estimated that as many as 10 per cent of the 220 million-plus population are illegal aliens. Due principally to militant agitation by residents with Mexican roots, US officials now cosmetically refer to those that came in without visas as "undocumented aliens".

US land borders are unguarded and unfortified. The US prides itself on this fact and seems to go to great measures to avoid changing this image. Thus, illegal entry on foot or by vehicle over countless dirt trails is both possible and widely accomplished. The Rio Grande River, separating the US and Mexico, is little more than a muddy creek in many places. Wading across the river at night into Texas has given many Mexicans the appellation "wetback".

Coastal surveillance is more vigilant, but entry by small boat from Mexico, Cuba or even Central America is also a common occurrence. Reportedly, fifty per cent of the entire population of Belize is in the US illegally.

Recent increasing concern in the US about international terrorism and drug smuggling is causing far closer surveillance of the land border with Mexico and some coastal areas. But as yet, few walls or fences have been erected, so crossing in either direction remains relatively simple.

One of the glaring discontinuities in US law is that although illegal aliens are subject to capture and instant deportation, many welfare and social services agencies cannot withhold benefits from them while they are otherwise illegally in the country. Typically, one government agency fails or refuses to communicate with another, thereby creating this paradox.

As a result, many illegal aliens openly receive welfare benefits for months or years without the dreaded INS being informed. This, plus assistance from organized church groups makes the US a very attractive destination for Mexicans, Haitians and Central Americans who seek education, medical benefits and subsistence until they find a job or start a business.

SUMMARY AND RECOMMENDATION

The bottom line is that while illegal immigration is easy, for peace of mind and economic security, the best status in the US for our typical reader would be that of treaty trader, non-quota immigrant visitor or businessman. If you are seriously contemplating permanent residency leading to citizenship, you should retain skilled tax and immigration attorneys. If you have a good lawyer to recommend, please let us know. We will add them to our list.

Dual-citizenship until 1990 was actively discouraged for new American citizens. Foreigners are still, as part of the naturalization process, required to renounce all former allegiances before obtaining US citizenship and a passport. As of 1991, **after** acquiring a US passport, one cannot lose it by acquiring another nationality, with or without an oath of allegiance.

Everyone agrees that having any dealings with the INS is like banging your head up against the wall. The whole situation reminds one of Kafka. Consider the middle-aged Italian-born wife of a Tufts University professor. In Boston, she had her handbag stolen and with it her immigration papers. She arrived at the INS office with photocopies and sought an official replacement. After being shunted between bureaucrats and forced to stand and wait (without any progress) for most of the day, she finally lost her patience and shouted: "You treat us worse than the Nazi bureaucrats in Italy did during the war". Her fellow supplicants, all waiting in the same INS chamber of horrors, burst into applause.

FOR DETAILS OF IMMIGRATION LAWYERS SPECIALIZING IN THE US, SEE ADVERTISEMENTS IN QUALITY NEWSPAPERS WORLDWIDE.

Here are three US immigration firms currently advertising:

US Immigration/Visas: Through investment, buying a business or real estate or starting US branch co's. Or through family, student, profession. Help with legal, financial, taxes, jobs. New law offers opportunities. Temporary green cards possible in 3-6 months, then permanent later. Lawyer J. Wachs. Benefit from my skill and 20 years experience. 130 W 42 St, 28th Flr. NY, NY 10036, USA.

Former US Immigration Sr. Examiner, Attorney representation: Employment based immigrants, intra-company transferees, family based immigrants, labor certifications and all other categories. Send resumé for free evaluation! T&D Associates, Inc., Post Office Box 870, Haymarket, Virginia 22060, USA.

US Immigration & Business Lawyers: 80-02 Kew Gardens Rd., Kew Gardens, NY 11415.

AMNESTY LAW WAS TO HAND OUT AS MANY AS 20 MILLION PASSPORTS – BUT IT DIDN'T!

Aliens who entered the US illegally prior to 1982 had one year in which to register under a new amnesty law. Immediate "legal residence" and "work permits" were granted. The amnesty registration period began May 6, 1987. The door remained open only one year from that point in time, till May 5, 1988.

INS offices were at first flooded with amnesty *inquiries* when the law was signed by President Reagan in October, 1986. To encourage trust, INS adopted a policy of not immediately deporting those who registered for amnesty, even if they were found not entitled to it. But applications ran 99 per cent less than expected. At year end 1987, under 100,000 residence permits were granted under the amnesty program. It appeared that most illegals in the US preferred to live with false identities rather than expose themselves and their families to possible deportation. The fact that it is the same agency, whose main purpose is to deport people, meant that it was not trusted by most illegal aliens. During the amnesty, INS and other US agencies were operating in an aggressive mode to capture and instantly deport anyone in an illegal status caught at or near the border. This activity caused a dilemma because some illegal aliens would otherwise have been eligible for amnesty. Why? They had briefly left the US to visit family back in Mexico or Central America and were caught returning to the US. US courts ruled that such persons otherwise eligible for amnesty could not be deported if apprehended under such circumstances.

Nobody really knows how many illegal aliens are currently in the US, although estimates still range up to 20 million. These are composed of three principal groups of people: Mexicans who have flowed across the border over the years, refugees from Central America who have crept in and a huge mass of foreign students who entered the US legally on university-sponsored visa programs, only to quietly submerge into the US work force after graduation.

INS, under US congressional probing, admits that they have not been able to keep track of thousands of student defectors. These students are principally from Hong Kong, Taiwan (Formosa), India, Africa, Iran, Pakistan and Turkey. In the 1991 Gulf war, thousands of Iraqi students in the US and elsewhere overstayed their visas and went underground – unwilling to be cannon-fodder in Saddam Hussein's war machine.

INS bureaucrats who wanted to sabotage the program privately expressed opposition and outrage with the amnesty: "It's a big loophole". "Once inside the USA," according to Michael D McMahan of the INS's Dallas, Texas office, "for about $1000, an alien can buy a packet of documents including school certificates, bogus income tax forms, baptismal certificates and such. These (documents) allow the person to apply for legitimate documents like driver's licences." McMahan added his personal fears that INS lacked sufficient staff to investigate all of the "bogus applications" that the amnesty had caused to flood in.

179

Illegal aliens who did apply under the amnesty faced an uncertain future. On one hand, many of these people have for years carefully avoided all paperwork or official contact with the government, especially the police. They believed that any documentation of their existence could lead to deportation. Faced now with a complete lack of documentation, these individuals are subject to denial of amnesty and ultimately, deportation.

Hundreds of Mexicans, for example, have been captured and deported out of Southern California well in excess of twenty or thirty times each. These individuals are known on a personal basis by INS officers and become routinely swept up in raids on their known residence in the US.

Many of these repeatedly captured individuals are briefly detained in the Federal government's "Metropolitan Correction Centre" or "MCC" prison in San Diego, some 19 miles north of the Mexican border. These enterprising individuals have openly dubbed this facility as the "Mexican Country Club" in a play on its MCC abbreviation. Some are in residence so frequently that they resume their bunks and "senior prisoner" privileges on arrival. Some appear before a US district judge and receive prison time before being deported. Others are simply loaded on to INS or US Marshal buses and dumped at the border.

Most illegal aliens in the United States decided to ignore the amnesty. They have opted to live under the protection of a false identity. There is virtually no way for the action involved in creating a false identity to be other than a felony. Prima facie, it is an intent to defraud the US and perhaps state and local governments as well. But with a low profile, detection is unlikely.

Our suggestion for our readers is to *enter* the US as a *tourist* with proper papers. Never stay there long enough at a stretch (four months) to be considered a resident for tax purposes. This is the "Permanent Tourist" solution we describe as the best way to live in our *PT* book (see back page). Come and go as you please. Make deals. The only thing you can't get is a 9 to 5 job.

US TO SELL 10,000 ALIEN ENTREPRENEUR VISAS. PASSPORT INCLUDED AT NO EXTRA CHARGE AFTER 5 YEARS

Starting on 1 October 1991, for the first time in history (and perhaps because of our suggestion in previous editions of this Special Report), the US began awarding "green cards" in exchange for "Proof of investment in the USA" of at least $500,000 and the creation of 10 new jobs for US citizens. Alien entrepreneurs who make this investment will not necessarily lose their half million (or more) and they will be able to withdraw their capital after two years. As might be expected, full details on the program are quite extensive and almost require a lawyer to interpret. Scope International can recommend a lawyer in Washington DC who will look at your situation and give you an opinion. But you can save your money because this is *our* opinion in most cases – the scheme is a rotten deal for the investor. Owning a green card will make most entrepreneurs a prisoner and hostage of the dreaded Internal Revenue Service. It will make the typical international entrepreneur a criminal subject to huge jail sentences if he does not fully and accurately disclose and pay taxes on every cent of wealth he owns all over the globe and every penny of worldwide income generated by him or any corporation in which he has more than a 5 per cent interest. It will subject him to criminal punishment for violation of several million laws (mentioned here and in *PT*) which are impossible to understand and which could be used to jail every man, woman and child holding a US green card or US passport. The only thing that keeps any single American out of jail is "selective prosecution", the euphemism describing the fact that the prosecutors and tax collectors only go after the big fish. And big fish is what the entrepreneurs who enter this scheme are going to be – these are the fish who will be skinned, gutted and deep fried. For an example of what happened to one typical entrepreneur, re-read the story of Aldo Gucci told elsewhere in our books. At the age of eighty, when he immigrated to the US, he was sued, screwed and stewed. He lost his money and his freedom, spending his last years in prison for "tax fraud". His feeling was that getting a "green card" or residence permit in the US was the biggest mistake of his life. There may be a few instances where it would be justified – but they would be A) If the person is or will soon be stateless, B) If the entrepreneur makes very good "special arrangements" to keep his worldwide assets and earnings beyond the reach of the US tax collectors and C) If the applicant is ready to spend one-third of his life with lawyers and tax accountants, embroiled in squabbles with US bureaucrats.

See also *The Tax Exile Report,* published by Scope International.

WHO IS QUALIFIED FOR AN IMMEDIATE US PASSPORT?

Only Americans or key alien employees of the US government can get instant American passports legally. The most important requirement is a **certified** copy of your birth certificate issued by the state or province where you were born. This birth certificate must show a file or reference number and the date of birth, as well as bear the official seal or other official certification of the issuing office. Only such copies, bearing the original seal are acceptable. Passport offices rarely check authenticity with birth certificate issuing offices. But they might check if a passport application looks "suspicious". Hospital birth certificates will not suffice for a US passport application. "Notification of Birth Registration" forms filed with US consulates abroad may be accepted without birth certificates on a case by case basis. But the original birth certificate plus a translation certified by a US Consulate abroad is usually required. If you were born as a US citizen abroad, with at least one parent who is a US citizen and who was a resident in the US in recent years, you will need a certified copy of a Consular Report of Birth or Certification of Birth. Naturalized US citizens also need either a Certificate of Naturalization or Certificate of Citizenship.

To prove your identity to the US authorities, you must show a valid current photo ID. Normally, only an American "officially issued" ID is acceptable. You can present an old expired passport, a driver's license or any government photo ID card. Alternatively, a business or industrial card or school/college ID with your photograph and name on it can be accepted at the discretion of a passport issuing officer.

As for passport photographs, the US has some of the most detailed requirements in the world: "Two pictures either color or black and white are needed. One for our files and one for the passport. These pictures must be absolutely identical and taken within last six months. Overall size is 2'' x 2''. Full front view. Plain white or off-white background. Image size between 1'' and 1⅜'' measured from top of head (including hair) and bottom of chin. Dark glasses which hide eyes are not acceptable. Hats or other headgear not to be worn. Photos from coin-operated booths not acceptable".

Some people can get exceptions made. A client of ours, "Pete the Patriarch", was allowed to wear headgear. Pete said he was the head of a spiritual sect, a religious order requiring

UNITED STATES DEPARTMENT OF STATE
APPLICATION FOR ☐ PASSPORT ☐ REGISTRATION
SEE INSTRUCTIONS—TYPE OR PRINT IN INK IN WHITE AREAS

1. NAME FIRST NAME MIDDLE NAME

LAST NAME

2. MAILING ADDRESS

STREET

CITY, STATE,
ZIP CODE

COUNTRY IN CARE OF

☐ 5 Yr. ☐ 10 Yr. Issue
R D O DP Date _____
End. # _____ Exp. _____

3. SEX **4. PLACE OF BIRTH** City, State or Province, Country **5. DATE OF BIRTH** **6. SEE FEDERAL TAX** SOCIAL SECURITY NUMBER
Mo. Day Year **LAW NOTICE ON REVERSE SIDE**

Male Female

7. HEIGHT **8. COLOR OF HAIR** **9. COLOR OF EYES** **10. (Area Code) HOME PHONE** **11. (Area Code) BUSINESS PHONE**

Feet Inches **12. PERMANENT ADDRESS (Street, City, State, ZIP Code)** **13. OCCUPATION**

FOLD

14. FATHER'S NAME BIRTHPLACE BIRTH DATE U.S. CITIZEN **16. TRAVEL PLANS** *(Not Mandatory)*
☐ YES ☐ NO COUNTRIES DEPARTURE DATE

15. MOTHER'S MAIDEN NAME BIRTHPLACE BIRTH DATE U.S. CITIZEN LENGTH OF STAY
☐ YES ☐ NO

17. HAVE YOU EVER BEEN ISSUED A U.S. PASSPORT? YES ☐ NO ☐ IF YES, SUBMIT PASSPORT IF AVAILABLE. ☐ Submitted
IF UNABLE TO SUBMIT MOST RECENT PASSPORT, STATE ITS DISPOSITION: COMPLETE NEXT LINE
NAME IN WHICH ISSUED PASSPORT NUMBER ISSUE DATE (Mo., Day, Yr.) DISPOSITION

SUBMIT TWO RECENT
IDENTICAL PHOTOS

2" x 2"

FROM 1" TO
1-3/8"

18. HAVE YOU EVER BEEN MARRIED? ☐ YES ☐ NO DATE OF MOST RECENT MARRIAGE
Mo. Day Year

WIDOWED/DIVORCED? ☐ YES ☐ NO IF YES, GIVE DATE
Mo. Day Year

SPOUSE'S FULL BIRTH NAME SPOUSE'S BIRTHPLACE

19. IN CASE OF EMERGENCY, NOTIFY *(Person Not Traveling With You)* RELATIONSHIP
(Not Mandatory)
FULL NAME

ADDRESS (Area Code) PHONE NUMBER

20. TO BE COMPLETED BY AN APPLICANT WHO BECAME A CITIZEN THROUGH NATURALIZATION
I IMMIGRATED TO THE U.S. I RESIDED CONTINUOUSLY IN THE U.S. DATE NATURALIZED (Mo., Day, Yr.)
(Month, Year) From (Mo., Yr.) To (Mo., Yr.)
PLACE

21. DO NOT SIGN APPLICATION UNTIL REQUESTED TO DO SO BY PERSON ADMINISTERING OATH
I have not, since acquiring United States citizenship, performed any of the acts listed under "Acts or Conditions" on the reverse of this application form (unless explanatory statement is attached). I solemnly swear (or affirm) that the statements made on this application are true and the photograph attached is a true likeness of me.

Subscribed and sworn to (affirmed) before me (SEAL) X
Month Day Year
☐ Clerk of Court or
☐ PASSPORT Agent
☐ Postal Employee *(Sign in presence of person authorized to accept application)*
(Signature of person authorized to accept application) ☐ (Vice) Consul USA .At _____

22. APPLICANT'S IDENTIFYING DOCUMENTS ☐ PASSPORT ☐ DRIVER'S ☐ OTHER (Specify) No.
LICENSE
ISSUE DATE EXPIRATION DATE PLACE OF ISSUE
Month Day Year Month Day Year ISSUED IN THE NAME OF

23. FOR ISSUING OFFICE USE ONLY (Applicant's evidence of citizenship)

☐ Birth Cert. SR CR City Filed/Issued:
☐ Passport Bearer's Name:
☐ Report of Birth
☐ Naturalization/Citizenship Cert. No.:
☐ Other:
☐ Seen & Returned
☐ Attached

APPLICATION APPROVAL

_____
Examiner Name
_____
Office, Date

24.
FEE _____ EXEC. _____ POST _____

FORM DSP-11 (12–87) (SEE INSTRUCTIONS ON REVERSE) Form Approved OMB No. 1405-0004 (Exp. 8/1/89)

182

NONIMMIGRANT VISA INFORMATION

I. IMPORTANT INFORMATION

A valid VISA is necessary for every person who is not a U.S. citizen or permanent resident who wishes to apply for entry into the United States. Under U.S. law, all persons seeking admission are presumed to be immigrants unless they establish that they are entitled to receive a visa in one of the nonimmigrant visa (NIV) categories. The most widely known NIV category is the visitor visa, which is used by persons who wish to enter the U.S. temporarily for business purposes (B-1) or for tourism, visit to relatives and friends or similar reasons (B-2). Other categories of nonimmigrant visas are required for persons with different temporary purposes of entry e.g. representatives of foreign governments (A & G), transit (C), crewmen (D), treaty traders and investors (E), students in academic or language programs (F), temporary workers and trainees (H), journalists (I), exchange visitors (J), fiance(e)s of U.S. citizens (K), intra-company transferees (L), and students in vocational or other nonacademic programs (M).

A nonimmigrant visa for a particular category is valid for entry **only** for the purpose for which it was originally issued. For example, a student visa cannot be used for entry as a visitor, nor can the possessor of a visitor visa enter to study.

A VISA DOES NOT GUARANTEE ENTRY INTO THE UNITED STATES. The bearer of a visa is subject to inspection at the port of entry by U.S. Immigration officials who have authority to deny admission. Therefore, the recipient of a visa should carry with him/her, for possible presentation to immigration inspectors, the evidence submitted to the consular officer when the visa was obtained.

The validity period shown in a nonimmigrant visa relates only to the period during which it may be used in making application for admission into the United States; **it does not indicate the length of time the person may spend in the United States.** The period for which the bearer of a nonimmigrant visa is authorized to remain in the United States is determined by the U.S. Immigration authorities at the port of entry. A nonimmigrant who remains in the United States beyond the period for which he/she has been granted permission to stay may become subject to deportation.

Certain categories of nonimmigrant visas require special documentation which can be furnished only by an authority in the United States. These categories include students, who must have a valid Form 1-20 A & B issued by the prospective school; exchange visitors, who must have a Form IAP-66 issued by the sponsoring organization; and temporary workers and trainees, intra-company transferees, and fiance(e)s of U.S. citizens, all of whom must have a specific petition filed on their behalf and approved by the U.S. Immigration and Naturalization Service.

> **IMPORTANT — A visitor (B-1/B-2) to the United States is NOT permitted to work. All forms of employment, even informal work in a household as a "nanny", "au-pair" or "mother's helper", are prohibited.**

There may be a fee charged for your visa. If there is a fee it is approximately the same as that which is charged by your government to a United States citizen for a similar type visa. (Currently the only fees charged to U.K. passport holders are for E-1, E-2 and L-2 Visas.)

Due to reduced resources we regret we cannot accept visa inquiries by telephone. Please mail any questions you may have.

II. TO APPLY FOR A NONIMMIGRANT VISA

1. Complete this application form by PRINTING all of the answers. **(A SEPARATE APPLICATION IS REQUIRED FOR EACH TRAVELER REGARDLESS OF AGE, INCLUDING BABIES.)** Be sure to sign and date the form.

   Submit your passport with the completed application form by mail. **WALK-IN VISAS ARE NOT ISSUED EXCEPT IN EMERGENCIES**. If the application is satisfactory, the passport with the issued visa will be mailed back to you. Your passport should be valid for at least six months longer than your intended period of stay in the United States. British passports are exempt from the six months validity requirement. A BRITISH VISITOR'S passport is **NOT** acceptable for American visa purposes since it is **NOT** valid for travel to the U.S.A.

2. **PHOTOGRAPH.** A recent photograph 1½ inches square with your usual signature written on the REVERSE side must be affixed (preferably stapled) to the application form in the space provided. Children under the age of sixteen are not required to submit a photograph.

3. Submit evidence substantiating the purpose of your trip and your intention to depart from the United States after a temporary visit. Examples of such evidence are: in case of business trips, a letter from your employer; in case of pleasure trips, documents outlining your plans while in the U.S. and explaining the reasons why you would return abroad after a short stay, such as family ties, employment, or similar binding obligations in your home country; for students a completed Form 1-20 A & B; for exchange visitors a Form IAP-66; and for temporary workers and intra-company transferees, evidence of an approved petition. **U.S. law prohibits aliens who are granted visitors visas, crewmen visas, and most student and exchange visitors visas from working in the United States.** They must therefore demonstrate that they have adequate funds of their own, or assurances that they will be supported there by some interested person. In this connection, evidence should also be submitted regarding the arrangements you have made to cover your expenses while in the United States and to provide for your departure from the United States. **Please do not submit marriage and/or birth certificates unless specifically requested to do so.**

   The above requirements are not inclusive, in that all persons will not be required to submit all documents, and some persons will be required by the consular officer to submit additional documents. In order to avoid delay, it is to your advantage to submit as complete documentation as possible when you first submit your visa application.

4. Detach this information sheet (do **not** send it in).

5. Include STAMPED ADDRESSED envelope (large enough for your passport(s) and any documents submitted) with sufficient POSTAGE. Failure to do so will significantly delay return of your passport.

OPTIONAL FORM 156 (Rev. 1/88)

IMPORTANT — TURN OVER PAGE FOR DETAILS

1. SURNAMES OR FAMILY NAMES *(Exactly as in Passport)*

                                                            DO NOT WRITE IN THIS SPACE

2. FIRST NAME AND MIDDLE NAME *(Exactly as in Passport)*

3. OTHER NAMES *(Maiden, Professional, Aliases)*

4. DATE OF BIRTH			7. PASSPORT NUMBER
DAY	MONTH (letters)	YEAR	

5. PLACE OF BIRTH *(City, Province, Country)*   DATE PASSPORT ISSUED

6. NATIONALITY   DATE PASSPORT EXPIRES

8. HOME ADDRESS *(Include apartment no., street, city, province and postal zone)*

9. NAME AND STREET ADDRESS OF PRESENT EMPLOYER OR SCHOOL *(Postal box number unacceptable)*

10. HOME TELEPHONE NO.	11. BUSINESS TELEPHONE NO.

12. SEX ☐ Female ☐ Male	13. COLOR OF HAIR	14. COLOR OF EYES

15. COMPLEXION	16. HEIGHT	17 MARITAL STATUS ☐ Married ☐ Single
18. MARKS OF IDENTIFICATION		☐ Widowed ☐ Divorced ☐ Separated

19. NAMES AND RELATIONSHIPS OF PERSONS TRAVELING WITH YOU *(NOTE; A separate application must be made for a visa for each traveler, including children and infants.)*

20. HAVE YOU EVER APPLIED FOR AN IMMIGRANT OR NONIMMIGRANT U.S. VISA BEFORE?
    ☐ No   ☐ Yes   Where?
    ☐ Visa was issued   When?
    ☐ Visa was refused   Type of visa?

21. HAS YOUR U.S. VISA EVER BEEN CANCELED?
    ☐ No   ☐ Yes

22. Bearers of visitors visa may not work or study in the U.S.

    DO YOU INTEND TO WORK IN THE U.S.?   ☐ No   ☐ Yes
    If YES, explain.

23. DO YOU INTEND TO STUDY IN THE U.S.?   ☐ NO   ☐ Yes
    If YES, write name and address of school as it appears on form I-20.

24. WHO WILL FURNISH FINANCIAL SUPPORT INCLUDING TICKETS?

25. PRESENT OCCUPATION *(If retired, state past occupation)*

26. AT WHAT ADDRESS WILL YOU STAY IN THE U.S.A.?

27. WHAT IS THE PURPOSE OF YOUR TRIP?

28. WHEN DO YOU INTEND TO ARRIVE IN THE U.SA.?

29. HOW LONG DO YOU PLAN TO STAY IN U.S.A.?

30. DO YOU PLAN FUTURE TRIPS TO THE U.S.A. IF SO, WHEN?

31. HAVE YOU EVEN BEEN IN THE U.S.A.?
    ☐ No   ☐ Yes   When?
                      For how long?

NONIMMIGRANT VISA APPLICATION

COMPLETE ALL QUESTIONS ON REVERSE OF FORM

OPTIONAL FORM 156 (Rev. 1/88) PAGE 1

184

32. (a) HAS ANYONE EVER FILED AN IMMIGRANT VISA PETITION ON YOUR BEHALF? ☐ No ☐ Yes
    (b) HAS LABOR CERTIFICATION FOR EMPLOYMENT IN THE UNITED STATES EVER
        BEEN REQUESTED BY YOU OR ON YOUR BEHALF? ☐ No ☐ Yes
    (c) HAVE YOU OR ANYONE ACTING FOR YOU EVER INDICATED TO A U.S. CONSULAR
        OR IMMIGRATION EMPLOYEE A DESIRE TO IMMIGRATE TO THE U.S.? ☐ No ☐ Yes

33. ARE ANY OF THE FOLLOWING IN THE U.S.? *(If YES, circle appropriate relationship and indicate what that person is doing in the U.S., i.e. studying, working, etc.)*

HUSBAND/WIFE_____ FIANCE/FIANCEE_____ BROTHER/SISTER_____

FATHER/MOTHER_____ SON/DAUGHTER_____

34. PLEASE LIST THE COUNTRIES WHERE YOU HAVE LIVED FOR MORE THAN SIX MONTHS DURING THE PAST FIVE YEARS
       COUNTRIES   CITIES   APPROXIMATE DATES

35. **IMPORTANT: ALL APPLICANTS MUST READ AND ANSWER THE FOLLOWING:**

A visa may not be issued to persons who are within specific categories defined by law as inadmissible to the United States (except when a waiver is obtained in advance). Complete information regarding these categories and whether any may be applicable to you can be obtained from this office. Generally, they include persons

— Afflicted with contagious diseases (i.e. tuberculosis) or who have suffered serious mental illness;

— Arrested, convicted for any offense or crime even though subject of a pardon, amnesty, or other such legal action;

— Believed to be narcotic addicts or traffickers;

— Deported from the U.S.A. within the last 5 years;

— Who have sought to obtain a visa by misrepresentation or fraud;

— Who are or have been members of certain organizations including Communist organizations and those affiliated therewith;

— Who ordered, incited, assisted, or otherwise participated in the persecution of any person because of race, religion, national origin, or political opinion under the control, direct or indirect, of the Nazi Government of Germany, or of the government of any area occupied by, or allied with, the Nazi Government of Germany.

DO ANY OF THESE APPEAR TO APPLY TO YOU?

                    NO ☐   **YES** ☐

If YES, or if you have any question in this regard, personal appearance at this office is recommended. If it is not possible at this time, attach a statement of facts in your case to this application.

36. I certify that I have read and understood all the questions set forth in this application, and the answers I have furnished on this form are true and correct to the best of my knowledge and belief. I understand that possession of a visa does not entitle the bearer to enter the United State of America upon arrival at a port of entry if he or she is found inadmissible.

DATE OF APPLICATION _____

APPLICANT'S SIGNATURE _____

If this application has been prepared by a travel agency or another person on your behalf, the agent should indicate name and address of agency or person with appropriate signature of individual preparing form.

SIGNATURE OF PERSON PREPARING FORM _____

DO NOT WRITE IN THIS SPACE

HAVE YOU COMPLIED WITH THE FOLLOWING?

1. Answered ALL 35 questions completely
2. SIGNED and DATED the form
3. Affixed ONE PHOTO
4. DETACHED and RETAINED the information sheet
5. Included ADDRESSED STAMPED ENVELOPE

37 mm × 37 mm
1½ inches × 1½ inches

———————— PHOTO ————————

Glue or staple
photo here

OPTIONAL FORM 156 (Rev. 1/88) PAGE 2   *(This form is free of charge)* members at all times to cover their heads with a huge Orthodox-type hat. At the passport office, clerks looked up the rules on hats and headgear in their books and read that "Hats and other headgear not to be worn unless specifically part of religious attire". Pete got to wear his regalia for the passport photo.

When you apply for a passport, please note that if you are older than 13, you must **appear in person** and sign the application in the presence of a US passport agent or consular official. Persons under 13 will not have to appear in person but can have a parent appear and sign for them.

If you have had a (previous) US passport, you may at the discretion of authorities be allowed to use Form DSP-82 (mail-in application).

VENEZUELA – SIMPLE APPLICATION

Venezuela is interested in improving its ability to compete in a world economy by luring highly-skilled labour from Eastern Europe and the former Soviet Union. They are currently offering large incentives. Qualified technicians are paid US $1,000 a month, which in Venezuela is a lot of money and compares more than favorably with the US $10 a month that workers receive in the rouble zone.

Venezuela is also one of the South American countries which has very simple application requirements for an instant passport. Passport holders obtain certificated citizenship, an ID card and driver's license. This country's documents are most valuable because of current "visa-free" travel to Canada, Germany, Netherlands, Belgium, Luxembourg and most of western Europe. In 1991 you could obtain standard Venezuelan passports for US $25,000 within 12 weeks. From summer 1992 – the position has been uncertain.

Comments, questions, additions and constructive criticism should be sent to:
Scope International, 62 Murray Road, Waterlooville, Hampshire PO8 9JL, Great Britain.

Part VI

TAX HAVENS
ODDBALL SITUATIONS
NEW COUNTRIES

TAX HAVENS

With the exception of the British colonies that are tax havens, it is too difficult and expensive to get a passport in a tax haven. In fact, as we often say, it is best not be a citizen of the country in which you actually live, and therefore tax haven passports are of little value. The reason this section has been added is because of the many inquiries we receive. Much time is saved by giving the information here. We have also written several Special Reports dealing at length with tax havens that individuals might find attractive as a "fiscal address". Reports available at the moment are on ANDORRA & GIBRALTAR, A CHANNEL ISLAND, MONTE CARLO, MONACO and CAMPIONE (Italy/Switzerland). These reports are £60 each or three for the price of two. See back pages for more information. Our reports on individual tax havens give detailed information on obtaining passports, residence permits, costs of living, communications and everything else you should know. This section is just a summary. See also *The Tax Exile Report,* published by Scope International.

However, there are most definitely some "interesting" options:

ODDBALL AND TAX HAVEN PASSPORTS

ANDORRA: Marriage by a foreign male to an "only daughter" is said to be the only way a foreign male can acquire citizenship. A woman can acquire the right to a passport by marriage to an Andorran. Residence is no problem. Just go there and live, PT style. Andorrans hold French and Spanish citizenship by birthright and can obtain a French or Spanish passport immediately upon application. Andorra is a great tax haven to live in, and there is a highly recommended Hill Special Report on Andorra and Gibraltar. See back pages of this book for a summary and outline. It is officially impossible for a foreigner to get a legal residence card for Andorra, but we know a lawyer who can arrange it, if you live there over six months.

BAHAMAS: Special arrangements are said to be possible, but the official residence period is set at five years, with residence permits difficult to get legally. Once a permanent residents permit is granted, the recipient is known quaintly as a "Belongee".

BAHRAIN, GULF STATES, KUWAIT, SAUDI ARABIA, etc: Females can get passports by marriage. Foreign males? Impossible, except by special dispensation of the ruling monarch. Residence and work permits are available, but you must have a job offer in advance!

BELGIUM: See LUXEMBOURG.

BRITISH COLONIES: Typically, administration and applications are handled by local people and the final decision on passport issuance is made by the Office of the Governor General. In prior years, British Subject Passports were equal in every way to those issued by the Home Office in the UK. However, as unwanted immigration of non-whites into the UK was perceived to be a problem, passports issued to inhabitants of colonies were changed to be good only for limited travel and not for domicile in the UK. These passports are generally titled: "British Overseas Subject". Normally visas are granted to prosperous-looking individuals without many questions. Visas can be multiple entry, good for the life of the passport. People in the colonies with British ancestors (i.e. white) can usually get full British passports. You may write to the British Home Office, Lunar House, Croydon, Surrey, UK, for full details on colonial passports.

Visas to reside in the colonies are granted by UK embassies or by the Governor General's Office serving tht particular colony. **Typically, after five years of legal residence one can become a citizen and obtain the passport**.

One unique situation is the Channel Islands, legally not part of the UK and legally not a colony. The Channel Islands were a possession of the first English King, William the Conqueror, before he took England at the Battle of Hastings in 1066. Thus, Channel Islanders today, as personal vassals of the British Queen, get a CI passport that (many feel) is slightly better than the British passport. It permits visa-free, in fact, passport free, ID card travel throughout the EC, UK and Ireland. As there are low taxes (or no taxes) in the Channel Islands, one could, for instance, have a home in London and not have to pay taxes in the UK. The details are far too complex to go into here. Just be aware of the general rule that five years of legal residence generally gets one a passport in a British colony. With a few exceptions, these passports require visas for European/US travel. There are the privileged few, such as Bermuda residents, who are generally prosperous folk and are welcome most places without visas. **Bermuda, like Canada, has an open border with the US**. In fact, there is no US customs clearance for Bermuda-originated flights to the US. A US customs officer checks people in Bermuda! For those not aware of British colonies also considered tax havens, this is the list: Bermuda, British Virgin Islands, Cayman Islands, Gibraltar, Guernsey CI, Hong Kong, Isle of Man, Jersey CI, Sark CI.

CAMPIONE d'ITALIA: A very unusual situation in that Italian law applies to this enclave *totally within Switzerland*. This means a ten year residence requirement for an Italian passport or immediate citizenship by marriage (six months processing time). Citizenship can be applied for three years after marriage if the couple does not live in Italy. We have published a special report on Campione. See back of this book for details.

CYPRUS: A former British colony now divided into two nations, one dependent upon Turkey, the other dependent upon Greece. In the present state of flux, either one might be open to suggestions of possible investment benefits in return for citizenship or the appointment of Honorary Diplomats. The Turkish Cyprus government has received very little diplomatic recognition and would be very likely to appoint an attorney or respectable person willing to do a little PR as an honorary diplomat. We have found that contacts made when a government needs all the help it can get are more fruitful than when you need the favor and they don't need you.

DUTCH ANTILLES: Same as Holland. Five to seven year residence. Residence permits easily obtained.

FRENCH POLYNESIA AND CARIBBEAN TERRITORIES OF MARTINIQUE etc: Not easy to get residence permit, but it is possible. Same rules as for France. EC citizens can live and work there without any permission.

GIBRALTAR: As Gibraltar is a British Colony, the United Kingdom is generally responsible for its immigration policy, and a similar program has been implemented. Thus, a person could take up residence in Gibraltar under the work permit scheme, acquire permanent residence after four years and one year later acquire a Gibraltar passport which is in all respects similar to the passport issued by the UK. However, as Gibraltar does not offer much by way of tax considerations for the individual (the top rate is currently a staggering 50 per cent), we see little sense in going to all this trouble. Gibraltar does have a great deal to offer as a tax haven for corporations and for one who plays the PT, i.e. lives there but is not a citizen. For more information seek *The Andorra and Gibraltar Report* which explains the situation in detail. See back pages for summary and outline.

GOVERNMENTS IN EXILE include: Poland, Estonia, Latvia, Lithuania, Ethiopia, Imperial Russia and a long list of others. Like the Republic of China (Taiwan) these are militarily defeated countries often without a population or control of the territory they claim. Their passports are not much good for travel without visas. The Byzantine Empire had its lights put out for good about five hundred years ago by the Turks, but Byzantine passports and noble titles are still being issued.

Bottom line: These documents are of little use for travelling. Even for banking, acceptance is rare. They can, however, now be exchanged for passports issued by the post-communist governments recently established in such countries.

LIBERIA: Special arrangements possible. See section on Black Africa. As of 1992 political instability and random violence, not to mention a population 80 per cent infected with AIDS, does not make this place our first choice for a place to vacation. But the passport itself is no worse than other Black African countries.

LIECHTENSTEIN: A female can become a citizen by marrying a male citizen. A male who marries a Liechtenstein citizen can obtain a residence permit, but grants of citizenship would be extremely rare. For all practical purposes, for a male, Liechtenstein citizenship is impossible to obtain – it may be possible if you are a lifelong close personal friend of the prince. Work permit or residence permit – rules similar to Switzerland's.

LUXEMBOURG: Belgium and Luxembourg are anxious to attract investors or entrepreneurs. If you would consider an investment of about $250,000 in Luxembourg or Belgium, apparently it can be managed in about one year! Work and residence permits are neither difficult nor expensive to get.

MALTA: After several years of a repressive, communist-oriented regime, Malta, as of summer 1987, reverted to its Western orientation. Malta is well known for appointing many honorary diplomats and issuing diplomatic passports to them. Worth an inquiry once the officers of the New Regime let us have a copy of what they tell you about residence and citizenship. We hear that "special arrangements" are common here.

THE ORDER OF MALTA: When during the Middle Ages, Crusaders went to liberate Jerusalem from the Infidels, a group of Samaritans known as the Knights of Malta set up an

Ambulance Corps and a chain of hospitals where wounded Christians could be nursed back to health. A letter of free passage granted by the Grand Master of this Order was normally recognized by all the Roman Catholic monarchs of Europe as an early diplomatic passport. The Kings themselves were usually members of and supported the good works of this meritorious Order. In the 19th century, when passports began to be used, a Knights of Malta passport was evidence that the bearer was usually a distinguished Roman Catholic philanthropist on a mission of mercy. But there were also rival charitable orders with the same name formed by Protestants. They still exist today, operating hospitals and rescue services in England and Scandinavia. The passports issued by these groups are generally recognized by Christian countries.

The passport issued by the original Roman Catholic order runs a close second to the Vatican passport in terms of elegance. It is in red leather, embossed in white with the Cross of Malta. It is issued in French, English or Italian and is stamped "Diplomatic Passport of the Sovereign Military Order of Malta". Inside: "The Grand Chancellor of the Sovereign Military Hospitaller Order of St. John of Jerusalem of Rhodes and of Malta, requests all those whom it may concern to allow the bearer to pass freely, etc." Thirty-two states recognize it for visa-free admittance. The US, Australia, Canada and Thailand require visas.

Even though the Knights of Malta do not have any sovereign territory, they carry a lot of weight because their members are, like officers of the International Red Cross, the (Moslem) White Crescent and (Jewish) Magen David, highly respected individuals (always Roman Catholic philanthropists) who financially support important charitable works. Members of all these organizations are still today issued passport-like documents whereby they can shed their national identity and work for the betterment of mankind. **The real documents are not passed out casually. Except for medical doctors on assignment and hospital administrators actually working for these groups, these passports are not a realistic option**.

The Roman Catholic Order is located in an impressive palace taking up a square block in downtown Rome. A polished brass plaque identifies it as SOVRANO ORDINE MALTA. It is located at 4/6 Cavalieri di Malta, Rome, Italy.

THE ORDER OF MALTA (BOGUS?): A number of entrepreneurs have placed ads and recruited members for their particular Orders. The most ambitious of these individuals manage to get official diplomatic recognition, from at least one small country. Often they sign up an impressive board of "name" directors. People line up for membership in these Orders up out of thin air each of whom is willing to contribute up to $50,000 for the "right" to call himself "Sir" something or other, or even Prince, Marquis or Duke. Each receives a "Diplomatic Passport" with his new title on it. These passports are accepted by some border officials whose instruction books show that Order of Malta passports are to be treated as legitimate. There is no effective method for a border official to distinguish quickly between a Rome Knight and members of the more recently organized Orders. To add to the confusion, Queen Elizabeth II heads an Order that Rome used to claim was bogus. This order, while it does not issue passports, does operate a large number of the ambulances in Great Britain. Rome claims that they have identified over twenty different bogus Orders, set up mainly to profit the founders by trading on the good name of the real Knights.

Some of these new Orders are headed by Prince Arnaldo Petrucci of New York City: In 1986, this Order had 400 diplomatic passports printed up by Garrods, a top London printer. They took delivery, sold the passports at big prices, but never paid Garrods their £6000 printing bill. While selling the passports (or investing new Knights, as Count Allessandro Protti, Knight's Minister Plenipotentiary, would have put it), Count Protti stayed at the Ritz Hotel and ran up a bill of £56,000 before absconding to Panama.

Prince Umberto Stefanizzi was named a Prince and Knight some years ago by Petrucci (above). He later declared himself to be head of a new Order of the same name. He received diplomatic recognition from the Seychelles government where he has one of the largest mansions on the island as his embassy. Because he has been in the Seychelles for several years, Prince Stefanizzi is scheduled to become the Dean of the Diplomatic Corps, thereby acquiring greater status under protocol than representatives of the UK, France or Japan. Prince Stefanizzi will gladly sell you a passport. His address is PO Box 267, Victoria, Mahe, Seychelles Islands. Phone: 78551 or Telex 2257 GMR of SZ.

Prince John de Mariveles d'Anjou has proclaimed himself the Grand Master of still another Order located in a fine mansion at Wentworth Estate, Virginia Water, Surrey, England. He issues diplomatic passports for $25,000 (negotiable) and for a time was partners with Count Nowina-Sockolnicki, President of the Republic of Poland in Exile. (Poland, Lithuania, Latvia, Estonia all had "governments in exile" and they too issued passports). But Prince Mariveles claims some sovereign territory. He calls it Colonia. It consists of 46,000 miles of underwater coral atolls in the South China Sea.

The *Wall Street Journal* did a humorous story in 1986 about many of the eccentrics who run the various Knighthood Orders of Malta. All give themselves magnificent titles, swords, medals and multi-colored plumed uniforms. They give many parties, and enjoy being listed in local phone-books as Princes, Grand Dukes and such. They are all fantasies and money-spinners for their founders. They sometimes even do a token amount of charitable work. Most try to enlist some religious leader as their "protector", and all give free membership and passports to genuine noblemen or "holy men" whose membership gives prestige and credibility to their organization.

Bottom Line: Would you want to travel on a bogus Knights of Malta Diplomatic Passport? The answer should be a resounding "No!" You want to cross borders with as low a profile as possible and a minimum of questioning. Because of greater publicity in recent years, diplomats are now less likely to give visas to Knights of Malta. Border officials will be more likely to detain travelers with oddball passports. For con-men with a fantastic ability to talk or bluff their way through anything, it might be OK to call yourself "Venerable Archbishop" or "Grand Vizier" – and to travel as a Knight of Malta or with a huge harem and suitable entourage. But fraudsters always seem to end up in prison eventually. That is not where we want you, dear reader, to be in a few years time.

MONACO: As difficult as Liechtenstein. Two Monegasque parents required. Without suitable parents, after twelve years residence one may apply, but few applications are granted, unless the individual has rendered meritorious service to the nation. Unlike Paraguay where meritorious services could be a thousand dollar donation, in Monaco, with its resident population of billionaires, it would probably involve something on the scale of a new twenty million dollar hospital. Why bother when all the advantages can be obtained with a free Monaco resident's card? See our separate *Monaco Report* for full information on how to become a resident for free. See the end pages of this book for further details.

NAURU: This Pacific Island republic does not grant full citizenship to anyone but natives. It has been known to issue provisional non-citizen documents and also diplomatic passports to Honorary Consuls. It is, in fact, actively looking for respectable individuals who can serve to show the flag in places where Nauru is not already represented. Nauru, by the way, is one of the wealthiest countries in the world due to rich phosphate deposits used for fertilizer by Australia. They pay Nauru large royalties each year. Nauru is a tribal kingdom inhabited by black people of gigantic size and girth.

THE NETHERLANDS: A unique "back door" to this EC country is having a "serious relationship" with a Dutch citizen. That relationship should involve living together (heterosexual, homosexual, lesbian or even with an informally adopted child or parent). Holland also is quite liberal about giving **asylum** to anyone claiming religious or other persecution. It is also one of the less difficult places to get a work permit in Europe (if you have a job offer or are self-employed). Five years of legal residence qualifies for citizenship and passport.

ROYAL ORDER OF THE WHITE EAGLE – POLAND: The following information comes directly from this organization: "The Monarchist Party of Poland respectfully asks that you mention in your next *Passport Report* the fact that we are raising funds to restore the legitimate constitutional monarchs in Poland and Eastern Europe by democratic process. For a substantial contribution of approximately $10,000 qualified candidates can be elevated to the nobility of Poland and made a Knight of our ancient and internationally respected Royal Order of the White Eagle. Accepted candidates will receive an appropriate set of medals and noble sash for formal and informal wear, an impressive certificate for framing and the right to use their own personal crest (coat of arms) on their car, crockery, silverware, etc. They will also receive a passport-like document containing their name and preceded by their new title, "Excellency". For a small additional donation, higher ranks can be achieved, i.e. Baron, Earl, Count, etc. These documents have no present legal status outside of the Order. The primary plank of our program is the integration of Poland into the European Community with the greatest possible speed. We favor a Libertarian style free market. The Royal Order of the White Eagle, associated with the monarchy for hundreds of years, has an international schedule of social activities. It supports many good works and as most of the funds raised will go for hospital and educational work, the contribution may be tax-deductible in many countries."

Don't try to travel on your "Polish Nobility Passport" for the time being. But it could become the equivalent of an EC passport some day soon. We like this the best of the "Oddball Passports", but at $10,000 it is the most expensive. Of course, with a noble title and party invitations thrown in, it may be of interest to those of our readers with money to burn on status symbols and good causes.

PUERTO RICO: This Spanish speaking colony of the United States issues a US passport to its residents. It may be easier for some individuals who speak Spanish to fit into society here and to acquire a passport by taking advantage of the residence period of five years, same as in the continental US.

SARK: This Channel Island is the only place in the world where one becomes a Member of Parliament by purchasing a home! There are no taxes, whatsoever. The passport is the best in the world with more visa-free travel than any other. The population of about 500 is by far the wealthiest per capita in the world. There are no local newspapers, cars, planes, servants or female dogs on the island. We have a lengthy separate Special Report on how to establish residence on this island for £600 a year. It is the perfect Libertarian Society, a Utopia that must be experienced to be believed. Banking is more private than in Switzerland. **One of the few crimes punishable by a 24 hours stint in the local dungeon is being a tax collector**. The Channel Islands passport is available and *free* after five years of physical residence. You can rent an accommodation address on this island for £600 a year. Why doesn't everybody live there? They would, but the door will close soon due to the unavailability of accommodation and rules prohibiting future building, which is why we do not wish to give this gem of a tax haven too much publicity. However, you can read all about it in the special *Channel Island Report* – see back pages for details.

SINGAPORE: Singapore was totally closed to immigration for some time, but during their current economic slump invited Chinese who were willing to invest (Singapore dollars) $1,000,000 to apply for residence and citizenship. We understand that quite a number of Hong Kong Chinese did in fact snap up the offer. Presumably, major investors from other places would be welcome. Singapore is a very well run little city state, but it is not very free or democratic. Some of the laws are a bit quirky – for a while it was a criminal offense to chew gum, for instance. The passport is good, allowing visa-free travel to most countries. Residence is now available to anyone of good character who will start a business there. See section on Singapore.

TONGA: The King of Tonga, Taufa'ahau Tupou IV, has been trying to sell passports as a way of raising revenue. Between 1987 and 1990 they were bought for up to Australian $46,078 each, mainly by Hong Kong and Taiwan Chinese, but with a catch. As few countries recognize the special Tonga protected persons passport, they are not much use for travel. It was reported that at least 20 Chinese with Tongan passports were trapped in Tonga because no other country would accept them.

Undaunted, the King has said he wants to stop the sale of these documents and sell a new and more expensive type of passport to attract millionaires to aid the economy rather than middle class people. They could be sold for up to US $35,000 and holders would be allowed to stay in Tonga for one year while they tried to migrate to another country.

THE UNITED NATIONS also issues a passport described on its baby blue cover as a ''certificate'' to employees. All member nations accept these documents for visa-free entry.

However, **UN passports are generally used only to attend international conferences or undertake specific short-term projects for international organizations**.

UNIVERSAL LIFE CHURCH: In some instances, being able to describe yourself as an ordained minister of religion can help get visas, immigration permits, even travel discounts from airlines. This church will ordain anyone by mail and has been held by many court decisions in the US to be a "Legitimate Church". For approximately $10 per certificate you can become a minister, bishop, archbishop or obtain any ecclesiastical title you can live up to. Write (with ten dollars donation please): Bishop Kirby Hensly, ULC Inc., 601 3rd Street, Modesto, California 95351, USA. Most European countries will give long-term visas to clergymen.

VATICAN CITY: Perhaps the most impressive and expensive passport in terms of its physical appearance, this brown leather bound document is embossed in gold with the crossed keys of St. Peter, surmounted with the Papal Tiara. Unlike all other passports, there is no request to allow the bearer to pass or to render assistance or protection. God provides that to all holders. How to get one? Become a Cardinal or have some reason to travel on Roman Catholic official business that the Holy Father in Rome (the Pope) thinks is vital to the interests of the Church. The Vatican Passport is generally recognized as a diplomatic passport. It is generally not available to the likes of you or me.

The passport, by the way, is issued by "Stato della Citta del Vaticano" and is no longer in Latin, but rather in modern Italian.

WHITE EAGLE: See Royal Order of the White Eagle of Poland.

WORLD SERVICE AUTHORITY: 1012 - 14th Street, Room 1011, NW WASHINGTON DC 20005, USA. Try the phone book if they've moved. The story as I heard it from author Douglas Casey goes like this: Way back in the 1950s or even earlier there was a group of Quakers (Christian Pacifists) who donated their time and money to help war victims and refugees. Associated with this group was an American named Gary Davis. He thought up the idea that to prevent future wars, people of the world should unite as "World Citizens" and ignore immoral laws and all governments. For a time, the organization he was identified with, the United World Federalists, was quite the fad with Do-Gooder Liberals of the sort who later went on to "Free Ethiopia", "Down With The Shah", Ecology and Free South Africa. Unlike many of the self-proclaimed leaders of the militant, liberal left, Gary was an idealist – definitely not a con-artist.

Around 1945-55, he articulated the concept that everyone should be a "world citizen" and refuse to apply for or travel on a document (i.e. passport) invented during the French Revolution solely to keep people from leaving France. We certainly agree that before the Proletariat took over France, creating an early version of "Socialist Paradise" that people would die to get out of, anyone could go anywhere without permission. Prior to the 19th century, passports were travel documents held only by very important people as sort of letters of introduction from one sovereign or Minister of State to another. Ordinary folks just got on a horse and went.

WORLD SERVICE AUTHORITY

1012 14th STREET, N.W., WASHINGTON, D.C. 20005
Tel: (202) 638-2662   Telex: 262214 WGOV UR

APPLICATION FORM • FORMULAIRE DE DEMANDE
FORMULARIO APLICACION

INSTRUCTIONS: 1. Mark in boxes which documents and postage chosen. **2. Sign ATTESTATION OF UNDERSTANDING below. 3.** Fill out form on reverse side in block letters or by typewriter. **4.** Have your signature authenticated. **5.** Send with photos, bank check, international money order or IRCs to: WSA, Washington, D.C. 20005. **No WSA document will be issued without payment or proof thereof.**

INSTRUCTIONS: 1. Marquer dans les cases les documents requis et le service postal choisi. **2. Signer L'ATTESTATION DE COMPRENHESION ci-dessous. 3.** Remplir la formule à l'endos en lettres majuscules ou à la machine. **4.** Faire attester votre signature. **5.** Retourner avec photos, cheque, mandat international ou CRI à W.S.A., Washington, D.C. 20005. **Aucun document WSA ne sera émis sans paiement.**

INSTRUCCIONES: 1. Indique los documentos y el franqueo que desea. **2. Firme el CERTIFICADO DE ENTENDIMIENTO al fondo. 3.** Llene el Formulario al dorso. Favor de hacerlo a máquina o en letra de molde. **4. Certifique su firma y solicitud. 5.** Envíe esta solicitud junto a la foto; giro bancario o postal, o Cupones Internacionales de Intercambio a: WSA, Washington, D.C. 20005. **Ningún documento de WSA será emitido sin pago o certificación del mismo.**

Send the document(s) to this address
Envoyez le(s) documents á cet adresse
Envie el(los) documento(s) a esta dirección

World Passport	Passeport Mondial	Pasaporte Mundial	8 years / 8 ans / 8 años $60 ☐	3 years / 3 ans / 3 años $35 ☐
World Donor Passport	Passeport de Donateur Mondial		Pasaporte Mundial de Donante	15 years / 15 ans / 15 años $300 ☐
World Identity Card	Carte d'Identité Mondiale		Tarjeta Mundial de Identidad	$12 ☐
World Birth Certificate	Certificat Mondial de naissance		Certificado Mundial de Nacimiento	$12 ☐

Certified Mail (U.S.A. only) / Courrier (E.U. seulement) / Correo certificado en USA   ☐ US $3
Registered mail anywhere / Lettre recommandée partout / Correo registrado en otros paises   ☐ US $7

ATTESTATION OF UNDERSTANDING

The applicant understands that the World Service Authority can accept no responsibility for the position of any government as regards the WSA passport and/or its other identification documents.

Important: Applicants under 16 years of age must have the **Attestation of Understanding** signed by a parent or a guardian.

ATTESTATION DE COMPREHENSION

Le demandeur comprend que le World Service Authority ne peut assumer de responsibilité quant à la position d'un gouvernement concernant le passeport du WSA ou de tout autre piece d'identité émise par le même bureau.

Important: Les demandeurs âgés de moins de 16 ans doivent faire signer **L'Attestation de Compréhension** par un parent ou leur tuteur légal.

CERTIFICADO DE ENTENDIMIENTO

El aplicante entiende que la WSA no puede aceptar la responsabilidad por la posición de cualquier gobierno en relación con el Pasaporte WSA o sus documentos de identidad.

Importante: Uno de los padres o el guardián de los aplicantes menores de 16 años debe firmar el siguiente **Certificado de Entendimiento.**

Signature and Date • Signature et date • Firma y fecha

Approximate size of photo.

Dimension approximative de la photo.

Tamaño aproximado de la foto.

ID

Passport

Submit 4 photos and sign your name on back of each one. Color accepted. Photos are for file, replacement if necessary, and ID card, in addition to passport.

Veuillez joindre 4 photos et signer votre nom au verso de chacune d'elles. Elles serviront aux archives et à la carte d'identité ou au passeport et au besoin au remplacement du document.

Envíe 4 fotografías firmadas en la parte trasera, como en el ejemplo. Se aceptan fotografías a color. Las fotografías son para nuestro archivo, para reemplazo en caso de necesidad, y para la Tarjeta de Identidad, además del Pasaporte.

Print or type • Tapez ou escrivez en lettres capitales • Escriba a máquina o con letra de molde

Last name • Nom de famille • Apellido	First name(s) • Prénom(s) • Nombre(s)
Street • Rue • Calle	City & Zip Code • Ville & code postal • Ciudad
State Province • Départment • Estado	Country • Pays • Nación
Place of birth • Lieu de naissance • Lugar de nacimiento	Telephone	Telex

Day • Jour Dia	Month • Mois Mes	Year • Année Año	M Sex F	Height • Taille Estatura	Color eyes • Couleur yeux Color de los ojos

Special Marks • Signes particuliers Caracteristicas especiales	Occupation • Profession • Ocupación

INFORMATION FOR WORLD BIRTH CERTIFICATE • INFORMATIONS POUR LE CERTIFICAT MONDIAL DE NAISSANCE
INFORMACION PARA EL CERTIFICADO MUNDIAL DE NACIMIENTO

Father's name • Nom du père • Nombre del padre	Mother's name • Nom de la mère • Nombre de la madre

I swear that my information in this form is true and correct.

Je jure sur l'honneur que les informations fournies ci-haut sont exactes.

Juro que esta información es veridica.

Signature • Firma: . . . .

CERTIFICATION OF SIGNATURE, OR PHOTOCOPY OF IDENTITY PAPERS OR PRINT OF RIGHT INDEX FINGER.
Certification d'authenticité de la signature ou photocopies des papiers d'identité ou l'empreinte digitale de l'index droit.
Certificación de firma, o fotocopia de documentos de identidad o impresión digital.

On this_____ day of
_____ , 19 _____ , before me
came_____ .
known to me and known by me to be the person who executed the foregoing application, and he/she thereupon duly acknowledged to me that he/she executed the same.

En ce_____ jour de
_____ , 19 _____ , s'est
presenté(e) devant moi _____
_____ la personne
connue de moi étant l'auteur de la présente demande, en foi de quoi elle attesté en bonne et due forme d'être conformée au règlement.

En este _____ día de
_____ , de 19 _____ , se
presentó _____ ,
conocido como el cual, quien cumplimentó esta aplicación y reconoció delante de mi haberla cumplimentado.

Certifying Official • Agent Officiel • Oficial de certificaciones

Fingerprint
Empreinte Digitale
Impresión Digital

Seal and signature • Sceau et signature • Sello y firma

WORLD SERVICE
AUTHORITY DIST. III
1012 14th STREET, N.W.
WASHINGTON, D.C. — U.S.A. 20005
Telephone (202) 638-2662
Telex: 262214 WGOV UR
WSA GA 21100 10-85

Send me _____ more application forms

Envoyez-moi _____ formulaires d'application supplémentaires

Envienme _____ más solicitudes

Of course, after World War One, in order to control their citizens and limit individual freedom, most "modern" states enacted compulsory passport laws. People were not allowed to leave or enter a country without one. Every country reserved the power to withhold a passport (and the right to travel) "in the interest of the state". Today, at least theoretically, the Helsinki Accords signed by most countries recognize a basic human right to leave a country without having to give any reason. In my opinion the activities of Gary Davis for three decades were at least partly responsible for Helsinki. But in 1948, Gary Davis was a lone brave voice in the wilderness – an idealist.

Figuring that border officials might respect an "Authority", Gary printed up a document resembling a passport. Instead of being issued by a State or a recognized agency like the Red Cross or United Nations, his "passport", printed in a dozen languages (like the International Driving License), was from the "World Service Authority". The World Service Authority was thus created by Gary, with the aid of a neighborhood printer and nothing more. Many of Gary's friends, especially Quakers working with international relief used these travel documents. For a time they even had some respectability. Perhaps if they were restricted to Quaker Relief Workers, the WSA passport would still be a good travel document. But it isn't! Gary gave them away or sold them to all comers, in any name one chose to use. His charge was $5 or some small price to cover printing and rent on his hole-in-the-wall office. In Europe, Gary sought publicity for his ideas by destroying his own US passport and renouncing his US citizenship. This caused him to be considered quite a troublemaker. Why? Because he couldn't be deported back to the US.

Officials in Europe didn't like Gary Davis spreading his passive resistance, one-world, anti-government ideas. Poor Gary then spent a decade shuffling in and out of jails for violation of immigration and passport laws – which doesn't say much for his WSA passport. Yet, in Africa and Afghanistan, liberal distribution of WSA passports enabled many natives in danger to get past semi-illiterate border officials by waving their World Service Authority documents and essentially pretending to be employees of an international agency.

Gary was very proud to show photocopies of his WSA passports bearing border-crossing stamps from almost every country. But the truth is that every stamp was just a "mistake" by a border official. Yet Gary claimed his passports had saved the lives of hundreds of thousands of refugees and persons fleeing oppression. Perhaps they did!

In 1991, I read an ad in the *Herald Tribune* offering "Passport – $2000". Responding to this most reasonable offer, I received an elaborate brochure promoting the World Service Authority passport as a "universally accepted document". Of course, I knew that was far from the truth. I couldn't believe old Gary had turned into a mail order thief. Contacting him directly under an alias, I was pleased to learn that he was still selling WSA passports from the above address, together with a "suitable for framing" one-world wall certificate, a multi-color plastic, personalized ID card (with photo) identifying you as a World Citizen and at no extra cost, a breezy, anarchistic newsletter – all for sixty bucks ($60)! The WSA passport was still free to anyone who needed one but had no money. Someone else was peddling a "forgery" of his limited value WSA document for $2000!

Should you buy a World Service Authority passport? If you realize the limitations, as explained above, why not? It's a good way to donate $60 to a good cause.

When is the WSA passport a good one to use on international trips? Since few countries recognize the WSA, it can very seldom be used as a dependable way of entering countries without a visa. But sometimes having one CAN mean the difference between imprisonment and freedom.

Mr "Achmed", an Iraqi opposed to the Saddam regime, in 1990 entered the US with a false (i.e., stolen) US passport. He went to jail in the US. Because he lacked any travel documents, the American Immigration and Naturalisation Service (INS) would not let him out on bail. He feared persecution in Iraq if he returned home and therefore remained in detention throughout the adjudication of his asylum claim. His way out? While in jail, he purchased a $300 leather bound passport from the World Service Authority. With this in hand, he received a visa to the Dominican Republic. Even though the Dominican Republic does not recognize the WSA passport "de jure" or as a matter of law, most of its embassies and consulates will grant visas on a regular basis to the holders of WSA-documents.

Mr Achmed submitted the passport stamped with a Dominican Republic entry visa to the INS administrator handling his case. He was then allowed to leave the US on the first plane out, bound for the Caribbean. The US was glad to be rid of him, and he was glad to have to chance to go anywhere that wasn't jail. Once free in the Dominican Republic, he felt he could make other arrangements to acquire a legal passport there. He did this with our assistance.

Editor's Note: A letter from the World Service Authority to the *Passport Report* stated: "WSA passports may be purchased from $60 for the ordinary model, to $300 for our delux, leather-bound version. We also have a $12 per year newsletter. Your readers are invited to contact us at WSA, #1101, 1012 14th Street, NW Washington DC, 20005. Tel: 1-202-638-7929 or Fax: 202-638-0638. We also supply birth certificates." Application forms are reproduced here.

CAMOUFLAGE PASSPORTS

THE EASIEST SECOND PASSPORT YOU CAN GET IS A FAKE!

For US $550, you can buy documents to create a whole new bogus identity. This sum buys you a phoney passport and two ancilliary pieces of identification, all delivered within days. At first glance, the "camouflage" passport looks richly authentic. It's burgundy, textured-vinyl cover is stamped with gold lettering that might read, "PASSPORT, REPUBLIC OF CEYLON", or perhaps it is from some other non-existent country. Ceylon is history. Its successor is Sri Lanka. All these camouflage passports are from non-existing nations like New Hebrides, Upper Volta, British Guyana and Patagonia. They are sold as protection in case of hijacking by the American firm "International Document Service". Scope International will arrange for any non-criminal to acquire these "passports" by mail.

Apart from Ceylon, IDS sells passports from another twelve "dead" countries that have changed their names. Your identification package will include a passport from such a fictitious country. Other less imposing documents such as library cards are furnished as back up ID. Documents can be supplied based on a fictitious personal history created by you. Passports come complete with numerous false entry and exit stamps. The passports are dated to be "valid" for 10 years. A well-used look will add to their authentic appearance.

Camouflage passports have been succesfully used by over 400 American businessmen and a surprisingly large number of government officials for half a dozen years. Why? To conceal their identity when travelling in troubled areas. In some countries, it is not always wise to be an American or whatever you really are. The Middle East is famous for its hijackings and hostage takings. South America abounds in episodes involving the kidnapping of rich businessmen. With a camouflage passport, you are not automatically singled out on a hijacked ship or plane as a rich target or a hated enemy. Rather, the package from IDS creates the appearance of a not very interesting person from a not very interesting country.

IDS insists that its passports are "legal". They say that the US Justice Department for instance has assured them that no particular law bans carrying such documents so long as they are not used for fraud or to enter or leave the US. IDS's rival in the passport business, the State Department, professes no objection to US citizens holding decoy papers – as long as holders present *only* their American passports when they enter or leave the country.

IDS claims its most numerous customers are federal officials. To date, they say, well over 400 of their passports have been sold. One hundred of them to US Government officials. An additional 120 have gone to military personnel.

A camouflage identity, they say, is a "must" for every traveller. Having received a sample, we can testify to the remarkably authentic appearance. It could be a lot safer to be from an uncontroversial country in the event of a hijacking or other situation (as in 1991 Kuwait) where hostage passports were collected. Or use your "CP" to check into one of those third world hotels with zero security where they insist upon confiscating your passport for the night and then leaving it exposed in an unattended registration desk pigeon hole from where anyone could steal it.

Your camouflage passport could even be a life saver. Nothing is guaranteed, but such an option could come in handy some day – it may be the only option you have in a tight spot.

Terrorists are usually in a hurry. They have no extensive resources to check whether a passport is real or not. Many of them even have trouble with reading or writing at all. The Achille Lauro (PLO) hijackers confused Australians with Austrians, Viennese with Venetians.

To get your own set of IDS travel documents, write to Scope International. Enclose three passport size photographs and US $550. Half-price for subsequent documents ordered for the same person at the same time. Group discounts of 25 per cent available for 5 or more documents ordered at the same time for different people. Please note that IDS will select your country for you. We will have your order filled with documents from IDS.

Be sure to also include ALL of the following:
1. NAME: Your name and personal history can be entirely fictious, but you may have to remember it under VERY stressful conditions. It is a good idea for your name, birthday and personal history to be familiar. You might do a "blend" with your real identity. If your name if John Barrett, you could change it to Giovanni Barretelli or Jean Barre. If you have trouble translating your name, leave it to the author. Specify this wish for a translation into the lingo of your new camouflage country. You may of course choose any name.
2. SEX: Male or female (not how often!).
3. HEIGHT.

4. COLOR OF EYES.
5. DATE OF BIRTH.
6. OCCUPATION: Choose something low profile like "accountant".
7. MULTI-DIGIT ID NUMBER: A familiar, long number of six or more digits, to use as an ID number. This number will be used on an identification card from your camouflage country and should be familiar to you. But as many people do not know their serial number, don't worry about it.
8. STREET ADDRESS NUMBER: Select a familiar number and street address. We may have to change the street name to jibe better with a real street, in a city of your "camouflage" country.
9. IDENTIFYING MARKS OR VISIBLE SCARS.
10. NAME OF WIFE/HUSBAND.
11. NAME OF CHILD/CHILDREN.
12. NAME AREA(S) OF WORLD IN WHICH YOU PLAN TO TRAVEL. This will help us decide which of the "fictional" countries would be best for you. We will choose a place on the other end of the earth from where you expect to use your camouflage passport.
13. COUNTRY OF RESIDENCE: Your country of residence is NOT the same as the country of your passport. Many people who hold the passport of one country live and work somewhere else. Your country of residence could be the US, Canada, England or any other country in the whole world. Include your "real" street address if you wish for easy memory.
14. Be sure to finally include the exact name and address to which you want to have your ID package sent.

Is $550 too much to spend? That's up to you! Would you like a "jacket" for your real passport that acts as a decoy slipcover for your American passport. The cost is a mere $20 extra for one from France, England or somewhere of our choice. Of course, if a hijacker opens the decoy cover of your real document, he will discover the disguise. And then you will be up the creek without a paddle. But if you don't want people standing in line at a hotel or airline terminal to know what country you are from, consider getting a cover-case from us or any major stationery store in a country you are desirous of using as your decoy.

Remember the camouflage passport is *not* good for crossing borders, nor cashing bum checks nor any other illegal purpose. It is sold with the understanding that it is only to be used by honest people to try and fool criminals such as hijackers and kidnappers. Neither the author nor Scope International can take any responsibility for the consequences of your use of a camouflage passport for any purpose.

"NEW COUNTRY" PASSPORTS

Various individuals have attempted to start new countries and as part of their activities have issued passports. These passports have generally been considered much the same as World Service Passports. At most international borders, manuals are consulted, and if visas are required of any countries at all entrance is refused.

There are a very few off-the-beaten-path countries that will admit anyone regardless of what identification document he carries. You can find out about these through a publication known as the *Travel Information Manual* (explained in more detail in the VISA REQUIREMENTS section). If you are a fugitive, you may want to know about these places, but believe me, in most cases jail would be better! In any event passports from "new countries" are almost worthless for travel but could be of some help as banking documents or for getting one out of a tight spot. For instance, in Kuwait, if you were a stranded potential captive/hostage with an American passport, your life was in danger. But if you had a World Service Authority or other passport-like document, you might have been better able to talk your way around a teenage semi-illiterate Iraqi border guard.

There have been dozens of "new country" set ups in the past fifty years but none of them have proved to have any staying power, and none ever achieved any degree of sovereignty or international recognition.

Just in case you ever respond to a sucker ad in a place like the *International Herald Tribune's* classified section and are offered a "legally issued recognized passport", noble title, ID card, set of stamps or coin or ambassadorial appointment. If it is from any of the following "countries" it is probably not worth the paper it is printed on:

ARAGON started by swindler Robert Vesco off Barbuda, who abandoned the project when he accepted an offer by Cuba to run his operations from headquarters there.

ARAUCANIA & PATAGONIA the oldest unrecognized country. It was founded in 1860 and currently has a population of 1, the ruling Monarch, Prince Philippe D'Araucanie who issues coins, stamps, medals and appoints ambassadors.

ARYANA military style neo-Nazi kingdom on a secret, perhaps non-existent, Pacific island, which offers ID cards and noble titles. The operation is said to be promoted by some loonies from Los Angeles who believe that everyone except blond blue-eyed individuals should be exterminated.

ARYAN NATION survivalist camps for well armed fugitives and others in North American wilderness areas – more neo-Nazis.

ATLAND an underwater plateau at Grand Banks, Newfoundland, Canada.

ATLANTIS [SILVER ISLAND, GRAND CAPRI REPUBLIC, TRIUMPH REEF] various projects of Charles Silver to build a gambling casino outside territorial waters off Florida.

ATLANTIS, NEW founded in 1965, by Leicester Hemingway, brother of novelist Ernest. It is said to offer passports, postage stamps, tax haven services, quick divorces, immigration assistance services and matrimonial services, i.e. finding obedient oriental wives for dirty old men, and is located on a floating platform off Jamaica. Last known mailing address is: 11 East San Marino Drive, Miami Beach Florida, USA 33139. Let us know of your experiences with Mr Hemingway.

ATLANTIS OPERATION founded by wealthy industrialist, Werner K. Stiefel. It is based upon the libertarian principles of writer Ayn Rand and was founded around 1969 with a fleet of ferro-cement boats bearing colonists to an uninhabited island near the real country of Anguilla. The project is reportedly floundering, and the current capital is said to be the Sawyerkill Motel, RD5, Box 22A, Suagerties, New York, USA 12477.

BALDONIA, OUTER founded 1948 by "Prince" Russell Arundel on Bald Tusket Island, off Nova Scotia Canada).

BIFFECHE rebel kingdom inside Senegal, Africa which issues passports and noble titles.

BURKE, SHIRE founded around 1980. It is based in Australia and offers passports for US $10. Send inquiries to: Shire Clerk, Civic Center, Burketown, Queensland, 4830 Australia.

CALIFORNIA FREE STATE offers to print up impressive 24 page "passports" for $20 per *dozen* in wholesale batches. The model California passport looks normal, except that under "age" it says "not to be filled in till you grow up." Actually, an interesting "country" to print up your passports if you wish to found your own country! Write Gil Moore, 4226 Folsom Street, San Francisco, CA 94110 or contact Sword Printing, South San Francisco.

CASTELLANIA This is not a real country with borders, people and such usual accoutrements of nationhood. It appears to be a figment of the imagination of "Prince" Ralph Hubner of Vienna, an insurance salesman who sells noble titles, passports, postage stamps and so on. He will be glad to appoint you Ambassador, Exarch, Grand Vizier or Imperial Potentate of Castellania – for a small fee. His "Commercial Representative" in the US can be reached at PO Box 1132, Fremont, California 94538-1132. If you want to impress your friends with a knighthood or diplomatic credentials from Castellania, send for a brochure at US $700. But don't try to use these credentials to cross borders or get into the Queen's annual Buckingham Palace dinner for the diplomatic corps. Latest information is that passports are available only to "persons of demonstrated value to the Principality and the Free Templer Order". Previous passport holders can have their documents renewed for five years. Applicants can become naturalization candidates for a two-year period.

CORTERRA As a destination for people wishing to emigrate, the Federal Union of Corterra sounded like a Utopia in the sun. A 1991 ad in the *South China Morning Post* said, "This group of 12 small islands in the Pacific, close to Tahiti and Hawaii, has a multiracial population of only 80,000". Ads seeking potential immigrants were placed in Hong Kong newspapers.

"The people love democracy and freedom, speak English and have a British-based constitution and legal system. There is no income tax and no residency requirement. Everything is duty-free."

Is Corterra an ideal haven in this troubled world? Sounds that way! There is only one snag – Corterra does not exist. While Corterran passports were sold for US $15,000 upwards, there is no state on any map bearing that name.

Corterra passports were simply printed up by a Salt Lake City, Utah businessman calling himself Patrick Watters. As a result, this passport is not a very good one to travel on. Corterra is one of the more enterprising attempts to con desperate Hong Kong people out of their money.

Details on Corterra first appeared in a Hong Kong Chinese newspaper in September 1990. An advertisement by a Hong Kong company, Cartiman Ltd, offered passports and said interviews would be conducted in Hong Kong by the Corterran Honorary Consul. There was "no need" the ads said, "to travel to Corterra itself".

Cartiman Ltd has now stopped doing business with the Republic of Corterra, apparently because "it was not profitable". It seems more likely, however, that the company was discouraged after police told it that the republic was entirely fictious and they'd be carted off to the pokey if they continued to sell passports obtained from their source in Salt Lake City, Utah, USA.

CLIPPERTON an uninhabited island 1,000 miles off the coast of Mexico and claimed by the French who evacuated some Mexican claimants to the island around 1922. Claimed by several pretenders who seem to have never visited the island, like Pitcairn, it is a fertile imagination stimulator for would be new country founders. Jacques Cousteau the author/explorer from Monaco did a documentary film about the island. The French say their permission is needed to visit the island, but no one is there to enforce this rule.

CREATIVE ANACHRONISM has a population of 6,000 members who stage medieval combats and claims the world as their empire, staging regular battles to settle border disputes between various kings, dukes, earls and barons. Write to: box 594, Concord, California USA 94522.

HAY, KINGDOM OF founded in 1977, sells passports for £1, knighthoods for £2 and poet laureate, herald and ambassadorial posts at similar prices. Write: King Richard de Booth, The Castle, Hay-on-Wye, Hereford, Great Britain.

HUTT RIVER PROVINCE ruled by his Royal Highness, Prince Leonard Casley who owns an 18,000 acre ranch and claims to be independent of Australia where it is located. He issues high quality gold and silver coins, stamps, passports, shipping licenses and currency pegged to the Australian dollar. Mailing address: 156 Edwards Street, Osborne Park, Western Australia 6017.

IROQUOIS INDIAN NATIONS This tribe was never conquered by the US Troopers – Really! Located in the Florida swamps they take their sovereignty very seriously. They send representatives to international conferences with their passports. Of course any document, or even a blank sheet of paper, with a Visa can be used to get into a country that invites you. But other countries, unless they want to annoy the US, do not take them seriously. Besides, only Iroquois can get these passports.

MACHAIS SEAL ISLAND "sovereignty undetermined" which makes this uninhabited island off the coast of Maine, USA and New Brunswick, Canada a possible new country site, claimed by many but actually uninhabited.

MALUTI libertarians advertising in *Reason Magazine* solicited $5,000 each from would be settlers of this island in an unknown location. Any readers who have further information about this project are invited to write the author.

MEVU CO-OPERATIVE REPUBLIC claims part of Antarctica. Write: Box 4405, N-4001, Stavager, Norway.

OLIVER, MICHAEL J. deserves a separate listing because he has been involved in trying to start several new countries since the 1950's. He raised money and supported the independence of the Turks & Caicos Islands, but the British and local residents ousted him when genuine sovereignty was ultimately granted. There was a replay with the New Hebrides in the Pacific which later became known as Vanuatu. Then, disappointed, because a local population wanted little of his plans, he started MINERVA by bringing in sand at a cost of $200,000 from Australia to build up a coral reef. When it was completed, the King of Tonga invaded the island from 260 miles away and claimed that the reefs had always been the property of his kingdom. Oliver was forced to abandon this project which he had financed with his own money and that of investors who purchased interesting bi-metallic gold and silver Minerva coins. Then, Mike Oliver supported a Free Abaco movement. Abaco Island was part of the Bahamas. This came to naught. Oliver was also involved with an independence movement in the Azores Islands (owned by Portugal) and the Isle of Man (a British Protectorate). The bottom line for Mike Oliver has been that with only a few hundred thousand dollars, his own money plus that of libertarian oriented investors, he has received reams of publicity, but never really had any significant or lasting role to play in any of the new countries he promoted. He currently promotes new countries as The Phoenix Foundation, Box 5085, 1007AB, Amsterdam, Netherlands.

OCEANUS was founded in 1970 by "Admiral" Ted Welles and a nucleus of believers. It claims all territory below mean high tide everywhere. Everyone on planet Earth is considered to be a citizen unless they specifically denounce citizenship in writing. (So far only one gentleman from Senegal has felt strongly enough to do so). In 1976, Oceanus adopted a constitution based on an American model, with three branches including one headed by a chief executive. Ted Welles himself filled this post until 1984 when according to the constitution he could no longer succeed himself.

One of the considerations for this presumed citizenship is the qualification for a passport. This document is issued for US $100 (US $50 of which apparently is used to cover delivery costs) and comes complete with ID card, birth certificate, medical certificate and driver's license. These documents have apparently been used to establish bank accounts and even for border crossings. The government of Oceanus is currently conducting a competition offering a US $500 award to the Oceanus citizen who collects the most stamps from different countries in his Oceanus passport.

The government of Oceanus has also informed us that they have embarked on a major advertising campaign, including classified ads in *The International Herald Tribune* under the heading, "BIRTHRIGHT: COMMON HERITAGE Oceanus Passport". This travel document just may help you get out of a tight spot, or at least provide some amusement. For more information write to: Oceanus Government via Post Office Manset-Seawall, Maine 04656, USA.

PALMYRA a Hawaiian island, uninhabited and under the control of the US Department of the Interior, although privately owned by an American. Morris C. Davis, a former partner of Mike Oliver has a scheme to move settlers there and then hold a referendum to achieve self governing Commonwealth status. We predict nothing much will come of the project but if you want to participate, write: Box 201, Orange, California, USA 92666.

PITCAIRN ISLAND settled by the survivors of Mutiny on the Bounty and then discovered 100 years later by the British who resettled the descendants of British sailors and Polynesian beauties to another island near Australia. About 200 of these relocated islanders decided they wanted to return to Pitcairn shortly after World War Two, which they did. But after a taste of civilization, the younger people all left lonely Pitcairn for other places throughout the Commonwealth where they were received as celebrities. As of today, the permanent population of the island is only 24 souls, and there are no youngsters. There is one radio-telephone, and the island is supplied by about four ships a year from Great Britain. There are about 4,000 descendants of Pitcairn settlers worldwide who are potential citizens of an independent Pitcairn, but no-one on the island is motivated enough to declare independence. Why? Because this would cut off the welfare dole shipments of necessities that come in. There is no port facility as the beaches are essentially cliffs. Longboats are launched and recovered from metal rails leading down to the sea. About one or two cruise boats a year visit Pitcairn. A small amount of income is raised by selling souvenirs and postage stamps printed in England to these tourists. The locals raise tropical fruits and vegetables and do some fishing. *National Geographic* did an interesting article on the place around 1983. These days, a visa is needed from Great Britain to visit Pitcairn – theoretically. But arrive in a yacht and no one really cares. The people on Pitcairn currently are a bit simple-minded and also physically weird as they are the products of inbreeding of families (known as incest in the West). With considerable enthusiasm they practice a kind of primitive fundamentalist Christianity. Their language is a peculiar English dialect.

QUAY, PEOPLE'S DEMOCRATIC REPUBLIC two Americans have claimed some uninhabited coral reefs about 1,000 miles east of New Zealand. If they made any serious development attempts, they would probably go the way of Minerva as New Zealand claims the territory. Address: Box 30335 Hialeah, Florida 33013.

REDONDA an uninhabited island, otherwise claimed by Antigua, ruled by King Felipe (otherwise known as writer Matthew Phillips Sheil) and six other competing self-appointed pretenders to the throne, most of whom live in England and sell noble titles. The country was described in a novel *Kingdom of Plaice* by the famous author, Laurence Durrell. No address.

ROSES, ISLE OF a privately built sea-platform of 4,000 square feet, 8 miles from Rimini, Italy, over water less than 20 feet deep. During the late 1960's it was a popular tourist attraction with a restaurant, bar, bank and tax-free store. The owner, Giorgio Rosa, an Italian, declared in 1969 that it was an independent republic the language of which was Esperanto, an artificial language once spoken by several hundred thousand idealistic "one world" minded individuals worldwide. After his declaration, suspecting that he would install a "pirate" radio or TV station to compete with the state monopoly, the Italian Navy evacuated and dynamited the structure. This shows us that existing nations will swiftly put an end to new country projects that they feel have the potential to cause them any trouble.

The Italians even limited the sovereignty of **SAN MARINO**, a genuine quasi-dependent long-existing independent enclave, by threatening to invade if they put up a proposed casino, radio station or even served as the site of a newspaper publishing plant. Likewise, the enclave countries of Monaco, Andorra and islands like Jersey, Guernsey and Sark are constrained by their protectors in how far they can stray. The Isle of Roses was outside the three mile limit then claimed by Italy, but the government did not hire a lawyer to dispute the matter. They just blew up the new country.

SEALAND is a similar platform off the British coast where Paddy Bates was a successful pirate radio station operator for years. He sold coins, stamps and passports and called himself "Prince Roy". Paddy actually lived on this abandoned World War Two British artillery platform with his wife Joan. Prince Roy spent hundreds of thousands of pounds in legal bills to establish and preserve his right to the island and resorted to firearms to ward off invaders more than once. His last known address: Sealand, Box 3, Felixstowe, Suffolk, Great Britain.

SHASHILAND, KINGDOM OF claims Limpopo Islands which is also claimed by South Africa, Zimbabwe and Botswana. The current potentate is Mr W.B. Coetzer, Box 5958, Johannesburg, South Africa.

SPRATLY ISLANDS uninhabited and located in the South China Sea are also claimed by China, Vietnam and the Philippines. The islands are thought to have valuable oil deposits and are claimed by many new country organizers, among them King John de Mariveles whom we have seen in these pages under the Knights of Malta heading. This is undoubtedly a complex and confused sovereignty question in which it is more likely that a major power will turn out to be the winner rather than a new country promoter.

One could write a very long volume on this subject since it is the realm of romantics, thinking individualists and various weird folk who have in fact, often been able to talk their way past amused border guards with some very strange documents. Let's make our summary short and sweet: there are approximately 230 countries or political entities in the world that are generally accepted and recognized as more or less "legitimate". Membership in the United Nations, a definite piece of land with borders, diplomatic relations with other countries and a population are a few of the most common requirements of nationhood. A "country" that issues passports without any or all of the foregoing is likely to be issuing a document of very limited value.

For those interested in the subject of new countries, a more comprehensive list and discussion is available in the interesting 167 page paperback *How to Start Your Own Country* from LOOMPANICS. We are grateful to them for having provided much of the information in this section.

CONTROVERSIAL AND UNUSUAL BOOKS: For anarchists, survivalists, iconoclasts, libertarians, mercenaries, investigators, drop-outs, law enforcers, law-breakers, researchers and those interested in the strange, useful oddball, and diabolical see the book catalogs section in the Resource List at the back of this Special Report.

A selected range of useful books is also available from Scope International. Please ask for the PT Booklist.

Comments, questions, additions and constructive criticism should be sent to:
Scope International, 62 Murray Road, Waterlooville, Hampshire PO8 9JL, Great Britain

Part VII

SPECIAL REPORT FOR
HONG KONG & SOUTH AFRICA
CITIZENS

SPECIAL REPORT FOR HONG KONG AND SOUTH AFRICAN CITIZENS

Most Hong Kong and South African citizens, at least the prosperous ones, would prefer to spend most of their time where they grew up and where their business is located. Moving is very unsettling and most people have no particular wish to leave their homes. But in Hong Kong, where most of the population has already fled once from the mental and economic slavery of communism, people are anxious to have somewhere else to go if life under the communists becomes untenable. While some South African and Chinese are PTs (Perpetual Tourists) and can be comfortable anywhere, the majority desire roots, a home, nearby friends, family and culture. They prefer to live in places where their community is already established with some degree of security. The plan of intelligent and far-sighted Chinese and South African leading families was to send a relative or two abroad to secure residence rights and perhaps a second passport while the rest of the family devoted considerable attention to a family business back home.

The favored destinations were and still are the US, then Canada, with Australia or Europe a third choice. Many free countries have accepted thousands of Chinese and South Africans, giving them second passports. Wealthier Chinese and South Africans have already discovered that every country has its loopholes. Even if direct immigration was officially discouraged or prohibited, there were many ways of obtaining second passports. Among the favorites was that virtually every country allows trainees and students to enter on a temporary basis. Once a student enters, it is relatively easy to arrange for a job or marriage that carries the right to citizenship and residence. Once any individual has such legal rights, parents, children, brothers and sisters can usually be squeezed in for "family reunification".

Besides marriage, a new company or corporation can be set up in most countries (usually by a talented immigration lawyer). This company then creates a job that "only" the would-be immigrant can fill. Or in some cases, certain categories of skills in short supply can qualify one for automatic admission. Thus, the Hong Kong person (or any would-be immigrant) receives a visa and work permit by filling a spot on a country's "want list". One common way is to set up a company which provides local employment or trains locals in a particular skill. In due course, the company founder applies for citizenship and brings in his extended family group.

Still another ploy is to get a job in the target country with a local company. That company goes to bat with the bureaucracy. It is well known that a given country, the US for instance, may have too many lawyers or medical doctors, but a good lawyer will know how to prepare an application so that a conservative doctor becomes an eminent practitioner and teacher of some obscure discipline currently in fashion. Thus a medical doctor in general practice becomes (on paper anyway) an authority on AIDS or acupuncture. He gets his admission ticket due to the talents of a skilled immigration paperwork preparer. In the US or Canada, a foreign medical doctor who is well informed enough to say he is going to settle in some remote rural area having no doctors receives an immediate entry permit. One who says he wants to move to New York, Vancouver or San Francisco finds only a "Do Not Enter" sign. But *once inside* any country, any immigrant can usually settle wherever he pleases. It is all form and little substance when one deals with governments!

Although we do not recommend this approach, it is well known that in most countries it is not difficult to arrange for a local birth certificate. Official records may have been burned in a fire. If so, false information cannot be proven to be false, except perhaps by the individual who procures or prepares it. Clever individuals use documents in a way that will never be challenged. For instance, it is not necessary to obtain a birth certificate proving you are an automatic citizen by virtue of birth in a country. Often, a birth certificate of a parent or grandparent can be arranged in such a way that the would-be immigrant can remain exactly who he is, born where he was. Example: A person born in Turkey would normally have an uphill battle to get German immigration papers. He would have to wait at least a dozen years until he received a passport. But if proof of a German grandparent born in communist East Germany can be arranged in the vital statistics department, the uphill path is transformed into a downhill slalom. A black African does not get much of a welcome from US immigration, but if his father or mother was an American citizen, that is another story. It is not difficult to find the name of some American citizen (probably dead) who is "adopted posthumously as a parent and replaces the real parent on the records in Africa.

It is a shame that talented and self-supporting people cannot simply just go to live wherever they want, without paying lawyers, telling lies, inventing ancestors, arranging marriages, setting up corporations or arranging for fraudulent papers to be filed. The United Nations collects billions to deal with "refugee problems". Much of this money goes to keep millions of innocent people worldwide in what amounts to concentration camps. The Vietnamese Boat People, for instance, are now behind bars in Hong Kong and Thailand (among other places) on subsistence rations. These refugees are confined in camps often with inadequate water, sanitation and food – surrounded by barbed wire fences. Cubans and Haitians in the US are in a similar position.

Vast amounts of hard earned taxpayer money is spent (flushed down a sewer, we would say) to classify people as either: A) "True refugees from political persecution" or B) "Undeserving persons who are just seeking a better life". As if it mattered! Neither Hong Kong nor South African citizens would be considered "true refugees" of course. They just want want to get out from under the heavy hand of government.

Few Hong Kong citizens or South African white people could prove that they would be facing death sentences for purely political activities. And thus they would not be eligible for resettlement as *bona fide refugees*. If Red China took over Hong Kong and started to squeeze, most Hong Kong residents would become unwanted human garbage – like the Vietnamese boat people. If South African whites are ousted from their country there will be little sympathy for them as well. Certainly no countries are willing to take in millions of refugees from either place.

According to the United Nations High Commission on Refugees, "Legitimate Refugees should be resettled, but those merely in search of better economic opportunities should be returned [forcibly if necessary] to their country of origin." For our typical Hong Kong or South African reader, to be classified by the United Nations as a "true refugee" will be harder than getting a triple PhD from Oxford, Harvard and the Ecole Polytechnique in Paris.

Accordingly, we are going to suggest other alternatives:

In the decade preceding the summer of 1989, the general consensus was that when Hong Kong reverted to mainland Chinese rule, they would be left alone to pursue their economic interests. It was felt that the communists "needed" Hong Kong as a thriving citadel of economic freedom and outlet for their goods. Hong Kong served China well as a source of investment capital and new technology. But this theory came unglued when the democratic movement in China's Tiananmen Square was suppressed by turning a bunch of non-violent, starry-eyed idealists into hamburgers. Fire hoses could have dispersed the students, but machine guns were used instead. Thousands were needlessly murdered. China's political leadership ignored "world opinion" – as leaders in unfree countries always do. The people of Hong Kong who wanted to believe otherwise, were given a preview of the reality of the kind of brute force that might soon be unleashed in Hong Kong.

The truth is that leftist politicians in general and all dictators (communist leaders in particular) never "need" anyone nor anything, except power. Again and again, once relatively prosperous countries like Czechoslovakia, Argentina, Syria, Soviet Ukraine, Burma and the Marxist States of Africa have been propelled into an economic tailspin by a Marxist ruling class. Productive people were murdered in genocidal campaigns. "Leaders" and bureaucrats can always squeeze enough out of any population to live comfortably themselves. The "good of the country" never weighs much against the need of those in power to keep themselves in power. Any analysis that assumes rational economic behavior on the part of politicians to **benefit** the masses is incorrect. Accordingly, people who love freedom and happen to live in Hong Kong or South Africa desperately need a second passport! If people have the option to leave, they can restrain those who hold the power.

This author predicts that at some time in the future, the white South Africans will have a rude awakening. We can't say exactly what it will be, but the writing on the wall is that in our lifetime, the South African whites will lose their position of privilege, power and property. Many may be killed. The few who were "loyal" and saw no need to make alternate plans and arrangements will be those who suffer most.

The ordinary Chinese individual quickly saw in the events of summer 1989 what he always suspected: The British government doesn't want more Chinese in England because there are, in its eyes, simply too many of them there already. Besides, it would be a politically unpopular move to allow Hong Kongese to "over-run" the small British Isles. The communist Chinese leaders would just as soon see their undisciplined brothers in Hong Kong made into sausages. The international community offers no help. Individual Chinese and South Africans who could pay a stiff price for a second passport will be able to obtain freedom. As to the rest . . . well who knows! Who cares?

The bottom line is, was and always will be that *in an unfair world, we are all on our own.*

Many governments have said in effect "any individual or family who has money can buy their way in". Canada took in the largest wads of cash with their investor programmes. But Canada imposed a lot of uncomfortable restrictions (see section on Canada). Some of the richest, smartest and most mobile people took the indirect route of buying property and establishing themselves as PTs in other countries. Then, once living in any new country, they looked around until they found the right opening elsewhere. Normally, the ownership of property and/or a business, even in a crowded country like Italy, Germany or France, puts one in the position to make the right contacts and gain sponsorship by local people of influence. Eventually the citizenship paperwork falls into place – if you have a goal and some spare cash.

What is our suggestion for the typical middle-class family? If cash resources exist, there are several programmes where you can obtain a fairly decent passport for travel *without the need to live in the country,* to pay any taxes there or to have a country that feels it "owns" you.

There are many plans for citizens desiring second passports. These exist in a number of countries of Central and South America. These programs are described elsewhere in this book. These deals all cost less than the rather sizeable investments required by the major *respectable* countries. Most of the Consulates in Hong Kong have at one time "sold" legitimate passports. Reportedly, Brazil, Paraguay, Portugal, Venezuela and even Tonga were selling "provisional" non-citizen travel documents in Hong Kong from $15,000 to $80,000. Their fountains gushed with these expensive little booklets. The supply and prices went up and sometimes even down with arbitrary fluctuations. The flow of documents was sometimes cut off abruptly! It still happens.

As to "investment programs", besides Canada, Singapore has had a deal for many years which gives residence and citizenship only to those Hong Kong Chinese or Asians who invested US $500,000 or more in a new Singapore business. See our section on Singapore for current information.

Yes, we agree that it is a shame that money talks and poor folks walk. In World War Two, Hitler for a time allowed any Jewish individual who had bribe money to emigrate. Poorer Jews could and did often smuggle themselves out of Germany or get out on nerve and wits. But 90 per cent of the Jews could not or would not leave. They were simply not accepted by other countries or were forcibly repatriated to certain death, as when Switzerland forced many of them out of their country at gunpoint. Hitler solved the "Jewish Problem" with death camps and genocide. The Chinese Communists have a track record for doing the same thing in Tibet. Black people, Asians as well as Europeans are all pretty good at murdering each other. How to escape?

The conventional approach is to have a second home abroad and money "offshore". We all need somewhere definite to go in the event of trouble. There is nothing wrong with this approach except perhaps that with only one passage or one plan, it is inflexible. With only one "back door" or escape route, if that one door is stuck, you may be stuck when the poison gas or bombs roll in. Another approach, the PT plan we perfected, is to have *several* escape routes and several sets of travel documents.

My book *PT* takes a long hard look at the problem of how to stay out from under the thumbs of those leftist bureaucrats of the United Nations (and their constituents) and political lunatics in general. The PT – Permanent Tourist answer is mainly having several passports, some assets strategically placed abroad and being comfortable with **no** fixed place of residence or stationary business.

The PT arrangement (given in outline form at the back of this book) works fine for anyone who has a "portable" occupation or enough capital to be able to trade and live on the profits. What is a portable occupation? Any job that does not require regular hours spent at a fixed location. For instance: promoter, builder, sportsman, private teacher, writer, actor, musician, boat owner, metals trader, currency broker, importer, exporter, computer programmer, consultant, stockbroker – all of these and people with about 6,000 other job classifications could survive anywhere. Because they are not "permanently resident" people with portable jobs (or assets). PTs are considered tourists by the country where they live. As a result, certain unpleasant obligations like military service or paying taxes can be reduced or avoided. Obviously, if one owns only one local restaurant, it is difficult to be a complete PT. Although with several restaurants in different countries, many PT-style advantages can be obtained. Transfer pricing can shift your company's profits to a no tax or low tax country from a high tax jurisdiction. There are always travel and freedom advantages in having several nationalities and multi-national businesses.

If I were a resident of Hong Kong or South Africa with a prosperous business or professional practice that I wanted to hold on to as long as possible, my personal program would be to start out by obtaining a legal "instant passport" at once. If next month there was a major unexpected event in my personal life, or in politics, I would *immediately* be able to get out and have somewhere to go without being at the mercy of some bureaucrat who could delay or withold my visa.

I'd start a second small business abroad and possibly rent or purchase a modest home in a different country that appealed to me. The home and the new business would be in two different places. In each case, I'd have the legal right to go and live at either. I'd keep expanding my options by trying to get a respectable passport, perhaps from Canada or New Zealand or some EC country, knowing that the project could take several years.

As mentioned elsewhere in this book, I'd plan to have access to *several* "target countries" on the assumption that one or more of them might not work out. With five sets of travel documents, I'd begin to feel secure!

I would start immediately on the paperwork for immigration from a country of residence *other than* my home country. Why? Because consulates in Hong Kong or South Africa have such a heavy backlog of applications that the odds of getting what is needed are much decreased when one starts at home, with only one passport. The favored method of emigrating to a desirable country, as previously mentioned, is usually best accomplished by setting up a business abroad in that country and then petitioning the Immigration and Labor Department of the target country with documents to prove that your presence is essential to the business. Naturally, the business itself must be one that is considered desirable, or better yet, *essential* for the country involved.

A skilled professional, usually an immigration lawyer, can normally help you bypass most frustrations. He can circumvent or expedite the lengthy delays that hold up ordinary immigration applications. In corrupt countries where such things are necessary, he can also disburse gratuities effectively. In uncorrupt countries, like Canada, he can advise you *against* offering bribes and thus save you from queering your application.

In other sections, I have spelled out how to make the right contacts. Normally, a countryman abroad who is a senior bank officer, contacts you'll make at a commercial club (like Rotary or Lions) or people you'll encounter at your place of religion (in the target country) can steer you to someone. The best channels are those already used by one or more friends. This author always trusts only those lawyers or agents who will work on a mainly *contingent* fee. **No delivery, no pay**. Too many crooks will just take your money without providing genuine services.

We know many people in many countries and can sometimes make referrals to passport experts. We do not become involved in the business ourselves, but will refer you to specialists that have, at least, not proved unreliable in such matters. Also, needless to say, if you have been helped by a particularly effective lawyer or otherwise, please let *us* know. We will then refer other clients to him based upon your good reports. It is our hope to help honest and deserving people get out from under the thumb of oppression and far away from those governments whose policies are life-threatening.

The Hong Kong situation, like the South African, may work itself out in a peaceful way. But as we note in *PT,* the odds are (in any country) that at least three times in your life you will face a crisis where it would help (and possibly save your life or your money) if you had a place to hide your ass and your assets for a time. You may want to go off and distance yourself from any conflict while riots or violent revolutions are in progress. There may come a time you'd like to get away until your spouse is no longer mad enough to sue you for divorce. It could be that the government or some personal acquaintance is out to destroy you for some good reason or just because of some mistake. There are many reasons to set up a PT style, alternate life support system for yourself and your family. There are just more obvious and immediate reasons if you live in Hong Kong or South Africa. Survival is the name of the game. You are free to make more moves with several sets of travel documents, well placed assets abroad, diversified business interests and the ability to earn a living and fit in anywhere.

Read *PT* for further valuable information. *PT 1* and *PT 2* are available from Scope International Ltd. (see back of this report for further details). See also *The Tax Exile Report.*

WARNING: TO HONG KONG CHINESE, REGARDING CON MEN

It is "buyer beware" in the passport business. Few vendors offer legitimate products, but this does not stop gullible people from shelling out tens of thousands of dollars in application fees for worthless paper.

These days, Hong Kong is the happiest hunting ground for passport peddlers. The pre-1997 rush to leave the colony has triggered dozens of cases of emigration fraud, among them the invention of a brand new republic (see "Corterra" in our chapter on ODDBALL and TAX HAVEN PASSPORTS).

The Panamanian consul-general in Hong Kong – a nephew of General Manuel Noriega, the deposed Panamanian dictator – was removed from office amid accusations that he was involved in a multi million dollar passport-for-sale business. It turned out that he had sold over 60,000 legitimate Panamanian passports at $8,000 each. Yes, he collected some five hundred MILLION dollars in fees!

In another case, the Venezuelan consul-general was arrested during late 1990 in connection with an investigation into stolen or fake travel documents.

The Irish consul-general had to leave his London office in a 1989 sex-for-passport scandal involving several hundred nubile Asian beauties giving their "all" for a passport to the West.

Several third world countries have become what amounts to participants in the rip off of Hong Kong citizens. Belize, Fiji, Tonga and even communist China itself have been selling passports. These are often non-resident passports, carrying numerous restrictions. These limitations become clear only after the money has changed hands. Passports on offer from Tonga, for instance, do not entitle their bearers to travel *outside* this tiny Pacific group of islands!

Another currently advertised scheme claims that a change in legislation on American Indian self-determination is imminent in the United States. Red Indian chiefs, the Chinese are told, will soon have the power to grant American citizenship to investors in their reservations. Several Red Indians, approach "investors" and collect application fees. These con-men visit Hong Kong on a regular basis and are today collecting substantial sums for "pie in the sky".

Comments, questions, additions and constructive criticism should be sent to:
Scope International, 62 Murray Road, Waterlooville, Hampshire PO8 9JL, Great Britain

Part VIII

BACK DOORS

INDIRECT ROUTES: TRY THE BACK DOOR WHEN THE FRONT IS LOCKED

In many instances you may not be successful in landing the first choice of passport you seek. This could occur for many reasons. To avoid being confronted with this situation, you should actively explore alternatives. In some cases, an indirect approach may produce better results than the direct would.

CANADA AND THE US – ALL THE BENEFITS WITHOUT THE HASSLES

As the US is regarded as the land of unprecedented economic opportunity for the entrepreneur, United States immigration normally requires representation by an expensive immigration lawyer. For nationals from most third world countries, getting a US residence permit is next to impossible without an arranged marriage to a US citizen.

The US quota system allows greater numbers of people to come in from Europe than from Africa or Asia. The wait for Filipinos or Hong Kong Chinese lacking appropriate occupational or family preferences can last twenty years.

For the entrepreneur, the self-employed person who earns a living by making deals or running his own investments, *it is inadvisable to become a US resident or citizen*. High US taxes can be avoided by the simple expedient of becoming a Canadian.

A Canadian resident or citizen needs no visa for a stay of up to six months a year in the US – and it is considerably easier to get Canadian than US residence and citizenship. Some Canadians work by day in the US and sleep in Canada. In fact, 90 per cent of all Canadians live within commuting distance (i.e. fifty-five miles) of the US border!

Investment income from the US and capital gains are not totally tax-free for Canadians. However, Canadians can avoid some of their own country's taxes by spending less than six months a year in Canada, thereby becoming non-residents. A 15 per cent Canadian non-resident tax is automatically withheld at source from all income (even the smallest sum), earned by a non-resident. With a Canadian passport one can come and go anywhere in North or South America, visa-free and have all the benefits of US citizenship without the burdens of taxation or military service. Although universal military service is not currently required, the US has imposed military conscription on and off during its history. HIGH TAXES, THE MAIN DRAWBACK TO US CITIZENSHIP OR RESIDENCE, ARE AVOIDED WITH A CANADIAN PASSPORT.

CASE HISTORY – THE 3 DAY PER WEEK BANKER

A well known Canadian millionaire investment banker generally worked in New York from Monday through Thursday. He spent the rest of his time on business travel or entertaining at his condo in Acapulco. He was careful to count the nights and never slept more than a total of 182 nights per annum in the US. *(Note: As of 1987, the permissible nights per year has been reduced to 122)*. He entered and left the US at least once a week. Wary of nuclear war, he kept a substantial home and sheep ranch in New Zealand and left his New Zealand passport in a Swiss Bank custodial account. It could be sent to him by courier anywhere in the world within 24 hours. This combination of passports permitted him to get in and out of almost any country without a visa.

On an income of several million dollars a year, this banker pays no income taxes whatsoever! Yet he is a welcome non-resident foreign investor in the US and also in Switzerland – where he keeps most of his personal money invested through nominee or agency accounts*. He is a welcome vacationer and non-resident in Acapulco. He seldom visits his home in New Zealand, but is welcome to move there anytime.

Our non-hero has no wish to join any army or send his children into war on behalf of Mexico, the US or New Zealand. Is he a human multi-national we should emulate? If you think so, read *PT 1* and *PT 2* for further details on this sort of lifestyle.

US VIA A LITTLE KNOWN BACK DOOR:

People who once considered obtaining US citizenship are amazed and astonished to learn that there is another way to acquire all the benefits, but none of the disadvantages (confiscatory and confusing taxes, discrimination, currency controls, severe moral laws and all the rest). As mentioned above, a Canadian has the right to cross the US border without a visa, but a Canadian does not have the automatic right to hold a job in the US nor to stay more than six months at a time. But citizens of certain places can come and go in the States without a visa. They can stay as long as they wish and can get any job they want or even obtain welfare and educational benefits without a work permit or ever registering as an alien. If a large number of foreigners were to take advantage of this route, like a herd of cattle at a water hole, they would muddy the drink for everyone else. Still, I will give you enough information to enable you to do it on your own if you want to undertake a bit or research and travel.

This is the theory: St. Pierre and Miquelon citizens enjoy all rights of Frenchmen without military service, taxes or other burdens. Nationals of the Channel Islands enjoy the same relationship with the United Kingdom. There are also several small semi-independent islands that were once colonies or protectorates of the US, starting to get the picture? They include, but are not limited to, such places as Palau, Guam, American Samoa, US Virgins, Roncador Cay, St. Thomas, St. Croix, Serrana Bank, Howland, Jarvis, Baker, Swain's, Conton, Wake, Johnson, Phoenix, The Marshalls, Carolines, Tokelau and of course Christmas Island. These islands are little known. Most are relatively undeveloped tax havens. Residence permits, citizenship and possibly diplomatic appointments (with passports) are often available under various local investor/benefactor programs. In some places the actual passports are printed on the same stock as US passports. They closely resemble US passports and are overprinted with the name of the island. Who gets them is typically decided by the local government, not the US. The holder of these island passports needs no visa to enter the US. There are usually direct flights to Hawaii (or in the Caribbean, to Miami). There is generally no customs clearance between these islands and the US ports of entry.

So long as these islands become the second home of just a few dozen international businessmen per year (who presumably will help the islands), the US is willing to accede to present arrangements. A big reason for this generous attitude on immigration and tariffs is that the US government feels guilty about exploiting and abusing the natives during its

---

*Would you like to know how the super-rich invest internationally with nothing held in their own name? Read *The Tax Exile Report* by Marshall J. Langer.

imperialist era. Many islands were actually used for target practice and even for the explosion of early atomic bombs. The US tries to make up for past sins with concessions allowing easy immigration and no customs barriers. If and when journalists ever make a "big deal" out of the "abuses inherent in the situation", one can be sure that some congressmen, full of righteous indignation, will seek to forbid US access to any citizens whose grandparents were not born on the islands. This will shut off any incentive to attract new blood and the small investment flow to the islands. It will ultimately cost the US taxpayers much more in foreign aid, but that is how the world is.

Right now the door is open a crack. For roughly $35,000 and a lot of paperwork, any reputable businessperson (plus family) can get the equivalent of a US passport. Contact Scope International if you learn and wish to share any of the finer points of the various island programs.

SHOULD YOU GET A US PASSPORT FROM A US PACIFIC BASIN POSSESSION?

Ever heard of the Federated States of Micronesia? Or the Republic of Palau? These tiny nations, islands in the Pacific Ocean are just two of a great number of US possessions and trust territories. Some of them offer great benefits and very low tax rates when compared to mainland US.

This is a brief review of the tax status of citizens legally domiciled in the following US possessions: Guam, American Samoa, Commonwealth of the Northern Mariana Islands, Federated States of Micronesia, Republic of the Marshall Islands and the Republic of Palau. As a general matter, citizens of Guam, American Samoa and the Mariana Islands are subject to US tax rates as if they ARE residents of mainland US. There are exceptions for local source income derived in such possessions. However, citizens of Micronesia, the Marshall Islands and Palau are generally considered by the US as NONRESIDENT ALIENS under the US Internal Revenue Code (the "US Code"). A more detailed discussion follows.

1. GENERAL BACKGROUND: Guam, American Samoa, the Mariana Islands, Micronesia, the Marshall Islands and Palau are all generally referred to as US "possessions". But not all of these territories are, in fact, true possessions of the US. The issue of whether a territory is a possession revolves around the question of "sovereignty". Due to the nature of the agreements transferring control of Guam, American Samoa and the Marianas to the US, the US is deemed to have sovereignty over those territories. Therefore, those regions are deemed to be "possessions" of the United States.

In contrast, the agreements transferring control of Micronesia, the Marshall Islands and Palau to the US were entered into under the auspices of the United Nations. Under those agreements, the US was charged only to *supervise* the territories on behalf of the United Nations. Thus, **the US is not deemed to have *sovereignty* over those territories**. Therefore, they are not classified as possessions of the US

Although these distinctions of sovereignty seem minor, they have **significant tax ramifications**:

2. TAXATION OF POSSESSIONS. (Guam, American Samoa and the Mariana Islands). Prior to 1986, Guam, American Samoa and the Mariana Islands were required to adopt an internal revenue code that "mirrored" the US code. Pursuant to the new 1986 code, these possessions were given the right to adopt independent internal revenue codes with respect to income generated in those possessions. However, prior to being released from the mirror code obligation, each possession was obliged to enter into an implementation agreement with the US designed to prevent tax avoidance and discriminatory taxing. To date, only American Samoa has entered into such an implementation agreement, although Guam and the Mariana Islands are conducting negotiations in this regard.

Under 1986 law, bona fide residents of US possessions are taxed in the same manner as US residents. However, in the case of such individuals, gross income for US tax purposes will not include income derived from sources within any of the three possessions or income effectively connected with the conduct of a trade or business by that individual within any of the three possessions. (The individual possessions will be entitled to tax this local-source income as they see fit, limited only by the terms of the implementation agreement.) However, under the 1986 law, even a bona fide resident of Guam, American Samoa or the Mariana Islands will be required to file a US return and pay taxes to the US on a net basis if he receives income from sources outside the three possessions (i.e. US or foreign source income).

Unless you have substantial investments in the possessions themselves, it is likely that the majority of your worldwide income would be subject to US income taxation if you became a citizen of Guam, American Samoa or the Mariana Islands. Accordingly, for PTs, these islands offer no tax advantages that we can see.

3. FOREIGN TERRITORIES UNDER US SUPERVISION. As discussed earlier, Micronesia, the Marshall Islands and Palau are deemed to be **foreign territories** under US **supervision**, but **not** under US **sovereignty**. As such, **they are not possessions of the US.**

Citizens of these three foreign territories will be treated as non-resident alien individuals for purposes of the US revenue code. As non-resident aliens, citizens of these foreign territories would generally be subject to US tax only on US source income. But for purposes of travel documents, i.e. passports, citizens of these islands are US citizens. They have the right to enter, leave or live in the US, travel abroad on a US passport and be regarded internationally as US citizens.

Accordingly, you would be able to enjoy the benefits of US citizenship in any of these foreign territories, while simultaneously preserving your tax status as a non-resident alien under the US code. We have now investigated the procedure for **acquiring** citizenship in these three foreign territories. Such citizenship would provide a US passport and easy access to the United States. You should discuss this matter with local island officials who will or *might* give you detailed information about acquiring citizenship in any of these territories. Lastly, the low tax rates or informal procedures in these three foreign territories could offer many tax avoidance opportunities. We suggest you contact the "Big Five" accountancy firms mentioned elsewhere in this book. Get their "area handbooks" on taxes in these jurisdictions. Let us know what you discover for future issues and for the benefits of our private clients. We will reciprocate with an exchange of information on related subjects.

Whatever you do, just be sure that you don't end up paying $100,000 for a "maybe" passport deal with some Palm Tree Republic (like the Cook Islands). Be sure your funds are placed in escrow and not paid out till you get a passport *you can use*. If you really want a US passport from an obscure Pacific Island, you may have to spend a few weeks, months (or years?) hanging out with the island locals. You could end up making a private deal to get the passport of your dreams for the price of a new Jeep. Or perhaps you'll end up married to the Chief's 300 pound daughter, Pocahantis. Bottom line: For a serious and busy businessman, there are better passports and faster, more interesting ways of obtaining them. Still, if you find that staying on such an island to over-eat, make love and get drunk with local natives is stimulating and pleasant, then a US Pacific Island passport is an option you might wish to pursue on your own.

SWITZERLAND VIA THE (ITALIAN) CAMPIONE BACK DOOR

Assume you want to live in Switzerland, enjoy the fresh mountain air, take advantage of efficient, confidential communication/banking and perhaps avail yourself of the fine recreational activities. But you don't like the idea of paying large sums to a lawyer for a residence permit. Perhaps you can't pass Switzerland's stringent financial and background requirements. Maybe twelve years is too long for you to wait for a Swiss passport. There are also the matters of an annual two month military service for life and high Swiss income taxes. Can these be avoided?

The back door lies with a tiny enclave in the southern Swiss province of Ticino. Campione, as it is called, is just inside the Swiss border near Como, Italy. It doesn't even appear on major touring maps of the area. Legally, Campione is part of Italy.

Obtaining residence there is no more complicated than leasing or purchasing an apartment. With your lease or deed in hand you register in person (at Como) and get a Campione residence permit. The process is automatic and takes one to three days. In Italian, Campione has a double meaning: "champion" or "sample".

As a non-Italian Campione resident, you are not subject to most Italian taxes. Likewise, Switzerland does not tax non-Swiss residents of Campione.

The beautiful part of this arrangement is that this enclave is surrounded by Switzerland. You are now eligible for Swiss auto registration license plates (Canton of Ticino) and a Swiss driving licence. You may enter and depart Switzerland at will and may also make full use of Swiss banks, postal services and telephones serving Campione. Your postal address is Swiss, and you are listed in the Ticino (Swiss) phone books.

Ten years residence in Campione will get you an Italian passport. Because the Italians are very loose about such things, no one really checks or cares how much or little time you actually spend in Campione. About once a year there is supposed to be a mandatory police check to see that the apartment or house you are registered at is in fact "properly furnished" and not regularly occupied by somebody else.

This annual residential verification was imposed recently after a Swiss newspaper exposé showed that two dozen German multi-millionaires were allegedly residing full-time in one tiny damp unfurnished Campione basement. The reality was that the German industrialists who never saw their "home" were operating major Swiss headquartered businesses from a Campione post office box (on a tax-free basis) while actually living in their usual homes in Germany.

Switzerland, which usually calls the shots on such things, made it clear that only "legitimate" residences occupied by no more than one resident and his family would be allowed in the future.

With about 1,200 homes or apartments in Campione, the back door to Switzerland is still open. But the cheapest apartment now costs close to US $650 per month to rent. For purchase, the cheapest Campione condo apartment is about US $135,000. Mail forwarding and telephone answering is still about US $100 per month, but you can no longer get a Campione resident's card on that basis alone. You must now have proof of a real home or apartment.

For the benefits of Swiss residence without the burdens of taxes or military service, consider Campione. Your Italian passport is a free bonus. We have an extensive special report, *The Campione Report.* If you are interested in obtaining it, please write to Scope International, 62 Murray Road, Horndean, Hants PO8 9JL, UK, and you will receive further details, or see the end pages of this book for more information and an order form.

See also *The Tax Exile Report* published by Scope International.

SPAIN AND THE COMMON MARKET (EC) – VIA SOUTH AMERICA

Suppose you want to obtain the valuable right to live, work or run a business in the Common Market. Spain will give citizenship in two years to those of "Spanish blood" or people who are descended from "Safardic Jews". Spanish blood is normally taken for granted whenever an applicant is a citizen of a former Spanish colony or has a Spanish surname and speaks Spanish.

The obvious fast back door to Spain and the EC is the acquisition of "instant citizenship" available for a price from Central and South American countries. This is followed by the acquisition of a house or apartment in Spain and a Spanish residence permit. After a reduced period of residence, you can apply for a Spanish passport. Obviously, learning Spanish somewhere along the line is a prerequisite.

To become a Safardic Jew is not difficult, but will take a little time and requires that you join a Safardic (Spanish-Jew) congregation. This works much like the standard path to Israeli citizenship,which requires that you spend approximately one year in Israel. See the section on Israel in part V. To later obtain Spanish nationality, you must also prove a "Spanish connection". Safardic Jews speak a language known as "Ladino", a sort of Spanish written with Hebrew letters.

All Common Market countries including Spain issue the new maroon colored EC passports. Qualify for one and you can live and work in any EC country.

BACK DOORS TO AUSTRALIA OR NEW ZEALAND

If you felt that Australia was your land of opportunity, but were turned down for immigration, you need not give up. Instead, use the back door. Just as there is a great open border between the US and Canada, there is a similar open border between Australia and New Zealand. An Australian or New Zealand citizen can go back and forth between these countries. They can work or get welfare benefits without visas, impediments, or delay.

Once issued, passports of Australia and New Zealand are for all practical purposes, interchangeable.

As of 1993, the business migrant to Australia must transfer into Australia the equivalent of US $350,000 (A $500,000) and meet all sorts of other requirements.

New Zealand has a new points system for immigrants, where a proposal to transfer NZ $500,000 (US $250,000) to develop a new business or industry in New Zealand would be taken very seriously, and would certainly be approved in a much shorter time. Also, for those without money NZ is a relatively easy country to immigrate to. The New Zealand citizen is for all practical purposes also an Australian. See the New Zealand section in Part V.

THE COMMONWEALTH

When the British Empire disintegrated after World War II, most former colonies became members of a group of nations called The Commonwealth. For English-speaking passport seekers the Commonwealth has a special significance since any Commonwealth passport usually creates a preference on behalf of its holder and thus constitutes a back door for other Commonwealth passports or residence permits.

1. All English-speaking nations are members with the exception of Ireland, South Africa, the US and former US colonies (i.e. the Philippines, US Pacific Trust territories and the US Virgin Islands).
2. The Common Law (British) is dominant. This means that usually citizenship is obtained by either birth in the country, by descent from parents or after a one to five year residence period. The residence period is usually shorter for Commonwealth citizens than for others. The UK itself, in a racially discriminatory new rule, limits birthright under a "grandfather clause" designed to deny citizenship to some blacks, Asians and non-Europeans.
3. Immigration and trade barriers between Commonwealth countries are generally eliminated or reduced in a Common Market arrangement. *No visa is usually needed for touristic or short business visits within The Commonwealth.*
4. One quarter of the world's population lives in The Commonwealth. Virtually all races, religions and languages are substantially represented. One would have no trouble "fitting in".

We have reproduced overleaf a map showing the location of Commonwealth members and associates.

BACK DOOR BRAZIL – THE PRICE: ONE "LOVE CHILD"

Brazil reportedly grants passports to those who make the effort to find a politically well connected lawyer and pay him about US $35,000. The prices we have heard quoted range from $3000 to $100,000. Because a special relationship exists between Brazil and Portugal, the passports of either country are good for travel or residence permits in the other. After a short period, "equality status" can be granted. Thus one citizenship is a back door to the other.

A special Brazilian rule is that the father of a Brazilian child may never be extradited at the request of another country. Even accused murderers will not be deported. Instead, they will

THE 49 MEMBER COUNTRIES AND 17 ASSOCIATED STATES OF THE COMMONWEALTH

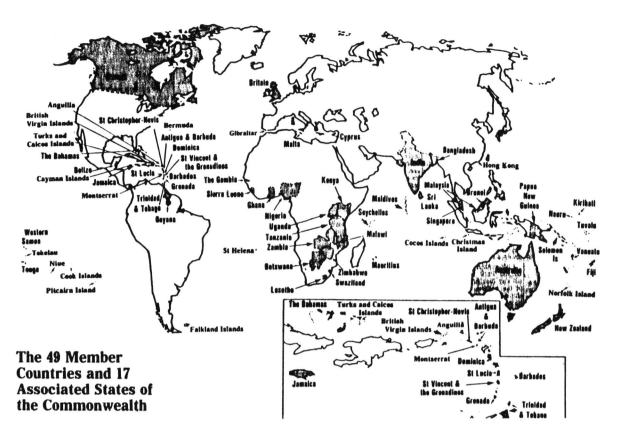

The 49 Member Countries and 17 Associated States of the Commonwealth

The Commonwealth is made up of 49 member countries, ranging in population from India's several hundred million to the few thousand of Nauru and Tuvalu.

They include people of many different cultures, languages and religions all over the world.

The newest member of Brunei Darussalam, which joined the association three years ago. Fiji dropped out in 1987.

Of the present 49 members, 26 are republics and 18, including New Zealand, are monarchies with Queen Elizabeth as their Head of State. Five members have their own monarch. However, Queen Elizabeth is recognized as the Head of the Commonwealth.

The Commonwealth also includes several associated states, such as the Cook Islands.

It is the work of the Commonwealth Secretariat in Pall Mall, London to co-ordinate all of this inter-governmental work and to oversee Commonwealth aid programmes in developing countries.

be granted a Brazilian passport after the normal five year residence period if they demonstrate good local behaviour.

It is not necessary to be married to your young Brazilian's mother. There are many nubile young ladies in Brazil who eagerly seek to have a child sired and supported by a wealthy foreigner. If you desire a family and wish to obtain a Brazilian/Portuguese passport, fathering a Brazilian baby offers one interesting possibility, for those who fear extradition. For all others, just go there, hire a lawyer and you should be able to become a citizen in a year or two for very small change.

No need for divorce either – just an understanding wife who doesn't mind you having a Brazilian girlfriend – or perhaps a wife who'd like to have her next child in Brazil. In this case, as with anyone born in Brazil, your child becomes a Brazilian at birth. Your own citizenship problems are solved. You don't receive citizenship because of your baby . . . you only get the right to stay in Brazil and support your child. If you behave yourself for five years, *then* you will receive a passport.

If having a child doesn't appeal to you, we have heard from a Brazilian lawyer who says that special arrangements and other creative approaches are possible. Once again, if you *go there* and snoop, we'd estimate that within six months you'd have a dynamite girlfriend (or boyfriend) and a passport without much expense.

FIND YOUR PERSONAL LOOPHOLE AND TELL US!

While marriage appears to be the most common way to change nationality, we found that each country has many particular quirks. Some countries allow immediate nationality through marriage, others require that one remains married for a certain number of years, and still others require a certain period of actual residence. As we continue our research and inquiries, this report will continually be updated to reflect our latest findings.

As a rule, traveling to the target country and talking to local lawyers will be your best source of information. Contacting a consular official or people from the target country in your own area is second best. But be warned that many consular officials are actually citizens of the country where they are working. It is a known fact that these employees often serve two masters by passing along information gained in the service of their employer to the authorities of their own country.

Some consuls are helpful (British usually), others will always say 'no' (Americans usually).

If you learn something useful, or make an interesting contact for getting a fast passport, by all means send it along to the editor. If we publish or use your idea, we will be happy to send you one of our publications, or the next edition of this book, gratis. Don't worry, we won't publish your name! Tell us what book you would like!

A reader desperate to change citizenship got his new European Community passport and work permit because of a personal loophole. Let's say he was South African. He wasn't, but he did have a passport that was burdensome. His ancestry was of no help. His present wife and children all had the same passport that he did. At a personal conference we discussed his language abilities only because a working knowledge of Hebrew, Portuguese or Turkish could lead to a fast passport. Even a knowledge of German could shorten the residence waiting period. But he had none of these, no children born abroad, and no languages but English. Then I asked for his life story – looking for any connections that might help. It turned out that one of his four ex-wives had been a citizen of a country in Europe, that (like many in these days of "Women's Lib") recently changed its laws to permit husbands to get instant passports of the wife's home country. The problem was: 1) He had never lived in the country and 2) More significantly, he had been divorced for fifteen years! As every good lawyer would suggest, I urged him to write this letter (saying nothing untrue) to the Consulate of (let's say) Italy. It was not Italy, but was an even better choice. Belgium? Portugal? Ireland? Luxembourg? Netherlands? It could have been any of the six.

> "Dear Consul General, I am enclosing a certified photocopy of my South African passport, my birth certificate and my marriage certificate to 'Maria Montessori'. You will note from the marriage certificate, that at the time of our marriage twenty years ago, she was a citizen of your country. If on the basis of this marriage I am able to acquire citizenship, please send me the appropriate application forms and further instructions.
> Yours hopefully,
> A. CITIZEN''

The Consul General wrote back:

> "Our law, like that of other Common Market countries, now allows spouses of either sex to acquire dual nationality as a result of their marriage. If the parties live together in our country, the non-citizen spouse can get citizenship immediately, although the processing can take up to six months. If the non citizen spouse lives abroad, we (currently) require the marriage to last three years before issuing a passport. The enclosed application forms plus required photographs and the nominal fees and stamp duties should be submitted to the Consulate closest to your present residence.
> Signed:
> A Very Nice Consul General''

Our client sent in his photographs, etc. and received his passport three weeks later! Just to satisfy our curiosity, your author went to a different Consulate pretending to be in the same fact situation – but this time mentioned that after five years of marriage we were divorced. Though I didn't get a definitive answer, the consular officer said that the law didn't say anything about divorces and if I had been married for over three years, I could probably get a passport. In view of the unusual circumstance however, he would have to go to higher-ups for a second opinion. Based upon past experience, I might wait ten years for an answer. He suggested I go to another Consulate and not mention the divorce since he felt duty bound to get the higher ruling. What's the moral of this story? If I have to spell it out for you, you'd better get some expert advice before proceeding on any quasi-legal matter. *Saying too much could thwart your objectives.*

Explore possibilities on the phone anonymously before you commit yourself on paper! Once you have been denied citizenship or a passport there is a record on the computer that will haunt any later application. Get it right the first time! Hiring an expert to assist you is a lot cheaper than a denial followed by a lengthy appeal process.

Comments, questions, additions and constructive criticism should be sent to:
Scope International, 62 Murray Road, Waterlooville, Hampshire PO8 9JL, Great Britain

Part IX

THE NUTS & BOLTS

PASSPORT PRICE GUIDE

STRATOSPHERIC – $1,000,000 and up: Liechtenstein, Monaco, Switzerland.

HIGH – $100,000 and up: Austria, Australia, Belgium, Canada, Italy, Jamaica, Mauritius, New Zealand, St. Kitts, Singapore.

MODERATE – $20,000 to $100,000: Argentina, Bolivia, Brazil, Cape Verde, Costa Rica, Dominican Republic, Ecuador, El Salvador, Haiti, Honduras, Mexico, Nicaragua, Panama, Paraguay, Portugal, Uruguay.

Most Central American and South American countries are in this price range.

LOWEST – $500 to $15,000: Most Black African countries and the poorest Asian countries.

FREE – With qualifying ethnic background or religion: Brazil, China, Germany, Ireland, Israel, Lebanon, Portugal, Spain, Taiwan, Thailand, Turkey, UK, US.

NOTE: This list has been prepared from reliable information and is intended only as a guide for those considering new citizenship. **We do not offer any passports for sale, but can only make referrals to attorneys and government representatives authorized to issue passports.**

This list refers to legally issued passports only.

The author and publisher strongly recommend against using stolen, forged or fraudulently obtained documents.

SHOULD YOU HIRE A LAWYER OR AGENT?

Do you need a lawyer or other representative to obtain a passport? The answer is "it depends". It is preferable to deal directly with Consular officials or government representatives. From an economic point of view you eliminate the middleman. With one less person to pay, your costs will generally be less.

Another reason to deal directly with your source (i.e. the government representative) is to avoid being defrauded. Unfortunately the passport business is loaded with swindlers, some of them claiming to be lawyers. They will gladly take your money and if you manage to find them again, they will profusely offer excuses and then promptly disappear again. That is why we recommend using escrow agents (see the following section) and only competent reliable agencies. You may obtain our recommendations of those who can assist you in acquiring a second passport upon request to Scope International. Do beware the crooks who habitually run sucker ads in certain international newspapers or magazines. Please tell us good or bad experiences you have had with them. Send us your own tearful story or happy ending, and we will *give* you some useful information in return.

ESCROW AGENTS
What is an Escrow Agent?

Losses may be avoided by making a fee deposit with a trusted third party such as a bank or other escrow agent. This third party holds your money, usually in the form of a certified check, payable to them. The escrow agent will receive your passport (or whatever) from the source and will then permit you to inspect it.

Upon your full satisfaction that a genuine passport or other document desired has been delivered, the escrow agent pays your cash to the procurer and simultaneously delivers the passport to you. The escrow agent also retains a small fee for his services. Escrow fees are typically one to ten per cent of the transaction value.

BEWARE OF ADVANCE FEES

Cut-rate lawyers who advertise and other unqualified agents often ask for a fee 'up front' for expenses such as a background check on you. Chances are you will neither see your money again nor receive benefit of any services you paid to obtain.

Sometimes an advance fee is warranted and necessary to pay for an investigation of you, the client. Most agents prefer not to represent unrecommended strangers. Should you turn out to be an infamous fugitive, terrorist, murderer or major dope dealer, most government officials (even corrupt ones) will not knowingly issue a passport – except, we must cynically observe, perhaps at a much higher price. Our experience has been that legitimate operators who can help you get a second nationality and passport are well backed financially. Whenever large sums are involved, and you are willing to place them in escrow, expense advances are seldom required. Middlemen who stay in the field want **clean business**, and **only fly-by-night operators will cater to lunatic fringe or underworld figures**.

Caveat emptor ("Let the buyer beware") is a fundamental expression in Anglo-Saxon law. This principle applies without exception in dealing with passports. Don't pay any fees (except into an escrow account) until you have the genuine documents in hand – or unless you are extremely satisfied with the bona-fides of the firm you are dealing with.

HOW TO DEAL WITH AGENTS OR LAWYERS

When applying for immigration as an *Entrepreneur* or *Investor,* you will probably deal with the government through an agent or attorney who specializes in such matters. You should use those recommended by reliable sources who have a clearly established practice. Retainers and advance fees *are the rule* rather than the exception in this situation.

When using a specialist, you are paying for professional services on your behalf. There will be no guarantee of a favorable decision. Fees are due for time spent representing you, win or lose! Generally this is money well spent.

You may draft your own business proposals. If there are doubts or grey areas, your odds will be far better if you obtain professional help from a lawyer or consultant. These specialists will know what bureaucrats require and what peculiar emphasis may be in vogue at the moment. You are unlikely to have access to such information. This would be particularly true in Austria, Australia and the US.

Finally, it frequently happens that lawyers or agencies have special relationships with passport authorities and diplomats. Some agents have legitimate and often exclusive authority to handle passport transactions on behalf of their clients. If you can assure yourself that everything is legitimate and that you won't risk your money, you may choose to pay a reasonable advance or make a deposit with such an agent.

Because of the confidential nature of the passport business, satisfied customer references are rarely available. Bank and professional references for agents can be supplied. They should be checked very carefully.

Perhaps the agent you are considering will be willing to have a satisfied client make contact with you. This could be a scamming confederate, however. Thus, prudent business practices are advised before you part with any money. An escrow arrangement or contingent fee is the least risky course to take – when acceptable to both you and the passport agent. As mentioned, we are familiar with the few reliable people in the business and most of the crooks too. We don't supply lists of crooks any more since the crooks would sue us for libel and we'd waste too much time defending ourselves.

PLAY BY THE BOOK, OR ELSE . . .

There are certain rules in getting citizenship. The governments of most countries try to keep these rules a secret. Why? So that applicants will not invariably be able to give all the 'right' answers on the government questionnaires. Thus, in our opinion, it is best to hire an expert – perhaps a former or retired immigration officer to help you with your application. You must get your application right the first time. Normally, once an application for citizenship has been refused, it is almost impossible to get an adverse administrative decision reversed.

Do make an effort to seek out a reliable immigration specialist who knows the ropes in the country of your choice. There may be ways to circumvent tough immigration rules: many countries have reciprocity deals with other countries, which offers a ''back door''. For example, persons who are citizens of some former colonies or overseas possessions of European countries often have the ''right of abode'' or similar rights in Europe. The rules are complex, but play your cards right and you will usually win the prized passport that you seek!

Please drop us a line and let us know of good or bad experiences you have with lawyers and immigration specialists.

BUREAUCRATS ALWAYS SEEK POLITICAL SELF-PROTECTION

The subject of passports is a delicate matter that can embarrass politicians. During the administration of US President Richard Nixon, there was an allegation that his financial supporters received diplomatic passports, Presidential pardons, and other favors. Such benefits and political spoils are distributed to patrons in all countries, but if notorious felons are discovered to be on the receiving end of passports authorized from high places problems arise. Princes, palaces, Presidents and politicians can tumble.

Neither governments nor bureaucratic public officials like the heat which can be generated by journalists and others who disclose illicit passport arrangements. This is especially sensitive when passport corruption has resulted in highly publicized undesirables becoming citizens.

Once the word is out that underworld characters are traveling on a certain nation's passport, the credibility of that document is hurt for all, including the innocent, who come later.

For these reasons, you may be required to show any lawyer you hire a certification of your own good conduct or to pay for a background check. This may not fully protect agents and countries against your possible passport fraud, but a police certification of your good character does protect the passport officials from accusations of knowingly giving passports to criminals. Get your "Good Conduct Certificate" today. You may need it. If you run into trouble next month or next year, you might not get this document so easily. Just go to your local police and ask for a letter stating that you have no criminal record. Normally you get it instantly and free, with the notable exception of the UK where such documents are never issued.

TYPICAL DOCUMENTS NEEDED TO SUPPORT A PASSPORT APPLICATION AND HOW TO GET THEM

If your source for a passport is unofficial and informal, the only things you will need are photographs and a bag of cash. Your passport may be ordered with any name, date of birth or any other particulars you choose. No other documentation is sought or desired. It is best if your suppliers never know your true identity. We do not encourage this, but cannot pretend that it does not go on.

On the other hand, working through normal, formal channels, you may encounter demands for some document you have never heard of. The documents to be discussed in this section are the only ones normally sought by official passport inspectors. If you are asked to produce your kindergarten academic transcript, you are probably being solicited for a gratuity. Your proper response would be along the lines, "It would be quite difficult for me to get that document. I wonder if $100 would cover the cost of your handling it for me?"

You are likely to receive one of three responses:
1. Acceptance – The official will waive the requirement or claim to be able to settle it with his superiors.
2. Indignation – Apologize! Explain that you thought the official could obtain the document or a waiver from another government source at your expense. "I didn't intend any offense, good sir."
3. Hesitation – Probably because the official expected a much higher gratuity. Ask if more money is required. If the higher price is acceptable, pay it.

Is this illegal? The plain truth is that in most countries, underpaid public officials expect gratuities. Your personal objections to this way of life won't improve things one iota and may well cause you serious harm in the long run. On the positive side, a moderate surcharge is well worth expedited service or special considerations being granted.

YOUR PRESENT PASSPORT
In many cases you will be asked to surrender your present passport for cancellation. The official policy of most countries is to allow citizens to hold and travel on only one passport, even if dual-citizenship is permitted. The common way to *keep* your old passport is to "lose" it before applying for your new one. Then you turn in the "lost" passport for cancellation. *We can't recommend this procedure because it is fraudulent.*

If your new country does not report your obtaining new citizenship and passport, you may also replace a surrendered passport from your "old" country at a future time. Check with the Consulates concerned.

Most countries do not report. All will tell you their policy, if you ask.

BIRTH CERTIFICATE

Legitimate birth certificates are easy to obtain. They are issued by the Bureau of Vital Statistics, Registrar of Public Records (or equivalent) upon request. A nominal fee is charged. In order to obtain a copy, it is usually necessary to provide only your name, birthplace, birthdate and your parents names.

Delayed birth certificates may be issued in cases of children's births at home that were never registered. Affidavits from relatives or friends may be required. This method also prevails if the place where original records were maintained was destroyed for some reason. Church or religious records are often used, particularly in Roman Catholic areas: France, Quebec (Canada), Louisiana (US), Spain and Ireland.

In general, usage of **false** or **forged** birth certificates to get a passport is a bad idea. Passport offices often verify public records. This takes them but a few minutes via phone or telex.

CLEAN POLICE RECORD

This document would be requested by you from the police of your present country (of citizenship) or from the country of last or present residence. Nations who are members of Interpol will check your name and birthdate through that organization, thus opening the possibility that "foreign" crimes will be discovered. They have only the information you supply to go on.

The mechanism used to initiate the investigation is your personal history statement. Sometimes a fingerprint card is requested. If you have a problem, or don't want your fingerprints on file, there are some alternatives. One is to apply by mail for your "Good Conduct Certificate". More often than not, you will get one back as a routine reply.

If a criminal record *is* involved in your past, indirect inquiry should be made with the new country to ascertain if your particular crime would be a bar to obtaining a passport. In many cases, political crimes against unpopular and toppled regimes would not be a problem. Tax and currency violations are almost universally ignored outside the country of offence.

Drug offences are ignored by some countries like the Netherlands (Holland) and considered grievous felonies by others. Likewise for sexual matters – in the US, homosexuals and communists may not become citizens. Most free countries do not enquire about sexual preferences or past political affiliations.

If there is a problem, it is best to initiate your passport quest by moving initially to a country that is not concerned about your past or does not consider your past offences to be a fatal flaw. There, a police certificate can be obtained and used in your next move. It should also be noted that any person with access to a sheet of any police department stationery can produce a letter saying what a good citizen they are. Like letters of recommendation, they are in reality, quite meaningless since even the worst criminals can get them.

MEDICAL CERTIFICATES

Most immigrants are required to produce medical certificates at some point in the process. Properly endorsed United Nations World Health Organization (WHO) certificates almost always suffice. WHO certificates include your blood type and immunization records along with notations of allergies and chronic conditions. These days an AIDS blood test is starting to be commonly required of potential immigrants.

Perfunctory medical examinations and WHO certificates are available almost anywhere in the world. After getting the medical forms from your target country you make an appointment with any doctor for the required examination. Most doctors charge a minimum fee and pay minimal attention to you, as you are whisked through the process. So long as you do not reveal any medical condition when making your medical history statement, problems without strong external symptoms may go undetected. No blood tests, urine samples or X-rays are usually taken. If you don't appear to be ready to expire, you'll pass. **Don't worry about the medical examination requirement unless you really do have a serious communicable disease**.

FINANCIAL STATEMENTS

If you seek admission under an entrepreneurial or investor category, you will be required to produce some evidence of having the specified amount of unencumbered capital. If you have the money, there is no problem. Your banker will be more than willing to provide required documentation.

In almost all cases, requisite capital will have to be transferred to your new country at some point in the process. A country that requires an investment for citizenship will not accept mere good intentions.

The principal problem is that whenever you provide financial statements to any government, you have no way of controlling access to this sensitive information about you. There may be tax implications in your new or old country, to cite but one obvious ramification.

The preferred method in such cases is to isolate the *minimum necessary funds* in a totally *separate account*. The best choice would be to deposit the investment required in a bank with branches in your new country. When inquiries or disclosures are made, they are limited to revealing that you have no more money than you will eventually have to produce in any case. Having asset verification made or a letter of credit worthiness issued through a local bank usually sits better with the officials of your new country as well. **It is always better to understate your assets than to brag**.

CHARACTER REFERENCE

This is a trivial requirement unless the government imposes restrictions on whom you may cite as a reference. In any event, if you cannot get flowing praise from several apparently prominent, qualified people, you need more drinking buddies than you now have.

OATH OF ALLEGIANCE

Your **new** country will often require such an oath to be taken. It is up to you as to whether your conscience will permit this, but I presume that someone seeking a second passport will not become unduly patriotic before taking this final step in the passport process.

The principal problem with such oaths is that former countries often interpret your new allegiance as a renunciation of *their* citizenship. Some countries, such as South Africa, go so far as to regard this as an act of treason! Thus, one should ascertain whether the country in which you seek citizenship reports this fact to your previous country and whether your previous country cares what oaths you take.

One little known fact involving the reporting routine is that some countries, notably the US and the former USSR, maintain extensive intelligence networks in foreign countries. It is reasonable to assume that the activities of citizens having business with foreign immigration authorities might come under their surveillance. Whether formal government-to-government reporting exists, informal leaks to officials of your old country might occur – particularly if you are a citizen of the US.

RELIGIOUS CERTIFICATE

Many countries require citizenship applicants to make statements of belief in a particular religion. Some require documentation in addition to your assertions on the subject. It is prudent to make specific inquiry regarding such requirements and the identity of religions which are both acceptable and unacceptable to your new country. If survival is a compelling need, you may have to join an "acceptable" church or temple or mosque in order to obtain the necessary religious certificate.

PERMISSION OF SPOUSE

This is a relatively common requirement whenever it appears that one parent may be absenting himself from a family group or is seeking to take a minor child with him. Other countries demand documentation and permission from non-emigrating spouses on the subjects of court-ordered custody and child support.

Solutions are straightforward. Be as honest as possible. If you are making a solo trip, an assertion that you were never married usually precludes demands for documentation proving spousal permission, divorce or widowhood. **If you are taking your minor child with you, there are many interesting twists far beyond the scope of this book.** For example, in most of the world, fathers get custody of male children in the event of divorce or separations. **What may be regarded as illegal, such as a criminal kidnapping, under the laws of England would be a perfectly proper act in Jordan, Morocco or Brazil.** Also see our report *PT 1* for an extensive chapter on this subject. A synopsis of *PT 1* is at the end of *this* Special Report.

WHY YOU SHOULD USE COURIERS AND SPECIAL HANDLING SERVICES

Timing your passport applications to coincide with peak periods is important. Bureaucratic work expands to fill time available, so applications during slow periods can be subjected to extensive checking and verification. When applications pile up, the approval process becomes automatic and the chances of sliding an otherwise questionable package through improve dramatically.

To improve your odds further, consider using the services of the largest travel agency in town. They will leniently perform the screening checks, allowing you to present information in a form that omits details which could otherwise spoil your chances if you were at the passport office yourself.

The answer as to why travel agents are so accommodating is obvious. If you purchase expensive travel and lodging accommodations through them, the agency stands to lose its commission if you subsequently cancel out. Not having a passport is a common reason for cancellation. Agencies will work hard to help you get a passport or visa. One important word of caution. **Do not ever use a known mail drop or forwarding service as your address on a passport application**. Countries with concern that an application is legitimate usually take time to check your application address against lists of known mail drops. Even fully legitimate applications may be delayed or disapproved (and law enforcement officers may seek you out) if a known mail drop is used.

It may be best to establish a legitimate address, even if only a boarding house, for a few weeks covering application until receipt. Leave a stamped, addressed envelope for the landlady to use in forwarding mail to you at your "field working site".

SHOULD YOU HIRE AN AGENCY TO GET YOUR VISAS? – A TIP FOR THOSE IN A RUSH

In our opinion, the world should have no guarded borders, no passports and definitely not any visa requirements. Getting entry and exit visas is an unnecessary impediment to travel.

For weary travellers, there is hope. Travel agencies and specialized visa services can often get you required passports and visa stamps, sometimes in a matter of hours. No need for you to stand in line at various embassies and consulates, wasting your precious time.

In London, Worldwide Visas Ltd, 9 Adelaide Street, London WC2, UK, offers to get the visas you need. For most countries it is "same day processing". Seven working days are needed for embassies and consulates not represented in the United Kingdom. The shop – a one stop service for all visas – will do everything for you by mail. Give them your itinerary and your passport and they will obtain all necessary visas. No charge for waiting time at embassies. There is the added convenience of having them check applications before submission to the embassy or passport office. For those in a rush, airport delivery (at extra cost) is available.

For "five-star" service, request a referral through Scope.

Criminals too can use the services of others to obtain their visas. An African friend of a friend once thought he might have trouble entering the United States. Why? A small matter – he was wanted under a different name than he was now using by the FBI, but he needed to go to the States on some monkey business. His problem was getting the visa. He feared that upon entering the local US embassy, he might be arrested in London if they had been informed of his new alias. The solution? He had his travel agent go to the US embassy, get the visa and bring the passport back to his office. From a distance, he watched the courier bring the passport back from the embassy. He waited a while and made sure that the courier wasn't followed. Then, he entered the travel agency, paid his $20 for the service, picked up his visa stamped passport and left for New York. He was reasonably sure that his present assumed identity was not on the American national criminal identification computer.

IS ANYONE LOOKING FOR YOU?

Just in case you wondered about it, every country has a "watch-for-this-person list" of political activists, fugitives, parole violators, narcotics dealers, pending bankruptcy subjects. Persons ordered not to leave the country – and many other categories are on it. Normally this list is computerized and contains the full name, known aliases, last known address, birthdate and a "rap" sheet of arrests and convictions. If there is a warrant out for your arrest – even for traffic tickets (or alimony non-payment) – a passport application in the country where you are "wanted" is very likely to trigger a late night visit from the gendarmes. Outside of your home country, Interpol international files are certainly not concerned with traffic violators, tax offenders or non-dangerous types. So if you didn't pay all your taxes, alimony or parking tickets – **don't worry, nobody is looking for you** on the international level.

WORLD'S GREATEST PASSPORT PHOTOGRAPHER?

What does it take to get named as "The Best" in this prestigious *Passport Report?* This "splendiferous" title goes to a little hole in the wall in London that provides the world's best service, fast delivery and cheap prices. They offer detailed knowledge of all the different color, background, size, shade and paper requirements for just about every single nation's passport and visa photos.

There are thousands of eager contenders for this prestigious award all over the globe, but we have found (so far) only ONE whom we deem worthy of the great honour:

THE BEST PASSPORT PHOTOGRAPHER IN THE WORLD
"Passport Photo Service"
449, Oxford Street
London W1, England
(Opposite Selfridge's main department store)

A fringe benefit – while waiting for photos, you can go across the street and enjoy a wonderful buffet at Selfridge's restaurant during the 40 minutes it takes Passport Photo to get your prints developed.

Another fringe benefit – at Passport Photo, you'll see a full wall covered with photos of just about every celebrity in the English speaking world. They've all been to this dinky, 2nd floor walk-up studio to get "shot". No appointment necessary!

For trivia fans, note that Sean Connery, Clark Gable, Patrice Lumumba and yours truly are all wearing the same tie! "Passport Photo Service" still has this 30 year old (now somewhat motheaten) tie as its standard prop for those who show up tieless! *What a thrill* to have your neck in the same noose that once adorned all these world famous celebrities.

Do you want to know what your author looks like? Just go to ''Passport Photo Service''. Look for the picture of the handsome fat guy with the blue ''prop'' tie with grey checkerboard squares.

And if you, dear reader, stumble across another contender for the title of World's Best – or even a runner up (in your home city) – please let me know. We shall list them in future editions of the *Passport Report*.

Comments, questions, additions and constructive criticism should be sent to:
Scope International, 62 Murray Road, Waterlooville, Hampshire PO8 9JL, Great Britain

Part X

WHEN YOU NEED A
SECOND PASSPORT FAST:
FRAUDS & OTHER MURKY METHODS

ILLEGAL AND QUASI-LEGAL METHODS

Who uses illegal passports? Government agents probably constitute the largest group. They are spies, terrorists or other secret agents who move about, shielded by fake passports, often from countries other than their own. Known criminals in the US get false passports in connection with the "Witness Protection Program" that shields informants.

STOLEN, FORGED AND GHOST PASSPORTS

Now we will take a look at various false and illegal passports. Let's see how they are used and how they are obtained. **We do not condone, suggest or encourage illegal activities.** We present this information as a public service so that readers will not be cheated by operators who pawn off illegitimate passports as the real item.

STOLEN OR PASSPORTS SOLD BY THEIR LEGITIMATE OWNERS

This is the most common source of illegal passports. Pickpockets, government employees, burglars and purse snatchers all have contacts who will purchase and resell almost any passport. Rates are well established throughout the underworld.

A buyer places his order with a source and then waits a few days until one in stock is prepared or one is stolen and prepared. Existing photographs are carefully removed and replaced with photos of the buyer.

Even the new tamper-proof passports (where embossed plastic covers the photo page) can be altered to look like the genuine article. These passports can be used until expiration and can often be officially or unofficially extended or renewed while abroad. Not every obscure consular official has time to verify passport status. As an alternative, bogus rubber stamps are commonly affixed to renew or extend an expired passport.

Estimates place the number of stolen passports in use at the ten million mark on a worldwide basis. Since border officials rarely perform more than a cursory look at the document and the bearer, there is no way (except in the country of origin) to detect stolen, altered or well-forged passports.

Travelers have been known to sell their passports for US $500 to US $3,000, depending on how current the passport is and if the general description of the owner is common. They, in turn, report the loss or theft and obtain replacement documents from their consular offices.

Altered and stolen passports are seldom used to enter or exit the country of origin. The reason is obvious. Immigration officials are likely to spot the imperfections and strange variations in their own passports. With the advent of the computer age, they can also punch in the passport number and obtain an instant readout of any reported loss. Greater use of special inks is also making life difficult for those travelling with fake documents. Ultra-violet light scans of passports will throw up forged or tampered visas and passports.

COUNTERFEIT PASSPORTS

Many countries passports are printed on specially manufactured security paper. Security features include watermarks, embedded silk threads, holograms, secret marks, coded entries, intricately engraved designs, color blends and other sophistications. It is often beyond the capability of even a skilled artist to successfully counterfeit intricate types of passports. It is often easier to counterfeit a country's currency. Remember, experts can always tell a genuine document from a bogus one. **We advise you to steer clear of forgeries.**

If cloak and dagger is your game, join the CIA. Otherwise there are proven methods fictionalized in *The Day of the Jackal* or detailed in Barry Reid's *The Paper Trip*. These bestsellers have made the world aware of "ghosting" and the details of illegal passports.

CREATIVE GENEALOGY AND REBIRTHS

A few years ago, when I began research for the original *Passport Report,* a gentleman in the business of supplying passports explained to me that there were two basic ways in which to get **legally issued** passports:

1. **The Naturalization Method** differs in each country, but the common element is that a "foreigner" meets certain requirements, usually including a period of residence, and often a language/history test. After a period of one to twelve years the applicant can become "naturalized". This is the process by which a non-citizen or "foreigner" usually becomes a loyal citizen of the country involved. Normally it involves taking an oath of allegiance to the "new" country and renouncing all loyalty to the "old" country. In some South American countries and Canada, the ownership of property and/or the making of an investment can lead to residence and citizenship, or in some cases, *immediate* citizenship. Various governments institute legal citizenship programs for non-residents from time to time. They vary in their requirements but these commonly involve giving employment to locals or making a substantial investment. Even the US has a program to "sell" green cards (residence permits) and eventual citizenship to foreigners who set up businesses and employ locals in the US.

Since the other method, "REBIRTH" involves fraud being used to obtain a legally issued passport, *I was initially horrified* that it was apparently regarded by some immigration lawyers as an equally desirable means of getting a passport. Yet as time passed and I saw the perfidy and thefts committed by governments against their "naturalized" citizens, or investors, I gradually came to believe that the second method "rebirth" was, in some cases, actually better than the 100 per cent "legal" route, for reasons I will now explain at length.

2. **The Rebirth or Creative Genealogical method of obtaining citizenship** involves fraud, no doubt about it. Making false oaths and procuring false documents is usually a (minor) criminal offence in the country where it is done. In the US it is a felony, but the US makes almost everything a felony these days. Simply put, the passport applicant (in whatever country is involved) obtains a "delayed birth certificate" or an equivalent document (i.e. Baptismal or religious record). This is done with the help of a lawyer, or as a do-it-yourself project in the country where one desires a passport. As that great philosopher and author of *The Paper Trip* Barry Reid once said, "Give them the papers they want, and they will give you the papers you want." Citizenship papers (i.e. a passport) will be granted to an applicant due to the fact that he was born (possibly out of wedlock to a female citizen) in or out of the country. The cover story is that because of the illegitimacy, or perhaps the poverty and ignorance of the family, or just plain bureaucratic bungling, the birth was not properly registered at the time.

One variation is to have the applicant born when and where he actually was born, but to arrange for "proof" that one or both parents were citizens of the desired country. Under the citizenship laws of most countries a birth outside the borders to parent(s) who are citizens usually gives their child either citizenship or the option to apply for it.

Still another variation for an unmarried adult who wants a foreign passport is the "arranged marriage". In France, for instance, there are advertisements in the daily papers by persons wanting or willing to make a "marriage blanche" that confers residence rights and eventual citizenship. We do not arrange such things, but you will see advertisements in newspapers and magazines across the world for people seeking partners for "arranged" marriages to enable them to obtain citizenship or the right to live in another country.

GENUINE PASSPORTS TO CREATE A NEW "BORN AGAIN PERSON"
– GHOSTING

This so-called "Paper Trip" is illegal in many countries, including the US. Thus it is emphatically not recommended. It consists of the following steps:

1. Search gravestones, newspaper obituaries or public records for a person born at approximately the same time as you, but who died in infancy. Be alert to matching your race and ethnic background if birth documentation includes this data.
2. Obtain a certified birth certificate from the appropriate office. Obviously, don't use a birth certificate that has been marked "subject deceased".
3. Become this deceased person's "ghost" by obtaining secondary documents such as driving licences, governmental registration and identity cards, leases and credit cards in the name of the deceased infant.
4. Apply for a passport, preferably by mail. In-person encounters should be at peak business hours at some post office, not a passport or immigration center if at all possible.

Remember – the major risk in ghosting is that someone else may have already used the dead person's identity.

THE DANGERS OF THE DAY OF THE JACKAL

One of the dangers of simply assuming the identity of someone who has died is apparent from this story which appeared in the press in the summer of 1992.

Two IRA terrorists who had escaped from prison in Belfast in 1983 had assumed the identities of US twins Kevin and Patrick Keohane who died aged 11 and 13 of congenital heart disease. The two terrorists obtained details from San Francisco death records, carefully choosing two people of Irish descent and applied for passports in their own names.

The stories in the papers led everyone to believe that these fugitives were caught because a fingerprint check was made for fugitives following the extradition from the US of two other Irish terrorists. The story goes on to explain that the fingerprints of one of the terrorists who had assumed the name of Kevin Keohane, who had died in September of 1970, matched those of a known terrorist, Kevin Artt. Other checks revealed that Keohane's twin brother, who died in 1968, applied for a passport in 1986. This search led to the IRA terrorist, James Smythe.

However, this is far from the case: **It is not commonly known that California began cross-indexing births and deaths on computer in about 1975**. Today, the indexing job is complete. Thus, an infant who was born in California and who also died in California is a poor choice for a rebirth. On any application for a US passport, California driver's licence or public assistance, some of the things automatically verified by computer are:

1) Birth certificate validity
2) Social security status
3) Income tax records of the applicant
4) Use of known mail drops

The Irish terrorists set of at least two sets of alarm bells by applying for a US passport. The social security and tax files showed that no social insurance nor income taxes had ever been paid. The birth certificate check with California Vital Statistics showed that the applicant had died in his youth. This rung bells and blew whistles even before the fingerprints were checked. In fact, fingerprint checks are not automatic as it is necessary to have a data-base of suspect prints to check against. In other words, before one can do anything with a fingerprint, there must be a target print or group of prints.

Thus, it was not really the fingerprints that got them in trouble, but rather the fraudulent passport application. Many fugitives don't know that any California source applications for US passports are automatically subject to a computer check with state archives and social security to verify that the birth certificate is genuine and that the applicant is a taxpayer.

FBI agents staked out the brothers houses in San Francisco and San Diego respectively for nine weeks. The brothers were arrested and extradition proceedings for the return of the two fugitives to Ireland are currently in hand.

The fact alone that California requires fingerprints to issue a driver's license should be enough to scare off any PTs. Be careful, Big Brother is getting stronger. We do not condone the practice of IRA terrorists living incognito and assuming the identities of dead persons, and hope that readers will be dissuaded from following such a course by this salutary tale.

DELAYED BIRTH CERTIFICATES

Delayed birth certificates (any name, any date) can sometimes be arranged. Usually the person needing such a document is the child of an unwed mother. For this reason, embarrassment, the birth wasn't registered (even for 40 or 50 years!). Of course, these documents can also be obtained through fraud. While it is a "victimless crime" it is not as "legal" as using one's own birth date and birth place and being 'naturalized'. Of course if anyone KNOWS the birth was falsified or the passport holder tells anyone, he cooks his own goose. We are not ADVOCATING falsification of documents, but just commenting upon our observations.

BIRTH DATE CHANGES

Obviously, one's place and date of birth are a FACT. We do not advise people to change their birth dates on official documents. One can have false documents, but that doesn't change facts. If the holder of false documents tells ANYONE the FACTS, he will always be open to blackmail and problems. If he keeps his mouth shut, anyone can pretend to be anyone he pleases. If you must change your birthday, don't let vanity get in the way. If you are really sixty-five, it is hard to pass for 39! Be born-again only within 1-5 years of your real birth-date if you are going to go this route successfully.

LEGAL NAME CHANGES

Name change is another story entirely. Anyone can legally call themselves any name they please in English-speaking, common law countries. However, in Roman Catholic countries (for instance) it is usually a major crime to use a different name than the one you were born with. In Italy it takes a PRESIDENTIAL DECREE (almost impossible to obtain for under US $100,000) to change one's name from John Smith to John Smythe. In the US and the UK, you just do it, and that's your new name, legally. Scope International can supply a name change kit customized for you with proper forms for Great Britain, the US or Canada (your choice). Please see the Resource List in the back of this report.

TWO WAYS TO GET LEGALLY ISSUED PASSPORTS

When citizenship is acquired by "right" of birth or marriage, usually no oath of allegiance is required. The new citizen gets his new passport and can also usually keep his old citizenship and passport. Normally, upon **naturalization** one must surrender old passports. Keeping one's old citizenship and passport can be a great advantage in many cases. *The more travel documents a person has, the more he is able to rise above political systems that do not appeal to him and maintaining the freedom of travel, being able to "vote with his feet".*

THE HIGH RISKS OF GAINING CITIZENSHIP LEGALLY

One would think that the risks and negative aspects under totally legal naturalization would be nil. This is not true. A country always treats all its citizens as a "natural resource" to be milked, squeezed, drafted, exploited and lied to. But at least native born citizenship cannot be taken away too easily. A *naturalized* citizen has all the disadvantages (responsibilities?) of citizenship, but at the option of the country, he can usually be arbitrarily deprived of any RIGHTS that go with citizenship.

In the US for instance, if a newly *naturalized alien,* for business, romantic or any other reason decides within three years after naturalization he must leave the US, it is possible that he will not be able to renew his US passport on the grounds that he **misrepresented his intention to reside permanently in the US**. Obviously, this can be avoided by leaving and entering the US without passport stamps and, after ten years, applying for a passport renewal from *within* the States on the basis of a "lost" document. The point is, the average man has not read *The Passport Report* and is blissfully unaware of the many pitfalls and several different ways he could lose his "new" citizenship and become stateless. We do not mean to use the US as an example of a particularly bad or unreasonable government – many others are far worse. In another scenario that has happened all too frequently, the new citizen gets involved in a dispute with any government agency or politician. His original citizenship application is exhumed and gone over by investigators with a fine toothed comb. The slightest misrepresentation about academic credentials, dates of attendance at schools, marriages, children, lawsuits or political affiliations serves as grounds for revocation of citizenship and deportation. Undisclosed brief membership in political organizations has resulted in thousands of such deportations from the US. As mentioned in *PT* and *The Passport Report,* the US more than any other country in the world, makes many activities considered normal and legal in other countries very serious criminal offences. There are thousands of victimless "crimes" in the US. These include – conspiracy, "stock parking", overpaying or underpaying taxes and failure to file thousands of informational documents (such as environmental impact reports). Many forms of sex or birth control between consenting adults are also a crime in many states. So is selling some vitamin pills or sexy videos – even if the same items are common as dirt in other countries. Once convicted, civil rights including the right to a passport can be taken away. Accordingly, obtaining a US citizenship by "Paper Trip" methods, for some people may be infinitely faster, less aggravating, and far less risky that the naturalization route for some people. If citizenship obtained by a rebirth is taken away, one can simply go underground and repeat the process. Yes, that makes the person a "criminal", but in many countries there are so many laws and restrictions that one must be a criminal three dozen times a day merely to do business and/or survive.

WHAT ABOUT GETTING A PASSPORT IN THE THIRD WORLD?

In Central and South American countries, there is a tendency for one political administration to set up a "legal immigration" and citizenship program to attract money and or skills and for the next administration to take back the program retro-actively. For instance, Costa Rica had a "Pensionado" program about eight years ago. A foreigner who did not need a job and had a proven income could make a substantial deposit (around US $50,000) in a Costa Rican bank. The Costa Rican deposit was *unconditionally guaranteed* by the government! The Pensionado was then allowed to buy a retirement home and bring in one tax free car which was given a special license starting "PEN". He received a "Provisional Passport" good for worldwide travel for five years and after that was promised the right to renew the passport or become a full dual-citizen, with the right to work locally, vote, etc. About 75,000 individuals, mainly Americans, bought into the program, bringing nearly a billion dollars into Costa Rica. Then the next administration pulled the rug out from under them! To make a long story short, this former opposition political party blamed all local problems on the pensionados. "Evil foreigners" became scapegoats for an economy that was falling mainly because of vast overspending (financed by inflation – i.e. running the government money-printing presses). A public works program and generous social benefits passed out to Costa Ricans were way out of line with the local economy's ability to pay.

In hysterical polemics the politicians pointed to the Pensionado's "big cars" and "big houses" and all their young pretty girlfriends. The Costa Rican voters responded favorably to this attack. "Throw out the foreigners!" How often have we heard that? The fact was that Pensionado deposits and remittances were the mainstay of the economy. The "bad foreigners" were bringing in most of the country's foreign exchange and giving locals some 500,000 jobs directly and indirectly. Yet the rabble-rousing politicians claimed with a straight face that the "PEN" cars bought and paid for in the US were "stolen from the people". The *interest* on the foreigners guaranteed bank accounts was also "being paid for with the blood of Costa Rica".

Politicians always have a fine time when they can create and shear a scapegoat class of individuals without political clout.

As a result of these relentless attacks, a new administration came in, dedicated to the proposition that Costa Rica needed to be cleansed of foreign influence. Thus foreigners dollar bank accounts were confiscated. The passport/citizenship deal was cancelled. Once the new administration took power, foreigners were beset by hostility and buzzing, biting bureaucrats. Pensionados (whether naturalized or not) who had been originally granted tax freedom on foreign source income were hit on every side by horrendous tax claims. They took huge losses and were forced (in most cases) to abandon their beautiful Costa Rican properties and leave the country.

Once the new party took power and, in effect, declared war on the Pensionados, the Costa Rican economy went into an even more rapid tailspin. The United States (naturally) rewarded the new leftist regime for its crimes against Americans, not by sending in the Marines, as Teddy Roosevelt might have done. No, they made economic grants, i.e. gave Costa Rica some big handouts. But the free money didn't do the country any good. It only went into the politicians foreign bank accounts. Four years later in 1988, a new government said it wanted to *restore* the Pensionado program and install a new variety of passport program. Offers of this sort are still attracting new capital from suckers who didn't bother to study their history. Some rich folks will believe and buy anything. Similar stories can be found throughout this report. New groups of investors are continually being fleeced by "legalized" thefts and confiscations. (See Costa Rica in section IV for the whole story.)

How about Uncle Sam?

Even the US is implementing a program whereby millionaire foreign investors can get residence and citizenship. Should you trust the US with your money or your life? Look at the way they treated Ferdinand and Imelda Marcos – invited foreign guests of recent vintage. Or Aldo Gucci, sent to jail for tax evasion in California at the age of 80. Trust any government? *You'd have to be crazy to believe that any venal politicians will ever look out for YOUR best interests! Only YOU can do that.*

We advise the person who is thinking of settling or investing anywhere to BEWARE. Even in Spain, where millions of Europeans (attracted by low or non-existent taxes) invested in winter homes on the south (Costa del Sol) shores. Once the area was fully developed with foreign money, property taxes were raised by 6,000 per cent. In a single jump! But the locals weren't satisfied with just that. The worldwide income of retirees spending more than six months per year in Spain was taxed at 60 per cent! "Hacienda" (Spanish) agents were sent abroad to study IRS - Gestapo techniques. After training their bureaucrats in Denmark, Germany and the US, Spain is now implementing a fiendishly efficient tax system combining all the worst features of the most oppressive regimes on earth. (See Spain in Section IV for details).

The moral of all of this is that perhaps one should not be anxious to jump into a "legal" or government authorized program involving investments and/or naturalization. Why? Governments have a way of backing out of their contracts and breaking their promises. Sometimes this is done only with new taxes. If a private person breaks his word one can usually sue and perhaps get some justice in a court or by arbitration. Governments cannot be sued! They have the unquestionable right to confiscate all assets within their jurisdiction and to deal in any way they want with the human beings (citizens or otherwise) who find themselves within their borders. Thus, the equation "A + A = PT" still means that one in today's world, must be able to *move one's ass and one's assets out of any jurisdiction within minutes of perceiving danger.* Achieving this objective and being ready, willing and able to move at the first whiff of trouble means having several sets of travel documents. It mandates that assets be registered under several names and that you be able to choose from a bouquet of nationalities. It also means keeping aware of current trends and politics – staying informed so that you can be gone long before "Clancy lowers the Boom". It also means that if you own a factory or property, or other fixed assets, you should stay *leveraged* or geared to the hilt. If all that can be confiscated is a tiny or non-existent equity supported by locally borrowed (hopefully State guaranteed) money, your own capital is more likely to be untouched and safe.

Since no government on Earth wants to lose its most productive and wealthy citizens, they all have laws to discourage (and make illegal) the avoidance of taxes and to limit the unfettered mobility of their own citizens. Paradoxically, almost every country wants to attract PTs from other countries. They put out the welcome mat (or "sets traps" – depending upon your point of view). Thus the bottom line is that it may be possible to be "legal" where you are going, but you will generally be, by definition, "illegal" – a deserter, a defector, a currency-law violator or tax evader in the place where you are FROM. With a great deal of care, study [and possibly lawyers and consultant fees], one can reduce the risk of criminal prosecution. At least such risks will be considerably less than the risks faced by people who have no choice – no options but to stay behind in their native country. After all, the PT can always vote with his feet. *Being nimble and quick is the best protection against government, the greatest danger to your health.* As we say in *PT* the *biggest cause of premature death in human beings is not AIDS, cancer or heart attack – it is and always has been* **GOVERNMENT!**

Comments, questions, additions and constructive criticism should be sent to:
Scope International, 62 Murray Road, Waterlooville, Hampshire PO8 9JL, Great Britain

Part XI

OTHER TRAVEL DOCUMENTS

MISCELLANEOUS CATEGORIES OF PASSPORTS

There are several miscellaneous categories of passport-like documents which often suffice quite nicely in their stead.

NON-CITIZEN PASSPORTS

Passports are usually issued only to nationals (subjects or citizens). Many countries, however, also have special categories of non-citizens entitled to passports. For example, stateless persons in a United Nations refugee camp will be issued a passport-like document which, with a visa, permits travel. Adopted children from these camps also receive the same type of documents which permit one-way travel to their adoptive parents country.

MARRIAGES OF CONVENIENCE

Females often receive preferential treatment in these matters because most countries will grant immediate citizenship to women who marry their male citizens. Males marrying a female national, on the other hand, usually must undergo a residence period of from six months to twelve years. Stateless residents usually receive a provisional passport until they become citizens. See our Nationality Survey chart for the rules regarding citizenship acquisition via marriage.

PROVISIONAL PASSPORTS

Some Latin American countries routinely grant citizenship to property owners after a short waiting period. During the waiting period, a ''Cedula'' or national identity card can be obtained. If the property owner needs to travel beyond the liberal scope of his cedula, a provisional passport will then be issued. These documents appear to be identical with regular passports, but holders may not vote until permanent citizenship is granted. The Dominican Republic, Costa Rica, Portugal and Tonga are well known for liberality in granting provisional passports.

HONORARY DIPLOMATS

Honorary Consul diplomatic passports are often awarded to friends of a country or to international businessmen who may be in a position to represent or assist a particular country. These are diplomatic passports in every sense of the word and are respected as such at every border crossing in the world.

Most Central American countries, Iceland, Austria, Turkey, Malta, Burkina Faso, Volta, Monaco, and San Marino liberally issue this category of document.

Honorary diplomatic appointments are usually obtained by cultivating favor with a political leader. Those rewarded with honorary diplomat status are expected to reciprocate by hosting important visiting personages and sponsoring social events.

For example, if a Third World country was interested in financing and building an aluminium refinery and needed support abroad, the government might seek out and appoint foreign industrialists in the aluminium field who as honorary consuls would then be expected to create and foster activities which would bring about the national goals. Thus, becoming an honorary consul normally carries with it some financial and social obligations. The passport is considered a fringe benefit.

SERVICE AND DIPLOMATIC PASSPORTS

Many countries allow foreign nationals to be employed by the government in various critical programs. Service passports were issued by the US to many former Nazis who, in between 1944 and 1946, became involved with US rocket research or intelligence programs in Germany. This was known as "Operation Paperclip".

Individuals of the caliber of rocket expert Werner von Braun received diplomatic passports instead. This provision allows such valued individuals to travel to international conferences under the highest auspices. While mere Service passport holders may be detained by police for questioning, holders of diplomatic passports with full immunity are quickly and politely ushered through all borders with minimal formalities. Personal friends of important politicians (and most politicians) have no trouble obtaining diplomatic passports for themselves and their relatives.

REFUGEE PASSPORTS

Whenever a stateless or persecuted person qualifies for residence in a particular country, but wants to travel through other countries in order to reach his destination, a refugee passport is normally issued. In order to enter or pass through any country, visas must be obtained. While the document appears to be a national passport, it is stamped with a legend to the effect, "Bearer is not a citizen – Refugee Passport". These documents are routinely issued in Berlin, West Germany; Vienna, Austria; Stockholm, Sweden; Paris, France and Mexico City to persons who make a claim for political asylum. They are better than nothing, but as a visa is required to go anywhere, being a refugee or stateless person is not a desirable situation.

DOCUMENTS USABLE IN LIEU OF PASSPORTS

Many identity documents are much easier to obtain than passports and they are accepted in lieu of passports for travel across friendly neighboring borders. Most of these documents are printed on inexpensive cardboard and have the bearer's photograph attached with staples or glue.

Alternatively, every local health department or bureau of vital statistics throughout the English-speaking world will issue a certified copy of a birth certificate to anyone who asks for it and pays a nominal fee. Often these birth certificates are printed on pocket sized ID cards. Such a card, obtained in the US or Canada is good for travel in 20 countries.

The same is true in Spanish-speaking countries where the identity card is called a Cedula. These are almost always included with a passport "package deal". In fact, they are necessary to get a passport or have one renewed and are usually all that is required to do so in a Spanish speaking country. A Cedula is normally issued at the local police station. As requirements vary widely, it is best to have a local inquire for you as to what papers you will need in order to obtain a Cedula. This ID is good for crossing the borders of most Central and South American countries.

In the EC, one can travel between countries (including non-EC countries within Europe) with only a European identity card. Normally the process of obtaining a card is far simpler than the one for obtaining a passport.

In the United Kingdom, there is no national identity card for travel purposes. The UK issues a ''British Visitor's Passport'' to its citizens. These cardboard cards are issued on the spot at most Post Offices. It is necessary to show a birth certificate plus the same documentation as needed to get a public library card, i.e. bills addressed to you, a lease, medical or bank card or a copy of a tax return. The Visitor's Passport is good for one year as a passport throughout Europe and even Bermuda. Any Bermuda ID, like a driving license, gets you into the US sans passport.

Similarly, Americans can leave and enter the US via Canada or Mexico with only a birth certificate. Generally, such ID is only necessary to return to the US. One reader recently wrote to inform us that Bellingham, Washington in particular is an easy entry point for the US, where customs/immigration checks are minimal, and tourists in cars are normally waved through. Other tourist spots, such as Niagara Falls operate in a similar fashion.

An identity card is never stamped at borders. Thus, unless the country requires you to fill in an arrival or departure form, there is no record of your movements, if that is a matter of importance to you.

If you have a passport without any pocket ID (National Identity Document) something is possibly wrong. Although, generally outside of their area of issue, these documents are never used or needed, a passport alone is sufficient identification for all purposes.

CROSSING BORDERS WITHOUT A PASSPORT

In most countries, there is usually one or more routes into a neighboring country that HAVE NO BORDER STATIONS. These unmanned crossing points are usually small backwater roads. Sometimes they are no more than dirt roads used by local farmers.

It is not illegal to use these border crossing points. But of course, officials of the countries involved have the right to ask for proper travel documents in the event that you are unlucky enough to be apprehended or stopped in a spot check. The usual penalty for improper entry is simply deportation. In a typical motorist case, the driver would be asked to return to the country he came from and possibly given police escort in that direction.

This could lead to a ''domino effect'' where the prior country illegally entered is informed of your situation, and they in turn may send you back to your country of origin.

DRIVING LICENSES BY MAIL

Driving licenses are available by mail from the Dominican Republic, Paraguay and Costa Rica through reciprocity. If you already have a driving license, you can get a new one without examination. These are for the usual term of about 4 years. But on the basis of one driving license it is easy to get another in almost every other country in the world, always on the basis of reciprocity. An international driving license, obtainable from any auto club in the country issuing the driving license is only a **translation** of your driving license and not a license itself, though most police don't know that. Your driving license doesn't have to match your passport as to country. But name, birthdate and photo should match. Most countries recognize any foreign driving license if you have it translated into the local language. With only a passport as ID one can always take the driving test (usually written and driving) and get one in person. I think that only in Switzerland and Great Britain does one get a lifetime or very long term license. Britain's expires when you are about 65. Then you just need an eye test.

TRADITIONAL COUNTRIES OF REFUGE

Many nations, by long tradition, will theoretically accept and give refuge to all persons in need (Switzerland, Thailand, the US, Sweden, Australia, Portugal, Finland and The Netherlands) or by direct constitutional provision (France, Mexico, Paraguay, Bolivia, Germany).

Although these countries may serve as a temporary port in a storm, it does not mean, however, that they will give you a passport. Still, every country that grants refuge has provisions for the eventual granting of full citizenship rights to long-term residents.

Most of these generous refugee policies were established in a different era when masses of poor people were tied to their land as agricultural workers. Also, as might be expected, countries that considered themselves underpopulated were the only ones who then (and still today) welcome any **large** influx of foreigners. In today's world, the cold climate countries tend to be underpopulated and able to support a larger populations than they have. Thus, the individual (without too much money or a special occupational skill) looking for a place that would accept him is best advised to concentrate on underpopulated countries. With a few exceptions, they are short on sunshine. Spain, Greece and Italy have liberal admission policies for those who simply arrive as tourists. If you decide to stay, government inefficiency in those countries and totally devastating taxes have created large black markets in labor. This makes it possible for the "illegal" immigrant to find work or start a low profile business and earn a living without ever having any contact with the government. Obviously, if a license or permit is needed or if tax returns were filed one could be discovered. Many individuals who operate "normal" businesses would never consider going "underground". However, approximately 25 per cent of the population of Europe and 75 per cent of the population of South and Central America only know the underground or black economy. According to an article in *Fortune Magazine* even in the former Soviet Union and China, there are quite a few very prosperous people running major underground businesses and traveling back and forth to the West without proper papers.

Very few countries have a large or effective special force of police devoted to ferreting out illegal immigrants and shipping them home. Where such efforts are made, normally only highly visible individuals of minority races or those in strange foreign garb are targeted. Thus in France, police will ambush black Africans and hooded veiled Muslim women emerging from the metro (underground transport in Paris) to demand "papers". Illegal immigrants and fugitives who look and speak like locals are caught only if they are involved in traffic accidents, bar brawls or arrested by accident.

In the US, the target of the Immigration and Naturalization or "Migra Policia" is typically the dark skinned non-English speaking Mexicans in California – people who look and sound like they "do not belong". These include undocumented Haitians who've arrived by clandestine boats in Florida. The police may get a tip that a factory or restaurant is operating with a large number of undocumented aliens. Then a "Migra" raid is made. Aliens (in the US) are then placed in holding camps until they can be shipped back to their home countries. Anywhere, a person who does not flock with a group of other illegals, but blends in with the population can easily buy or otherwise obtain some local identification such as a driving license, voting registration and a few charge cards. If one learns the local language without an obvious accent, anyone can live almost anywhere all of his life. In English speaking countries where identification cards are not mandatory, it is even easier. **In countries where by law, one must carry national identification, the problem is solved by obtaining a foreign driving license and having a good cover story to the effect that one is just a tourist and merely "Passing Through" the country**. A policeman cannot generally prove otherwise, and will let the "tourist" pass on his way within the country. Thus, the only problems come up when crossing borders. Most countries will not admit foreigners without a passport and, in many cases, a visa issued by the consulate of that country. If someone without any papers can raise the money to buy passport(s) from third countries, then even the travel problem is solved. Unrestricted mobility and international movement, at will, becomes possible, if one has money and a passport.

Before cheap airplane fares, usually only in the case of religious wars or famines were common people likely to move permanently. There was a mass migration of people to North and South America in the nineteenth and twentieth centuries. Some twenty million black slaves were "imported" by force. They got only a one-way ticket. Oriental and Indian laborers were recruited as cheap labor. Most such laborers eventually returned to their country of origin, but a large number stayed on. There were a number of unusual circumstances that led to quite a melange and blending of the population in Europe. For instance, when the huge Spanish Armada destined to invade England foundered and sank, vast numbers of Spanish sailors managed to swim ashore in Ireland! Because any enemy of Protestant England was a friend to most Roman Catholic Irish, these Roman Catholic sailors were hidden, protected and rapidly assimilated into the local population.

In the old days, refugees were likely to be the elite lords, warriors, nobles or highly educated people in neighboring countries, who made enemies of those in power. Generous refugee policies were in part political – a local prince or king would give refuge to the enemies of his neighboring king. Those who were sheltered would usually be helpful if and when they ever resumed a position of influence. It was unthinkable in times past that millions of poor people of a different race, religion, language and culture would descend from the skies *en masse* upon a country and expect hospitality, employment and full social services. When cheap charter flights and a disparity in the wealth of nations caused such immigration, local politicians in richer countries typically passed exclusion laws. Thus in Australia and the US, there were (until recently) laws specifically prohibiting the immigration of "inferior races". In recent years, racism has become internationally unpopular, but current policies of most First World nations (Europe, the US, Japan) do discriminate against people whose "grandfathers" were not of the "proper" race or religion. Grandfather clauses and such are a cute way of saying "we don't want you". No need for posting crude signs of the sort you see in Guatemala or South Africa saying simply, "No Blacks!" The message may be the same, but the delivery method is more subtle today. Canada, to its credit, seems to have become color blind in the last few years, and is one of the few "white" countries not discriminating against other races in matters of immigration. In our perfect imaginary world, anyone should be able to go anywhere. The reality is that only money and careful preparation will ensure mobility and freedom.

In Geneva, on the main street, a huge stone bas-relief depicts a liberty type female figure welcoming refugees from neighboring war ravaged countries. The carving is several hundred years old. **The Swiss still like to think of themselves as generous hosts to the oppressed**, but the reality is that Swiss law and practice will grant resident status only to Nobel prize winners, ex-kings and dictators who are still rich and multi-millionaires. **Nowhere on Earth are people more xenophobic than in Switzerland. Thus reality contrasts with theory**. In the United States, the famous Statue of Liberty beckons welcome to the "miserable huddled masses of foreign shores" but the reality is far from the inscription on the statue. To enter the US one must be diabolically clever enough (or have a diabolic lawyer) who will fill out a mountain of forms to get a would-be immigrant past a bureaucracy whose main job it seems, is to say "no".

THE BEST COUNTRIES FOR PEOPLE WITHOUT PAPERS

Few countries of the world have a vicious police force that has as its only purpose the ferreting out of illegal aliens. In Europe, aside from Germany, there is much more of a live and let live attitude. Most countries have huge refugee and illegal immigrant populations. The "undocumented aliens" usually work for cash in the "black economy" often as child-minders, domestics, nurses for old people, manual labourers and so on. If one is in the higher economic brackets and of the same race as the local people, the odds of ever needing or being asked for papers (except to cross borders) are nil.

When this author set out in 1977 to become a PT, we felt it was absolutely essential to have the "proper papers". This idea was shattered when we became friendly with a very high priced international lawyer who had been living in and running his business from Geneva, Switzerland quietly for 35 years without being "registered". He showed us that being a "Passing Tourist" was the best status one could have. Though Switzerland's immigration laws allow only a three month stay, one can rent a house or apartment as a tourist and stay forever. Passports and identifying documents from "somewhere" are needed only for crossing international borders. The most important thing our lawyer friend explained, was simply, "stay out of trouble and avoid having neighbors' complain to the police about you."

We have met "illegal aliens" from all walks of life and economic brackets. Ten years ago we would never have thought it possible to live "illegally" in a computerized, bureaucratic country like France. Then we heard this story from a cleaning lady in Paris, a North African woman who had been in France for thirty years, without papers.

She told us: "Once I was picked up for jay-walking and the police discovered, by asking me, that I was an illegal. What did they do? They just asked me for an employer reference from any legal resident I ever worked for. They called one madam I cleaned for and she gave me a good reference. So the police let me go. That was it. I wasn't told to leave or get papers, or anything. They have this big amnesty program in every country in Europe every ten years or so where you can get legal residence papers, but who needs it? I don't want to be in their lousy social security and tax system. I go back to Morocco every year with my passport and crossing to Spain the French don't care that I over-stayed. They don't even look at it going out. Coming back, I have friends who get me in on a regular ferry boat that goes every day and is full of illegals. It lands in Italy where they don't check passports. I don't worry about papers or visas. Still, I have an old Moroccan passport. It doesn't have my real name or birthday in it because the government charges more than I want to pay. Mine is an expired, stolen one I bought for ten dollars.''

The cleaning lady gave us the following list of places where, ''somebody without papers can get along just fine:''

PORTUGAL: Best in Europe. Police don't care about papers. If you want papers you can buy them cheap.

ITALY: Almost as good as Portugal. Especially in the south, if you have a good employer, they take care of everything by paying small sums to the police. You can even get a regular ''white'' job.

FRANCE: The police never stop white people, but they sometimes look at us (North African types) and ask questions. But the money is better in France. I have lots of jobs and friends here now. Sometimes they deport people, but it is pretty rare and only if they are unemployed. Many of the peddlars, street sweepers and restaurant workers in France are illegals.

We would observe that the person who doesn't need a regular registered job with income tax deductions can live almost anywhere in the world for as long as desired. Passports are not normally checked for overstaying. In Europe, passport checks and stamps in passports are given on a random and irregular basis even to visitors from outside the EC. For instance, Americans arriving in Nice, France or Shannon, Ireland or most places in Switzerland are seldom stamped. It is impossible thus for a country to know when you arrived and when you left. Passport stamps can be ''structured'' to give the image you want by **asking for stamps** to legally establish that you left on a certain date and returned on another – even though you may have made twenty border crossings that were not recorded! This sort of thing could be important in connection with avoiding ''tax residence''. But with a low profile rented apartment and no locally registered car, the odds of a tax challenge are also almost nil in most countries. For more information on this concept we suggest you read the book the author regards as his best, namely *PT 1*.

WHAT DOES THIS ALL MEAN TO YOU?

In our opinion it means that as a practical matter, **it is not a good idea to wait for the crisis to take place before taking out an insurance policy**. It is folly to depend upon generosity and theoretic open immigration policies. When there is civil war or an individual is on the run, in trouble and broke, he is at the mercy of random forces beyond his control. **An intelligent individual should and must provide himself and his loved ones in advance with assets on**

deposit (or invested) abroad and the necessary paperwork completed. That way, in times of political turmoil, plagues, personal problems or persecution of any sort, he has a comfortable place to go. Knowing which countries extend a theoretical welcome (those named above, for instance) is valuable. Why? Because at least in times of peace and normality, when not too many people are trying to batter down the gates and get visas to somewhere other than where they are, it is possible to arrange for the needed paperwork. *PT 1* deals with the questions: Where to go? How to make a living? How to transfer and protect assets? *PT 2* is the practice of how to communicate, bank, transfer money etc. confidentially.

Comments, questions, additions and constructive criticism should be sent to:
Scope International, 62 Murray Road, Waterlooville, Hampshire PO8 9JL, Great Britain

Part XII

POSSIBLE PROBLEMS

DUAL NATIONALITY – PROBLEMS AND BENEFITS

Many private individuals are stuck with dual nationality whether they want it or not. Most countries take the position if you were born a citizen of their country, you remain one for life. Unless, of course, you formally renounce that citizenship.

Some countries establish age related rules regarding dual citizenship. Foreign-born children of US citizens have until their 21st birthday to declare their preference under US law. The US did not formerly permit dual citizenship. Now a US citizen can hold more than one citizenship and under certain circumstances, more than one passport.

Under dual nationality laws, it is possible to create serious negative circumstances for oneself in a totally innocent manner. Certain acts, though committed abroad, are considered treason by some countries. The United States government announced in 1989 that like the Russians under Stalin, it had the legal power to kidnap anyone in the world and bring them "to justice" in the US, regardless of local laws.

DOES THE ACQUISITION OF A FOREIGN PASSPORT CAUSE A US CITIZEN TO LOSE HIS US CITIZENSHIP?

We asked this question of several immigration lawyers in Washington DC and we relay their composite answers (with permission) below:

"The acquisition of citizenship of another country is no longer an automatically-expatriating act for a United States person. Expatriation only occurs now, for all practical purposes, if the individual files a formal oath of renunciation. Similarly, a US citizen's acquisition of another country's passport is not prohibited, even if there was an "oath of allegiance" to the new country.

The State Department takes the view that US citizens may use a non-US passport for travel between foreign points. The State Department considers it improper for a US citizen to use a non-US passport to enter the United States. This view is probably legally incorrect, but it remains official US policy.

Thus, there are no negative consequences to a US citizen obtaining foreign citizenship as regards to his United States status. Many Americans today have dual citizenship and multiple passports."

MILITARY SERVICE

Military service may also be a definite problem for dual nationals. If your residence has been in one country all of your life, but you are of draft age and happen to be discovered within your other nationality's borders, you may find yourself conscripted into that army. Many countries have peacetime conscription. Only a few do not.

US CITIZENS NO LONGER LOSE CITIZENSHIP
BY ACQUIRING A SECOND PASSPORT
EVEN IF THEY TAKE AN OATH OF ALLEGIANCE
TO A FOREIGN POWER

In an important change of policy (July 1990), The United States State Department changed its regulations so that an American Citizen who applies for and is granted another citizenship is now presumed NOT to have intended to renounce his or her US nationality. Even signing a written or printed statement disavowing any further allegiance to the US does not lead to a loss of US citizenship. Even taking citizenship combined with employment under a foreign government in a non-policy making position does not cause a loss of citizenship.

How can a US Citizen divest himself of citizenship?
1)   By formal renunciation before a US consular official abroad.
2)   By taking on a policy level position in a foreign state.
3)   Upon conviction of treason.
4)   In very rare cases where conduct is so inconsistent with retention of US citizenship that it compels the conclusion that the individual intended to relinquish US citizenship.

The above policy is to be retroactive, and thus approximately 10 million Americans who live abroad and who have acquired other nationalities (and who may have given up their US passports in the process) may now be entitled to have their citizenship restored. This will make their children US citizens in many instances. The IRS (US tax collectors) have not yet issued a policy statement as to whether these restored US citizens will be considered "taxpayers" during the time their citizenship was in doubt or whether the requirement of filing annual tax forms will begin only when their new passports are issued.

These new regulations came about in response to a court decision involving an American fugitive who took up residence in Canada and was, after three years, granted citizenship in Canada. Later the ex-fugitive applied for a visa to visit the US with his Canadian passport. He was apparently turned down. He then re-applied as a US citizen. The court ruled that there is a presumption that a person who acquires another citizenship did *not* intend to relinquish US citizenship, and the applicant must be re-admitted to the US. The expat was held to be still a citizen entitled to a passport, *despite his oath of allegiance to Canada.*

Among those countries *without* a peacetime draft are the US, Canada, Australia, New Zealand, UK, Spain, Benelux countries and Austria. **"Tax Haven" countries are usually under the protection of a major regional power and never have a military establishment of their own**.

Dual nationality would seem to imply that you would be entitled to apply for a second passport if you wanted one. But the laws are very tricky.

Whenever you become a citizen of any country by naturalization, you are often required to renounce all allegiance and loyalties you have previously had. You are often required also to surrender all prior passports.

The tricky part is if you later acquire a different country's passport based upon dual nationality or other right. **Acquisition based upon "right" will not cause you to lose your naturalized citizenship. However, if you actively seek citizenship and take an oath of allegiance, you may be stripped of your new citizenship if they find out about your second passport.**

Confused? Here's an example. A naturalized American of Jewish ancestry born in Argentina of a Paraguayan mother and Swiss father and descended from an Irish grandparent could obtain *all* of these countries passports without losing his naturalized US citizenship. However, if he obtained a foreign passport by serving in any of those armies, he could be deprived of his US citizenship.

Notice I did not comment upon whether holding all of those passports at the same time would be "legal". The laws of each nation vary, but as a general rule, few countries permit their citizens to hold a "foreign" passport. To my knowledge, only the UK, Canada, New Zealand and a smattering of Commonwealth countries are unconcerned with the number of other countries passports you hold.

CROSSING BORDERS AS A DUAL NATIONAL

One should never cross any border with multiple passports on one's person or in one's baggage. Border officials will hit the panic button almost automatically whenever they discover a multiple passport situation. Legitimate possession of more than one passport is a rare situation for them. They automatically assume criminal activity or fraud.

What usually happens is that border officials will immediately confiscate all passports and then turn you over to the governmental police force responsible for prosecuting passport violations. You may be able to satisfy their aroused curiosity, but only after a harrowing ordeal, lost time and a thorough check with all of the countries or agencies that issued your travel documents. If your encounter occurs at the start of a weekend or a long national holiday, you may be on ice for quite some time.

Many countries don't practically (as opposed to officially) care if you hold two passports. In fact, one diplomat I knew hoped to encounter these situations for his personal profit. He was a Costa Rican Consul General stationed in the United States. Whenever he dealt with US Pensionados, he first got possession of their Costa Rican provisional passports. Then he casually asked, "May I please see your US passport?" If one was produced, he instantly confiscated the Costa Rican document. His game was to enforce Costa Rican law which, like most other countries laws, prohibits holding more than one passport at a time. Of course he enforced the law just strictly enough to extract a US $2,000 ''ransom'' from the retiree in exchange for return of his Provisional Passport.

If you hold another passport and your US passport is ever confiscated at a US port of entry or at a US diplomatic post, you'll probably pay far more than US $2,000 in lawyers fees before you get it back. You may also trigger an investigation into your travels, taxes and business dealings.

BE SAFE, NEVER TRAVEL WITH MORE THAN ONE PASSPORT!

TREATIES ON DUAL NATIONALITY

Many nations, especially those who want to exercise maximum authoritarian control on their citizens, enter into agreements with other nations so that if any citizen of one country acquires a passport of the other, it will be reported to the original country of citizenship. In some countries, a treaty provides that the obtaining of another citizenship and passport will result in the automatic loss of the first citizenship. Such a treaty exists (dating back to 1930) between Iran and Germany, for instance. But although a treaty may exist, if relations between the signing countries are no longer friendly, co-operation and information exchanges simply stop. If and when they are resumed, normally old information is not exhumed, but only new cases are reported.

Normally, a consular officer will have no hesitation in informing anyone who asks, if their country reports the acquisition of citizenship to the country of original citizenship. As a general rule, we know the following countries are very tight lipped about their citizens and will not report names and passport numbers to anyone except in the case of major wanted criminals and even then, there is no reporting if the ''crimes'' are of a political nature: Belize, Ireland, Switzerland, Israel and most Spanish-speaking countries.

Here are some of the countries that love to exchange information on their citizens and will tattle-tale on foreigners who have come to live in their country: the US, the former USSR, South Africa, Germany, Japan, Australia and Scandinavian countries.

We find that the same groups of countries are eager to exchange tax and financial information.

Canada and the United Kingdom are ''mixed''. They exchange information with the US and the EC, but not with most other countries.

The way to circumvent the problem is simple. If you do not want your country to know you have acquired a second passport, this is the procedure:

1.   Acquire the passport of a tight-lipped country like Ireland or Israel. For greater security, use an alternate identity or variant on your name for the ''intermediate'' document.

2.   Using that passport, acquire the passport of the loose-lipped country which will report (if at all) only to the country of your latest citizenship. For example: Mr. South African desires to become a German. First, Mr. South African becomes a Paraguayan or Belizian with the name Mr. Touth Nafrican. Then Touth becomes a German. The Germans don't report to Paraguay or Belize because there is no reciprocity, South Africa never finds out anything.

Is it legal? Generally speaking, there are no laws that require a person to report the acquisition of a new nationality. Thus, unless we hear otherwise, in our opinion, the above procedure is legal. Naturally, as stated elsewhere in this book, one should leave and enter one's home country only with local identity documents. Above all, don't take our word for anything. **Always** consult a local legal expert.

PASSPORTS AND TAX TREATIES?

Tax treaties (being pushed by high-tax countries like Scandinavia, Germany and the US) mean that if the individual who is a citizen somewhere else (i.e. foreigner) files an income tax return in treaty countries under his home country name and identifies himself as a foreigner, the government will turn over a copy of his local tax return (usually a few years later) to the home country.

What does that have to do with travel documents? Nothing! But the new financial information exchanging between certain countries is a good reason to have a "Banking Passport". See our section on that subject.

Any passport you purchase should normally be renewable for life. However, a lot depends upon how the request is presented, and who is doing the renewing. Best to have it done at a consulate abroad by mail. Have a very good letter composed in the appropriate language. We suggest it be sent with a colour COPY of the old passport, which is perhaps "lost or misplaced". Consulates have a way of losing original documents and thus extorting extra fees for research and replacement. That's the way it's done in South America or Africa. Incidentally, any client should always keep several color copies of important documents like driving licenses and passports. These are to be kept in a safe place so that duplicates can be obtained in case of loss or theft. Encased in plastic, your copy of any legal document except passports can often be used as an original.

First use of a passport should be in a country that does not stamp passports coming in. Switzerland is one such country.

It is less risky for all if a second passport is used only for BANKING and not for travel. Even an expired passport is good for banking and identification.

IS YOUR REAL REASON FOR WANTING A SECOND PASSPORT RATIONAL?

Some people just want to "get away from it all", "make a change" or "give up their citizenship". People, particularly under stress, can go off half-cocked and spend lots of money on things that really do not help them achieve their true objectives. They "burn their bridges" because of emotional considerations, with no real appreciation of the situation as it really is. People often assume things that just are not true.

Thus we are going to make some observations on commonly recurring matters so that you "know what the score is". These comments may cover questions you didn't think about asking.

First thing, any American who gets a second travel document is probably going to be breaking quite a few laws. Whether these laws are moral or justified – or whether everybody else is doing it – is not the question. The point is that every reader should realize that finding a dollar on the street and putting it in their pocket without reporting it and paying an income tax is a crime. In the US, it is theoretically punishable by 5 years in the pokey. Whether one has any real chance of getting caught or getting prosecuted is another thing. In most other countries, simply not reporting income is not a crime. Nor is having a "secret" second or unreported passport a crime anywhere else but in South Africa and a few despotic dictatorships.

Having a secret passport based upon a residence, marriage, parentage or birth (that never happened) is like finding money and not reporting it as income or like having a secret bank account abroad when the laws of your country make it obligatory to report the existence of such an account. *You probably won't get caught if you use common sense and elementary precautions, but you are technically speaking, a criminal, and this is something many people don't want to admit, even to themselves.*

Unique in the world's legal systems, any person, American or not, at home or abroad, who participates in any however insignificant way in helping an American citizen or resident to break the law (no matter how trivial) is part of a "conspiracy". This conspiracy is another crime usually considered more serious than whatever is being done. To put it in perspective, if a Frenchman in Paris advises an American to show his contempt for his own government by spitting on the sidewalk in front of the nearest US embassy, the Frenchman is guilty of a conspiracy to commit misdemeanour. This is a felony under existing US laws. Under those same US laws, his (French) home can be raided by US law officers and searched. Any of his property can be confiscated by US agents even if they are illegally in France and even if those US *agents are breaking the laws of France*. Further those US agents can, legally under US laws as in the recent Noriega case, legally KIDNAP the Frenchman and legally torture him on the way back to the US in order to legally extract a false confession to a more serious crime. The kidnappers can also legally secure *fraudulent testimony* to convict. They can legally arrange to have him placed in custody with known rapists and killers and have him physically and mentally abused by other prisoners and interrogators. It is all legal (from a US point of view). One cannot but wonder whether the Frenchman is the criminal or the *legal system* in some countries is lacking in morality.

To put it in proper perspective, Thoreau, Oscar Wilde, Winston Churchill, George Washington, Tom Paine, Ben Franklin, Lech Welesa, Mahatma Ghandi, all those who rose up against the Communists in eastern Europe, the present Pope, Socrates, Martin Luther, Martin Luther King and millions of heroes who stood up against oppression were all during most of their lives, *criminals by definition*. They often paid a high price for doing what they thought was right. The prime example of an individual who challenged the state and was crucified for it was Jesus Christ! Thus, it is obvious that someone can be doing the morally right thing and still face punishment.

Our view has been that governments are usually the "criminals". They, like the mafia, make you pay (taxes) for "protection" that is worthless. Thus, it is best to decide at the outset that what you are going to do is worth the price you may have to pay. Many people have been imprisoned or murdered (legally!) by governments for simply wanting to leave a jurisdiction, avoid being made into a murderer (military service), engaging in peaceful protest or attempting to protect assets. If these things are done with proper planning and mature common sense, there need be little risk, as explained more fully in *PT 1*. A second passport gives you the right to hold an unpopular opinion or eccentric way of life.

Now, comments about SOME of the things that are most commonly misunderstood regarding my books and the programs I have mentioned or recommended:

Second passports from many countries are currently available and can be granted on the basis of residence, parentage, property ownership over a period of years or many other factors. If the passports are "instant" the backup facts are generally going to have to be worked out **creatively** with someone If those backup facts are not true or if they are ever questioned in an in-depth way, the holder of the passport may well be unable to renew.

A person who visits Brazil with a passport based upon birth there should normally speak fluent, accent-free Portuguese and look the part. Why? At border control points there could be embarrassing questions he can't answer, like, "Why don't you speak our language?" Naturally, some people can memorize and get away with a good cover story, "I was taken to St Louis Mo. as a small child, etc." The person must be cool, confident, well rehearsed and well drilled in all possible questions. His story should 100 per cent match the documents he carries. Sometimes it turns out (or can be arranged) that a parent had citizenship which was passed to the child. In such cases, the bearer of a passport may not speak the language or know anything about "his country".

Even the dumbest border official has some sense of "who belongs" and who doesn't. As the typical reader is certainly not a professional criminal (and if they were we wouldn't want to know them, they are no good at fibbing). Thus as a general rule you shouldn't use a travel document to go to the country where it was *issued*. The place of issue is the country you are most likely **not** to fit in. A suspicious character will always be grilled. If a client says, "I paid a lawyer to get me the document and I never visited the country," he is ipso-facto, by definition, travelling on fraudulently obtained papers. What does this mean? It means trouble! It means you should *fully understand the legal basis by which your passport was issued!*

TRUE STORY: A young girl (let's say from Germany) recently went to the US on her sister's (US) passport. She had all the right papers and looked like the photo, but the customs official asked, "Where did you go to school?" When the girl said she went to the school her sister had gone to in the US (for 5 years), they didn't believe her. Why? Because her English was not as good as a person who really went to school in the US for 5 years. She then admitted the fraud and was sent from the New York City Airport to the Federal Detention Centre jail for 2 days. Then she was deported. Her passport was confiscated. She spent another two nights in jail in Germany, finally being released without charge. The point of this story is that *if you don't fit the documents you are carrying, if you go to the country that issued them, you are facing the biggest risks. If you don't speak fluent Spanish and travel with a Spanish speaking country's passport to places where they **don't** speak Spanish, you are generally going to be OK*. It is not a good idea to use such a passport anywhere that Spanish is spoken, likewise with Brazilian documents and Portugal. Since the Belize program shut down in late 1989, we know of no other country where English is spoken and where instant passports can be acquired. Sorry! We have heard that Liberia, Nigeria and Gambia (all English-speaking African countries) are a possibility, but, as you can tell from our *Passport Report*, we don't think much of African countries since you require a visa to go anywhere just about. If you hear of any interesting passport availabilities, prices or contacts, please let us know. We are interested in all such programs – even Africa.

Many readers don't seem to recognize that they should never (in our opinion) get (legally or otherwise) the passport and citizenship of the country they really want to live in or spend time in. I take 500 pages to explain all this in my *Passport* and *PT 1* reports, which our clients should always read cover to cover before taking any action in this sphere. On the other hand, if you just want to go somewhere and be a regular wage-slave or small business owner, you are talking about immigration and residence.

WHY YOU CAN NEVER "OWN" A PASSPORT

Technically, all passports belong to the issuing country and not to the individual. As a result, any government official can seize a passport on any pretext if the document is physically within their country or presented at a diplomatic post.

A diplomatic post is legally an extension of the home country. Honorary diplomats are also on "foreign soil" when in that space set aside for the purpose of transacting diplomatic business.

Obviously this means you should hide your second passport well or store your spare passport safely outside of the country in which you legally reside. This is because you can be ordered to surrender all passports "in your possession". You should consider keeping it outside the country of issue because it can be revoked or confiscated. Remember the general rule: a government has power and "jurisdiction" only over people and things within its borders.

Unless you are wanted by Interpol, any country where you surface as a tourist will rarely detain you at borders on a passport question. They have no records of lost or stolen passports outside their own. Unless you call attention to yourself with outlandish dress or behavior or have stamps in your passport showing visits to known drug-exporting countries, you usually will not encounter any flaps. The usual question is only to determine if you have a round trip ticket and enough money to live on during your planned touristic sojourn.

Comments, questions, additions and constructive criticism should be sent to:
Scope International, 62 Murray Road, Waterlooville, Hampshire PO8 9JL, Great Britain

Part XIII

CASE HISTORIES

PASSPORTS FOR ATHLETES, AUTHORS, ENTERTAINERS AND OTHER HIGH PROFILE PEOPLE

Because of its former policy of apartheid, or racial separation, South Africa has been barred from the international sporting community. Restrictions eased in 1992, but the situation is still not entirely clear. International sporting codes prohibited South African athletes from competing anywhere outside their country and some countries have maintained this ban. Most countries also imposed lengthy bans on any athlete who competed *in* South Africa, but with South Africa's return to the Olympics even this is becoming passé.

Other countries have similar problems. Israel, Iran, Iraq and several ex-Communist Eastern Bloc countries among them. The former Soviet Union itself and many more nations have been barred from competitions on and off. The US refused to participate in the 1980 Olympics in Moscow, referring to the Soviet invasion of Afghanistan. Taiwanese athletes cannot compete in any meets where mainland China is a participant and vice versa. Libyan and to some extent Syrian athletes are considered terrorists wherever they go. Thus they can't get visas to play in the games.

And so goes this crazy world. To make matters worse, not only the sports community is infected with this problem, but entertainers and other performers are hit with many restrictions and hard choices as well. The same can be said for some authors and a long US list of more than 300,000 ''undesirables''. Graham Greene, considered by many to be one of the greatest novelists in the world, was barred from entering the United States. Why? He (like your author) said one too many nasty (but true) things about the US.

In 1990, a British industrialist was accused of having ''imported'' six Czech soccer players ''illegally'' into the United Kingdom by means of obtaining Bolivian passports for them. They got into the UK without visas on their Bolivian passports.

It turned out that Bolivian passports can be had quite legally by mail order through proper official channels. There was nothing shady about the scheme. So why couldn't six Czech athletes travel into the UK on their own Czech passports? Reason: Because Czechoslovakia, like most ex-communist East Bloc countries, does not facilitate visa-free travel to Great Britain. It is almost impossible (even today in 1993) for residents of some former Soviet Bloc countries to get exit-visas or passports to travel abroad freely. Bolivia and most Central and South American countries are relatively liberal in granting their passports. No exit visas are needed. No entry visas are needed. Once legally in England, it is possible to acquire UK residency and later citizenship, provided one has powerful sponsors.

With political factors now dictating do's and don'ts in the arts, sports and many other fields, restrictions on freedom have spawned a whole cottage industry of travel document specialists. Usually, they are team coaches, sports managers or consultants. Sometimes they are show business impressarios, but they all have one thing in common – they can help their ''names'' or clients get different identities and different nationalities.

CASE HISTORY: FRUSTRATED FISHERMAN RUNS TO SWAZILAND

With the right documents, banned athletes can enter competitions with alternate identity papers naming them as someone else. One athlete, the black South-African 1,500 metre runner "Fred Fisherman", heard that he could get Swazi citizenship in time to compete in the 1984 Olympics. He went to Swaziland, a small independent country on the border between Mozambique and South Africa. There he met with the head of the country's sports council. He was told, "It would not be difficult for such a fine runner to represent Swaziland at the Olympics."

He went back a second time and met officials of the country's track and field federation. Then he talked to the Swazi Olympic Committee. After six months of negotiations, "Fred Fisherman" began noticing that the more Swazi officials he met, the more it was costing him. Finally he just approached officials in the Swazi passport office with a small packet of cash.

It paid off. "Fred Fisherman" and two other South African athletes received Swazi passports for a total of 50 Rand, about US $25. Much cheaper than endless meetings with officials.

Still, the passports were not enough. The LA '84 Olympics had come and gone and still our runner didn't have his officially required *certificate of citizenship*. Also, he was running out of money. He had already bribed officials to get a Swazi residence permit, about 1,200 Rand. But a residence permit was not the same as citizenship. Without a *certificate of citizenship* in addition to his passport, he could not register to compete.

"Fred Fisherman" was frustrated. It was time to see the top banana: His Royal Highness, the Swazi King.

After three months of negotiations, he arrived at the appointed time for the audience. He waited. The King, a teenager, never showed. The King's counsellors had little to say to Fred about this. "This sometimes happens," they told him.

That night, he invited members of the Swaziland Olympic Committee to a dinner. Twenty-five "officials" showed up. The next morning, as he was checking out of his hotel, he noticed a disrepancy in his bill. It seems that his dinner guests had checked into eight different hotel suites with call girls and charged substantial expenses to his account.

Today, he has his Swazi passport. It is good to travel with. But he still does not have the Swazi citizenship papers needed to compete in the Olympics.

Athletes and other people like "Fred Fisherman" are twiddling their thumbs all over the world. They are desperate and rightly feel that the time has come for policians to stop meddling with the world of sports. Athletes, black and white, are suffering because politicians – as usual – cannot distinguish between individuals and the accidents of birth that make them citizens of "pariah" countries. Professional athletes have been exploited and shoved around as pawns for many years. Today, they are all too often simply victims left dangling in the hands of stupid and arbitrary politicians.

CASE HISTORY: PAUL GETS IT RIGHT IN LESOTHO

In South Africa, Paul Coetser (real name) is the man athletes talk to when they want to gain their freedom to compete internationally. Coetser runs "Sports-Mark", South Africa's only sports management company. To make his business profitable, he often has had to get second travel documents for his athletes. This is the only way he can get them into international games.

He gets some of his passports in Lesotho, an independent African country surrounded by South Africa. This is cumbersome because the Kingdom is hard to reach. There are no airports, no railways and not even many roads to Lesotho. Also, a very special and sometimes delicate approach is required. Coetser recalls a typical instance in 1990 in which he had to get a Lesotho passport for Annette Falkson. She is white and one of South Africa's best women marathon runners.

It took Coetser nine months and quite a bit of money to set up the trip to Lesotho. After finding the right village and the right local chief, they all sat in a circle. Coetser told the chief that he had come from afar to seek the chief's wisdom on a certain matter.

The matter, he said, involved one of the chief's people, a girl who had grown up in this village. He told the chief that he had brought the girl, now a woman, before him to identify.

Coetser said that if the chief confirmed that this woman and her parents before her had come from his town, then this woman could get a Lesotho birth certicate, which was very important to her.

The chief thought about "the problem". They continued to sit and smoked a pipe for some time. Then someone brought in some of the chief's homebrew beer. They drank that. The chief said he wasn't sure he could remember this one woman from among so many people in his village.

Coetser said he understood how an elder with such responsibilites could have this problem. Coetser pulled out a US hundred dollar bill. The chief thought about this. Coetser pulled out another bill. The chief peered intently at Miss Falkson. The more money Coetser extracted from his pocket, the more the chief seemed to recognize Falkson.

The chief suddenly recalled that Falkson and her blood kin had been respected residents of his village for generations. More money. He then even remembered her first words as a baby.

A little later, Paul Coetser and Annette Falkson left Lesotho with exactly what they had wanted, a Lesotho passport and birth certificate for Falkson, formerly a South African citizen.

For another athlete, Coetser spent about US $25,000 and obtained – quite legally – a Paraguayan passport. The athlete this time was a young black welfare officer in a platinum mine in South Africa, marathon runner David Tsebe. He was entered in the Honolulu marathon as Brandt Nava, a runner from Paraguay. Coetser – his coach – passed himself off as Paul Stefanos, a Greek national living in London.

Fifteen miles into the race, Gianna Poli of Italy made a break. Nava/Tsebe went with him, in the lead. Poli caught him at 22 miles and Nava settled in behind him. To most, Nava looked fresh and Poli was laboring.

But Poli won. Nava was a close second with a time of 22 hours 15 minutes and 12 seconds. Still, Nava was entitled to a substantial cash prize.

Among the reporters was ex-runner Alberto Salazar, assigned to do television commentary. Salazar, who speaks Spanish, approached Nava for an interview. Salazar then spoke Spanish to Nava. Remember, the second place winner was supposedly a Paraguayan whose native language would have been Spanish. Nava didn't appear to understand any Spanish. Salazar then spoke to him in English. No response.

It turned out that David Tsebe didn't have the right language to go with his new passport. The charade unravelled. They were forced to hand back the second prize money and leave Hawaii. He was placed second fair and square. He was of the black race the boycott against South Africa was supposed to protect, but he couldn't keep the money he had won fair and square. This was one result of the ban on South African athletes.

ON MARRYING FREEDOM

Some athletes have entered into marriages of convenience to get other citizenships and second passports. South African sports defector Zola Budd gained British citizenship in time for the 1984 Olympics, then ran a race "back home" in South Africa and as a result was again banned abroad.

Black long distance runner Sydney Maree, Pretoria, became a US Citizen and a two-time Olympian.

Frith van der Merwe married a complete stranger solely to get to compete internationally. Van der Merwe has never lived outside of South Africa, but is widely considered the best female ultra-long distance runner in the world.

What does this all mean to you?

Sports figure or tycoon, as long as governments unfairly restrict travel, some creative people will find ways to get new identities and second passports. These people are not criminals. They will be aided by other individuals like your author who feel that travel is a basic human right. That right must be facilitated for moral reasons, personal profit or both. It is unfortunate that corrupt bureaucrats usually hold the key to freedom in the form of the ability to grant passports, visas and other documents needed for travel. Our observation is that a strong willed individual who wants to get from point A to point B will always find out HOW to do it (perhaps by reading a book like this). He'll refine his own plan by consulting with experienced experts. Finally he will implement his plan, eventually circumventing all artificial restrictions and unjust laws. When such barriers stand in the way of righteous and legitimate aspirations, *all good people have the moral duty to help themselves and all others overcome them. The United Nations charter recognizes the right to travel and to move freely as a basic human right. Why then do most member nations make exercising this right a crime for many people of the "wrong" race, place of birth or parentage? Why indeed? With your contribution of information and case histories like these to future editions of* Passport *and* PT, *WE SHALL OVERCOME!*

CASE HISTORIES

The following case histories are true. They are drawn from the author's own experiences, from readers who have submitted their stories for this report and from other reliable sources.

Because these histories portray situations as they actually occurred and thus describe how various laws and regulations actually interact, we have taken care to verify any critical details that are presented. We point out, however, that nobody associated with the production of this report is offering legal advice of any kind. Nor, for that matter, is anybody recommending that the reader take any particular course of action based upon information contained in this report.

Instead, we urge the reader to consult with competent legal and financial advisors according to your needs.

While the countries and details of each character presented in the following histories are properly identified, we have purposely changed the names of individuals and business establishments. While we feel that the information to be presented is of value to the reader, we do not wish to create hardship and inconvenience for the subjects themselves who have been so willing to share information with us.

THE AUSTRALIAN JOCKEY WHO CAME IN TOO LATE

''Tiny Tim'' was one of Australia's leading jockeys. He raced mainly in Australia and New Zealand. His colorful personality got him an offer to race for a two month season in Hong Kong, followed by two months in England and another two in the US. If all had gone well, his earnings would have been about US $30,000 per month.

Tiny never thought about a second passport, and his accountant kept his taxes low by investing in Australian livestock and homegrown tax shelters.

When Tiny got to Hong Kong he was surprised to be invited to a meeting of jockeys and owners where **he was told that he would win his first Hong Kong race**. Expressing surprise that the race was apparently going to be **fixed**, he was told that in Hong Kong, horse racing was more like American TV wrestling. It was the show that people came to see, and racing was more theater than competitive sport in Hong Kong.

Tiny **won** on schedule. A few days later he was **arrested**. The police, alerted by the Hong Kong Racing Board, were investigating allegations of pre-arranged winners and losers. **Tiny told the truth**, was brought before a magistrate and was ordered to **forfeit his passport** and remain in Hong Kong until his trial.

It appeared that Tiny had arrived in Hong Kong at an **inopportune time** when race fixing was about to be investigated. In order to deter future culprits, those involved were to be punished. For his part in the conspiracy, Tiny faced a five year jail sentence. Any conviction would put an end to his career as a jockey.

Even though **he personally agreed to nothing but to do his best to win**, Tiny's crime lay in **not reporting the conspiracy to the police**. Tiny had considered going to some authority about the meeting, but since everyone who was anyone in the Hong Kong racing establishment was present and seemingly in cahoots, he felt that **it was not his place to upset the order of things**.

Tiny had only his Australian passport. He was ordered either to surrender it or to remain in jail until the trial. Unable to leave without a passport, he cannot fulfill his professional obligations to race in England and the US. This represents an immediate loss of US $120,000. He will spend a like amount presenting a defense in his upcoming trial – a charade that will result in his being convicted and serving some time in jail. Tiny is clearly going to become an example to others.

Tiny is now thinking that if he had a second passport, he could simply leave Hong Kong via Macau and continue his racing tour. Instead, he is wasting time and money waiting for his no-win trial. Since he had lived in New Zealand, he could have easily obtained a second passport without even surrendering his Australian one.

Tiny learned that it is easier to obtain a second passport when nobody is watching and when you are not in dire need of one. Had he observed the Boy Scout motto, "Be Prepared", some simple steps taken a few years ago would have stood him in good stead today.

A GERMAN TAX LAWYER IN SWITZERLAND

To "Gunther Beckman", Switzerland was a magnet. It was politically neutral, clean, prosperous, anti-leftist and perhaps the closest place to Utopia that he could possibly imagine. The problem was that while the Swiss love tourists, it is almost impossible to get a Swiss passport. Residence and work permits are likewise unattainable by the typical German lawyer.

Swiss law requires that in order to qualify for any of these privileges, you must have two Swiss parents, be a Head of State, a major author or movie star, a Nobel prize winner or an individual having superior characteristics and international fame that will bring credit upon Switzerland.

Gunther is a brilliant and creative international lawyer. Switzerland already has an excessive number of native lawyers. Gunther knew he could best serve his clients with tax havens, corporations and delicate business negotiations from a Swiss base of operations. Confidentiality is well respected there. Plus, Gunther loved skiing, sailing and the whole Swiss outlook on life. On the other side of the ledger, Gunther recognized that Swiss taxes were high and that lifelong service in the National Guard is required of Swiss citizens.

As a result of wanting the advantages without the negative factors, Gunther sought a back door to Switzerland. He bought a home in Campione, a small Italian enclave located physically inside Switzerland. As a resident of Campione, he was entitled to Swiss telephone and postal service, a Swiss driving license, Swiss plates on his automobile and full membership in Swiss professional associations. His Italian Campione residence card was endorsed by Switzerland, thus allowing him unrestricted access both to Switzerland and to all of Europe.

Best of all, Gunther's **tax situation improved radically. He owed no Swiss taxes on his six figure income because he wasn't a Swiss citizen; Italy didn't tax his income because it wasn't earned in Italy; Germany didn't tax him for the same reason**. Gunther feels that he is in a **perfect situation**.

Gunther was aware of Swiss difficulties and he remembered his own hunger in World War II. As a result he was determined to find an even safer haven to fall back upon in the event another European war was waged. Because of his wealth and status and **because of Paraguay's hospitality** to right wing Germans, **Gunther was able to arrange for a Paraguayan passport**.

This was done through a meeting in Switzerland with German-speaking Paraguayan diplomats. A short visit to Paraguay and a small land investment were required. He keeps his Paraguayan passport in a safety deposit box in nearby Lugano and now has his last ditch emergency retreat to South America completely provided for.

Gunther recently purchased a fine penthouse in Buenos Aires, Argentina during the current real estate depression. The price was US $20,000. He exchanges use of this apartment for similar benefits in expensive vacation homes elsewhere in the world. See *PT 1* for details on how to exchange vacation properties.

As a Paraguayan, Gunther qualifies for permanent residence status and a work permit in Argentina. He is already working with an Argentine-German law firm that will generate profitable business.

Gunther has attained his goals in life. He has assured his personal safety; he is paying essentially no taxes; he has diverse real estate investments and business associations well lined up. Best of all, no government can misuse him. He has found freedom in an unfree world.

THE MEXICAN IN AMERICA

"Pedro Sanchez", age 33, was anxious to find a way to live legally in the United States. He grew up near the California-Baja border and considered it unfortunate that he was born on the Mexican side instead of a few hundred feet to the north in the United States. Pedro began his career as a wetback harvester at age 13. He found that the pay was far better in the US for his unskilled agricultural labour.

Working without proper papers meant that he would be deported on many occasions. After twenty years of illegally working in the US, he had gained a Mexican-born wife, four US-born children and a mortgaged US home. Despite his **willingness to pay US taxes** and having learned to speak passable English, Pedro lived in **constant fear** of being caught and deported again. Each time this happened, he lost his job and had to start over again once he crept back across the border.

The Immigration and Naturalization Service ("Migra") border police forcibly put his wife and four children across the border. Housing and employment in Mexico are always bleak problems. Pedro's children did not even speak Spanish, further alienating his family from the homeland in which the Migra would have them reside.

Getting back across the border was no problem, but Pedro realized that La Migra would be looking for him at his old home. Immigration lawyers could not discern a loophole for Pedro to slip through. Finally, Pedro met a man who promised him a US passport for $5,000.

The process involved using the birth certificate of a deceased US-born infant named Manuel Estrada. Manuel (the dead infant's name) was changed in court to Pedro Sanchez. Then Pedro, using his lifelong name and the birthright of Manuel Estrada, applied for and received a US passport. He remarried his wife in a California civil ceremony, thereby giving her a US resident's card and ultimately citizenship. This will protect her from ever being deported again.

Pedro will never tell even his wife or his children how this miracle was worked because he doesn't want to take any chance of being discovered. **He knows that what he has done is illegal, but he also knows that he wants the opportunities for his wife and children that only the US can bring him**.

Fearing any further contacts with La Migra, he is one of the twenty million illegal immigrants in the US who **did not** apply for the 1986-87 amnesty.

A SOUTH AFRICAN BECOMES A SOUTH AMERICAN

"Abe Levin", age 34, was a prosperous businessman in the metal casting industry in South Africa. South Africa's laws forbidding foreign bank accounts and the exporting of capital worried Abe, as he viewed the deteriorating racial situation. He carefully developed export customers in Europe and South America. He could now justify frequent foreign travel.

While abroad, he established illegal foreign bank accounts and devised ways to divert some of his revenues to them. These were **serious criminal offenses**, but Abe reasoned that if things did go up in smoke in South Africa, **he needed a means to support his family**.

Abe then began to plot how to provide for a rapid exit in the event one became necessary. Being of Jewish ancestry, he explored the possibilities offered by Israel. Learning however, that there was **no way to avoid Israeli military service for himself or his sons**, he considered Spain.

Spain appeared to be an ideal place to relocate both his business and his family, but immigrants from South Africa were being **flatly refused by Spain**. Then Abe discovered Ecuador, a **back door** route into Spain.

Ecuador's immediate "Entrepreneur's Passport" was the perfect choice. By setting up a small enterprise in **Ecuador** that employed several locals, Abe qualified for a passport. Once this was firmly in place, he was able to travel to **Spain**, reside there and conduct his business there simply because **he was holding a passport issued by a former Spanish colony**. No visas, no permits, no hassles. By joining a Safardic Jewish congregation in Spain, he became eligible for a Spanish passport in one year, and **can now live or work anywhere in Europe without a visa or permit**.

A CANADIAN WHO DIDN'T NEED A SECOND PASSPORT

"Bill Wayne", age 45, was a Canadian tycoon who was ready to move on to other challenges. He built a small oil company into one of Canada's largest privately held business conglomerates.

Bill intended to float a public stock issue and then concentrate on how to spend and invest the US $10,000,000 he expected to reap from the transaction. Then his tax consultant gave him the bad news. Under Canadian law in effect at the time, he would lose about US $7,500,000 to taxes. This was too much, so he began searching for an option.

Bill discovered that if he became a legal resident of tax-free Bermuda and relocated before the stock deal took place, he could avoid all Canadian taxes, keeping the full $10 million. He could always return to Canada after his money was safely transferred and invested through a Bermuda bank, but the cold winters had a chilling effect on those thoughts. Bill stayed in Bermuda, but now keeps an apartment in nearby Manhattan and another in London.

US citizens are faced with similar tax problems and could follow Bill's pathway to financial freedom. The only rub in this case, however, is that **US citizens would have to renounce their citizenship**. Otherwise, they would still be subjected to taxes because **under US law worldwide income is taxable regardless of** their **place of residence**.

Many US capitalists with large sums of money at stake, shortly before taking any large capital gains, become Canadian citizens first and then make the residence move to Bermuda.

Bermuda is a resort-playground and tax haven for the US, European and Canadian millionaires. It is a short flight from major US, Canadian and European cities.

Other Caribbean tax havens worth looking into are the Bahamas, Cayman Islands, British Virgin Islands and Turks and Caicos. See also *The Tax Exile Report,* published by Scope International.

AN AMERICAN ENTREPRENEUR IN SAUDI ARABIA

"Jack Armstrong" was born in the US in 1946. He spent his childhood with his father, whose engineering business took him to the Middle East. Jack returned for about seven years in order to attend Princeton University and then the Massachusetts Institute of Technology. He eventually succeeded to the family business.

Armstrong Engineering USA Inc. generated over one million dollars per year in net profit for many years. **As a US citizen, Jack paid out 40 per cent to 90 per cent of Armstrong's net income in US taxes**.

Jack finally recognized what was happening and sought out skilled tax advice. He was told to obtain Uruguayan citizenship and then renounce his US citizenship. Jack's Uruguayan passport was obtained and the US Consul in Jedda, Saudia Arabia endorsed it for unlimited business trips to the US.

Jack was now saving over US $500,000 in annual tax payments. He also found that he was **now free of dozens of other US business regulations ranging from providing equal employment opportunity to anti-bribery laws that prevented him from engaging in customary Arab practices**.

Reincorporating in Liechtenstein, Armstrong Engineering Ltd now enjoys a **200 per cent increase in profits** after taxes and a **newly found administrative efficiency** that would have been impossible when operating under US laws.

FRENCHMAN IN MONACO BECOMES A NEW ZEALANDER

"Marcel Martin", now aged 85 and retired for more than 20 years, was born in France. He is a patriot and a former hero of the World War Two French Resistance. Marcel owns successful retail stores in Nice, France and his palatial seafront apartment is in Monte Carlo, Monaco.

The Principality of Monaco is bounded on three sides by France and on the fourth by the Mediterranean Sea. It is a tax haven and a retirement retreat for the very wealthy. There are no property taxes, income taxes or estate taxes.

Shortly after Marcel retired to this fiscal and climatic paradise France concluded a treaty with Monaco that permitted France to collect their extremely high income and "wealth" taxes from French citizens in Monaco. Marcel's investments in Switzerland provided about US $100,000 in annual income. France was about to lay claim to well over US $60,000 of this previously untouchable income.

Marcel sought a way out. His live-in girlfriend of some 20 years held a New Zealand passport, and this gave him "the answer". **He married her at age 80, took a short trip to New Zealand and gained citizenship there by virtue of being the spouse of a New Zealander**. He then **returned to Monte Carlo, again free from income taxes on his Swiss deposits**.

Only the US and the Philippines tax the worldwide income of their citizens, even if they reside abroad. France only taxes the income of French citizens abroad if they reside in Monaco.

For Marcel, the Resistance hero, **to renounce his French citizenship was an emotionally trying episode, but the economics of the situation dictated this course of action**. With his Monaco identification card, **Marcel still feels French. By walking across the street**

from his apartment, he can actually breathe French air, stand on French soil and be in France. Of course, he is US $60,000 per year richer, and when he dies, France won't take 70 per cent of his estate either.

AN IRANIAN IN THE US

"Mohammed Reza" was **born in Iran**. He became a **multi-millionaire** under the Shah's regime. When the house of cards began to collapse, he **moved to California**. Eventually, he **became a US citizen**.

Because of the anxiety Reza had over getting resituated after a narrow escape when the Shah's regime crumbled, he didn't pay attention to the tax consequences of US citizenship. His income from New York bank investments and occasional land transactions was not previously taxed by the US. **When he gained citizenship, he also gained a staggering tax bill.**

Reza rethought his situation and opted for Canadian citizenship. After changing, he bought or rented homes in various countries around the world. He now pays no taxes on his income, yet he enjoys the benefits of traveling on one of the world's best passports. **He is free to come and go to the United States without a visa, but never stays more than four months at a time.**

THE CHINESE MAN IN PORTUGAL

"David Ling" was born in mainland China fifty years ago. He owns several cargo ships, both freighters and tankers. His net worth is well in excess of US $1,000,000 and his annual income is over US $100,000. David lives in Hong Kong and has a Hong Kong British passport. He also has serious concerns.

David is worried about what may happen when the Peoples' Republic of China takes over Hong Kong at the expiration of the treaty in 1997. Unless he makes some clever moves right away, he may lose his shipping interests to a Chinese communist corporation. His lifestyle and freedom may also become curtailed, as there is no reliable way to predict what the communist Chinese will do. He fled the mainland before Chiang's defeat and doesn't like to face new uncertainty now.

David does not want to leave his Hong Kong home and friends, yet he realizes that his economic and personal future might force making such a move. Several years ago, David purchased a home in Macau. After gaining a working knowledge of the Portuguese language, he was able to obtain Portuguese citizenship and a passport for himself and his family. This opens all of Europe to him because Portugal is in the European Economic Community.

David was fortunate in having moved so quickly. In 1985 a British treaty with Portugal slammed the Macau back door shut by limiting the number of Hong Kong Chinese who could obtain Portuguese citizenship via Macau to 100,000. That quota was already filled when the treaty was inked.

David's story is living **proof of striking while the iron is hot. Many slower-moving Hong Kong Chinese are now desperately casting about for other alternatives, but few are so simple or satisfactory as the Macau route was.** Belize offered a legal passport in return for a bond purchase ($25,000) from 1985 to 1989 and then again from 1992 to 1993. This door closed abruptly both times because of internal political disputes.

A RUSSIAN BECOMES A DISPLACED PERSON

In 1985, before the days of Glasnost, Perestroika and anti-communist uprisings, "Walter Ivanovich", 19, was a Russian citizen, a lover of pop music and fast cars. He had secretly dreamed of moving to the West since early childhood. He joined the Russian merchant marine and managed to jump ship, locating a route of defection while his ship was docked in Italy.

His first attempt to defect was in an Italian police station, but there he was threatened with being returned to his country. Walter knew that would mean 40 years at hard labor or even death.

To obtain asylum somewhere became literally a matter of life-or-death. The US Consul in Rome refused his application for asylum since he had nothing of interest or value to offer to the US. Walter then found good advice from a refugee organization. Saying he wanted to go to America and own a Porsche was the wrong script. He could say he **escaped for political or religious reasons,** and he would then receive an Italian refugee passport and safe transit passage to one of three countries – Austria, Sweden or West Germany. Additional inquiry also revealed that South Africa, Canada and Australia offered free passage, asylum, and eventual citizenship. These countries were just names on a map to him – America was still his goal.

Without Western friends or money, Walter had to accept whatever deals were offered rather than selecting his destination. He spent some time in an Austrian refugee camp, safe at least. Where his efforts to secure permanent residence somewhere in the West were aggressive and determined. With youth, health and a bright ambitious mentality working in his favor, Walter connected with a good sponsor and residence after a brief period. Author's Note – "Walter" writes from Santa Barbara, California, "I own a Porsche now, have a home with an ocean view, and I have political freedom. Thanks to *The Passport Report.*"

A FILIPINO BECOMES AUSTRALIAN

"Arturo Madera", 42, was loyal to the second-to-last Phillipines revolution and to President Marcos. For his valuable loyalty, Marcos ensured that Madera received an inside track ultimately gaining a major interest in the national airline. Madera became wealthy through this liaison. Madera, like most Filipinos, realized that Marcos' reign would eventually falter. He embarked upon a careful plan of hiding much of his assets in stable foreign countries to prepare for that eventuality. Investing in an animal feed pellet manufacturing business in Australia, Madera qualified for citizenship under the entrepreneurial program by spending a few months each year in Sydney, running his business.

When Marcos' regime collapsed, Madera joined his wife and family in the state of New South Wales, Australia where he had already sent them at the first signs of trouble. Had he not planned ahead, Madera might have been murdered as an enemy of the new state. What few assets remained in the Philippines were confiscated, **but he had already secretly moved the bulk of his fortune out of harm's way**.

Instead of suffering the uncertain and meandering course of his deposed patron, Madera is now safely at work in his new country. Because he **anticipated the future and did something about it early enough, he had his passport and safe haven ready and waiting when he needed it**.

THE BANKRUPT AND THE BILLIONAIRE

In recent years, the story of two wheeler-dealers made the front pages of all the financial newspapers of the world. Ivan Boesky was a leading corporate raider and receiver of "greenmail", while Marc Rich traded oil and other commodities on a global scale. The lawyers for both men probably warned them many times that they could be heading for trouble with various regulatory and tax agencies. Neither were criminals in the same sense as thieves or swindlers. However, a thicket of regulations makes it difficult, these days, to make any deals without violating some law or other. In the US most violations carry stiff criminal penalties.

Marc Rich was eventually accused of income tax fraud and a host of other crimes. Ivan Boesky's main offense was insider trading. **Both men at their peak were on their way to billionaire status,** when **government agents swooped in to confiscate all their assets and business records.** The immediate **effect on Boesky was the complete inability to continue doing business. He had only one office (in the US).** Marc Rich who also did most of his business from Wall Street was more **prepared.** Rich (according to newspaper reports) kept his most **sensitive records in a second office in Zug, near Zurich, Switzerland. He held both Belgian and Spanish passports, and a legal residence and work permit for Switzerland.** For both men, a criminal indictment must have been unpleasant. **But Boesky was totally wiped out.** He **paid a hundred million dollar fine and pleaded guilty to criminal charges.** He was also persuaded to turn State's evidence on dozens of his closest business associates. His friends would also do jail time and be ruined financially. **Rich was inconvenienced,** but by simply leaving New York for good he was able to do business as usual from Zug. **Rich is now reportedly a billionaire, living the good life in Europe.**

The moral of the story and its implications for you should be clear. You may not be a big time operator, but **anyone can run afoul of the bureaucracy. It may not be** *fair* **that one violator gets away with something scot free and another loses everything, including his freedom, but that's the way life is! Those who are prepared for possible eventualities survive.** Those who do not prepare fall by the wayside. Our books and special reports are all about preparing! Develop **alternative residences** (A Channel Island, Monaco, Campione, Andorra, Brazil), alternative incomes (Lloyd's etc), and generally prosper and survive in a difficult world. **We are not writing for "criminals" but for people who have the degree of wealth or success that makes them targets for unjust persecution or lawsuits.** If you are in this category, it will take more than reading this book to protect yourself. **You must obtain your second passport, an alternative residence and a safe haven for some of your assets** *before* **the trouble starts.** The author hopes you will do it soon.

Comments, questions, additions and constructive criticism should be sent to:
Scope International, 62 Murray Road, Waterlooville, Hampshire PO8 9JL, Great Britain

Part XIV

PARTING WORDS

THE LAST WORD

The Passport Report, now in its 8th Edition for 1993, has been a labor of love – certainly not a source of instant wealth for the author. We are committed to maintaining this publication as the world's most current and authoritative book on the subject. Nothing better is available from any source at any price. The plagiarists and copyists are at work, and we've seen our own outdated and now wrong information being circulated – long after our new edition has come out with the latest news. We get the information at source. The competitors copy us and each other. This edition came out in early 1993. About one year later we expect to produce another version. As a registered report buyer, you may acquire the new edition for half price.

A great deal of work and massive research expenditures are needed to keep up with over 239 different political entities.

We would like to feel that our readers are part of a group of friends, who pool information for mutual benefit. Sharing information can only help us all. If you discover a new source of passports or a thieving swindler in the business who takes money and does not deliver, please let us know. Such information will save our friends a lot of grief. This sort of data goes into our Special Information Sheets.

Finally, each person's need and personal situation is quite different. We find that in spite of our efforts to bring order and clarity to a welter of information, some people will still do things that are completely wrong for them. You must read all you can on the subject, verify your information and, before you take the irreparable steps, probably take individual counselling. Anyone who has visited a good lawyer knows that his charges are seldom under £600 for a preliminary consultation.

We can recommend a specialist consultant with considerable experience in the field who will be pleased to evaluate your goals, review your present residential and financial position and analyse your plans. He will then make recommendations. This service was free to buyers of the first edition, but it soon became apparent that a substantial charge was needed just to cover overhead, handling and postage. We also found that our replies to a detailed written request (use a pen name if desired) were far more effective than phone conversations where misunderstandings were common. Also, off the cuff telephone answers may not take important variables into consideration.

If you write to Scope International enclosing £200 or equivalent in cash or bank check, we will make referrals to help you achieve your objectives. **Personal conferences at £700 per session can be arranged, preferably after an initial exchange of correspondence.** Finally, you must state, **"I am neither a criminal, government employee or journalist and the information being sought is for my personal use only, and will not be published nor revealed to any third person without your written permission."**

We also suggest you read *PT 1* before asking for a personal consultation. It may answer all your questions a lot more inexpensively.

Please include your name and registration number in any communication and tell us if your mailing address or name is different from that which was originally registered. As you know from other Special Reports, I recommend that for any subscriptions, mail order items, etc. you use a "pen-name" and an address other than your home, such as a private post office box.

Our minimalist records are (of course) secure and **our mailing list is not available to any government agencies,** thus ensuring your privacy. Also, incoming foreign mail in any country can legally be opened and copied by government agencies. This is rarely done, but an ounce of caution is worth a pound of cure. Our responses are sent in neutral looking envelopes.

We sincerely hope that this Special Report and the others in our PT series take you where you want to be. When you've got your second passport, let us know how it feels to be free!

W.G. HILL

Comments, questions, additions and constructive criticism should be sent to:
Scope International, 62 Murray Road, Waterlooville, Hampshire PO8 9JL, Great Britain

UNIVERSAL DECLARATION OF HUMAN RIGHTS

All members of the United Nations have agreed to this Universal Declaration of Human Rights, 10th December 1948.

This book was written to help individuals obtain these basic rights when governments abrogate or deny them.

PREAMBLE

Whereas recognition of the inherent dignity and of the equal and inalienable rights of all members of the human family is the foundation of freedom, justice and peace in the world.

Whereas disregard and contempt for human rights have resulted in barbarous acts which have outraged the conscience of mankind, and the advent of a world in which human beings shall enjoy freedom of speech and belief and freedom from fear and want has been proclaimed as the highest aspiration of the common people.

Whereas it is essential, if man is not to be compelled to have recourse, as a last resort, to rebellion against tyranny and oppression, that human rights should be protected by the rule of law.

Whereas it is essential to promote the development of friendly relations between nations.

Whereas the peoples of the United Nations have in the Charter reaffirmed their faith in fundamental human rights, in the dignity and worth of the human person and in the equal rights of men and women and have determined to promote social progress and better standards of life in larger freedom.

Whereas Member States have pledged themselves to achieve, in co-operation with the United Nations, the promotion of universal respect for and observance of human rights and fundamental freedoms.

Wheras a common understanding of these rights and freedoms is of the greatest importance for the full realization of this pledge.

Now, Therefore,
THE GENERAL ASSEMBLY proclaims
THIS UNIVERSAL DECLARATION OF HUMAN RIGHTS as a common standard of achievement for all peoples and all nations, to the end that every individual and every organ of society, keeping this Declaration constantly in mind, shall strive by teaching and education to promote respect for these rights and freedoms and by progressive measures, national and international, to secure their universal and effective recognition and observance, both among the peoples of Member States themselves and among the peoples of territories under their jurisdiction.

Article 1. All human beings are born free and equal in dignity and rights. They are endowed with reason and conscience and should act towards one another in a spirit of brotherhood.

Article 2. Everyone is entitled to all the rights and freedoms set forth in this Declaration, without distinction of any kind, such as race, colour, sex, language, religion, political or other opinion, national or social origin, property, birth or other status.

Furthermore, no distinction shall be made on the basis of the political, jurisdictional or international status of the country or territory to which a person belongs, whether it be independent, trust, non-self-governing or under any other limitation of sovereignty.

Article 3. Everyone has the right to life, liberty and security of person.

Article 4. No one shall be held in slavery or servitude, slavery and the slave trade shall be prohibited in all their forms.

Article 5. No one shall be subjected to torture or to cruel, inhuman or degrading treatment or punishment.

Article 6. Everyone has the right to recognition everywhere s a person before the law.

Article 7. All are equal before the law and are entitled without any discrimination to equal protection of the law. All are entitled to equal protection against any discrimination in violation of this Declaration and against any incitement to such discrimination.

Article 8. Everyone has the right to an effective remedy by the competent national tribunals for acts violating the fundamental rights granted him by the constitution or by law.

Article 9. No one shall be subjected to arbitrary arrest, detention or exile.

Article 10. Everyone is entitled in full equality to a fair and public hearing by an independent and impartial tribunal, in the determination of his rights and obligations and of any criminal charge against him.

Article 11. (1) Everyone charged with a penal offence has the right to be presumed innocent until proved guilty according to law in a public trial at which he has had all the guarantees necessary for his defence.

(2) No one shall be held guilty of any penal offence on account of any act or omission which did not consitute a penal offence, under national or international law, at the time when it was committed. Nor shall a heavier penalty be imposed than the one that was applicable at the time the penal offence was committed.

Article 12. No one shall be subjected to arbitrary interference with his privacy, family, home or correspondence, nor to attacks upon his honour and reputation. Everyone has the right to the protection of the law against such interference or attacks.

Article 13. (1) **Everyone has the right to freedom of movement and residence within the borders of each state.**

(2) **Everyone has the right to leave any country, including his own, and to return to his country.**

Article 14. (1) **Everyone has the right to seek and to enjoy in other countries asylum from persecution.**

(2) This right may not be invoked in the case of prosecutions genuinely arising from non-political crimes or from acts contrary to the purposes and principles of the United Nations.

Article 15. (1) **Everyone has the right to a nationality.**

(2) **No one shall be arbitrarily deprived of his nationality nor denied the right to change his nationality.**

Article 16. (1) Men and women of full age, without any limitation due to race, nationality or religion, have the right to marry and to found a family. They are entitled to equal rights as to marriage, during marriage and at its dissolution.

(2) Marriage shall be entered into only with the free and full consent of the intending spouses.

(3) The family is the natural and fundamental group unit of society and is entitled to protection by society and the State.

Article 17. (1) **Everyone has the right to own property alone as well as in association with others.**

(2) **No one shall be arbitrarily deprived of his property.**

Article 18. Everyone has the right to freedom of thought, conscience and religion; this right includes freedom to change his religion or belief, and freedom, either alone or in community with others and in public or private, to manifest his religion or belief in teaching, practice, worship and observance.

Article 19. **Everyone has the right to freedom of opinion and expression; this right includes freedom to hold opinions without interference and to seek, receive and impart information and ideas through any media and regardless of frontiers.**

Article 20. (1) Everyone has the right to freedom of peaceful assembly and association.

(2) No one may be compelled to belong to an association.

Article 21. (1) Everyone has the right to take part in the government of his country, directly or through freely chosen representatives.

(2) Everyone has the right of equal access to public service in his country.

(3) The will of the people shall be the basis of the authority of government; this will shall be expressed in periodic and genuine elections which shall be by universal and equal suffrage and shall be held by secret vote or by equivalent free voting procedures.

Article 22. Everyone, as a member of society, has the right to social security and is entitled to realization, through national effort and international co-operation and in accordance with the organization and resources of each State, of the economic, social and cultural rights indispensable for his dignity and the free development of his personality.

Article 23. (1) Everyone has the right to work, to free choice of employment, to just and favourable conditions of work and to protection against unemployment.

(2) Everyone, without any discrimination, has the right to equal pay for equal work.

(3) Everyone who works has the right to just and favourable remuneration ensuring for himelf and his family an existence worthy of human dignity, and supplemented, if necessary, by other means of social protection.

(4) Everyone has the right to form and to join trade unions for the protection of his interests.

Article 24. Everyone has the right to rest and leisure, including reasonable limitations of working hours and periodic holidays with pay.

Article 25. (1) Everyone has the right to a standard of living adequate for the health and well-being of himself and of his family, including food, clothing, housing and mecial care and necessary social services, and the right to security in the event of unemployment, sickness, disability, widowhood, old age or other lack of livelihood in circumstances beyond his control.

(2) Motherhood and childhood are entitled to special care and assistance. All children, whether born in or out of wedlock, shall enjoy the same social protection.

Article 26. (1) Everyone has the right to education. Education shall be free, at least in the elementary and fundamental stages. Elementary education shall be compulsory. Technical and professional education shall be made generally available and higher education shall be equally accessible to all on the basis of merit.

(2) Education shall be directed to the full development of the human personality and to the strengthening of respect for human rights and fundamental freedoms. It shall promote understanding, tolerance and friendship among all nations, racial or religious groups, and shall further the activities of the United Nations for the maintenance of peace.

(3) Parents have a prior right to choose the kind of education that shall be given to their children.

Article 27. (1) Everyone has the right freely to participate in the cultural life of the community, to enjoy the arts and to share in scientific advancement and its benefits.

(2) Everyone has the right to the protection of the moral and material interests resulting from any scientific, literary or artistic production of which he is the author.

Article 28. Everyone is entitled to a social and international order in which the rights and freedoms set forth in this Declaration can be fully realized.

Article 29. (1) Everyone has duties to the community in which alone the free and full development of his personality is possible.

(2) **In the exercise of his rights and freedoms, everyone shall be subject only to such limitations as are determined by law solely for the purpose of securing due recognition and respect for the rights and freedoms of others and of meeting the just requirments of morality, public order and the general welfare in a democratic society.**

(3) These rights and freedoms may in no case be exercised contrary to the purposes and principles of the United Nations.

Article 30. Nothing in this Declaration may be interpreted as implying for any State, group or person any right to engage in any activity or to perform any act aimed at the destruction of any of the rights and freedoms sct forth herein.

RESOURCE LIST

RECOMMENDED CONSULTING SERVICES ON CITIZENSHIP, PASSPORTS, RESIDENCE REQUIREMENTS AND ALL PT-RELATED MATTERS

DO YOU NEED A CONSULTANCY?

Due to an excess of work and recent ill-health Dr Hill is no longer offering either personal, written or telephone consultancies, but Scope International can offer you the services of three expert consultants who will answer your questions and advise you equally well.

Indeed, we would say that the three consultants we are now using have been recommended by Dr Hill because they are engaged in actually putting into effect the advice which they offer.

The first, Peter Thompson, is a PT whose specialities include knowledge of worldwide company incorporation and advice, maildrops in various parts of the world and imaginative answers to legal, accountancy and tax questions, including the kind of advice that you *really* want to know. He also has many useful connections around the world.

If you have any general PT type questions or require advice in the areas mentioned above then we highly recommend Peter. His consultancy fee is £200 for a letter, fax or telephone consultation plus the cost of the call or £700 for half a day (four hours) plus travel costs according to where you require him to go. You may visit him in Europe where he is often to be found. If you can arrange to meet in the same country that Peter is in at a particular time, or wait until he is going there, travelling expenses will be minimal or nil.

Please send your written consultancy together with cheque, cash or draft payable to Peter Thompson to Scope International Ltd, 62 Murray Road, Waterlooville, PO8 9JL, UK and we will forward it on immediately. If you require a personal consultation, please telephone our office on 0705 592255 and we will arrange a convenient appointment on behalf of Peter Thompson and yourself.

If you need to discuss confidential movement of funds, bearer shares, secret numbered bank accounts, or simply financial secrecy with minimum risk of loss or disclosure, then Robert Stirling could be your ideal consultant. He leads an international group of currency and banking specialists and has great experience in legal world currency movement.

If you would like to discuss your particular requirements with Robert Stirling, arrangements can be made through Scope. The fee is £700 for a half day (4 hours) plus travel and associated costs.

If your consultancy is of an immigration or passport nature then we can recommend an expert firm of immigration specialists who can offer you passport and immigration consultancies. They can also arrange second passports on your behalf in a variety of countries as well as offer diplomatic passports and honorary consulates.

If you would like a consultancy with an international immigration lawyer, please send £200.00 (US $350.00) together with your written questions and as much background information as you can provide. We will forward this for direct reply from our international immigration consultant.

If you seek to come to the UK we can offer you the services of a firm which specialises in UK immigration. The services offered by this firm are explained in part V of this report. Please contact Scope International for the appropriate referral.

If in doubt as to which consultant you need, please ring Scope International and discuss the nature of the advice you seek and we will be able to advise you.

Please note that before spending money on consultations, you will invariably find it cheaper to read the specialised Scope Reports which deal with particular subjects (especially *PT 1* and *PT 2*) because the answer is probably within. It is much cheaper and cost effective for you to obtain information from the Scope Special Reports than from a personalized response. Reading *PT 1* may also make you think about avenues of which you had never thought about previously.

Scope International Ltd, 62 Murray Road, Waterlooville, Hants PO8 9JL, UK (International Code: +44 705) Tel: (0705) 592255   Fax: (0705) 591975

Harry D. Schultz: Consultant on all PT and investment matters. US $40 per minute. Send advance payment (minimum US $200) in US dollars to FERC, PO Box 622, CH-1001, Lausanne, Switzerland with questions and your phone, fax or telex number. Minimum charge of $200 is for a five minute phone conversation. Retainer $112,000 per year. Harry Schultz is the world's most expensive investment advisor, listed as such in the *Guinness Book of Records*. Since his newsletter takes about 200 hours to produce each month it is therefore quite a bargain at $275 per year. Send £10 or equivalent in cash to cover postage and handling for a couple of sample back issues.

Mark Skousen is a good man to have on your side! He is resident in the US. Which means some limitations on the advice he can give on a personal basis. He does still give out his best ideas without fear of prosecution in his books and newsletter. Skousen knows the PT ropes, speaks at many foreign seminars and conferences (best time to talk with him) and has a highly recommended newsletter. He's promised to send a free sample issue to our readers! Mark is also the author of a dozen books on financial privacy, survival, Swiss banks and so on. We suggest you tell him you are a follower of Bill Hill and ask for whatever he has of interest to PTs. Write him at PO Box 2488, Winter Park, Florida 32790, USA or 7811 Montrose Road, Potomac, Maryland 20854, USA.

CHANGING YOUR NAME – OBTAINING ALTERNATE IDENTITIES

It is possible to legally change your name, usually without employing a lawyer and usually without spending more than the price of a good lunch. You can then get the new name entered into your passport, driving license and other identity documents. The name-change procedure varies from country to country and within the USA, from state to state. You can choose any new name for any (legal) reason. Many ethnic people are changing their names back to ancient names, while those with hard-to-remember names are simplifying.

If you send Scope International a summary of your basic objectives in changing your name, we can supply a complete name change kit customized for you with proper forms for the

UK, US or Canada (your choice) for US \$50/£30. Please do not tell us you want to evade your creditors or escape prosecution for a crime since those are not considered legitimate purposes, and we could not send you forms. However, for any other purpose, you can change your name by merely filling in a few forms and filing them with the relevant public officials – possibly outside of your home country. In England and some US states, there is not even any requirement to file your name change.

RECOMMENDED TAX LAWYER

Marshall J. Langer: Tax lawyer with Schutts and Bowen, 100 Chopin Plaza, Miami, Florida 31131, USA. Very ethical, responsible and professional. A high recommendation from your author, Hill. Charges are the usual lawyer rates at about US \$250 per hour. Good for setting up offshore corporations and all international tax planning. Langer is author of *Practical International Tax Planning,* published by the American Practicing Law Institute available from Scope International, price £125/\$250 airmail post free, *The Swiss Report* and *The Tax Exile Report* published by Scope International.

CHEAPEST ACCOMMODATION ADDRESS ON A TAX HAVEN

£600 per year on the Channel Island of Sark includes: mail receiving and forwarding, electronic telephone forwarding, fax and confidential banking. Our discovery of this service and the tax freedom and privacy it provides is so important that a Special Report has been devoted to it. See *The Channel Island Report* for a full discussion of this unusual situation. Order direct from Scope International Ltd at £60 or equivalent in any currency. Add £15 for airmail postage outside of Europe. Order form in the back of this report.

TAX HAVENS

The best book on the subject is *The Tax Exile Report* by Marshall Langer, published by Scope International. Another recommendation is *Tax Havens And Their Uses* published by *The Economist,* 25 St. James's Street, London SW1A 1HG, GB. Price £75.00.

The standard reference work on tax havens, expatriation and so on is Marshall Langer's *Practical International Tax Planning*. Please request further information from Scope International.

A comprehensive report, highly readable and amusing is *Fiscal Paradises of the World* by French lawyer, Edouard Chambost, 51 Ave. Montaigne, Paris 75008, France. It is currently only in French. An English version should be out by the time you read this. Price not set. Write to the author, Chambost, not Scope.

For a most comprehensive treatment consider: *Diamond on Tax Havens,* the original "old standard" for offshore operations. Publisher, Matthew Bender, 11 Penn Plaza, New York City, NY 10001, USA.

Barry Spitz's *Tax Haven Encyclopaedia,* Butterworth's, 88 Kingsway, London W2B 6AB, GB. Both of these are expensive loose-leaf books usually found in business libraries.

For FREE! Almost every major accounting firm publishes useful booklets for distribution to clients and *potential clients* (that's you) covering tax laws and business conditions in selected jurisdictions. Merely call the 'librarian' of the firm in any major city for a list of publications. Try any major certified public accountants (called ''Chartered Accountants'' in the Commonwealth). For instance: Touche Ross, Price Waterhouse, Peat Marwick, Pannell Kerr Forster, Arthur Anderson, Arthur Young, etc.

HOW TO KEEP BURGLARS OUT OF YOUR HOUSE, CAR OR STORAGE LOCKER

We suggest copying this sign on yellow paper, coloring the skull and crossbones red and pasting it where burglars will see it!

WARNING

POISON GAS

DO NOT ENTER!

INSURANCE CARRIER DISCLAIMS ANY LIABILITY DUE TO SERIOUS INJURY OR DEATH AS A RESULT OF UNAUTHORIZED ENTRY.

RECOMMENDED NEWSLETTERS

One of the most offbeat publications we have come across is the *Expat Newsletter.* The price of a one year trial subscription is US $70. Their monthly rag has wonderful classified ads on places to rent, mating agencies and many other weird and wonderful things. Send subscription to Scope International.

Low Profile edited by Mark Nestmann. Excellent US newsletter dealing with privacy and the threat to your wealth from government. Highly recommended. Annual subscription US $99.00. Send to Scope.

Harry Schultz International Newsletter: Issued every five weeks, this newsletter is an interesting mixture of investment advice, political updates and philosophy. It is also the only newsletter in the world that has a regular PT section! I strongly suggest a trial subscription to this stimulating newsletter of original ideas. It's also a mind-boggling guide to profitable international investments. One year subscription for US $275. Sample back issue or two free if you mention W.G. Hill. See Consultants for details.

International Living Newsletter: Wonderful monthly bulletin with interesting ads. A subscription is not expensive – but write for current rate as it was due to change. Many ads on vacation home rentals and exchanges, etc. Great travel articles, plus section on travel bargains. News of interest to nomads not found elsewhere. Highly recommended! Send US $2 for sample back issue to William Bonner, Publisher, 824 East Baltimore St., Baltimore, MD 21202, USA. Mention W.G. Hill when asking for sample.

Adrian Day's Investment Analyst: From one of the few intelligent financial journalists in the world. His perceptive stories and sound financial advice has often produced good results for me. Free sample issue if you mention Hill. Write to: Box 3217, Silver Spring, Maryland, USA 20918.

Wayne Phillips International Government Grant & Loan Alert, 136610 N. Scottsdale Road, No 10-105, Scottsdale, Arizona 85254, USA. A strange and erratic jumble of information on many subjects by the world's most financially successful author, PT and former jazz musician. Well worth the price of a postage stamp because it is totally free if you mention Hill!

Larry Abraham's Newsletter, PO Box 609, Wanna, Washington 98395-0609, USA. Highly recommended by Harry Schultz. Special offer to Hill readers only. Send US $2 for postage – free sample issue.

Ken Gerbino's Newsletter, 9595 Wilshire Boulevard, Beverly Hills, California 90212, USA. Also recommended by Harry, same US $2 offer for free sample issue.

BOOKS FOR PTs

The World's Best by Marian V. Cooper. A "How To" source book for the international traveler. Recommended. Costs US $20.00 which includes surface mail postage in the UK. Add 40 per cent for airmail outside of the UK. This superb book has a wide range of things in it like the best beaches, banks, bars and bird watching in the world. And that was just the "Bs"! 300 pages of goodies. Also recommended are: *The World's Top Retirement Havens* (172 pages for $15), *Paris Confidential* (135 pages for $15). All available from the Scope International PT Booklist.

The Hong Kong Bank (contact branch nearest you) has an excellent (free) series of books on investing and doing business in most countries. The Hong Kong Bank is also known as The British Bank of the Middle East and the Crocker Bank in the US.

Information Libraries run by consulates and information services of the US, Great Britain, Australia, etc. are all good places for free information on a wide variety of topics of interest. There will be a government bias to their material, but if you read between the lines and ignore the propaganda, you can get some valuable data.

VACATION HOME EXCHANGE ORGANIZATIONS AND DIRECTORIES

While many individuals may be afraid to let "strangers" use their homes, home exchangers are not the same as rental tenants. Normally the people who trade homes for a month or three are experienced exchangers who will take the same care of your home and property as you do. They will exchange references with you. Since you are using their place, and perhaps their car, while they use yours, there is naturally a high degree of responsibility. This author has had many wonderful experiences exchanging properties in Paris, London, Hong Kong, South Africa, Bangkok, San Francisco and Monaco. The beauty of an exchange is that instead of an expensive hotel room, you get a fully furnished apartment, books to read, etc. If you are lucky, the owner of the home you trade for will leave you a list of the best restaurants and reveal many non-touristy secrets of his city. Plus, depending upon the terms of the exchange you may get fringe benefits, like the use of a summer cottage, a regular cleaning person, a car, boat, horse, etc. You can always advertise for an exchange in a newspaper of the town where you want to go – but the home exchanging clubs are probably a better deal. The people in them tend to be upper-middle class retired folks or teachers with attractive places to offer. If you have an open mind and will consider offbeat locations you might otherwise not have on your list of first choices for visiting, you will definitely enjoy some enriching experiences.

The Arthur Frommer publishing organization has a paperback called *Swap and Go*. It's full of info on the subject of home exchanges. They have a superb bargain offer including this book, *Europe on $40 a Day* a one year subscription to their newsletter, *The Wonderful World of Budget Travel* and the *Frommer Guide to New York City*. The price of the entire package is US $25. Send to: $25 A Day Travel Club, Frommer/Pasmentier Publications, 1230 Avenue of the Americas, New York, NY 10020, USA.

The best home-trading organization in our experience has been the *Vacation Exchange Club,* 12006 111th Ave., Youngtown, Arizona, 85363 USA (Phone: 602-972-2186). They have a large "catalog" of homes and apartments which over 6,000 subscribers have listed as being available for exchange. You can either buy the directory and write to the people listed in it or you can list yourself and expect to receive many tempting offers for the periods you designate, and from the places you want to go. The cost of the service is quite inexpensive, about US $20 for the directory and another US $10 to be listed in it. The second largest organization is *International Home Exchange Service,* PO Box 3975, San Francisco, California 94119, USA (Phone: 415-382-0300). They have about 4,000 subscribers with the price of their books slightly more than Vacation Exchange Club. It doesn't hurt to join both for best exposure since the benefits of one exchange could pay for the club membership a hundred times over.

TRAVEL BARGAINS

Experienced travelers know that seats on the same plane starting and stopping at the same points can vary tremendously in cost. This author once had an argument with a client who said,

"I always go first class because I can afford to." A few weeks later, we were sitting side by side on a first class flight, getting exactly the same service, heading for the same destination. He had paid US $2,600 for his ticket, while I had paid US $500 for mine. For what was saved by not just buying a point to point ticket, yours truly could buy a new car. Of course one doesn't get much of a car for US $2,100 unless he's read the Hill *Free Car Report*. Not doing a bit of comparison shopping for airline tickets, cars or any major item is to my mind, extremely foolish, no matter how much money you have. I hate to be "taken for a ride". Here are a few secrets known to all experienced travelers:

1. Always ask your travel agent to *look for the cheapest way to travel*. Go first class if you must, but try to get it at a discount. Usually a travel agent can do better than the first price quoted if asked to "look for a cheaper way".

2. Look at ads particularly in Sunday newspapers (travel sections) and in travel/entertainment/leisure magazines. Best ads are in *Time Out* published in London and available in magazine stores worldwide. *Time Out* ads are always offering bargain flights, package tours, cruises, home exchanges and so on. The best deals on discounted plane tickets can usually be purchased in London, Singapore or Hong Kong. Travel agents who sell these tickets are locally known as "Bucket Shops". In London some of them even have elaborate full color brochures and catalogs. Particularly recommended is *Trailfinders,* 42 Earl's Court Road, London W8 6EJ, GB. Phone: (44-71) 938-3366. They specialize in "round-the-world" tickets, usually good for year, with a huge number of stopovers. The price of such a ticket can be as low as £650. Send for free catalog.

3. Overflight routings should be checked. For example, sometimes one can get a super bargain flight from say London to San Francisco. Assuming where you really want to go is London-Salt Lake City, a good travel agent may be able to sell you a San Francisco ticket at the bargain rate, and you simply get off the plane in Salt Lake throwing away your coupon to San Francisco (or you might sidle over to a line of people waiting to buy tickets and try to *sell* your coupon for San Francisco).

4. Due to IATA monopolistic price controls, a flight including a hotel package may be considerably cheaper than a flight without accommodation. You can always throw away or give away any hotel room vouchers you won't be using.

5. Casino Gambler Flights are usually subsidized. Thus if you are going to the US, East Coast or West Coast, you could probably get a super-bargain "High Roller" flight to Atlantic City, New Jersey or Reno, Nevada. If South Africa is your destination, tie it in with Sun City, and you can probably get a big discount deal on a round trip ticket.

6. Business conventions, academic conventions, etc, all may have group package flights and hotel deals that are less costly than a do-it-yourself, point to point ticket.

7. Travel passes, such as the Eurail Pass in Europe or the Unlimited Flight Passes available to foreign passport holders in most countries, always work out cheaper than buying point to point individual tickets – if you are going to be moving around quite a bit.

8. Look into becoming a travel agent or owning a share in a travel agency. Travel agents always get discounts on everything. There is no reason why you couldn't be a travel agent (part-time). You *can't* just print up a calling card and get away with passing yourself off as

a travel agent. Why? Because you need an IATA ID number. But if you *know* a travel agent who lets you use their number, well . . . why not?

9. Currency conversion deals. Where a currency has appreciated suddenly, as the US dollar did in 1985, the pricing of tickets in the home currency remains the same, but a ticket purchased somewhere else could be had at half price. For instance, due to the high value of the Yen, in 1989, a sensible Japanese person who wanted to go to Europe or the US would take a short flight to anywhere outside of Japan and be able to get his air tickets for half the price of those bought within Japan. As the dollar was "low", the US was a fairly good place to buy tickets in 1991. In countries with a two tier market in currency, like South Africa, it is possible to change money with a friend there and buy an air ticket with "cheap money" to give youself a 75 per cent saving.

10. Other sources of discounts? They exist for anyone in the hotel or travel business and are obtained by showing a calling card identifying you as such. Then too, there are special prices for those with "student ID". Your author has been carrying around student ID for forty years, as a result of enrolling in some adult education course or other. For the over 55's there are "Senior Citizens Discounts" for which your author will also soon be eligible. In summary, with a little effort, your travel and hotel accommodation bills can be cut by half without compromising your comfort in the slightest.

11. LAST MINUTE BARGAIN SPECIALS: Our personal best deal came when passing a travel agency in Genoa Italy. We saw advertised in the window a three week Mediterranean cruise "Leaving Genoa in Three Days". The announcement was in magic marker on a handwritten poster. It said, "$12 per day per person in a four-person cabin, with window on the sea." I went in to inquire. It turned out to be on a brand new Russian ship. They were having trouble filling it up because a similar ship had just sunk off the coast of Australia. The usual rate for a cruise (with full meals and free nightlife activities) was at least five times that price. I quickly called up a friendly ex-wife and told her to pack up the kids for a surprise fun trip to Cairo, Tel Aviv, Odessa, Istanbul, Dubrovnik, Athens, Cyprus, Palma de Majorca, Morocco, Libya, Sicily, Monaco, etc. The price was certainly right! I couldn't stay at home for $12 a day.

Moral: If you keep your eye open for bargains and are flexible, you can usually find them. Sometimes calling a cruise line direct and asking about last minute bookings works wonders. I have bought last minute tickets at 20 per cent to 50 per cent off the regular price several times.

As Woody Allen once said, "The only sin in my family was paying full retail price for anything!" Travel books and newsletters often have sections on how to get different travel bargains. A book may cost a few dollars but it could save you thousands. Knowledge is cheap, ignorance is expensive.

RECOMMENDED TRAVEL BOOKS

When you visit a new country, the best way to know where to stay, what to do and see is by purchasing a good travel book. Many such books are a waste of time and money. We once bought a guide book where much of the ink was wasted on fancy phrases like, "The dining room is papered in a nonchalant mauve. '' Who cares? I want a practical guide to good values, good times and an intelligent discussion of such things as prices or quality of food and service. What are the special attractions locally? Where is a coin-op laundry or an American Express office (for cashing checks and receiving mail)?

For down-to-earth travel books and guides to good value we highly recommend:

South American Handbook, published annually and in our view *the best travel book and the best value for money published today.* If you are going to visit or live anywhere from Argentina to Mexico, or the Caribbean, this portable, pocket-sized 1,500(!) page book has EVERYTHING you need to know. Beautifully organized and indexed. Costs about $40. Published by Rand McNally in the US and is on sale at most bookstores. To order by mail write (in Great Britain), Mendip Press, Parsonage Lane, Bath BA1 1EN, England.

Arthur Frommer $25 A Day travel guides. They are available in all English Language bookstores or by mail order from 1230 Avenue of the Americas, New York City, NY 10020, USA. The books are very inexpensive paperbacks priced at around $10 each. They cover most countries and major cities. There is another series called the *Frommer Dollarwise Guides.* These are less oriented towards budget-minded travelers, but still discuss the best places to see, things to do and places to stay with an emphasis on getting good value for money. Highly recommended. We have been using them personally for thirty years!

LET'S GO Budget Travel Guides. Available in most bookstores or by mail from Harvard Student Agencies, Thayer Hall B, Cambridge, MA 02138, USA or in England: Columbus Books, 29 Elmfield Road, Bromley, Kent BR1 1LT, Great Britain. While the *LET'S GO* series of books to most European countries, Canada, the US and Mexico are aimed at backpackers and impoverished students, they also have vast amounts of information good for PTs such as train schedules, hours of admission at tourist sites, maps, museum guides, etc. These very fat paperback books are about $10 to $12 in the US.

Michelin, Baedeker, Fodor, Fieldings and Birnbaum's guides. Not as good as the above, but better than nothing.

BOOK CATALOGS

For unusual and hard to find books about personal freedom, individual liberty, alternate identification, survival, etc. we highly recommend sending $5 or equivalent in any currency (refundable with first order) to cover postage and handling to all of the following:

Scope International Ltd, 62 Murray Road, Horndean, Hants PO8 9JL, Great Britain. Fax: (44-705) 591975. Publishers of all works by W.G. Hill. We also select the best of all books of interest to PTs and offer these in our PT Booklist. Available free.

Loompanics Unlimited, PO Box 1197, Port Townsend, Washington 98368, USA.

Paladin Press, PO Box 1307, Boulder, Colorado 80306, USA.

Eden Press, PO Box 8410, Fountain Valley, California 92728, USA. Especially recommended. Don't be put off by the somewhat sleazy tabloid look of the catalog. Most of the books sold by Eden are unavailable elsewhere and quite good.

Laissez Faire Books, 942 Howard Street, San Francisco, CA 94103, USA. An excellent free catalog. We especially recommend the *Amazing Bread Machine,* a book about a man who invents a terrific product, markets it, becomes a millionaire and goes to jail for violating various technical laws. It is fiction but more true than anything you've seen on the TV news.

NEWSPAPERS AND MAGAZINES FOR EXPATRIATES

FREE subscription available to very good magazines upon application: *The International Investor,* published by the Financial Times Business Information Ltd., 102-108 Clerkenwell Road, London EC1M 5SA, Great Britain. Free to anyone interested in investments.

The Offshore Advisor by the same publisher, free to investment advisors, stockbrokers or lawyers or accountants based outside of Britain.

Not free, but worth looking at:

Resident Abroad, "The Magazine for Expatriates". Terrific classified ads and good articles. Thick, slick, monthly magazine at £51 per year, or £36 in the UK. RA, 27 Park Street, Croydon, CR0 1YD, England, GB.

Investment International, Consort House, 26 Queensway, London W2 3RX, Great Britain.

For an interesting **free** monthly magazine concerning refugees and stateless persons, and how the United Nations High Commissioner for Refugees spends its budget of one half billion dollars per year, ask for a subscription to *Refugees* from: UNHCR, PO Box 2500, CH-1211 Geneva 2 Depot, Switzerland. The magazine is glossy, full of photographs and will make you glad that you have several passports and are not a refugee! Ask for it in any of the following languages: English, Italian, Greek, Spanish, Japanese or German. An interesting feature is regular stories of famous refugees like the scientist Albert Einstein and Victor Hugo, the French novelist. **There are articles of direct interest to the passport seeker from time to time.**

For an up to date, thick monthly bulletin of about 400 pages on passports, visas, exit permits, currency controls, pets, how many cigars you can import duty free – and information about a **zillion stupid rules and regulations you never knew existed** go to any major travel agent and ask to look at their *TIM* or *Travel Information Manual.* It is a joint publication of the fourteen member airlines of the IATA. Almost all airline ticket offices and travel agents subscribe. For most people, you won't need a personal copy if you just want to get the rules in a couple of countries. If you want one for your own personal reference and don't want to subscribe for a year at 246 Dutch Guilders, write to: **TIM, PO Box 902, 2130EA Hoofdorp, Netherlands.** If you mention Bill Hill's *Passport Report* and include 42.50 Dutch Guilders (approximately US $20) **they will send you a single copy.** It offers a complete explanation of the visa requirements of every country on earth. Unlike *The Passport Report,* it says nothing about *how* to obtain passports, etc. **The purpose of the TIM book is mainly to enable airline employees to check the documents of passengers and refuse passage to those whose documents are not in order** or who are carrying things that are illegal in the destination country. In many cases, airlines must pay huge fines for people they transport (£1,000 per passenger in the UK for example, plus a free return trip) who arrive in a country without proper papers.

RECOMMENDED NEWSPAPERS FOR THE PT

The International Herald Tribune, Paris.
The Financial Times, London.
The Wall Street Journal, New York.
The European, London.

These are available at all international hotels and magazine stores.

Also, almost every international anglophile community has local English language newspapers. These are very good for finding apartments, handymen, concerts, art exhibits, etc.

INFORMATION AND INSPIRATIONAL BOOKS FOR THE PT

BOOKS BY W.G. HILL
Currently in print: *The Lloyd's Report* – How To Become a Member of Lloyd's of London. *The Monaco Report* – Live Like a Prince in Monte Carlo, Monaco for $500 per Month. *The Campione Report* – Switzerland's Semi-Tropical Tax Haven. *Gibraltar/Andorra. Think Like a Tycoon* – How to Make A Million in Three Years or Less. *The Free Car Report.* All are available from Scope International Ltd, 62 Murray Road, Horndean, Hants PO8 9JL, Great Britain. Fax: (44-705) 591975. Any single report £60. A current brochure is FREE.

PT 1 and *PT 2* are of course my best and longest reports. Once you have a second passport you'll want to know WHERE to live, WHO can manage your money, HOW to earn a substantial tax-free income, WHAT businesses are suitable for a person tied to no particular country, WHEN are the best seasons and WHY you need to have two or three places to live in order to avoid taxes and take advantage of the best the world has to offer. The price of each is £60.00 (US $100). See the back pages for further details and an order form. These reports are a continuation of *The Passport Report* and an expansion of the concepts here. *PT 2* has only been recently released. It is a great hands-on companion to *PT 1.*

The Bridge Across Forever and *Jonathan Livingston Seagull,* by Richard Bach, published by William Morrow, New York. International best-sellers available in most bookstores.

How I Found Freedom in an Unfree World, Harry Brown, published by Avon Books, 959 Eighth Avenue, NYC, USA. Paperback available in bookstores. We regard this as another source of inspiration for PTs and recommend it most highly!

Free to Choose, Milton Freidman, also published by Avon Books.

AIRCRAFT, YACHT AND CAR LICENSES

The PT has special problems in this regard and there are some unique special solutions to get licenses, insurance and so on in such a way as will insulate and allow your personal whereabouts and net worth to be private. Please contact Scope International for advice. Give the year and make of your boat, aircraft or car and where it is usually used. Please include the standard consultancy fee of £200 and we will refer you to a specialist consultant.

DIPLOMATIC APPOINTMENTS

It violates the PT's rule about low profile to be an Honorary Consul or diplomat. However, this disadvantage may be overcome by the diplomatic immunity, special passports, greater credibility, official status, free car license plates and tax-free status.

There are three ways to gain diplomatic appointments:

a)   Campaign for them (since they are like any other political appointive offices) and hope for the best.

b)   Make a well placed donation (US $25,000 to US $50,000) to the favorite charity of some politician who has the power to appoint you and get your appointment instantly.

c)   If you wish to spend US $20,000 - US $80,000, Scope can recommend an agent to handle your application.

We know that any candidate who has a presentable home, knows how to eat with a knife and fork and above all has a net worth of at least US $750,000 can get appointments ranging from Ambassador to Minister Plenipotentiary. For those with lesser ambitions, the post of Honorary Consul General is available in most places from a large variety of countries. Contact Scope International for details.

TITLES OF NOBILITY

Have you always wanted to be a real Count, Knight, Prince, Duke or Earl? There are many crooks in the business who will sell you worthless paper. Also, you could call yourself anything you wanted to, but a genuine title of nobility can be acquired in about six months. Through purchase, *marriage blanche* or adoption, you can legally get a title from the lowest (Lord of the Manor) at about £50,000, to the highest – Prince Pretender to the Throne of Albania (if not already taken). Recently, a Dukedom in Sicily was for sale, carrying with it a castle, moat, fortifications, small private army, art collection, antique furniture, the right to appoint Abbotts of certain churches and about 1,000 acres of vineyards. The price was a mere $2 million – a bargain for the land alone. Quite a few opportunities to obtain "ceremonial titles" exist in France, Germany, Italy and other republics.

More expensive opportunities carrying with them real status and an actual (usually ceremonial) role in government exist in Spain, Belgium, Netherlands, Luxembourg, Liechtenstein, Monaco and The Vatican. There, hereditary monarchs and an aristocratic class still exist and have certain privileges recognized by law.

Titles are arranged by purchase, marriages, appointment, donation or adoption. They can be passed on to your heirs, and you in turn can adopt other people. Gucci, Pucci, The Prince of Liechtenstein, The King of Sweden, Lord Rothschild, the Seigneur of Sark and in fact most aristocrats (or their ancestors) acquired their titles by adoption, direct purchase or by doing financial favors for those with the power of appointment – just as you would be asked to do. Don't waste your money on professional advice unless you are prepared to spend at least £3,000 on the project to gain a title.

The use of a legal aristocratic title is sometimes an economic benefit. Obviously, in promoting some snob-appeal item the Prince of Liechtenstein's personal cuvée, estate bottled wine will command a higher price than "Padrone Corleone's Chianti", or any other *vin ordinaire*.

All previous providers of titles have proved unreliable or are scams, As at the time of going to press in 1993 we cannot recommend any legitimate source of titles. If you know of one, please drop the editor a line.

Comments, questions, additions and constructive criticism should be sent to:
Scope International, 62 Murray Road, Waterlooville, Hampshire PO8 9JL, Great Britain

OTHER REPORTS
PUBLISHED
by
SCOPE INTERNATIONAL LTD.

PT VOLUME ONE – THE PERPETUAL TRAVELLER
A COHERENT PLAN FOR A STRESS-FREE, HEALTHY AND PROSPEROUS LIFE WITHOUT GOVERNMENT INTERFERENCE, TAXES OR COERCION
4th Edition Revised and Expanded for 1992/93
by Dr. W.G. Hill

PT stands for Prepared Thoroughly, Perpetual Tourist, Prior Taxpayer and much, much more.

People of intelligence and wealth owe it to themselves and their descendants to have five 'flags'. No one with common sense should give all their assets or allegiance to just one flag. Why? Because no country nor any government has ever survived more than a few generations without totally annihilating itself or its own middle and upper classes. Even in that 'last bastion of capitalism', the USA, people of property were thrice forced to flee the country. In 1775, one third (the entire middle and ruling class), was forced to move to Canada; these were the Tories who supported England in the Revolution. In 1865, it happened again; all large land owners (who supported the Confederacy in the Civil War) were forced to migrate to Mexico, Europe or South America. In the post 1917 period, prohibition, confiscatory taxes, compulsory military service, and suffocating government regulations once again caused wealthy Americans (and Europeans) to seek new flags. **Five million of the wealthiest and most productive Americans now live abroad.** Eighty-five percent of all liquid private wealth is already anonymously registered 'offshore'. CAN **YOU** AFFORD TO HAVE ONLY ONE FLAG? - NOT IF YOUR NET WORTH IS OVER US$ 250,000.

THE FIVE FLAGS OF THE PT

Flag 1. BUSINESS BASE. These are the places where you make your money. They must be different from the place where you 'legally reside', your personal fiscal domicile. Your business base should be in a place that gives a tax holiday to your business, freedom from over-regulation, and good access to contacts, labour markets or materials needed for conducting your business. London, Tokyo, and New York are the Big Apples for Finance and Insurance. Zurich, Hong Kong, Singapore, Frankfurt and Milan are among the second-rank contenders.

Flag 2. PASSPORT AND CITIZENSHIP. These should be from a country unconcerned about its offshore citizens or what they do outside its borders. There must be no tax or military requirement for non-residents. PASSPORTS MUST BE AVAILABLE TO FOREIGNERS.

Flag 3. DOMICILE. This should be a tax haven with good communications; a place where wealthy, productive people can be creative, live, relax, prosper and enjoy themselves, preferably with bank secrecy and no threat of war or revolution. Monaco, Campione, The Channel Islands, Andorra, Bermuda, Thailand and Gibraltar are all recommended.

Flag 4. ASSET REPOSITORY. This should be a place from which assets, securities and business affairs can be managed by proxy. Requirements are: The availability of highly competent financial managers, confidential banking, no taxes on non-residents, or non-citizens. One of the best places in which to plant your fourth flag would be Liechtenstein. Other possibilities would be Austria, Luxembourg, Switzerland, New York or London.

Flag 5. PLAYGROUNDS. These are places where you would actually physically spend your time. Normally, because of legal restrictions on how long one may stay without being inducted as a taxpayer, it is necessary to have from two to four playgrounds. One might try to avoid spending more than 90 days per year in any one of them. We look for quality of life. **For 'no nukes' and good fishing:** New Zealand. **For the most interesting sex life imaginable:** Thailand, Costa Rica or the Philippines. **Superb climate:** California. **Best food:** French Riviera or Hong Kong. **Stimulating cities:** Paris, London, San Francisco. **To buy the best things at the cheapest prices:** Singapore, Hong Kong (or Denmark, for cars).

PT fully explains all Five Flags. It is a complete guide to getting the most out of life that this Earth can offer. Each individual should have at least two, but ideally three toeholds in each 'flag'. For example:

1.   A BUSINESS OR SOURCE OF INCOME IN New York, London and Singapore.
2.   A PASSPORT FROM Canada, Brazil, Italy and Australia.
3.   A LEGAL OR FISCAL ADDRESS IN Monaco, Campione or the Channel Islands.
4.   A BANK ACCOUNT OR OTHER ASSETS REGISTERED ANONYMOUSLY IN Liechtenstein trusts or foundations.
5.   FRIENDS AND FUN IN Paris, Bangkok, Manila, Buenos Aires, Sydney and San Francisco.

ISBN 0 906619 24 6.

How to do it? . . . Read *PT – The Perpetual Traveller,* available from Scope International Ltd, 62 Murray Road, Waterlooville, Hampshire PO8 9JL, UK. Price – £60 UK Sterling (or equivalent) by credit card, cash, cheque or banker's draft. Price includes postage and packing, and please allow 6-8 weeks for surface delivery outside UK. For quicker air mail add £15 or equivalent (allow 3-4 weeks for delivery). Ordering details and order form are supplied on the last two pages of this Report.

REMEMBER: Consultations with specialists are available to all purchasers and our no nonsense money back guarantee applies to all our publications.

PT – VOLUME II
THE PRACTICE: FREEDOM AND PRIVACY TACTICS FOR THE NINETIES – AND BEYOND
1st Edition, NEW for 1993
by Dr. W.G. Hill

Now is the time to take proper precautions, says W.G. Hill, father of P.T. and the world's leading expert on personal tax havens, in this startling book. Contrary to the popular image projected by mainstream media and most governments, your taxes are shooting up and your personal freedom is being taken away, bit by bit. Anyone with a visible pocket will become a victim. The most dangerous place on earth is wherever *you* are. But in this hands-on guide to low profile and privacy, PT-style, W.G. Hill shows you how to regain your lost freedom. In more than 200 fact-filled pages, he teaches you the little-known tactics and techniques of living tax free. For the first time ever in print, he gives away all his privacy secrets and shares with you unique insights on how to escape what he terms "the scam called government". This explosive volume deals with matters that no other books ever dared in a practical, hands-on manner. You will learn all the world's unknown ins and outs of getting, and keeping, a life free from problems, frustrations, harrassment, extortion, lawsuits and the implications and ramifications of all of these – the works.

DO YOU HAVE THE ESSENTIAL KNOWLEDGE FOR A FREE LIFE?
Answer these simple questions to determine if you have the information and tools necessary for a rich life in complete freedom:
* Do you know the world's six best ways to transfer cash across borders? Do you know how to triple your interest earnings and gain when currencies change?
* Do you have a collection of untraceable credit cards? Do you have foreign credit cards in a selection of names other than your own?
* Do you know the how-to of no-name bank accounts, where ID is not needed?
* Can you name the ten best low profile mail tips? Do you have a "dead drop"?
* Do you own and operate at least one PT—PC in a foreign jurisdiction?
* Will you be able to keep your money safe despite the coming world tax-squad, the new OECD treaties and the international laws already in place? Do you even know all the dangers of the nineties and beyond? Are you willing to run the risk of asset stripping and long jail sentences for a "crime" you did not commit' a so-called crime invented by money-grabbing world governments?

If you answered "no" to one or more of these questions, please do not waste any time in getting *PT Volume II*, the all-new 1993 tome for tax exiles and perpetual travellers. In five lengthy parts, W.G. Hill thoroughly covers ALL privacy and low profile questions – even those you never dared ask. From such simple things as securing your cars or using all the unknown loopholes of air travel, Hill firmly moves on to invisible ink 1993-style and words guns, crossing borders *sans* passports and what he calls the Ten Privacy Tenets. This book even gives you the inside facts of essential low profile gadgets and some privacy paraphernalia that would probably be illegal if your government knew that they existed!

Contents also include... True, tried and tested: W.G. Hill's own telephone tactics, now with a PT shortlist for phone secrecy... All about mobile phones, Super Phones, add-on gadgets for your phones... How best to transmit faxes... The art of compartmentalizing your life... Never-before-told maildrop secrets... Secure communications... Also: The secret trust, onshore or offshore? And so much, much more. **Stop Press:** This volume now comes complete with a bonus – W.G. Hill's complete guide to banking worldwide, including some secret, supersafe havens for smart money only. Plus a complete course in bearer shares and bonds.

In his introduction, Dr W.G. Hill writes: *This book is dedicated to showing people of intelligence how to stay FREE in every sense of the word. While you may consider yourself a "free man" (or woman), chances are that you are not. The bad news is that even if you are currently living a fairly normal and happy life, events may conspire to turn against you and wind up stealing your money, your freedom – and ultimately, your life. Today, you are a sitting duck – unless you take precautions now. The good news, on the other hand, is that there are plenty of things that you may do yourself to thwart whatever dangers are likely to pop up – in advance, and with just a modicum of effort and expense.* Are you ready for true, undiluted, unrestrained freedom in all personal and financial matters?

Do you believe that "an ounce of preparation is worth about a ton of cure"? If so *PT Volume II ("The Practice")* is for you. If you are not content just "letting things happen" then it makes perfect sense to make sure that they don't – or, if they still do, that this will not be to your extreme disadvantage.

ISBN 0 906619 40-8.

PT - Volume II is available from Scope International Ltd., 62 Murray Road, Waterlooville, Hampshire PO8 9JL, UK. Price – £60 UK Sterling (or equivalent) by credit card, cash, cheque or banker's draft. Price includes postage and packing, and please allow 6-8 weeks for surface delivery outside UK. For quicker air mail service add £15 or equivalent (allow 3-4 weeks for delivery). Ordering details and order form are supplied on the last two pages of this Report.

Right now, in his brand new first edition of the PT-sequel, W.G. Hill gives you the low down, no-nonsense, straight facts about how to set up those seemingly elusive safeguards that may shield you in times of trouble. If you put the information in this book to practical use you will find that you, too, can keep your money, your freedom and your life. And forever be Home Free, PT.

REMEMBER: Personal consultations are available to all purchasers and our no nonsense money back guarantee applies to all our publications.

THINK LIKE A TYCOON
HOW TO MAKE A MILLION OR MORE IN THREE YEARS OR LESS!
3rd Edition Revised for 1992/1993
by Dr. W.G. Hill

Do you sincerely want to be rich without knocking yourself out? Do you want respect? Do you need love?

Learn the incredible secret that will bring you the *happiness only money can buy.*

You CAN become a millionaire in three years or less while, at the same time, having three times more fun out of life. Of course you are sceptical. So read on.

My name is W.G. Hill. I did not make my millions (like some authors) by writing books about things I have not done myself personally. Starting from scratch, without money, special skills, contacts or luck I founded eight totally unrelated part-time FUN businesses. I saw **each** of them earn me over a million Pounds **each** in three years or less.

While I was making all this money, I managed to go to an average of five parties a week, plus two or three concerts, plays or movies. **SEX!** My love life didn't suffer either – as I had more "companionship" in a year than most men have in a lifetime. What was the sex-appeal secret of a grumpy, overweight, middle-aged bald guy with crooked teeth and thick glasses? **I was doing things that appeared exciting and glamorous to women. I *was* the action and they *came* to me.** There is no Aphrodisiac that comes anywhere close to the appeal of **MONEY** and **POWER!**

When thousands of people depend upon you economically, some will fawn and dote upon your every word. Some try to gain your good will with gifts, sexual favors, bribes and offers you can't refuse. *When you can refuse, you know that you have arrived.* When you can go to the best restaurants in town with your friends and order anything you fancy without considering the price, when you can travel the world free as a bird, you know that you have ARRIVED! If you can *live anywhere* in the world, have any partners and friends you want, Tell off or ignore government bureaucracy, union officials, politicians and former bosses, then you know that you have found FREEDOM!

With money, everything else will fall into place. *Try it!*

Would you trade your present life for what I have just described? Then read on. Years ago I was broke, physically in bad shape and seriously in debt. Then I found concealed in a window box a dusty tattered old book. It had been hidden in the summer cottage of my close friend's father. He was a very rich and powerful man. Later on I discovered that he owed his good fortune to his own discovery of this book many years earlier. Reading the timeless volume I discovered an amazing formula that every single super-rich person seems to have used to gain wealth. It was so incredibly easy to understand that I started to apply it within twenty four hours. In six months I was a millionaire. I never had to work again.

In Chapter One I learned how to avoid mistakes that keep 94 per cent of the population just plodding along in a miserable rut – dissatisfied with everything. In Chapter Two I discovered how to "Think Like a Tycoon" – how to set and achieve goals. Chapter Three taught me how to *achieve these goals quickly* – not by moving up some corporate ladder for 30 years. I saw how to make things happen *fast* plus how to strike it very big in two or three years (at the most). Chapter Four taught me how to use credit and borrow unlimited funds (usually interest free) from bankers and investors. Another important chapter told me why all the "investments" I thought of as sound are really only for suckers.

Although the book I read was written two hundred years earlier, it was like Aladdin's Magic Lamp for me and changed my life dramatically. After two hours of reading I never earned less than a million a year for the next 30 years. Other millionaires went up and down like a yo-yo, but I just kept having more and more fun by getting richer and richer.

Now after many adventures, at the age of 49 I have retired (in great comfort I might add) to write my memoirs. Before doing so I wanted to pass on to other ambitious lads the age-old secrets that made me a millionaire at the age of 24.

I took the original timeless secrets of wealth, transformed them into modern English and added my own experiences and witty humor. Then I tested out the formula on my best friend, a poverty stricken but talented jazz musician. Let's call my buddy "Warren Trumpet". For years my friend had been insisting that he sincerely wanted to be very rich. I gave him the manuscript of my book. In six months he was a millionaire. In two years more he had gross annual earnings of over FOUR MILLION DOLLARS. As a jazz musician, even with a hit record, *The Girl From Ipanema,* he had never earned more than twenty thousand a year. Warren never had much of an IQ. A highschool dropout, he used to read and write like a ten year old. But that didn't stop him from using my unpublished manuscript to become one of the richest men in the world.

If he can do it, you can do it.

Truth is, I'd like to give away these secrets. If everyone used them, the world would be a richer, more productive and happy place. But I learned from the SPCA (Society for Prevention of Cruelty to Animals) that if you give away a puppy dog, that dog is more likely to be mistreated and kicked around than if you *SELL* that same dog for $100.

I want to give you respect, value and seriously apply this incredible, exciting formula. *I will not give it to you for free.* On the back page is the order form you must complete and send to Scope International now, if you want to get a copy of my sumptuously bound, gold blocked, limited edition of *Think Like A Tycoon. How to Make a Million or More in Three Years or Less.* (Personal registered copy, not for resale).

ISBN 0 906619 30 0

THE CAMPIONE REPORT
SWITZERLAND'S SECRET SEMI-TROPICAL TAX HAVEN
3rd Edition Revised and Expanded for 1993
by Dr. W.G. Hill

W.G. Hill, the world's leading expert on personal tax havens predicts that Campione, a strange accident of history, anomaly of geography and climatic freak, will be one of the most fashionable tax havens of the next decade.

This report shows anyone how to become a legal resident of this soon-to-be discovered enclave of the super-rich. *Campione is a unique semi-autonomous community located entirely within Switzerland.* But as a separate country, it is **not subject to any Swiss laws, taxes or tax treaties**. Strange as it may seem, becoming a resident of Campione gives one all the advantages of being Swiss, but none of the disadvantages. No compulsory lifetime military camps, no heavy Swiss income taxes, none of the disadvantages of being (as Switzerland is) *outside* the European Community.

Campione is a part of the EC with all the benefits of passport free, visa free travel. Its citizens have the right to travel, work, engage in commerce or perform services anywhere in the EC. Best of all, Campione has "in practice" no income taxes. This Special Report shows you how to achieve these tax benefits even without acquiring residency.

Campione also is one of the few places in the EC where there is no VAT (value added tax), which seriously reduces the price of goods and services.

The Campione Report tells all the secrets, but here's some more highlights:

Campione enjoys a freak Mediterranean climate found only in the small Italian Swiss Province of Ticino, where Campione is located. Because it is on lovely Lake Lugano and considerably lower in altitude than the rest of mountainous Switzerland, it's white sand beach supports a small grove of tropical palm trees. Your 'sea-view' villa in Campione will be gently caressed by balmy yet non-humid tropical breezes. However, although Campione is in a 'Banana Belt', nearby ski slopes are clearly visible. Half an hour on the local funicular railway takes you up to the powder runs!

The cost of living is less than half that of Monte Carlo, Paris, London or New York. There is no pollution, industry or crime. The mountain and lake scenery is breathtaking. The sub-Alpine climate and year-round temperature is second to none. A vibrant social and cultural life is a few minutes away in Lugano or Locarno by regular ferry boat. Take the superhighway due south from Campione and in forty five minutes you can hear the world's best grand opera at La Scala or visit the fabulous shops of downtown Milan. There are more bankers and stockbrokers locally in Lugano and Chiasso than you can count. The area is second only to Zurich in the proliferation of financial services. All Tokyo, London and Wall Street publications are available at many stands on the day of publication. Locally you can eat in several hundred ethnic gourmet restaurants and see first run English language films in a movie palace the likes of which no longer exist in most big cities. Most of the action is in Lugano, ten minutes across the lake by 'vaporetto' bus-boat, or over the one mile long causeway by car.

Shopping, dining, night clubbing, golf, horses, tennis clubs, spectator sports, every pleasure known to man is available. Modern hospitals and internationally known clinics attract the wealthiest people of the world to the area for a variety of cures and treatments. As to morality and personal eccentricity, local Italian Swiss are easy-going and more tolerant than their German Swiss brothers fifty miles to the north.

For an inexpensive, stress-free, tax-free life, Dr. Hill suggests, "Move to Campione this year. Buy property soon, before it is over-publicised and discovered." *You could probably make twenty times on your money over the next decade in this semi-autonomous town that practically pays you to live there.*Only a short drive from Italy, France, Austria, Liechtenstein and Germany, Campione is still a sleepy peaceful and unspoiled tax haven. But it appears to be heading rapidly towards becoming another Monaco. The ground floor is now. The present population of 3,000 is just 10 per cent of Monaco's. Monte Carlo has 35,000 people on a similar square mile of waterfront. Campione in 1993 is like Monte Carlo in 1949, before it became 'in' and developed into a mini-Manhattan.

This Special Report gives the who, what, where, when and why. Hill feels that Campione is a great place to escape to, while it is still relatively uncongested. In five or ten years as it becomes overcrowded, it will be the place you can escape from. But your little villa would hopefully be a million dollar hotel or apartment site by then. In the meantime, you have a conveniently located European home base, you can pick up an EC passport and you can enjoy life in Campione, one of the most unusual spots on Earth.

The Campione Report is available from Scope International Ltd., 62 Murray Road, Waterlooville, Hampshire PO8 9JL, UK. Price £60 UK Sterling (or equivalent). See last two pages in this report for ordering details.

ISBN 0 906619 22 X

THE MONACO REPORT
HOW TO BECOME A LEGAL RESIDENT OF TAX-FREE MONTE CARLO, MONACO
5th Edition
Revised and Expanded for 1992
by Dr. W.G. Hill

There are many places where you could live and be free of income taxes, inheritance and estate taxes and real estate taxes. But most are isolated, too cold, too hot, too Third World, or simply too dull. Monaco is the only tax haven located a short drive from several truly major cities, and at the same time in a resort area well known for its glitter and the non-stop action of major gambling casinos. It boasts fine beaches, golf and tennis clubs. This report looks at tax havens in general and compares Monaco with the runners-up: Andorra, Bermuda, Campione and Liechtenstein. It provides a simple test to see if Monaco is 'your cup of tea'. Tax havens are discussed in a way that shows how they may be used to advantage by middle class people (not just the very wealthy) fed up with high taxes and government controls. But more importantly, a new possibility is discussed: the option of being a 'Permanent Traveller', spending up to six months a year in the most enjoyable places of the world, being able to avoid taxes entirely because you are legally classified as a tourist. The report also goes into the question of how to earn a living, manage a business, handle investments, form corporations or trusts, etc.

The Monaco Report documents how, contrary to popular belief, it is possible to live in a hotel, eat regularly, and have a pleasant month in Monaco on a budget of £10 a day. But as a practical matter, a liveable apartment with a sea-view will cost about £300 a month – considerably less than half the price of similar accommodation in New York or London. And the weather is far better! There are a few problems in paradise, one of them being the French Government. But for those who read this Special Report, the effect of French fiscal measures can be completely and legally avoided by not making the mistake of transferring substantial assets to Monaco banks and fiduciaries. The moves to win the game are all in *The Monaco Report*.

The surprisingly simple legal steps to take to become a resident and obtain the coveted Monaco Identity Card are revealed. It is absolutely free, the main requirement being the ability to support yourself without taking away a Monegasque's job. There is no net worth requirement and once in Monaco, many interesting jobs and opportunities are available. Also covered are such questions as whether to buy or rent; how to buy a luxury car for less than half the usual price, and register it tax-free in Monaco; exchange controls; what will happen in 1992; meeting new friends or single men and women; why Americans have a particularly good deal in Monaco; even advice on getting a good parking spot . . .

The Monaco Report is masterfully written and is designed to spare many months of seeking answers and save many thousands of dollars getting the wrong ones!

A comprehensive appendix includes: Attorneys, stockbrokers, management, business and finance consultants, banks, medical practitioners, dentists, motor dealers and garages, supermarkets, hotels (with price ranges), restaurants, cinemas and theatres.

ISBN 0 906619 20 3.

The Monaco Report is available from Scope International Ltd., 62 Murray Road, Waterlooville, Hampshire PO8 9JL, UK. Price – £60 UK Sterling (or equivalent) by credit card, cash, cheque or banker's draft. Price includes postage and packing, and please allow 6-8 weeks for surface delivery outside UK. For quicker air mail service add £15 or equivalent (allow 3-4 weeks for delivery). Ordering details and order form are supplied on the last two pages of this Report.

REMEMBER: Consultations with specialists are available to all purchasers and our no nonsense money back guarantee applies to all our publications.

THE LLOYD'S REPORT
HOW TO EARN A SUBSTANTIAL SECOND INCOME
UNDERWRITING INSURANCE
6th Edition
Revised and Expanded for 1992
by Dr. W.G. Hill

How would you like to earn an additional £10,000+ a year? No investment, time nor expertise is required, but a minimum net worth (or means) of UK £250,000 is needed to qualify. There is no work to do; no expertise is required. Quite simply, you fill out a form, and in due course you become a member or 'Name' at Lloyd's. You could expect an income of up to UK £200,000 per year for the rest of your life; doors will open to excellent asset management opportunities, plus much invaluable business information and social contacts.

But what about the risk? You have read stories about members who have been driven into bankruptcy by their unlimited liability. Let's put those horror stories into perspective: In round numbers, Lloyd's has about 26,000 members. In an average year, a few hundred of them walk away with up to a million dollars in profit (without any investment whatsoever). Thousands of others might deposit cheques in excess of $100,000; and the average Joe Member could expect to make around $30,000 from an exposure of £350,000 for which a letter of credit of £136,500 is required. In a bad year like 1988, and the two we have just experienced, 1989 and 1990 (Lloyd's always take 2-3 years to close an account), most Names will have taken out stop-loss policies to limit their loss to 10 per cent of their total allocation; but some will find themselves writing cheques in excess of $100,000 after experiencing losses on some syndicates in excess of 100 per cent of their individual allocations.

Compare this with an average year in the stock or commodities markets: A very small percentage of the players (usually insiders) make millions or even billions. The majority are lucky to earn 10-20 per cent on capital they are risking. In a bad year like 1987, almost everyone lost from 30 per cent to 100 per cent of their money. In any year, like all gamblers, those on the margin are typically wiped out eventually, with the figure in commodities being around 87 per cent of all leveraged speculators losing 100 per cent (or more) of their capital in four years or less. A typical stock market player lasts a little longer.

There are no sure things in life, but Lloyd's membership as we explain in more detail in the Report, comes close. No investment, a double return on capital. Every twenty years or so, it is likely that a Name will have to dig in his pocket to cover a loss; but this can be hedged by setting up reserves which receive favourable tax treatment in the UK; taking out personal stop-loss insurance; joining mutual insurance pools; or choosing syndicates very carefully with help from experts as well as reputable members agent. Clients of Dr. Hill will probably have to "dig" less deep than the average Name because we can recommend expert sources that can steer Names away from poorly rated syndicates and badly run underwriting agencies.

The bad publicity is really quite unreflective of the true situation. It simply isn't nearly as bad as it is painted. Yet the current rash of newspaper horror stories do provide an opportunity! Faint-hearted, newer, easily panicked members are in fact dropping out like scared, exhausted rabbits. With just a bit more stamina they could finish in the money. Their departures are your opportunity. For the first time in many years, there are many openings on better syndicates. Instead of waiting five or ten years to get a good spread of profitable, highly rated syndicates, a new member today, with proper guidance can position himself on the ground floor. New members can get set for a real whiz-bang ascent when the self-adjusting insurance market recovers and again becomes profitable – as it always does.

Dr. Hill thinks Lloyd's at the bottom, in the midst of all the bad news is a better bet now than at any time since the last trough, in the mid 1960s.

When Hill was first asked by a potential Lloyd's candidate to investigate Lloyd's, he was very skeptical of such a 'perfect arrangement'. However he accepted the challenge of doing an in-depth study of Lloyd's as a business opportunity. The client paid $6000 for a Special Report, that, with his permission we have published, now in its sixth edition.

Surprisingly, Hill concluded that although a Lloyd's membership was not a one-way street to riches, it was one of the better and least risky business opportunities in the world today. He discovered a secret about all the bad publicity: It was very much like the frequent public relations releases of a Las Vegas Casino announcing big winners. Insurance underwriting is much like owning a gambling casino. Big losses are good business. Rates are set to cover losses and yield a profit. Without losses there would be no insurance industry. Hill's client eventually joined Lloyd's. This client's later experiences show all the positive and negative aspects of Lloyd's membership.

There were some surprises, and the procedure for becoming a member was an unusual experience, to put it mildly. In many conversations with people connected with Lloyd's the client was discouraged from joining. The reason for this is another secret Hill discovered in the course of his investigation . . . .

Exact steps to be taken and sources to contact are provided in the report including the names, addresses and telephone numbers of all the Underwriting Agencies at Lloyd's. Here is all you need to know. We found this to be possibly the most fascinating of Dr. Hill's superior reports.

ISBN 0 906619 18 1.

The Lloyd's Report is available from Scope International Ltd., 62 Murray Road, Waterlooville, Hampshire PO8 9JL, UK. Price – £60 UK Sterling (or equivalent) by credit card, cash, cheque or banker's draft. Ordering details and order form are supplied on the last two pages of this Report.

REMEMBER: Consultations with specialists are available to all purchasers and our no nonsense money back guarantee applies to all our publications.

Two reports in one volume – Double value for money:
THE ANDORRA AND SECRET ENCLAVES REPORT
UNDISCOVERED FISCAL PARADISES OF THE PYRENEES
&
THE GIBRALTAR REPORT
IDEAL BASE FOR YOUR OFFSHORE COMPANY?
2nd Edition Revised for 1993
by Dr. W.G. Hill

W.G. Hill, the world's leading expert on personal tax havens has found another place where real estate values should double in a very short period. It is the ultimate personal tax haven of Andorra, a medieval principality secluded from the rest of the world, yet a short drive from sparkling beaches, mountain lakes and the Mediterranean. The nearest big city is that bustling European economic powerhouse, Barcelona. Andorra is a hidden haven for the few in the know. Property is still affordable. Living costs are low. Natural beauty, powder snow in winter, miles of ski and hiking trails plus the lowest prices in Europe on a huge selection of goods makes this Mini-Switzerland the top personal tax haven in Europe. It's a place important for what it doesn't have: Andorra has never had an economic depression, nor AIDS, nor random violence, nor police intimidation. No nuclear plants are in the vicinity. Andorra has no leftist political parties and hardly has any government at all. Of the 60,000 people that inhabit this alpine tax refuge, the number employed by the state is less than 100, or 0.4% of the population. There are no taxes whatsoever! Labor unions are strictly forbidden. There is no hint of a "socialist mentality" among the natives. The unregulated banking system is among the safest in the world. It is sound, prosperous, computerised, streamlined, discreet and very customer oriented. Some of the wealthiest people in the world prefer Andorra's low profile banks to those of secretive Switzerland.

In the all new second edition which has been revised and expanded for 1993, W.G. Hill reveals the secrets of two Spanish enclaves. Os and Llivia are both small, provincial towns hidden in the mountains of Andorra. In fact, they are only accessible via Andorra. These secret enclaves could be your key to tax freedom. For those interested in becoming prior-taxpayers of North European countries (Sweden, Denmark, Germany), these little spots could provide the ideal solution. As most of our readers are aware, these countries mandate that if one of their citizens moves to a tax haven, he must continue paying taxes to his country of origin. By implementing the plan spelled out in this report, you could achieve the best of both worlds, all the conveniences of a tax haven, but the fiscal address of high-tax country. Best of all, property prices are even less than those in Andorra-proper.

Dr. W.G. Hill shows you where, how and when to buy bargain property in this unknown alpine paradise and its enclaves. Now is the time to get in, he says. The prices in Campione tripled within two years of his special report being issued. Will it be the same in Andorra? In Andorra there is no crime. There is free health care for everyone, including old age pensions. Mail is free, too! Schools are free for everyone. Most entertainment is free. Dining out in a first class restaurant before a free classical music concert is cheap. Andorra has 250 restaurants, some of Europe's best skiing and the largest number of Mercedes limousines *per capita* in the world. Its people are affluent. They do not pay any taxes at all. Andorra is cosmopolitan. More than two-thirds of all residents are wealthy, selfmade foreigners, most of whom moved to Andorra because they were fed up with government red tape and destructive bureaucracy.

Chapters include: Andorra as a Sex Haven, Shopping in Europe's Bargain Basement (where they give you a discount when you buy with credit cards), Why you should **not** form an Andorran corporation, How to get local passports, and much, much more. Andorra is located on the north eastern border of Spain, facing southern France.

On the Spanish *Costa del Sol,* on the south west coast, is Gibraltar. This sovereign British Crown Colony is fast becoming the preferred European tax haven for offshore corporations. "The Rock of Gibraltar" is the ideal place to register your tax haven company, your trust, your car, yacht or airplane. In this report, W.G. Hill examines in great detail the financial advantages of Gibraltar. He also considers quality of living, the real estate market, where to get the most interesting car deals in Europe and how to get the best out of life in Gibraltar. This corporate tax haven is prospering after a 25 year border embargo with Spain. In more than 20 in-depth chapters, Dr. Hill covers all the secrets of this unique place where you can drive without a driving license. Where setting up a tax haven corporation "offshore" and buying Branston Pickle, British Bangers or H.J. Heinz tinned soups is easy. He answers questions like: "Yachts, casinos – Is this another Monaco?", "Gibraltar, the new Hong Kong?", "Is Gibraltar a Sex Haven?" and "Should you get a Gibraltar Passport?" Other chapters include: Confidential Banking in Gibraltar, How to Set Up Your Own Tax Haven Corporation, Owning a Home in Next-Door Spain plus Gibraltar Secret: Why the British Army Pays Your Bills when you Live on Gibraltar.

The Andorra & Gibraltar Report, is available from Scope International Ltd., 62 Murray Road, Waterlooville, Hampshire PO8 9JL, UK. Price £60. See last two pages in this report for ordering details.

ISBN 0 906619 31 9

THE FREE CAR REPORT
HOW TO OWN A NEW LUXURY CAR EVERY YEAR OF YOUR LIFE, FOR FREE
3rd Edition Revised and Updated for 1992/1993
by Dr. W.G. Hill

In this unique and original report the author shows readers how, during the past thirty years he has owned a free Rolls, Ferrari, and several Mercedes – a new one each year – spending absolutely nothing for these fine motor vehicles. Hill shares his secrets explaining how he learned where cars could be bought "tax free" at the lowest factory list prices in the world. He reveals WHY prices in DENMARK are as low as half of what they are in other countries. Yes, the biggest part of this confidential registered report is buying tax-free at Denmark's low prices. Now that you know this secret, why buy our newest special report? The answer is simply that there is more to it than just buying a car in Denmark:

For instance, without knowing what's in our exciting new book, you'd automatically get Danish Tourist license plates expiring in six months. In the process of "exporting" from Denmark, you would lose your price advantage by paying duties easily and legally avoided. After you read this exclusive report you'll know how to get 2 year Danish or cheap renewal tax-free plates in Germany, Andorra, Gibraltar, USA and England. You will be able to use your car legally all over the world!

Another secret is that *you don't have to go to Denmark to get your tax free ultra-cheap car. Your Danish-origin car can be delivered to you* – while you take your summer vacation in say, sunny Spain. This report includes a list of recommended dealers plus warnings about a few sharks. The alternatives – making your next car deal in the Netherlands, Belgium, Switzerland, Gibraltar or Andorra (better for a few brands of cars) are also discussed.

Insurance on your car can cost as much as £4000 per annum, depending upon your driving record and whether you can say the "magic words". *What Magic Words get you 50 per cent OFF ON YOUR INSURANCE,* and a two year license plate instead of six months? You will learn these secrets only in this special report. For instance, W.G. Hill recently paid only £70 per annum for his full-coverage car insurance and £45 for his annual license plates. Do you spend this sort of nominal fund as the entire cost (besides gas and oil) of a brand new car? Finally this special report shows (after a year of fun driving and pride of ownership) *how to sell your car at a considerable profit* over the purchase price. Then you simply repeat the process again and again to have a free luxury car every year of your life!

LIMITATIONS

Can this technique work for everyone? The answer is that it will work for "almost everyone". It will NOT WORK 100 per cent for a 9 to 5 working guy who lives in the country of his origin, has only one passport, and never parks himself or his buggy anywhere outside the town he was born in. As with most Hill techniques, the "free car" gambit works best for PTs who have at least one of the five PT flags, i.e. a secondary residence. Do you spend play-time in a country different from your domicile? Then you can benefit! The scheme will also be more difficult for those who insist upon British style right-hand drive steering wheels. As Hill's technique involves buying in one country tax-free with a low factory list, and selling in another, the choice of cars and sales price-flexibility is restricted with a right-hand drive auto. But for the individual who lives part time outside of the UK and doesn't mind a left hand drive, this scheme will work! More importantly, even for nine-to-fivers who never travel, the techniques explained in this book may be used to make *considerable savings,* even if not realizing the full benefits promised by the title. Any reader should save at least ten times the price of the book, on the purchase, insurance and licensing of every car he buys for the rest of his life. The author feels that this fact makes his new report quite a bargain! We think that as with all of Dr. Hill's original ideas for PTs you'll get more than your money's worth from this special report. If you don't agree, send it back. We promise you a full refund (with a smile)!

ISBN 0 906619 29 7

How to Own a New Car Every Year Free, for Life is available from Scope International Ltd., 62 Murray Road, Waterlooville, Hampshire PO8 9JL, UK. Price £60 UK Sterling (or equivalent) by credit card, cash, cheque or banker's draft. Price includes postage and packing, and please allow 6-8 weeks for surface delivery outside UK. For quicker air mail service add £15 or equivalent (allow 3-4 weeks for delivery). Ordering details and order form are supplied on the last two pages of this Report.

REMEMBER: Consultations with specialists are available to all purchasers and our no nonsense money back guarantee applies to all our publications.

THE CHANNEL ISLAND REPORT
HOW TO ESTABLISH AND MAINTAIN A TAX HAVEN DOMICILE
ON A CHANNEL ISLAND (UK) FOR £50 PER MONTH
1st Edition
by Scope International

A businessman, weary of government red tape, lawsuits and domestic problems, arranged to sell his business and investments for a sizeable sum. If he could keep the proceeds he would enjoy financial security with a very comfortable income. But if he had to pay all the required taxes his economic base would be cut in half.

Being both ethical and cautious, he rejected the appeals of tax shelter promoters and schemes that sounded fraudulent. ''If only there was a way to keep my hard-earned money working for me instead of seeing it taken away.'' So he endeavoured to determine whether establishing a tax haven domicile was a good idea for him, and how much time one actually had to spend at such a residence. His findings were:

1. IS MOVING TO A TAX HAVEN LEGAL?

    Generally, yes. Almost all countries permit the free movement of their citizens. In peacetime, most nations also permit assets to be transferred abroad. But more importantly we discovered this basic principle of international law: *A government has jurisdiction (power to control) only over those people and property within its frontiers.* Once someone removes himself and the family jewels from a particular country, for all practical purposes that jurisdiction ends. (Exceptions are deportation and extradition for serious crimes).

2. DOES IT MAKE ECONOMIC SENSE?

    For this particular client, yes indeed! We concluded that anyone who enjoyed travelling a few months a year and who was not absolutely tied down to a nine-to-five job in a high tax country should at least consider tax havens. A mere change of legal address could typically double the income of retirees. In most cases the tax savings alone could finance all travel and living expenses. Greater financial freedom and flexibility are also factors to consider.

3. HOW MUCH TIME MUST ONE SPEND AT A TAX HAVEN?

    You don't have to live there. Domicile is normally a question of personal intention, not physical presence. Thus, a person who calls a certain place 'home' can travel elsewhere for years, but his domicile will stay the same. True, some tax havens, notably Monaco, have fairly strict rules to the effect that to retain a resident's card one must actually be physically present six months a year. But many other tax havens don't issue residence cards or even keep track of their citizens. A domicile with this sort of informal approach is to be preferred. Residence is proved by such things as a mailing address, telephone listing, apartment lease, or house deed, etc.

This particular tax haven is 100 per cent English-speaking, and has far tougher bank-secrecy laws than Switzerland.

The government is perhaps the least intrusive of any nation on earth, and is a protectorate of a major power. It is politically stable, located within commuting distance of Paris and London. It is totally free of crimes of violence or fraud. Communications are excellent. This report contains all the information you will need to know about establishing your own tax haven domicile in this unique location.

ISBN 0 906619.

The Channel Island Report is available from Scope International Ltd., 62 Murray Road, Waterlooville, Hampshire PO8 9JL, UK. Price – £60 UK Sterling (or equivalent) by credit card, cash, cheque or banker's draft. Price includes postage and packing, and please allow 6-8 weeks for surface delivery outside UK. For quicker air mail service add £15 or equivalent (allow 3-4 weeks for delivery). Ordering details and order form are supplied on the last two pages of this Report.

REMEMBER: Consultations with specialists are available to all purchasers and our no nonsense money back guarantee applies to all our publications.

THE TAX EXILE REPORT
Marshall J. Langer

Are you fed up with paying confiscatory taxes? Are you willing to move and to do whatever else may be legally necessary to escape your present tax burden? If so, *The Tax Exile Report* is for you. This report is intended for the small minority of well-to-do individuals who are no longer willing to tolerate increasingly unfair tax systems and are prepared to **vote with their feet**.

Marshall Langer's brand new report tells you how to overcome the **tax octopus** – eight different criteria used by the United States and other high-tax countries to tax you on your income and your capital. To avoid confiscatory taxes you must eliminate each of the eight tax tentacles, one by one. Langer's report tells you how to do it.

Langer tells you how to change your **residence** and your **domicile,** and when and how to acquire another **nationality**. He explains how to cope with **community property rules**. His report also tells you how to change the **source of your income** and the **location of your assets**. He helps you to **watch your timing** and to deal with problems caused by **family members who remain behind**.

Should you become a **perpetual tourist (PT)** or should you move to a new homeland? The report will help you to make the right choice.

The Tax Exile Report deals with the special problems involved in leaving high-tax countries, including America (the US), Britain, Canada, Germany and the Nordic countries. Langer concentrates on demystifying the US rules and telling you how they really work. He tells you how to plan around the US **anti-expatriation rules** and the departure taxes imposed in other countries. His report devotes twenty chapters to a review of suitable destination countries, describing the benefits and pitfalls of each of them. Surprisingly these include some of the high-tax countries that others are seeking to escape. Langer explains that most high-tax countries play both ends against the middle. They constantly squeeze their captive 'customers' while seeking to attract new investment from abroad.

The depth of coverage can best be seen by reviewing the partial summary of the **table of contents** which follows.

Why is Marshall Langer uniquely qualified to write this Report?

He is a member of the Florida Bar, and practised law in Miami for more than 35 years. He has worked as an international tax adviser in Europe since 1985, living in Switzerland and in England. He was a partner in the law firm of Shutts & Bowen, Miami, and remains of counsel to that firm. He was also an Adjunct Professor of Law and the University of Miami for many years. In 1990, Langer received the Florida Bar Tax Section's award as **Outstanding Tax Attorney of the Year.**

Langer is a graduate of the Wharton School of Finance and Commerce of the University of Pennsylvania (B.S. in Economics) and the University of Miami School of Law (J.D. *summa cum laude*). He has lectured extensively at tax institutes and seminars throughout the US and Europe, as well as in Japan, Hong King, Australia, Canada, and the Caribbean. He has written numerous articles on international taxation and books on tax and other subjects. He is the author of *The Swiss Report,* published in 1991 by Scope Books. He is also the author of a leading book on tax havens and how to use them, entitled: *Practical International Tax Planning* (the third edition was published in 1985 and is updated annually). In addition, Langer is co-author (with Rufus Rhoades of Los Angeles) of a five-volume set of books on taxes and tax treaties called: *Rhoades & Langer, Income Taxation of Foreign Related Transactions* (updated four times a year).

The Tax Exile Report by Marshall J. Langer is available from Scope International Ltd. Price £60. See last two pages in this report for ordering details.

ISBN 906619 34 3

THE SWISS REPORT
by Marshall J. Langer
With Foreword by Dr. W.G. HILL

Some countries pride themselves on being 'like Switzerland', but there is only one Switzerland – the most respected small country in the world. *The Swiss Report* gives you an inside look at the country and the institutions that make it tick.

Switzerland is not exactly a tax haven but – it is the world's greatest *money haven*. Chances are you already keep some of your money in Swiss banks. *The Swiss Report* takes you inside this country that is deservedly called "the world's safest place for your money."

The report describes Switzerland's banks, its world-renowned bank secrecy, and attempts by other countries to end that secrecy. It discusses the controls that limit non-residents to buying small amounts of Swiss real estate. It describes the companies typically used by investors and how you can save money by using a limited liability company instead of a corporation.

Langer considers Switzerland to be both a tax planner's dream and his nightmare. Correctly used in the way spelled out in the report it can be a base for you to earn money at a tax rate of 11 per cent or less, but it is hard to get that money out of Switzerland without paying a 35 per cent federal tax.

The report tells you how to visit Switzerland – places to visit – where to stay – how to travel around – where to eat. Would you like to stay longer? The report also tells you how to live and work in Switzerland, or retire there. Sure there are restrictions on obtaining permits to live in Switzerland. If it didn't have them, millions more would try to live and work there. Residence permits are difficult to obtain, but not impossible, and *The Swiss Report* ttells you how to get them. It even discusses how you can spend up to six months each year in Switzerland as a 'Permanent Traveler' (PT), legally remaining a tourist instead of a taxpayer.

Dr. W.G. (Bill) Hill regards Marshall Langer as his 'tax guru'. Langer is a tax lawyer and the author of several books including the standard reference work on tax havens, *Practical International Tax Planning,* published by New York's Practising Law Institute. After more than thirty years of law practice in Florida, Langer moved to Europe. He lived in Neuchatel, Switzerland for five years and still operates a company from there. Dr. Hill has encouraged Langer to share his know-how about Switzerland with readers of these reports. Langer's clients have willingly paid him large fees for many of the insights he has learned as a Swiss-based international tax planner and which he now shares with you in *The Swiss Report*.

The Report answers the questons:

Is Switzerland more free than the USA or Great Britain?
Should you apply for a resident's permit or live there unofficially, as a PT?
Should you move there at all?
What's the real cost of living?
Regional variations?
How do you avoid or reduce Swiss taxes?
How can you use Swiss bank accounts and the Swiss secrecy laws to your advantage?
How safe and secret really are your financial affairs?
What are the Swiss really like?
Can anyone understand Swiss politics?
Will you have to do military service?
How long before you can apply to be a citizen?
Where can you get a good meal at a reasonable price?
Swiss punctuality and other peculiarities – how do they affect you?
Should you buy a home or rent?
Can you find more happiness in Montreux?
How can you benefit from Swiss tax treaties?
Can you survive with just English?
How long before Switzerland joins the European common market?
Can a foreigner own a Swiss company?
How can you negotiate a flat income tax in advance?

These and many other questions are answered in *The Swiss Report*. We highly recommend it.

ISBN 0 906619 28 9

The Swiss Report is available from Scope International Ltd., 62 Murray Road, Waterlooville, Hampshire PO8 9JL, UK. Price £60 UK Sterling (or equivalent) by credit card, cash, cheque or banker's draft. Price includes postage and packing, and please allow 6-8 weeks for surface delivery outside UK. For quicker air mail service add £15 or equivalent (allow 3-4 weeks for delivery). Ordering details and order form are supplied on the last two pages of this Report.

REMEMBER: Our no nonsense money back guarantee applies to all our publications.

THE TAX HAVEN REPORT
1st Edition NEW for 1993
Adam Starchild

The words "tax haven" bring to mind far off corners of the planet with millionaire populations. This population, of course, spends most of its day drinking daiquiris on the beach, its funds secure in various numbered Swiss bank accounts. Not so, according to Adam Starchild (well, he doesn't refute the daiquiri bit). Tax havens need not be the exclusive refuge of the ultra-rich. People of average means need no longer be captive slaves to the State in today's modern jet-set era. In his newly written Special Report for 1993, *The Tax Haven Report,* Adam Starchild reveals these secrets of the ultra-rich so that us lesser mortals can take advantage of the many benefits tax havens have to offer.

As modern governments continue to expand and swallow human rights, deficits and taxes grow. All free-minded individuals must seek a means to protect their assets from this monster out of control. As Starchild explains, it is legally possible to pay absolutely no taxes. Your government may want you to think otherwise. The media may love to tattle about the misery of a particular celebrity "tax evader", but a very important point remains unnoticed. While "tax evasion" is illegal, "tax avoidance" is not. This distinction is crucial, and thus Starchild explains it at great length.

Starchild goes on to cover this exhausting subject from start to finish in a clear, easy to understand style. No legal jargon here. He brings over twenty years of experience to the production of this report and doesn't hop on the bandwagons for the latest "fad" tax havens. (It is not commonly known, but tax havens are just as interested in finding you as you are in finding them.) He explains everything from the basic criteria you should use when assessing a tax haven to how you can put them to work to save you that big chunk of your income whisked off each year by Big Brother.

For entrepreneurs and businessmen, he explains the ins and outs of tax haven corporations and trusts, including how they are formed, how they are controlled, where they can be located, and, most importantly, how they can seriously reduce, if not eliminate, the tax burden of your business.

Starchild explains the basics of some of the known and not-so-known tax havens of the world. He divides them into easily identifiable categories, including:

No-tax havens: The Bahamas, Bermuda, The Cayman Islands

Foreign-source-income havens: Panama, Cyprus, Malta, The Isle of Man, Jersey, Guernsey, Gibraltar, Hong Kong

Double-taxation agreement havens: The Netherlands, Austria, Luxembourg

This report also includes detailed chapters on both Liechtenstein and Switzerland. In stark contrast with most tax experts, Starchild successfully argues that Switzerland no longer has a great deal to offer as a tax haven.

This report is essential reading for anyone interested in reducing his tax burden. With over 170 pages of vital information, we are certain that you can develop a successful plan to reduce your tax burden as a result of reading this report. We are so certain that we do not even hesitate to offer it with our standard money-back guarantee. Unless you are absolutely satisfied return it within 28 days for a full refund.

About the Author: Adam Starchild has been a business consultant for nearly two decades. He is the author of over a dozen books, four of which are on tax havens, the earliest having been published in 1978. He has also written hundreds of magazine articles, for journals around the world. Amongst the many publishing his articles have been: The Christian Science Monitor, Credit & Financial Management, International Business, The New York Times, The San Francisco Examiner, Tax Angles, Tax Haven & Shelter Report, Tax Haven News *and* Tax Planning International.

His consulting clients have ranged from wealthy individuals to banks, trust companies, investment companies, book publishers, import-export companies and tour operators. Often critical of the hype and inflated prices from some of the more famous tax havens, Starchild gives you the benefit of his many years hands-on experience in setting up trusts in many countries around the world.

ISBN 0 906619 39 4

The Tax Haven Report is available from Scope International Ltd., 62 Murray Road, Waterlooville, Hampshire PO8 9JL, UK. Price £60 UK Sterling (or equivalent) by credit card, cash, cheque or banker's draft. Price includes postage and packing, and please allow 6-8 weeks for surface delivery outside UK. For quicker air mail service add £15 or equivalent (allow 3-4 weeks for delivery). Ordering details and order form are supplied on the last two pages of this Report.

REMEMBER: Consultations with specialists are available to all purchasers and our no nonsense money back guarantee applies to all our publications.